Communications
in Computer and Information Science 68

AlpeshKumar Ranchordas
João Madeiras Pereira
Hélder J. Araújo
João Manuel R. S. Tavares (Eds.)

Computer Vision, Imaging and Computer Graphics

Theory and Applications

International Joint Conference, VISIGRAPP 2009
Lisboa, Portugal, February 5-8, 2009
Revised Selected Papers

 Springer

Volume Editors

AlpeshKumar Ranchordas
INSTICC, Setúbal, Portugal
E-mail: alpesh@insticc.org

João Madeiras Pereira
INESC-ID, Instituto Superior Técnico
Lisboa, Portugal
E-mail: jap@inesc.pt

Hélder J. Araújo
University of Coimbra
Institute for Systems and Robotics
Department of Electrical
and Computer Engineering Polo II
Coimbra, Portugal
E-mail: helder@isr.uc.pt

João Manuel R. S. Tavares
Faculdade de Engenharia
da Universidade do Porto
Departamento de Mecânica
Porto, Portugal
E-mail: tavares@fe.up.pt

Library of Congress Control Number: 2010922005

CR Subject Classification (1998): I.3, I.5, H.2.8, I.3.7, I.2.10, I.3.1, I.4

ISSN   1865-0929
ISBN-10   3-642-11839-9 Springer Berlin Heidelberg New York
ISBN-13   978-3-642-11839-5 Springer Berlin Heidelberg New York

springer.com

© Springer-Verlag Berlin Heidelberg 2010
Printed in Germany

Typesetting: Camera-ready by author, data conversion by Scientific Publishing Services, Chennai, India
Printed on acid-free paper   06/3180   5 4 3 2 1 0

Preface

This book includes extended versions of the selected papers from VISIGRAPP 2009, the International Joint Conference on Computer Vision, Imaging and Computer Graphics Theory and Applications, which was held in Lisbon, Portugal, during February 5–8, 2009 and organized by the Institute for Systems and Technologies of Information, Control and Communication (INSTICC). VISIGRAPP comprises three component conferences, namely, the International Conference on Computer Vision Theory and Applications (VISAPP), the International Conference on Computer Graphics Theory and Applications (GRAPP), and the International Conference on Imaging Theory and Applications (IMAGAPP).

VISIGRAPP received a total of 422 paper submissions from more than 50 countries. From these, and after a rigorous double-blind evaluation method, 72 papers were published as full papers. These figures show that this conference is now an established venue for researchers in the broad fields of computer vision, computer graphics and image analysis. From the full papers, 25 were selected for inclusion in this book. The selection process was based on the scores assigned by the Program Committee reviewers as well as the Session Chairs. After selection, the papers were further revised and extended by the authors. Our gratitude goes to all contributors and referees, without whom this book would not have been possible.

VISIGRAPP 2009 included four invited keynote lectures, presented by internationally renowned researchers. The presentations represented an important contribution to the overall quality of the conference. We would like to express our appreciation to all invited keynote speakers, in alphabetical order, David Hogg (University of Leeds, UK), Franz Leberl (Graz University of Technology, Austria), Dany Lepage (Ubisoft, Canada) and Patrick Wang (Northeastern University, USA).

We wish to thank all those who supported and helped to organize the conference. First and foremost we would like to acknowledge the collaboration from Eurographics and ACM SIGGRAPH. On behalf of the conference Organizing Committee, we would also like to thank the authors, whose work mostly contributed to a very successful conference and to the members of the Program Committee, whose expertise and diligence were instrumental to ensuring the quality of the final contributions. We also wish to thank all the members of the Organizing Committee, especially Bruno Encarnação, whose work and commitment were invaluable. Last but not least, we would like to thank Springer for their collaboration in getting this book to print.

December 2009
AlpeshKumar Narotam Ranchordas
João Madeiras Pereira
Hélder J. Araújo
João Manuel R. S. Tavares

Organization

Conference Co-chairs

João Madeiras Pereira   Instituto Superior Técnico, Portugal (GRAPP)
AlpeshKumar Ranchordas   INSTICC, Portugal (VISAPP and IMAGAPP)

Program Co-chairs

Helder Araújo   University of Coimbra, Portugal (VISAPP)
Paul Richard   Laboratoire D'ingénierie Des Systèmes
         Automatisés - LISA, France (GRAPP)
João Manuel R.S. Tavares   FEUP – Faculty of Engineering of University of Porto,
         Portugal (IMAGAPP)

Organizing Committee

Sérgio Brissos	INSTICC, Portugal
Marina Carvalho	INSTICC, Portugal
Helder Coelhas	INSTICC, Portugal
Vera Coelho	INSTICC, Portugal
Andreia Costa	INSTICC, Portugal
Bruno Encarnação	INSTICC, Portugal
Bárbara Lima	INSTICC, Portugal
Raquel Martins	INSTICC, Portugal
Elton Mendes	INSTICC, Portugal
Carla Mota	INSTICC, Portugal
Vitor Pedrosa	INSTICC, Portugal
Vera Rosário	INSTICC, Portugal
José Varela	INSTICC, Portugal

GRAPP Program Committee

Tomi Aarnio, Finland	Manfred Bogen, Germany
Francisco Abad, Spain	Ronan Boulic, Switzerland
Marco Agus, Italy	Willem F. Bronsvoort, The Netherlands
Marco Attene, Italy	Stephen Brooks, Canada
Dolors Ayala, Spain	Pedro Cano, Spain
Curzio Basso, Italy	Maria Beatriz Carmo, Portugal
Jiri Bittner, Czech Republic	Miguel Chover, Spain

Jung Hong Chuang, Taiwan
Ana Paula Cláudio, Portugal
Hervé Delingette, France
Jean Michel Dischler, France
David Duce, UK
Roman Durikovic, Slovak Republic
Francisco R. Feito, Spain
Petr Felkel, Czech Republic
Luiz Henrique de Figueiredo, Brazil
Julian Flores, Spain
Doron Friedman, Israel
Ioannis Fudos, Greece
Manuel Gamito, UK
Marina Gavrilova, Canada
Michael Gleicher, USA
Enrico Gobbetti, Italy
Jean-Yves Guillemaut, UK
Diego Gutierrez, Spain
Vlastimil Havran, Czech Republic
Nancy Hitschfeld, Chile
Andres Iglesias, Spain
Insung Ihm, Republic of Korea
Jiri Janacek, Czech Republic
Chris Joslin, Canada
Marcelo Kallmann, USA
Henry Kang, USA
Josef Kohout, Czech Republic
Ivana Kolingerová, Czech Republic
Martin Kraus, Germany
Caroline Larboulette, Spain
Frederick Li, UK
Joaquim Madeira, Portugal
Marcus Magnor, Germany
Stephen Mann, Canada
Michael Manzke, Ireland
Ramon Molla, Spain
Guillaume Moreau, France

David Mould, Canada
László Neumann, Spain
Gennadiy Nikishkov, Japan
Marc Olano, USA
Samir Otmane, France
Giuseppe Patané, Italy
Bernard Péroche, France
Steve Pettifer, UK
Denis Pitzalis, Cyprus
Anna Puig, Spain
Enrico Puppo, Italy
María Cecilia Rivara, Chile
Inmaculada Rodríguez, Spain
Przemyslaw Rokita, Poland
Daniela Romano, UK
Bodo Rosenhahn, Germany
Manuel Próspero dos Santos, Portugal
Frank Steinicke, Germany
Ching-Liang Su, India
Ayellet Tal, Israel
Matthias Teschner, Germany
Daniel Thalmann, Switzerland
Holger Theisel, Germany
Gui Yun Tian, UK
Walid Tizani, UK
Juan Carlos Torres, Spain
Pere-pau Vázquez, Spain
Luiz Velho, Brazil
Ivan Viola, Norway
Andreas Weber, Germany
Daniel Weiskopf, Germany
Alexander Wilkie, Czech Republic
Michael Wimmer, Austria
Burkhard Wuensche, New Zealand
Jian J. Zhang, UK
Richard (Hao) Zhang, Canada
Jianmin Zheng, Singapore

GRAPP Auxiliary Reviewers

Jean-Paul Balabanian, Norway
Selim Balcisoy, Turkey
Jesus Caban, USA
Carlo Camporesi, USA
Carlos González, Spain
Yazhou Huang, USA
Jorge Jimenez, Spain

Juan J. Jimenez-Delgado, Spain
Oliver van Kaick, Canada
Jorge Lopez-Moreno, Spain
Oktar Ozgen, USA
Guido Reina, Germany
Claus Scheiblauer, Austria

VISAPP Program Committee

Heinrich Niemann, Germany
Mark Nixon, UK
Yanwei Pang, China
Massimo Piccardi, Australia
Bogdan Raducanu, Spain
AlpeshKumar Ranchordas, Portugal
Carlo Regazzoni, Italy
Paolo Remagnino, UK
Alfredo Restrepo, Colombia
Eraldo Ribeiro, USA
Mariano Rivera, Mexico
Bourennane Salah, France
Joaquin Salas, Mexico
Ovidio Salvetti, Italy
Yoichi Sato, Japan
Gerald Schaefer, UK
Xiaowei Shao, Japan
Lik-Kwan Shark, UK
Li Shen, USA
Luciano Silva, Brazil
Georgios Sirakoulis, Greece

Mingli Song, China
José Martínez Sotoca, Spain
Joachim Stahl, USA
Peter Sturm, France
Changming Sun, Australia
Eric Sung, Singapore
Shamik Sural, India
Johji Tajima, Japan
Jinhui Tang, Singapore
Jean-philippe Tarel, France
Huiqiong Wang, China
Song Wang, USA
Tiangong Wei, China
Qingxiang Wu, UK
Pingkun Yan, USA
Tianhao Zhang, USA
Jianmin Zheng, Singapore
Ying Zheng, UK
Huiyu Zhou, UK
Xingquan (Hill) Zhu, USA
Zhigang Zhu, USA

VISAPP Auxiliary Reviewers

Bernhard Burgeth, Germany
Farid Flitti, Australia
Richang Hong, Singapore
Giovanni Puglisi, Italy
Chauã Queirolo, Brazil

Jon Rihan, UK
Ferdous Sohel, Australia
Levi Valgaerts, Germany
Alexandre Vrubel, Brazil
Henning Zimmer, Germany

IMAGAPP Program Committee

Amr Abdel-Dayem, Canada
Constantino Carlos Reyes Aldasoro, UK
António Luís Pereira Amaral, Portugal
Oscar Au, Hong Kong
Emmanuel Audenaert, Belgium
Reneta Barneva, USA
Arrate Muñoz Barrutia, Spain
Isabelle Bloch, France
Giulia Boato, Italy
Xavier Bresson, USA
Valentin Brimkov, USA
Mujdat Cetin, Turkey
Vinod Chandran, Australia

Chin-Chen Chang, Taiwan
Jocelyn Chanussot, France
Paulo Correia, Portugal
Olivier Coulon, France
Aysegul Cuhadar, Canada
Nedeljko Cvejic, UK
Mohamed Daoudi, France
Peter Eisert, Germany
Mahmoud El-Sakka, Canada
Arie Feuer, Israel
Mario Figueiredo, Portugal
GianLuca Foresti, Italy
Jordi Gonzàlez, Spain

Manuel González-Hidalgo, Spain
Michael L. Goris, USA
Bernard Gosselin, Belgium
Mislav Grgic, Croatia
Abdessamad Ben Hamza, Canada
Raouf Hamzaoui, UK
Nies Huijsmans, The Netherlands
Martin Kampel, Austria
Reinhard Koch, Germany
Andreas Koschan, USA
Constantine Kotropoulos, Greece
Arjan Kuijper, Germany
Maria Kunkel, Germany
C.-c. Jay Kuo, USA
Fatih Kurugollu, UK
Andreas Lanitis, Cyprus
Slimane Larabi, Algeria
Sébastien Lefevre, France
Chang-Tsun Li, UK
Xuelong Li, UK
SukHwan Lim, USA
Xiuwen Liu, USA
Miguel Angel Guevara López, Portugal
Alexander Loui, USA

Rastislav Lukac, Canada
Stephen McKenna, UK
Javier Melenchón, Spain
Todd Pataky, UK
AlpeshKumar Ranchordas, Portugal
Ana Reis, Portugal
Marcos Rodrigues, UK
Alessia De Rosa, Italy
Rajab Said, UK
Rudini Sampaio, Brazil
André Saúde, Brazil
Fiorella Sgallari, Italy
Timothy K. Shih, Taiwan
Bogdan Smolka, Poland
Jon Sporring, Denmark
Xue-Cheng Tai, Norway
Mengxing Tang, UK
Sabina Tangaro, Italy
João Tavares, Portugal
Shan Yu, USA
Yongjie Zhang, USA
Jun Zhao, China
Huiyu Zhou, UK

Invited Speakers

Franz W. Leberl   Graz University of Technology, Austria
David Hogg   University of Leeds, UK
Patrick Wang   Northeastern University, USA
Dany Lepage   Ubisoft, Canada

Table of Contents

Part III: Computer Vision Theory and Applications (VISAPP)

Invited Papers

Human Habitat Data in 3D for the Internet

Franz Leberl

Institute for Computer Graphics and Vision
Graz University of Technology, Graz, Austria
leberl@icg.tugraz.at

Abstract. In March 2005, at the occasion of his 50th birthday, Bill Gates went public with his "Virtual Earth Vision" for local search in the Internet and stated: *"You'll be walking around in downtown London and be able to see the shops, the stores, see what the traffic is like. Walk in a shop and navigate the merchandise. Not in the flat, 2D interface that we have on the web today, but in a virtual reality walkthrough."* This implies optimism that an enormous advance will be achieved in computing power, communications bandwidth, miniaturization of computing, increase of storage capacity and in the ability to model the human habitat (the Earth) in great detail in 3 dimensions, with photographic realism and at very low cost per data unit. Action followed this declaration by Bill Gates, and the transition of a then-10-year old Microsoft business segment called "Map Point" into a new Virtual Earth Business Unit was kicked off (recently renamed Bing Maps). The Microsoft initiative, along with similar initiatives by other Internet-providers, most visibly Google, can serve as an example and actually also as a driver for the future of computing and of computational thinking. Research in the complete automatic creation of 3D models of urban spaces has become greatly inspired and now is a very active field of innovation. The level of automation in creating 3D city models has benefited from an increase in the redundancy of the source data in the form of highly overlapping imagery either from the air or from the street. We explain in this paper that it is possible to create 3D models of an entire city from aerial photography fully automatically, and thus at a commercially acceptable cost. Using this as a geometric framework, detail can be added from street-level and indoor imagery or laser scanner data. Such data can be produced either systematically or by "us", the anonymous community of users. The result is a global geo-data base consisting of a combination of aerial data at perhaps 10 to 15 cm pixel size, street side data at perhaps 2 cm and indoor data of important or commercially relevant spaces at 0.5 cm pixel size. This will add up to a data base of thousands of cities, perhaps also of smaller communities, with more than 1 Exabyte to be created and maintained.

1 Introduction

If we want to see how photogrammetry has been evolving from a film-based activity to a fully digital workflow, we only need to review the quadrennial congresses of the International Society for Photogrammetry and Remote Sensing (Table 1). A digital approach is the basis for a fully automated photogrammetric 3D process by essentially

A. Ranchordas et al. (Eds.): VISIGRAPP 2009, CCIS 68, pp. 3–17, 2010.
© Springer-Verlag Berlin Heidelberg 2010

adopting computer vision algorithms to create mapping data. Full automation is also the basis for the creation of models of urban areas in 3 dimensions for photo-realistic rendering and applications: automation is feasible at such cost per data unit, say a building or tree, that a large scale data base development seems feasible and affordable (see also some early work, for example Gruber, 1997, [5]).

It appears that the technology to automatically create 3D models of urban spaces exists at a sufficient level of completeness and accuracy to serve as a basis for initiatives such as Bing Maps by Microsoft (formerly Virtual Earth).

Bing Maps is an Internet-based infrastructure to support search and navigation. It also is a Website supporting the search for locations, offering directions and supporting social interactions with maps and photos. It competes head-on with Google Maps and Google Earth. The interesting challenge in Bing Maps is the commitment to a World in 3 dimensions, essentially at an unlimited level of detail. Figure 1 illustrates the Bing Maps presentation of Vienna (Austria) in 3 dimensions as it currently is hosted on the Internet.

Table 1. The congresses of the ISPRS document the major milestones in the evolution of photogrammetry from a strictly film-based activity to a fully digital workflow and provider of geo-data for Internet applications (ISPRS, 2008, [8]).

1992 (Baltimore)	Film scanning to enable a digital vision process with photogrammetric images
1996 (Vienna)	Digital Stereo starts to replace the 100-year old optical stereo process;
2000 (Amsterdam)	Announcement of digital aerial cameras, awaiting any practical uses;
2004 (Istanbul)	First reports about uses of digital aerial cameras and about the advantages of digital sensing vis-a-vis traditional film based sensing;
2008 (Beijing)	The Internet employs and serves geo-data in 2 and 3 dimensions.

We review in this paper the 3D modeling technology and some of the business cases for a location-aware Internet, relying to some extent on the example of Microsoft's Bing Maps.

2 A Historical Perspective

Car navigation and travel planning, the latter on an office computer, have been the initial drivers for the emergence of 2-dimensional digital road maps. At first, this began in the form of stand-alone applications running on a personal computer. In Microsoft's case, this development began in the mid-1990s. The evolution from the original offering called "Streets and Trips" via "MapPoint" to "Bing Maps" is illustrated in Figure 2. The most successful system of this kind was developed by

Fig. 1. Vienna in 3D is being presented in Microsoft's Bing Maps website at http://www.bing.com/maps.

MapQuest, today operated by AOL. From the stand-alone shrink-wrapped software in 1995, these offerings soon evolved into web-based solutions by perhaps 2001, and today the drive is towards applications on smart cell phones.

Search rapidly augmented the initial application of location data, and rapidly surpassed navigation and travel planning as a business model. Search created an entirely new business, with Google as the clear winner in market share. Major competitors are Microsoft, Yahoo and Ask. To attract users to a particular search engine, it must offer excellence in the user experience. The vector-based street maps therefore began to get augmented by ortho-photos, to achieve the needed enrichment of the user experience. This was not only offered by the afore-mentioned 4 global players, but also by regional phone book providers. In Austria, it was Herold (www.herold.at) to cover all major cities with ortho-photos, in Germany Gelbe Seiten (http://maps.gelbeseiten.de/Kartensuche/), new regional providers were established, such as in Germany with Klicktel (http://www.klicktel.de/kartensuche/) , in England with Getmapping and Multimap (www.getmapping.com and www.multimap.com) and so forth. The idea to augment the user experience by means of oblique aerial photography started in 2006 at Microsoft with its "Bird's Eye Views" and was soon followed by Klicktel's EagleView (Germany) and others.

It seems that the step towards the 3rd dimension was only logical. Three-dimensional building models of entire large urban areas were first introduced by Microsoft in November 2006 as an essential and defining component of the Bing Maps system (see Figure 1, now bing.com/maps). While the focus remained on improving the user experience for searches, travel planning and navigation, there also was the business model based on an enhanced advertisement option with 3D models.

Location Based Services LBS further broaden the applications of mapping data into *"an information and entertainment service, accessible with mobile devices through the mobile network and utilizing the ability to make use of the geographical position of the mobile device"* (quoted from Wikipedia, 2009, [24]) . Car Navigation, Route Planning and Search thus evolve into LBS as the user's location is made part of

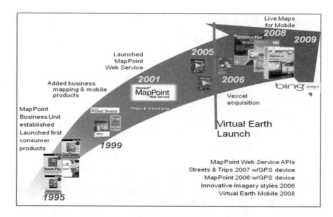

Fig. 2. Microsoft's mapping-inspired initiatives, 1995 to 2009

the application. LBS develop the Internet-use of geographical data into a new academic endeavor with conference series, academic discourse (Taylor & Francis, 2009, [21]) and educational training programs. Mapping data as an ubiquitous feature in everyday computer-supported life is rapidly becoming a reality far beyond its original emergence, with Internet-based commerce on e-bay, in real estate and with Amazon.com, in the daily news, in computer games, as a basis for the "*Internet of Things*" or as an enabling element of "*ambient living*". The interest and need will be for mapping data in the sub-centimeter range, and the resulting data quantities will reach beyond the magical Exabyte with enormous challenges in collecting and updating the geometric information, and to serve this globally to all places, at all times.

We do see a transition from digital mapping to a 3-dimensional Virtual Habitat, and a transition from the realm of expert users of mapping data to a dramatic democratization, making everyone of us a mapping expert evaluating, and contributing to, a global model of our environment, along the "neo-geographer's" paradigm promoted by Goodchild (2008) [1].

3 Defining the Concept of "Location-Awareness" on the Internet

When one marries maps with the Internet and applies the result to searches based on places, then one can denote this as an Internet that knows about locations, thus is it "location-aware". This does not necessarily imply that there is a user-position involved as well. We argue that location awareness is independent of satellite navigation or of mobile phone triangulation.

If we want to know something about Arles (France) and can indeed find its location by an Internet-search, on a digital map, with ortho-photos, a Bird's Eye view and perhaps even a 3-dimensional model of the city, we are in the midst of an Internet that knows location.

This may proceed to an ability to interpret news and find inside some search results an occasional pointer to geographic locations. If in a text one finds the word

"London", and this text is understood to refer to a place on Earth and can point us to this place or the many places that all are called "London", we are interacting with a location-aware system (Teitler et al., 2008, [22]).

"Location" traditionally has been the responsibility of professional cartographers and map makers, oftentimes employed by governments and serving the purpose of the sovereign. Under that responsibility, "location" has evolved into a highly structured matter of reliability and accuracy. The corner of a property has been and is being defined with certain accuracy, perhaps in the range of ± 10 cm, by virtue of governmental rules and methods derived to satisfy those rules.

By contrast, the Internet-based approach to location is "Wikipedia-like" – locations are not government-mandated but serve a business purpose by those providing the locations to the Internet-application. Data may be accurate or not, they may be outdated or current; the user will be the judge of the data's usefulness and violations in accuracy and completeness will be met with loss of market share.

4 Creating 3 Dimensional Models via Aerial Photogrammetry

4.1 Data

The ambition to proceed from the traditional 2-dimensional map-paradigm to a 3D augmented reality experience probably was first introduced as a result of competitive pressures to conquer market share in the brand-new business of map-based search. To be useful, all major industrial cities would have to be modeled in 3D. About 3000 cities have been mentioned in initial press releases by Microsoft when the Bing Maps initiative was first announced in March 2005. Let us assume that these 3000 cities are home to 1.5 billion people. The average number of people per city would be 500,000. Those assumptions track well with lists of cities of the World. At 10 persons per building, we would have to model 50,000 buildings per city, or 150 million in total. If we had available a total budget of US$ 100 million for the initial model of all buildings, we would operate with a budget of less than US$ 1 per building. Only a highly automated photogrammetric modeling process would be capable of supporting this cost. A high level of automation requires a high level of data redundancy. We are basing our assumptions on a factor of 10 for redundancy for a photogrammetric process based on 80% forward and 60% sideways overlap. Table 2 summarizes the assumptions and resulting computations.

4.2 Data Processing

Table 2 easily explains why full automation of the urban modeling process in 3D is a requirement. Such automation is available today provided that 8 important factors are being considered (see also Leberl, 2007, [11]):

a. Excellence in digital imaging from the air with a radiometry with a range of 7000 gray values to succeed in automation; such excellence is available from novel large format digital aerial cameras such as the UltraCam-series of cameras;

Table 2. Numbers defining the 3D modeling effort for 3000 cities (above). Given a budget of US$ 100 million for urban modeling, the cost per building is at US$ 0.7. At a ground sample distance GSD of 10 cm, one will need to work with about 10 million photographs. The entire Earth surface would be covered by 351 million photos at a GSD of 15 cm and a 10-x redundancy. This would represent a data volume at ~ 200 PBytes.

ITEM	VALUE	COMMENT
Population, global	1,500,000,000	The rich industrial world
Cities	3,000	Assumed
People per city	500,000	Computed
People per building	10	Assumed
Buildings, global	150,000,000	Computed
Buildings per sqkm	300	Assumed
Data budget, US$	100,000,000	Budgeted at will
Cost per building	0.67	Computed
Area per city	167	Computed
Area of 1 photo @ 10 cm pixels, sqkm	1.87	17K * 11 K pixel format
Photos per sqkm @ 10 cm Pixels	0.53	Computed
Photos per city, no redundancy	312	Computed
Redundancy factor	10	Assumed
Total number of photos per city	3,117	Computed
Total number of photos	9,350,000	Computed
Mbytes /image	1,496	2 bytes per each of 4 colors
Mbytes/image @ level 2 (compressed)	540	Pan @ full res., Color reduced res.
Terabytes all cities	5,051	Computed
The Earth's land area	148,000,000	Square kilometers
Area of 1 photo @ 15 cm pixels, sqkm	4.21	Computed
Photos for Earth, no redundancy	35,175,282	Computed
Photos for Earth, with redundancy	351,752,822	Computed
Terabytes for the Earth's land mass	190,025	Computed

b. Smart image data collection strategies to achieve high redundancy at little extra cost, to be achieved by high forward overlaps at 80% and high side-lap at 60%; this is available today with image repeat rates sufficiently high to obtain high forward overlap at no extra costs, and with on-board storage capacities accommodating the collection of thousands of images in a single airborne mission;

c. Fully automated aerial triangulation of large image blocks with 3000+ photos for a city; this is available today, for example in the UltraMap-system (Reitinger, 2008; [16] Gruber and Reitinger, 2008, [3]);

d. Ease of interaction with very large data sets encompassing more than 5 Tbytes per city; this is available today as a result of the Seadragon-approach to data management (see Livelabs, 2008, [14] and Reitinger, 2008, [16]);

e. Fully automated object classification into buildings, trees, vegetation, water bodies, circulation spaces; this is available from highly redundant image coverage;

f. Fully automated creation of Digital Surface Models DSM and separation into the Bald Earth Digital Terrain Model DTM and vertical objects (buildings, vegetation); this is available today from advanced "dense matching" (Klaus, 2007, [8]);

g. Very high geometric accuracy in the sub-pixel range to obtain excellence in the dense DSM/DTM and well-defined discontinuities along building edges (Ladstätter, 2009, [10]; Gruber and Ladstätter, 2006, [2]);

h. Intelligent computing acceleration to cope with large CPU-requirements; dense matching an area covered by a single image may take 1 hour of CPU on an un-aided computer; acceleration is available today in the form of GPU-aided personal computing and an acceleration factor of perhaps 400, or by large multi-hundred CPUs in a "parallel" blade computer arrangement.

4.3 Geometric Accuracy

Internet-inspired modeling of urban spaces should be directed towards the visual "experience" only and it surprises that a high geometric accuracy is a condition for success, as listed in the above item g. Two reasons exist: first is the need to fully automate the dense matching for a DTM that has postings at every 2nd pixel. Dense matching will work automatically only if the high overlap images are geometrically precisely connected. Second is the need to use photographic texture from multiple images over a precise 3D model of buildings which can easily degenerate in visually unattractive results along elevation discontinuities such as along roof lines. Figures 3 and 4 explain.

Fig. 3. Digital Surface Model extracted of a building from overlapping UltraCam-imagery with a GSD at 8 cm (right, "3D vision"). For comparison we present an Airborne Laser Scanner DTM (left, denoted as "ALS") collecting surface points with a final posting interval at 25 cm. This comparison is from the Vaihingen test area near Stuttgart, managed by the University of Stuttgart. Note the superior photogrammetric edges of the building.

Fig. 4. Typical errors in the photo texture due to inaccuracies in the DTM (left) and avoiding these effects via an accurate DTM (right)

Geometric accuracy implies a very accurate aerial sensor. In the case of the Ultra-Cam system, internal accuracies are in the sub-micrometer range, and system accuracy as defined via an aerial triangulation with a σ_0 right at a 1 µm value:

Laboratory-Calibration.. ± 0.5 µm
Merging 9 tiles into a single seamless image........... ± 0.6 µm
Field calibration via AT resulting in a σ_0 at................ ± 1.0 µm

Such accuracies require careful laboratory tests as illustrated in Figure 5.

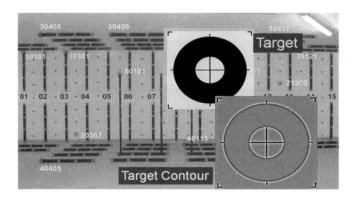

Fig. 5. Laboratory for factory calibration of an aerial camera UltraCam. Many hundred targets exist and are imaged onto 84 separate images. The targets are being automatically recognized and their coordinates get entered into a bundle adjustment for computation of geometric calibration parameters (Leberl and Gruber, 2007, [12]).

5 Limitless Detail

The competition between the various search providers has already shown how highly they regard the "human scale experience". This is reflected in the work to provide street-side images to the Internet user. The typical pixel size for street side data may be at 2 cm or so, driven by the desire to read signs. Google already is presenting its Street-View data, as shown in Figure 6, and Microsoft is working on a similar initiative, however very much concerned with the global furor of "invasion of privacy" resulting from this type of detail. A regional example is by Herold (2009, Figure 7).

While the 2 cm pixels of street-side imagery will support the human experience as it exists in streets, it is not complete. The building interior is of interest as well, for example in shopping malls, places of religion or culture. The inside of buildings requires an even higher geometric resolution, perhaps with pixel sizes approaching 0.5 cm (see Gruber and Sammer, 1995; [4] and Figure 7).

This appetite for detail is being matched with progress in bandwidth and computing to make such data quantities feasible. In Microsoft's case, and interesting development is its Photosynth system at http://photosynth.net (Snavely, Seitz et al., 2008, [18] and Snavely, Garg et al., 2009, [19]). Figures 8 and 9 illustrate the system which permits a user anywhere on the globe to submit private un-calibrated, yet overlapping photos.

Fig. 6. Google's Street View data offering, illustrated at 2949 10th Street, Boulder, Colorado. The street-view (above) is geometrically linked to the ortho-photo (below) for ease of navigation. See also Figure 10 for another view and context.

Fig. 7. Regional yellow-page provider Herold.at offers interactive urban views both of outdoor and indoor scenes. This illustration is taken from strassentour.herold.at and captures 2 arbitrary views of a Vienna street.

The website will triangulate those photos and return to the user a new arrangement of these photos in a local 3D coordinate system for easy interaction, and in a geometrically ordered fashion. One now can, as a user, travel through the space, be it outdoors in a street or indoors, much as if one had a 3D model of the scene. The Bing Maps system is expected to take advantage of such user-provided content and increase the level of detail significantly.

Both Photosynth and Figures 7 through 9 illustrate an interesting point of simulating 3D by a series of 2D views. This is currently used by Google's StreetView system and is an intermediate solution that leads to quick applications while putting off the solution of the complexities associated with a fully 3D world model.

One can easily show that the addition of 2 cm street-side data, also at a 10-times redundancy, and 0.5 cm indoor data will augment the total data quantity from the aerial 200 Petabytes to more than 1 Exabyte.

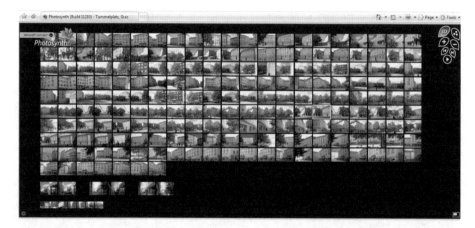

Fig. 8. Screenshot. A user submits his block of overlapping, uncalibrated images to the Photosynth website. They are then triangulated and a sparse 3D point cloud is being generated. The example shows 200 images of the Tummelplatz in Graz (Austria). The system is a service of Microsoft, but is now organized under the Bing Maps umbrella. The development originally was in cooperation with the Univ. of Washington (2008), [23] where the project has resulted in a companion solution called Phototourism. We can expect that this approach will lead to the user adding information about interior spaces, courtyards, shops, shop widows etc.

Fig. 9. Screenshot. The ~200 images from Figure 8 have been triangulated in accordance with the Photosynth-method. They are now in a 3D coordinate system and arranged for easy navigation in 3D space. Each photograph can be viewed separately or in conjunction with overlapping images, however all presentations are in 2D. The area: Tummelplatz, Graz.

6   Economic Justifications

Navigation, travel planning, search and the wide array of Location-Based Services LBS need to justify the costs of setting up, maintaining and serving everywhere on the globe such an all-encompassing 3D data base. "Search" is economically justified via advertisement. It is to be noted that the yellow pages and local paper advertisement do represent an annual business volume in excess of US$ 60 billion. It is this volume of business that is in the cross hairs of the global search providers. Yellow pages offer addresses of businesses, and so do the location aware internet websites.

Creative applications ideas get generated from the connection of data bases with maps. If one is interested in the value of a piece of real estate property in North America, one can ask www.zillow.com, as illustrated in Figure 10 for the same building that was shown in Figure 6.

Search, navigation, travel, games, smart cell phones, e-commerce, mixed reality and the so-called "Internet of Things" will all contribute new and exciting applications of maps on the Internet (see an example in Schall et al., 2009, [17]). Setting up global data bases will be the basis for grabbing market share as time progresses.

Strassenburg-Kleciak M. (2007), [20] expressed some disappointment at the unavailability of large area 3D urban models since car navigation would be ready to be a major user, has the technological capability, but needs to await the creation of such 3D data in the public domain or by commercial concerns.

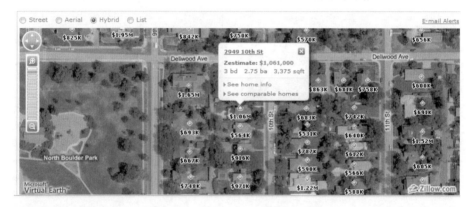

Fig. 10. Example of a Bing Maps application at www.zillow.com producing the value of real estate. In the USA this is available via the municipal public records of real estate values which are defined annually as a basis for property taxes.

7 Research Challenges

Of course the idea of a detailed 3D-model of the human habitat with in excess of 1 Exabyte of source materials presents numerous research challenges and opportunities for success. The desire to be more fully automated in extracting, and keeping current, dense geometric information from sensor data will continue to support method development at all levels of detail.

Work on the street side imagery has just begun (see an example in Irschara et al., 2009, [6]) In lieu of presenting imagery, it would be useful to "render" geometric models of street side scenes, thereby reducing the data quantities to be stored, maintained and served, as well as eliminating the legal threats due to suggested violations

14   F. Leberl

of privacy. Going inside buildings increases the challenges significantly, and research has hardly begun to address the need to deal with interior spaces.

As one fills the data repositories with initial content, the question immediately rises: "and what about data aging"? Automating the detection of errors, responding to user inputs about errors, investigating public records for documents on changes are all issues of interest. And once we know that changes have occurred, we then have the issue of automating the update of the 3D data repositories at far less cost than the budgets for the initialization of the systems.

Figure 11 illustrates work dealing with cars. In an ortho-photo, cars are not very meaningful because at one point in time they are in the street, a moment later they are gone. In a 3D model, cars do represent visual clutter. In a street side environment, cars also can be identified via their license plates, therefore one wants to remove the cars. They could, once removed, be replaced by graphics generated model cars. Recognizing cars and removing them can be achieved using a method called "boosting" (Kluckner et al., 2009, [9]). Cars can be recognized via their 2D-shape in the ortho-photo and color, but also via the 3D point clouds, and the fact that they tend to be on streets and other circulation spaces.

Fig. 11. An aerial photo to the left shows cars in parking lots and in streets. To the right is the same photograph with the cars automatically removed (courtesy Kluckner et al., 2009, [9]).

Fig. 12. Example of the Colorado Capitol in Denver in Bing Maps at http://maps.live.com with all trees recognized and replaced by computer-rendered vegetation.

Vegetation resembles the cars in that vegetation changes rather rapidly with time, for example from season to season, is complex and should be replaced by models of vegetation. Figure 12 illustrates that Bing Maps already operates with the detection of trees and has implemented a system of rendering vegetation, in lieu of using imagery.

Finally, Figure 13 presents in intermediate result of efforts to replace street side images by an interpretation of the imaged scene. The example shows a building with façade, roof, sky, vegetation and a circulation space. The appeal of a geometric model of a scene replacing the original photographic imagery is immediately evident: reduced amounts of data to deal with, independence from weather, applications-relevance of the information about windows or doors, number of floors etc. (see also Leberl et al, 2009, [13]).

Fig. 13. Street side imagery of Graz and its segmentation into objects such as facades, sky, roof, vegetation (from Recky and Leberl, 2009, [15])

8 Conclusions

A *"location-aware"* Internet is a natural consequence of merging the GIS, the Internet, search, navigation, travel planning and location-based services. Microsoft's Bing Maps at http://www.bing.com/maps and Google Earth at http://maps.google.com are the major current systems competing for market share, and both are eying the vast opportunities from advertisement. Both are augmenting the initial 2-dimensional approach based on the paper map and digital street maps by a view at the third dimension, mainly of urban areas where the market opportunities are concentrated. Both are aiming at a human scale data base showing the world as a human pedestrian or driver experiences it on foot or from a car, both have collected vast amounts of street side images and both are looking for ways to provide user-contributed content.

The development is that of a generation with vast future significance. The emerging *"Internet of things"* will track us and every object of any value using embedded miniature RFID chips, and provide the object's location via the Internet, at all times, at all places and accessible from anywhere.

For this to make any sense, the World needs to be modeled in the Internet to be able to offer "location" for any of the billions of tracked objects. If the World is being modeled in 2D in 4 color bands and at 15 cm pixel size, if the urban areas get modeled in 3 dimensions with a pixel size of 10 cm, and if the human scale is introduced by street side image sources at 2 cm, and indoor data at 0.5 cm, and if all this uses sources with a redundancy factor of 10 images per object point, then the resulting data base will have to cope with 1 Exabyte.

It remains unclear at this time how location data will be supplied and updated in such systems – how much will have to be collected systematically by a central provider, and how much will get contributed in a "wiki-mode" by billions of users. What is clear, however, is that all current players in this development have the user planned as a significant provider of information and as a source for quality control.

Acknowledgements. This paper is built on material that was developed since mid-2006. Heavy use is being made of insights provided by the team at Microsoft-Photogrammetry in Graz, represented by Dr. Michael Gruber, and of the research team organized under the name "Virtual Habitat" at the Institute of Computer Graphics and Vision at Graz University of Technology, for example from Stefan Kluckner, Arnold Irschara or Michal Recky. We want to express our gratitude for the generous help we have been receiving by these two teams.

References

1. Goodchild, M.: Assertion and authority: the science of user-generated geographic content. In: Proceedings of the Colloquium for Andrew U. Frank's 60th Birthday. GeoInfo 39, Department of Geoinformation and Cartography, Vienna University of Technology (2008)
2. Gruber, M., Ladstätter, R.: Geometric issues of the digital large format aerial camera UltraCamD. In: International Calibration and Orientation Workshop EuroCOW 2006, Proceedings, Castelldefels, Spain, January 25-27 (2006)
3. Gruber, M., Reitinger, B.: UltraCamX and a new way of photogrammetric processing. In: Proceedings of the ASPRS Annual Conference 2008, Portland (2008)
4. Gruber, M., Sammer, P.: Modeling the Great Hall of the Austrian National Library. International Journal of Geomatics 9/95, Lemmer (1995)
5. Gruber, M.: Ein System zur umfassenden Erstellung und Nutzung dreidimensionaler Stadtmodelle, Dissertation, Graz University of Technology (1997)
6. Irschara, A., Bischof, H., Leberl, F.: Kollaborative 3D Rekonstruktion von urbanen Gebieten. In: 15. Intern. Geodätische Woche Obergurgl 2009. Wichmann, Heidelberg (2009)
7. ISPRS (2008),
   http://www.isprs.org/congresses/beijing2008/Default.aspx
8. Klaus, A.: Object Reconstruction from Image Sequences, Dissertation, Graz University of Technology (2007)
9. Kluckner, S., Pacher, G., Bischof, H., Leberl, F.: Objekterkennung in Luftbildern mit Methoden der Computer Vision durch kombinierte Verwendung von Redundanz, Farb- und Höheninformation. In: 15. Internationale Geodätische Woche Obergurgl 2009. Wichmann, Heidelberg (2009)
10. Ladstädter, R.: Untersuchungen zur geometrischen Genauigkeit der UltraCamD/X. In: 15. Internationale Geodätische Woche Obergurgl. Wichmann, Heidelberg (2009)
11. Leberl, F.: Die automatische Photogrammetrie für das Microsoft Virtual Earth System. In: 14. Internationale Geodätische Woche Obergurgl 2007, pp. S200–S208. Wichmann, Heidelberg (2007)

12. Leberl, F., Gruber, M.: Ortsbewusstsein im Internet – von 2-dimensionalen Navigationshilfen zur 3-dimensionalen Mixed Reality. In: Tagungsband der 15. Geod, pp. S67–S79. Woche Obergurgl, Wichmann-Verlag (2009) ISBN 978-3-87907-485-3
13. Leberl, F., Kluckner, S., Bischof, H.: Collection, Processing and Augmentation of VR Cities. In: Photogrammetric Week 2009. Wichmann-Verlag, Stuttgart (2009)
14. LiveLabs, Seadragon, Microsoft Live Labs (2008),
    http://livelabs.com/seadragon
15. Recky, M., Leberl, F.: Semantic Segmentation of Street-Side Images. In: Roth, P., Mautner, T., Pock, T. (eds.) Proceedings of the Annual Meeting of the Austrian Assoc. for Pattern Recognition AAPR, "Visual Learning", Stainz, Austria, May 14-15, vol. 254, pp. 273–282 (2009), books@ocg.at
16. Reitinger, B.: Interactive Visualization of Huge Aerial Image Datasets. In: International Archive for Photogrammetry and Remote Sensing, Beijing, vol. XXXVII (2008)
17. Schall, G., Schmalstieg, D.: Einsatz von mixed reality in der Mobilen Leitungsauskunft. In: 15. Intern. Geodätische Woche Obergurgl 2009. Wichmann, Heidelberg (2009)
18. Snavely, N., Seitz, S.M., Szeliski, R.: Modeling the world from Internet photo collections. International Journal of Computer Vision 80(2), 189–210 (2008)
19. Snavely, N., Garg, R., Seitz, S.M., Szeliski, R.: Finding Paths through the World's Photos. In: ACM Transactions on Graphics, SIGGRAPH 2008 (2008)
20. Strassenburg-Kleciak, M.: Photogrammetry and 3D Car Navigation. In: Proceedings of the 51st Photogrammetric Week, pp. 309–314. Wichmann Verlag (2007)
21. Taylor & Francis, Journal of Location Based Services (2009),
    http://www.tandf.co.uk/journal/tlbs
22. Teitler, B., Lieberman, M., Panozzo, D., Sankaranarayanan, J., Samet, H., Sperling, J.: NewsStand: A New View on News. In: Proceedings of the 16th ACM SIGSPATIAL international conference on Advances in geographic information systems, Irvine, California (2008) ISBN:978-1-60558-323-5
23. University of Washington (2008), http://phototour.cs.washington.edu/
24. Wikipedia (2009),
    http://en.wikipedia.org/wiki/Location-based_service

Part I
Computer Graphics Theory and Applications (GRAPP)

Fast Spatially Controllable Multi-dimensional Exemplar-Based Texture Synthesis and Morphing

Felix Manke and Burkhard Wünsche

University of Auckland, Dept. of Computer Science, Graphics Group
Private Bag 92019, Auckland, New Zealand
fman020@aucklanduni.ac.nz, burkhard@cs.auckland.ac.nz
http://www.cs.auckland.ac.nz/~burkhard

Abstract. Texture synthesis and morphing are important techniques for efficiently creating realistic textures used in scientific and entertainment applications.
In this paper we present a novel fast algorithm for multi-dimensional texture synthesis and morphing that is especially suitable for parallel architectures such as
GPUs or direct volume rendering (DVR) hardware. Our proposed solution generalizes the synthesis process to support higher than three-dimensional synthesis
and morphing.

We introduce several improvements to previous 2D synthesis algorithms, such
as new appearance space attributes and an improved jitter function. We then modify the synthesis algorithm to use it for texture morphing which can be applied
to arbitrary many 2D input textures and can be spatially controlled using weight
maps. Our results suggest that the algorithm produces higher quality textures than
alternative algorithms with similar speed. Compared to higher quality texture synthesis algorithms, our solution is considerably faster and allows the synthesis of
additional channels, such as transparencies and displacement maps, without affecting the running time of the synthesis at all. The method is easily extended to
allow fast 3D synthesis and we show several novel examples and applications for
morphed solid 3D textures.

Overall the presented technique provides an excellent trade-off between speed
and quality, is highly flexible, allows the use of arbitrary channels, can be extended to arbitrary dimensions, is suitable for a GPU-implementation, and can be
effectively integrated into rendering frameworks such as DVR tools.

1 Introduction

Texture mapping is one of the most important techniques for increasing the realism of
a 3D scene by providing fine surface details. Exemplar-based 2D texture synthesis is
a powerful tool to generate large textures from a single input example. Texture morphing as an extension creates coherent transitions between entirely different materials
with a quality and flexibility that cannot be achieved using simple blending techniques.
The applications of texture morphing are manifold and include terrain rendering, scientific visualization, the creation of transitions in animal fur and between biomedical or
geological materials, and the simulation of aging processes.

3D solid textures have the advantage that, in contrast to 2D textures, objects can be
"carved" out of a 3D material resulting in more realistic results. Since the acquisition of

A. Ranchordas et al. (Eds.): VISIGRAPP 2009, CCIS 68, pp. 21–34, 2010.
© Springer-Verlag Berlin Heidelberg 2010

3D textures is difficult, the synthesis and morphing of solid textures from 2D exemplars is very important. However, the task is extremely challenging and usually requires long computation times.

In this paper, we present a new fast algorithm for exemplar-based 2D texture morphing and higher-dimensional texture synthesis and morphing. After presenting the method for generating morphed 2D textures from 2D exemplars, we extend the algorithm to support 3D solid texture synthesis and morphing from the 2D input. A generalization to higher-dimensional texture morphing is followed by an evaluation of our method and comparison with Kopf et al.'s algorithm [10].

Our texture morphing algorithm is based on Lefebvre and Hoppe's pixel-based texture synthesis algorithm [13], a real-time approach implemented on the GPU by utilizing the parallel synthesis scheme proposed by L. Wei [26]. In a second publication the authors introduce the *appearance space*, a high-dimensional space that carries much more information per pixel than only color [14]. Its information richness allows us to perform a very robust texture morphing between exemplars of different nature.

Because of the close relationship we will give a brief summary of the original synthesis algorithm for only one input exemplar in section 3. We then discuss our extensions for texture morphing of arbitrary many input exemplars in 2D (section 4), 3D (section 5), and higher dimensions (section 6). In section 7 we discuss our results and conclude with an outlook on future research in section 8.

2 Related Work

Texture synthesis and texture morphing are closely related fields in which numerous different algorithms have been proposed. Procedural techniques for both 2D and 3D texture synthesis [19, 24, 28, 29] proofed to be hard to control and, compared to exemplar-based methods, limited in the variety of materials that can be modeled. Parametric exemplar-based methods, as proposed in [2, 3, 7, 20], rely on models of global statistical properties which serve as constraint function while matching statistics of the input and target texture. Though extensions for 3D synthesis have been made [4, 7], parametric models are usually only successful in synthesizing homogeneous and stochastic exemplars. Mixing properties of different textures is possible, but for texture morphing not enough spatial control is offered. Patch-based methods paste random patches of the exemplar into the output texture and optimize the transitions between overlapping patches [5, 12, 21]. While these methods could probably be extended to use 3D texture patches as input, there is no straightforward way to generate 3D textures from 2D input patches. In fact, we believe it is questionable whether such techniques can be used to create texture morphing of acceptable quality at all (though Kwatra et al. placed flower textures onto a grass texture and optimized the grass seams [12]).

In contrast, by processing one pixel at a time pixel-based methods [1, 6, 13, 27] offer a control that is fine enough to allow high-quality texture synthesis and morphing in 2D, 3D, and even higher dimensions. A successful 3D synthesis has been shown by L. Wei [25, 26]. Finally, optimization-based approaches use the local similarity measures of pixel neighborhoods to define a global texture energy function that is minimized [11]. Recently, Kopf et al. demonstrated that energy-based methods can be used for 3D synthesis [10], though the synthesis times of up to 90 minutes are rather slow and a GPU implementation is non-trivial. Another specialized solution for synthesizing 3D composite materials based on stereology theories (the analysis of 2D cross-sections of 3D volumes) has been proposed by Jagnow et al. [9].

Algorithms specifically for 2D texture morphing have also been developed. L. Wei used his pixel-based method to create transitions between two exemplars [26]. However, the synthesis quality within the transition area decreased significantly. Liu et al. proposed a pattern-based approach that uses ideas of image morphing in order to generate metamorphosis sequences [15]. Both Zhang et al. and Tonietto and Walter used texton maps to support a pixel-based texture morphing [23, 30]. Unfortunately, all three publications show results only for very similar input exemplars, which makes it difficult to assess the quality of the approaches. Matusik et al. utilized a simplical complex model to build a neighborhood graph of input exemplars [18]. Though examples with several input textures are given, the approach relies on a texture database and is explicitly designed for similar textures only. To our knowledge, texture morphing in three dimensions using exemplars of very different irregularly textured materials has not been shown by anyone before.

3 Lefebvre and Hoppe's 2D Texture Synthesis

As most pixel-based methods, the algorithm proposed in [13, 14] performs an iterative optimization to minimize the difference of the synthesis result to the original exemplar, where the distance is measured using the sum of squared differences (SSD) of local neighborhoods. A standard multi-resolution approach is pursued by computing a Gaussian pyramid E of the exemplar and creating an "empty" pyramid S for the synthesis result. The synthesis is performed from the coarsest to the finest resolution, first establishing low frequencies and then defining the fine details.

A key difference of the algorithm to other methods is that S does not store image colors, but *pixel coordinates* into the exemplar E, which facilitates a GPU implementation. To pass the synthesis result of a coarse level S_{i-1} to a finer level S_i an *upsampling* of the coordinates is performed that distributes the value of $S_{i-1}(P)$ (that is, a coordinate into E_i) to four child pixels in S_i. In the correction phase, the synthesis error is minimized by searching the pixel coordinate Q with the best-matching local neighborhood $N_{E_i}(Q)$ in the exemplar for the neighborhood $N_{S_i}(P)$ around $S_i(P)$. The correction phase is accelerated using sub-passes, each of which optimizes only selected pixels, and *k-coherence* search [22] based on pre-computed candidate sets.

The texture synthesis can greatly benefit from using an *appearance space* [14], where pixels encode texture characteristics in addition to color. The high-dimensional appearance vectors are projected into a low-dimensional space defined by the first n principal components obtained from a principal component analysis (PCA). In tests we found that usually more than 95% of the total variance of an exemplar is explained by the first 8 components.

4 Our 2D Texture Morphing Algorithm

When dealing with texture morphing we have to synthesize a texture based on several input exemplars. The result should reflect the nature of all exemplars, though the influence of each input can vary spatially. To control the spatial influence of each of the m exemplars, we use scalar *weight maps* of the size of the synthesized texture S. Each weight map W^j encodes the weight of the exemplar E^j per position $P \in S$. To ensure a correct morphing, we normalize the weight maps so that $\sum_{j=1}^{m} W^j(P) = 1$. Note that, when specifying only one input exemplar, our algorithm behaves like a standard texture synthesis algorithm.

In the following, we will present the extensions we made for every single step of the original synthesis algorithm. Because the coordinate upsampling remains unchanged and is performed on each S_i^j individually, we do not include it in the discussion. Note that the modifications necessary for texture morphing still allow an implementation on parallel architectures.

4.1   Initialization

The initialization of the exemplars themselves remains unchanged, because they are independent from each other. For every weight map W^j that is associated with each exemplar, we additionally compute a Gaussian pyramid. Because the algorithm is based on manipulating exemplar *coordinates* rather than colors (and coordinates cannot be averaged or merged), we need a separate synthesis pyramid S^j for every exemplar. Instead of initializing S_{-1}^j with zero coordinates, we find the following initialization more intuitive (where s_{e^j} is the size of E^j):

$$S_{-1}(P) = P \bmod s_{e^j}.$$

This better reflects how the algorithm proceeds, especially when only a few pyramid levels are used.

4.2   Coordinate Jitter

Similar to the upsampling the coordinate jitter is also independent for each exemplar and could be carried over unchanged. However, the plot of Lefebvre and Hoppe's function $J_i(P)$ for different combinations of $\mathfrak{H}$ and r (see figure 1 (left)) shows that $J_i(P)$ always returns zero for randomness $r < 0.5$. In addition, for $r = 1$ the probability of $J_i(P) = 0$ is twice as high as for $J_i(P) = -1$ and $J_i(P) = 1$. We therefore propose the following equation that behaves more intuitive (see also figure 1 (right)):

$$J_i(P) = \left\lfloor j + \begin{pmatrix} k_x \\ k_y \end{pmatrix} \right\rfloor, \text{ where}$$

$$j = \mathfrak{H}(P) \cdot \mathrm{lerp}(0.5, 1, r_i),$$
$$k_{x|y} = \begin{cases} \mathrm{lerp}(0.5, 2/3, r_i) & \text{if } j_{x|y} \geq 0 \\ 1 - \mathrm{lerp}(0.5, 2/3, r_i) & \text{otherwise,} \end{cases}$$
$$\mathrm{lerp}(a, b, t) = a + t(b - a).$$

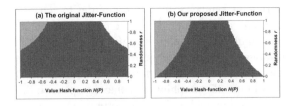

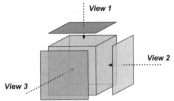

Fig. 1. Plots of the result of different jitter functions $J_i(P)$. Left: The original jitter function proposed in [13]. Right: Our improved jitter function. Color encoding: Blue $= -1$, Magenta $= 0$, Yellow $= 1$.

Fig. 2. Several 2D exemplars define different views of the solid texture being synthesized. Adopted from [25].

4.3   Correction Phase

In the correction phase the best-matching pixel for a synthesis pixel P is searched in the exemplar. However, now $S_i(P)$ must represent *all* input exemplars, weighted according to the weights $W_i^j(P)$. For the original 2D synthesis algorithm the neighborhood of P in the synthesis level S_i can be defined as the set:

$$N_{S_i}(P) = \{E_i(Q) \mid Q = S_i(P + \Delta_N)\}, \quad \Delta_N \in \mathcal{N}, \tag{1}$$

where Δ_N takes the values of offset vectors from the neighborhood's center to all pixels in the neighborhood as defined by the set $\mathcal{N}$ of all offsets:

$$\mathcal{N} = \{\delta \mid (P + \delta) \in N(P)\}.$$

For the texture morphing of multiple exemplars, we extend the neighborhood gathering as follows:

$$N_{S_i}(P) = \{C(i, P + \Delta_N)\}, \quad \Delta_N \in \mathcal{N}, \tag{2}$$

$$C(i, X) = \sum_{j=1}^{m} W_i^j(X) \cdot E_i^j(Q), \quad Q = S_i^j(X).$$

$C(i, X)$ is the synthesized color in level i at location X and is' the weighted average of all exemplar levels. Given the synthesis neighborhood $N_{S_i}(P)$ the best-matching pixel is searched for in each of the exemplars E_i^j and $S_i^j(P)$ where $N_{S_i}(P)$ is the same for all m synthesis levels $S_i^j(P)$:

$$S_i(P) = \operatorname*{argmin}_{Q \in E_i} SSD(N_{S_i}(P), N_{E_i}(Q)). \tag{3}$$

5   3D Texture Synthesis and Morphing

In the following, we will discuss how to generate textures with an additional spatial dimension and how to morph between different materials. As illustrated in figure 2, several input exemplars are considered as being different *views* of the solid texture cube that is to be synthesized [10, 25]. During the synthesis, the algorithm tries to generate a 3D texture that reflects the characteristics of all views. The close relationship to 2D texture morphing in terms of the use of multiple exemplars was already mentioned by L. Wei [25]. To create smooth transitions between entirely different materials within the solid texture cube, exemplar views need to be specified for each material. For 3D morphing the weight maps are used as in the 2D morphing to define the spatial influence of the materials. Our algorithm gives a unified tool for supporting 3D synthesis or morphing at the same time. It is not always necessary or appropriate to specify all three exemplars. Sometimes, for example when a material exhibits dominant directional features, it is better to define only two views [25].

The jitter step is not affected by our modifications, because the coordinates stored in a synthesis level $S_i^j(P)$ are still defined in $\mathbb{R}^2$. A minor difference is that the jitter function $J_i(P)$ and the hash function $\mathfrak{H}(P)$ now take 3D coordinates as input argument.

5.1   Initialization

In contrast to the 2D morphing, the synthesis pyramids S^j and the weight maps W^j are solid texture cubes. In S^j each voxel stores a 2D coordinate into the corresponding exemplar E^j. Because E^j represents only one particular view onto the solid target texture, the initialization of S_{-1}^j is modified in the following way:

$$S_{-1}^j(P) = P_{u,v} \bmod s_{e^j},$$

where u and v denote the two components of $P \in \mathbb{R}^3$ to which E^j is parallel.

5.2   Coordinate Upsampling

The coordinate upsampling cannot simply be extended by an additional dimension, because the synthesis pyramids still store 2D coordinates. Thus, we apply the 2D upsampling for every second slice that is oriented parallel to the exemplar view and duplicate the result for each subsequent slice:

$$S_i^j(2 \cdot P_{u,v|w} + \Delta_{u,v}) = S_i^j(2 \cdot P_{u,v|(w+1)} + \Delta_{u,v}) = \qquad (4)$$
$$(2 \cdot S_{i-1}(P) + \Delta_U) \bmod S_{e^j},$$

where w is even ($w \bmod 2 = 0$) and depicts the component of P that is orthogonal to the view. $\Delta_{u,v}$ describes a 3D vector with the same value in the u- and v-component as Δ_U and $w = 0$.

5.3   Correction Phase

When performing neighborhood-matching during the correction we have to compare neighborhoods around voxels in a 3D synthesis pyramid with neighborhoods of pixels of a 2D input exemplar. We exploit that the exemplars are oriented orthogonally to one of the principal axes of the solid cube that is synthesized. Since each exemplar represents only the view in this direction, the synthesis pyramid for an exemplar only needs to reflect the exemplar in that direction. Thus, we can align the 2D neighborhoods $N_{S_i}(P)$ to stand parallel to the exemplar, as it has also been proposed in [10, 25].

In consequence, we need to introduce several synthesis neighborhoods $N_{S_i|u,v}(P)$, one for each possible orientation of exemplars. Note that, as in the 2D morphing algorithm, $N_{S_i|u,v}(P)$ is a merged neighborhood that needs to represent all exemplars. Our definition in equation 2 is also valid for the 3D synthesis, except that $P \in S_i^j$ is now defined in $\mathbb{R}^3$. We therefore modify the definition to support oriented neighborhood gathering in 3D solid textures:

$$N_{S_i|u,v}(P) = \{C(i, P + \Delta_{N|u,v})\}, \quad \Delta_{N|u,v} \in \mathcal{N}_{u,v}, \tag{5}$$

where $\Delta_{N|u,v}$ gives the neighborhood offsets parallel to the current view (the w-component of $\Delta_{N|u,v}$ is set to 0). Notice the similarity to the upsampling step, which also depends on the view's orientation.

Interleaved correction for an improved convergence using sub-passes is still possible in 3D synthesis and morphing. However, because of the additional dimension we now have to define eight sub-passes as a pattern in a 2^3 cube.

5.4 A New Neighborhood

As discussed in section 3, the synthesis in the reduced appearance space makes it possible to use a very compact neighborhood consisting of only 4 corner pixels. However, 3D texture synthesis is a much more challenging problem. The algorithm generally has to deal with little information that is available for generating a solid texture from the 2D exemplars. We found that the reduced neighborhood is not capable of preserving the features of the input exemplars. Much better results can be achieved using a full 5×5 or even 7×7 neighborhood — of course at the expense of speed.

In order to improve the synthesis while keeping the computation time low we propose a new "half-reduced" neighborhood. The layout is shown in figure 3 (top). We still average several pixel values to compute the values for the individual neighborhood values (shown on the bottom of the figure). Note that the new neighborhood, consisting of 9 points, is a superset of the neighborhood proposed in [14]. Figure 4 shows a comparison of the results using different neighborhoods for 3D synthesis. Our new neighborhood is much better capable of preserving feature coherence than the original four-pixel neighborhood, which fails to produce acceptable results. The new neighborhood can also be used for 2D texture synthesis and morphing. We found that 2D morphing results are improved significantly for exemplars with large semantic features [16].

5.5 Synthesis and Morphing of Additional Channels

The synthesis and morphing based on texture coordinates makes it possible to restore the exact location in the original exemplar for each pixel in the synthesized texture. Instead of a color image, the result of the synthesis is a map of texture coordinates that is used to sample the exemplars and output the final image.

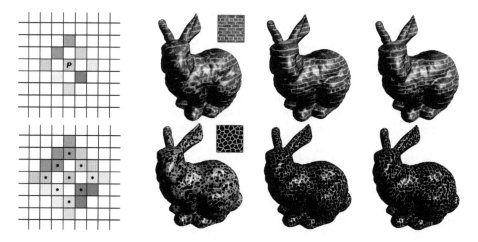

Fig. 3. Pixels used in our half-reduced neighborhood (top) and pixels for computing averaged values of the neighborhood (bottom).

Fig. 4. Comparison of different neighborhoods used during the correction phase of the 3D texture synthesis. First column: Reduced four-pixel neighborhood. Second column: Full 5×5 neighborhood consisting of 25 pixels. Third column: Our new half-reduced neighborhood consisting of 9 pixels.

Using this map of texture coordinates, we are able to sample arbitrary input images, and not only the color exemplar. Hence, additional channels — like alpha channels, displacement maps, specularity maps, etc. — can be synthesized without affecting the performance of the synthesis/morphing at all. This is an advantage over other methods that do not keep track of the original pixel locations in the input exemplars.

6   Higher-Dimensional Texture Synthesis

Our algorithm can theoretically be extended to support texture synthesis and morphing in arbitrary dimensions using also higher-dimensional input exemplars. Though it might already be hard to define what 4D texture morphing exactly means, a possible application could be the synthesis of material properties that change spatially over time, for example aging wood or rusted metal.

The idea for higher-dimensional synthesis generalizes the modifications we made in the previous section. For a target dimension N and M-dimensional exemplars, each exemplar defines a view onto an M-dimensional "face" of the synthesis texture, the $N - M$ remaining dimensions are not specified by this view.

The initialization of S_{-1} can be defined as $S_{-1}(P) = P_{x_1,\cdots,x_M} \bmod s_{ej}$. Similarly, the coordinate upsampling needs to repeat the upsampled coordinates for $N - M$ "slices". The extensions of the jitter function to M dimensions are trivial. For optimizing the synthesis during the correction phase the neighborhoods $N_{S_i|x_1,\cdots,x_m}$ need to be aligned with the exemplar's orientation, which can be achieved by defining the offsets in $\mathcal{N}_{x_1,\cdots,x_m}$ according to an M-dimensional neighborhood. An interleaved correction scheme would specify a sub-pass pattern in a 2^N-dimensional cube.

7   Results

We implemented our algorithm using C++ and execute it on the CPU in order to facilitate experimentation and integration into existing biomedical visualization software. As exemplars we used 64×64 or 128×128 pixel textures. For the 2D morphing, the target size is 512×512. Our generated solid textures have 128^3 or 256^3 voxels. We used the appearance space attributes discussed in section 3 and projected the 150-dimensional vectors onto the first eight components using the PCA implementation from [8]. Several new appearance space attributes such as neighborhood variance and principal direction of texture features were extensively tested. We found that RGB color, signed feature distance, and gradient estimates are best with respect to visual quality and computational cost [16]. We performed two full correction passes per synthesis level. We used the reduced or our half-reduced neighborhood for the 2D outputs, and the half-reduced or a full 5×5 neighborhood for 3D synthesis and morphing.

Figure 5 shows some of our 2D morphing results with two exemplars to demonstrate how the transition between structures is generated. Note how the algorithm gradually defines a coherent transition of features and morphs between them, even if the exemplars are extremely different. Morphing examples with several exemplars and complex weight maps are shown in figure 6.

Examples of our 3D synthesis, including one with an additional channel for displacement mapping, are given in figures 7 and 8. As can be seen, the generated 3D solid textures coherently reflect the characteristics of the materials. However, a smoothing of the fine details can be observed — a problem that is common in solid texture synthesis algorithms (compare for example to [10, 26]).

Fig. 5. 2D morphing results using two input exemplars and linear weight maps. The examples illustrate how the morphing algorithm finds coherent transitions between the features.

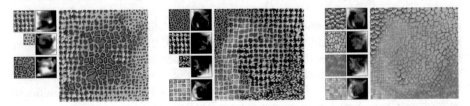

Fig. 6. 2D morphing results using three and four input exemplars and complex weight maps. Note that the weight maps are normalized and actually of the same size as the synthesized target texture.

Fig. 7. 3D texture synthesis results. The generated solid textures have been used to render different 3D geometries. Bottom-right: Intensity values used as additional channel for displacement mapping.

Fig. 8. 3D morphing results using two exemplars and linear weight maps. The last two examples use a morphed texture of size 256^3.

The charts in figure 9 illustrate how our algorithm performs using the settings stated above, executed using one core of a 2.13 GHz Intel® Core™ 2 Duo CPU with 2 GB RAM. The 2D morphing using two exemplars and a reduced neighborhood takes less than 12 seconds on average. With our half-reduced neighborhood the timings are still below 17 seconds. Our examples with three and four exemplars needed less than 18 and 25 seconds respectively for the morphing with a reduced neighborhood.

For 3D synthesis, even with a full 7×7 neighborhood (which we never use in practice) our algorithm needs no more than 15 minutes to synthesize a 128^3 solid texture cube, and 3D morphing with twice as many exemplar views takes less than 30 minutes. The half-reduced neighborhood performs with little more than 5 minutes for 3D synthesis and about 12 minutes for 3D morphing very fast while producing high-quality results. For morphing solid textures with a resolution of 256^3 voxels, our algorithm needs between 110 minutes (half-reduced neighborhood) and 140 minutes (full 5×5 neighborhood). Note that doubling the target resolution leads to eight times as many voxels in the solid cube. With an implementation on the GPU we expect a significant performance boost, possibly by several orders of magnitude.

Our algorithm has some limitations. As most pixel-based approaches the algorithm has difficulties to synthesize or morph textures with large features or where the features

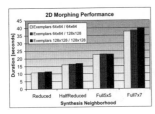
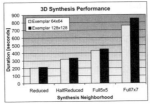
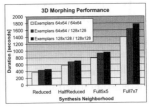

Fig. 9. Performance charts for our algorithm with different neighborhoods (without initialization times). Left: 2D texture morphing with two exemplars; Middle: 3D texture synthesis with one exemplar; Right: 3D texture morphing with two exemplars. The target texture size for the 2D tests was 512×512 and for the 3D tests 128^3.

have a semantic meaning to humans. Problems also occur with near stochastic textures such as clouds and slightly crumbled paper. Textures with features of very different scale represent a particular problem for the morphing, because no common structures can be found that could be morphed into each other. Currently, we are working on texture morphing supported by *frequency-dependent feature scaling* (FDFS), a spatially varying exemplar scaling based on the dominant frequency of the textures. Depending on the frequencies of the exemplars and their weights $W^j(P)$ we compute a scaling factor $s(P)$ for each exemplar in order to locally match the feature sizes to each other.

7.1　Texture-Enhanced Direct Volume Rendering

To further demonstrate the flexibility of the proposed morphing algorithm, we present examples of a new methodology termed *texture-enhanced DVR* [17]. In traditional DVR features of interest in a data set are classified by transfer functions (TF) that map data values to colors and opacities. Texture-enhanced DVR enriches this pipeline by supporting textures for encoding materials and conveying additional information. A new type

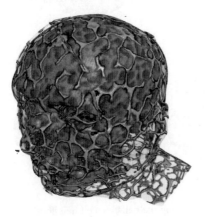
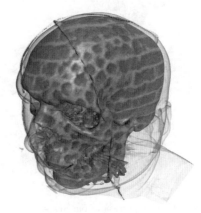

Fig. 10. Texture-enhanced Direct Volume Rendering uses textures to encode different materials and convey additional information. Left: Screen-door transparency effects; Right: Encoding imaginary materials using textures.

of TF, called *texture transfer function*, maps from data values to weighting curves for the input textures, and therewith provides the weights for a subsequent 3D texture morphing step, which coherently morphs materials in transition zones. Figure 10 shows two examples of texture-enhanced DVR. On the left we show how to exploit the synthesis of additional channels (section 5.5) for screen-door transparency effects, the example on the right illustrates the use of texture morphing on a single layer.

7.2   Comparison with Kopf et al.'s Algorithm

In figure 11, we compare the synthesis quality of our proposed algorithm with results of the algorithm based on energy minimization recently presented by [10]. Disregarding the different illumination settings, the results for the first two exemplars ("woodwall" and "animalskin") appear to be of very similar quality. Our result for the "woodwall" texture seems to have more structure than Kopf et al.'s result, which looks rather smooth. Although our result for "animalskin" shows more variance in the size of the features, it better reflects the structures within the blue spots. On the other hand, the boundaries between texture features look sharper in Kopf et al.'s solid texture, which can also be seen in the right hand image, where features (the tomatoes) are more distinct and the green leaves are not suppressed as much. However, our technique is significantly faster. Including the initialization, we need about 6 minutes when using the half-reduced

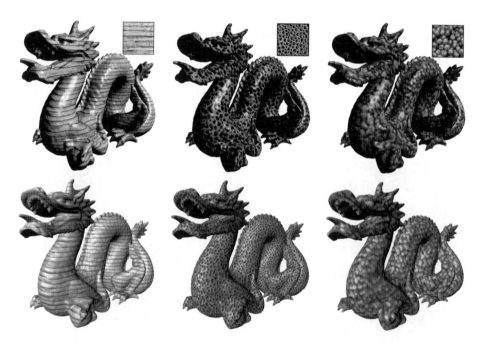

Fig. 11. Comparison of our 3D texture synthesis (top row) using the half-reduced neighborhood (left, right) and a full 5×5 neighborhood (center) with Kopf et al.'s (bottom row) algorithm using the same input exemplars and target resolution (from http://www.johanneskopf.de/publications/solid/results/index.html).

neighborhood and less than 9 minutes using the full 5×5 neighborhood. In contrast, Kopf et al. reported up to 90 minutes required for the synthesis. Another advantage of our method is that additional channels can be synthesized without affecting the running time of the synthesis at all. In contrast, the cost of Kopf et al.'s method directly depends on the number of channels in the exemplar. Furthermore, Kopf et al.'s algorithm does not allow a straightforward implementation on the GPU, because a continuous update of the histogram is required.

8 Conclusions and Future Work

We presented a new and fast exemplar-based texture morphing algorithm for two, three and theoretically also higher dimensions as an extension of the pure 2D synthesis algorithm proposed in [13, 14]. Because our modifications obey the design principles of the original algorithm, our new contribution still allows an implementation on parallel stream-processing hardware. Even without hardware acceleration our current CPU-based implementation is already faster than comparable 3D synthesis methods.

The steps of the original algorithm have been generalized to support morphing with arbitrary many exemplars and higher-dimensional synthesis. A more intuitive jitter function and a new compact neighborhood suitable for fast 3D synthesis have been introduced and its performance evaluated.

In the future we want to further improve the synthesis quality. Spatially varying scaling based on the dominant frequency of the exemplars could support the morphing to create better transitions between exemplars with structures of very different scale. Another interesting feature is the synthesis and morphing along time-varying vector and tensor fields.

References

1. Ashikhmin, M.: Synthesizing natural textures. In: Proceedings of I3D 2001, pp. 217–226. ACM Press, New York (2001)
2. Bar-Joseph, Z., El-Yaniv, R., Lischinski, D., Werman, M.: Texture mixing and texture movie synthesis using statistical learning. IEEE Transactions on Visualization and Computer Graphics 7(2), 120–135 (2001)
3. De Bonet, J.S.: Multiresolution sampling procedure for analysis and synthesis of texture images. In: Proceedings of SIGGRAPH 1997, pp. 361–368. ACM Press, New York (1997)
4. Dischler, J.-M., Ghazanfarpour, D., Freydier, R.: Anisotropic solid texture synthesis using orthogonal 2d views. Computer Graphics Forum 17(3), 87–95 (1998)
5. Efros, A.A., Freeman, W.T.: Image quilting for texture synthesis and transfer. In: Proceedings of SIGGRAPH 2001, pp. 341–346. ACM Press, New York (2001)
6. Efros, A.A., Leung, T.K.: Texture synthesis by non-parametric sampling. In: Proceedings of ICCV 1999, pp. 1033–1038. IEEE Computer Society, Los Alamitos (1999)
7. Heeger, D.J., Bergen, J.R.: Pyramid-based texture analysis/synthesis. In: Proceedings of SIGGRAPH 1995, pp. 229–238. ACM Press, New York (1995)
8. Intel® Corporation Corporation. Open Source Computer Vision Library, http://sourceforge.net/projects/opencvlibrary/ [checked: 07/24/2009]
9. Jagnow, R., Dorsey, J., Rushmeier, H.: Stereological techniques for solid textures. ACM Transactions on Graphics (Proceedings of SIGGRAPH 2004) 23(3), 329–335 (2004)

10. Kopf, J., Fu, C.-W., Cohen-Or, D., Deussen, O., Lischinski, D., Wong, T.-T.: Solid texture synthesis from 2d exemplars. ACM Transactions on Graphics (Proceedings of SIGGRAPH 2007) 26(3), 2.1–2.9 (2007)

11. Kwatra, V., Essa, I., Bobick, A., Kwatra, N.: Texture optimization for example-based synthesis. ACM Transactions on Graphics (SIGGRAPH 2005) 24(3), 795–802 (2005)

12. Kwatra, V., Schödl, A., Essa, I., Turk, G., Bobick, A.: Graphcut textures: image and video synthesis using graph cuts. ACM Transactions on Graphics (Proceedings of SIGGRAPH 2003) 22(3), 277–286 (2003)

13. Lefebvre, S., Hoppe, H.: Parallel controllable texture synthesis. ACM Transactions on Graphics (Proceedings of SIGGRAPH 2005) 24(3), 777–786 (2005)

14. Lefebvre, S., Hoppe, H.: Appearance-space texture synthesis. ACM Transactions on Graphics (Proceedings of SIGGRAPH 2006) 25(3), 541–548 (2006)

15. Liu, Z., Liu, C., Shum, H.-Y., Yu, Y.: Pattern-based texture metamorphosis. In: Proceedings of Pacific Graphics 2002, p. 184. IEEE Computer Society, Los Alamitos (2002)

16. Manke, F.: Texture-enhanced direct volume rendering, MSc thesis, Dept. of Computer Science, University of Auckland, New Zealand (July 2008)

17. Manke, F., Wünsche, B.: Texture-enhanced direct volume rendering. In: Proceedings of GRAPP 2009, Lisbon, Portugal, pp. 185–190 (2009)

18. Matusik, W., Zwicker, M., Durand, F.: Texture design using a simplicial complex of morphable textures. ACM Trans. on Graphics (SIGGRAPH 2005) 24(3), 787–794 (2005)

19. Perlin, K.: An image synthesizer. In: Proc. of SIGGRAPH 1985, pp. 287–296. ACM Press, New York (1985)

20. Portilla, J., Simoncelli, E.P.: A parametric texture model based on joint statistics of complex wavelet coefficients. Int. Journal of Computer Vision 40(1), 49–70 (2000)

21. Praun, E., Finkelstein, A., Hoppe, H.: Lapped textures. In: Proceedings of SIGGRAPH 2000, pp. 465–470. ACM Press, New York (2000)

22. Tong, X., Zhang, J., Liu, L., Wang, X., Guo, B., Shum, H.-Y.: Synthesis of bidirectional texture functions on arbitrary surfaces. In: Proceedings of SIGGRAPH 2002, pp. 665–672. ACM Press, New York (2002)

23. Tonietto, L., Walter, M.: Texture metamorphosis driven by texton masks. Computers & Graphics 29(5), 697–703 (2005)

24. Turk, G.: Generating textures on arbitrary surfaces using reaction-diffusion. In: Proceedings of SIGGRAPH 1991, pp. 289–298. ACM Press, New York (1991)

25. Wei, L.-Y.: Texture Synthesis by Fixed Neighborhood Searching. PhD thesis, Stanford University (2002)

26. Wei, L.-Y.: Texture synthesis from multiple sources. In: SIGGRAPH 2003: ACM SIGGRAPH 2003 Sketches & Applications, p. 1. ACM Press, New York (2003)

27. Wei, L.-Y., Levoy, M.: Fast texture synthesis using tree-structured vector quantization. In: Proceedings of SIGGRAPH 2000, pp. 479–488. ACM Press, New York (2000)

28. Witkin, A., Kass, M.: Reaction-diffusion textures. SIGGRAPH Computer Graphics 25(4), 299–308 (1991)

29. Worley, S.: A cellular texture basis function. In: Proceedings of SIGGRAPH 1996, pp. 291–294. ACM Press, New York (1996)

30. Zhang, J., Zhou, K., Velho, L., Guo, B., Shum, H.-Y.: Synthesis of progressively-variant textures on arbitrary surfaces. ACM Transactions on Graphics (Proceedings of SIGGRAPH 2003) 22(3), 295–302 (2003)

Extending Marching Cubes with Adaptative Methods to Obtain More Accurate Iso-surfaces

John Congote[1,2], Aitor Moreno[2], Iñigo Barandiaran[2],
Javier Barandiaran[2], and Oscar Ruiz[1]

[1] CAD/CAM/CAE Laboratory, EAFIT University, Medellín, Colombia
[2] VICOMTech, San Sebastian, Spain

Abstract. This work proposes an extension of the Marching Cubes algorithm, where the goal is to represent implicit functions with higher accuracy using the same grid size. The proposed algorithm displaces the vertices of the cubes iteratively until the stop condition is achieved. After each iteration, the difference between the implicit and the explicit representations is reduced, and when the algorithm finishes, the implicit surface representation using the modified cubical grid is more accurate, as the results shall confirm. The proposed algorithm corrects some topological problems that may appear in the discretization process using the original grid.

1 Introduction

Surface representation from scalar functions is an active research topic in different fields of Computer Graphics such as medical visualization of Magnetic Resonance Imaging (MRI) and Computer Tomography (CT) [1]. This representation is also widely used as an intermediate step for several graphical processes [2], such as mesh reconstruction from point clouds or track planning. The representation of a scalar function in 3D is known as implicit representation and is generated using continuous algebraic iso-surfaces, radial basis functions [3] [4], signed distance transform [5], discrete voxelisations or constructive solid geometry.

The implicit functions are frequently represented as a discrete cubical grid where each vertex has the value of the function. The Marching Cubes algorithm (MC) [6] takes the cubical grid to create an explicit representation of the implicit surface. The MC algorithm has been widely studied as has been demonstrated by Newman [7]. The output of the MC algorithm is an explicit surface represented as a set of connected triangles known as polygonal representation. The original results of the MC algorithm presented several topological problems as demonstrated by Chernyaev [8] and have already been solved by Lewiner [9].

The MC algorithm divides the space in a regular cubical grid. For each cube, a triangular representation is calculated, which are then joined to obtain the explicit representation of the surface. This procedure is highly parallel because each cube can be processed separately without significant interdependencies. The resolution of the generated polygonal surface depends directly on the input grid size. In order to increase the resolution of the polygonal surface it is necessary to increase the number of cubes in the grid, increasing the amount of memory required to store the values of the grid.

A. Ranchordas et al. (Eds.): VISIGRAPP 2009, CCIS 68, pp. 35–44, 2010.

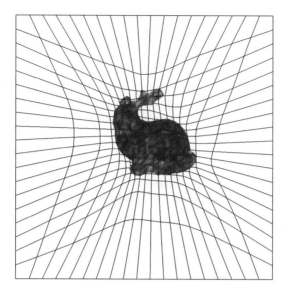

Fig. 1. Optimised Grid with 20^3 cubes representing the bunny

Alternative methods to the MC algorithm introduce the concept of generating multi-resolution grids, creating nested sub-grids inside the original grid. The spatial subdivision using octrees or recursive tetrahedral subdivision techniques are also used in the optimization of iso-surface representations. The common characteristic of these types of methods is that they are based on adding more cells efficiently to ensure a higher resolution in the final representation.

This work is structured as follows: In Section 2, a review of some of the best known MC algorithm variations is given. Section 3 describes the methodological aspects behind the proposed algorithm. In Section 4 details the results of testing the algorithm with a set of implicit functions. Finally, conclusions and future work are discussed in Section 5.

2   Related Work

Marching Cubes (MC) [6] has been the *de facto* standard algorithm for the process generating of explicit representations of iso-surfaces from scalar functions or its implicit definition The MC algorithm takes as an input a regular scalar volumetric data set, having a scalar value residing at each lattice point of a rectilinear lattice in 3D space. The enclosed volume in the region of interest is subdivided into a regular grid of cubes. Each vertex of all cubes in the grid is set by the value of the implicit function evaluated at the vertex coordinates. Depending on the sign of each vertex, a cube has 256 (2^8) possible combinations, but using geometrical properties, such as rotations and reflections, the final number of combinations is reduced to 15 possibilities. These 15 surface triangulations are stored in Look-Up Tables (LUT) for performance reasons. The final vertices of the triangular mesh are calculated using linear interpolation between the values assigned to the vertices of the cube. This polygonal mesh representation is the

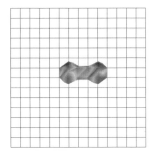 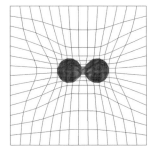 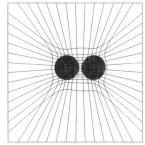

(a) Original Grid. The two spheres are displayed as a singular object due to the poor resolution in the region

(b) Intermediate Grid. Both spheres are displayed well, but are still joined

(c) Final Grid. The new resolution displays two well shaped and separated spheres with the same number of cubes in the grid

Fig. 2. 2D slides representing three different states in the evolution of the algorithm of two nearby spheres

best suitable one for the current generation of graphic hardware because it has been optimized to this type of input.

MC variations were developed to enhance the resolution of the generated explicit surfaces, allowing the representation of geometrical lost details during MC discretization process. Weber [10] proposes a multi-grid method. Inside an initial grid, a nested grid is created to add more resolution in that region. This methodology is suitable to be used recursively, adding more detail to conflictive regions. In the final stage, the explicit surface is created by joining all the reconstructed polygonal surfaces. It is necessary to generate a special polygonization in the joints between the grid and the sub-grids to avoid the apparition of cracks or artifacts. This method has a higher memory demand to store the new values of the nested-grid.

An alternative method to refine selected regions of interest(*ROI*) is the octree subdivision [11]. This method generates an octree in the region of existence of the function, creating a polygonization of each octree cell. One of the flaws of this method is the generation of cracks in the regions with different resolutions. This problem is solve with the Dual Marching Cubes method [12] and implemented for algebraic functions by Pavia [13].

The octree subdivision method produces edges with more than two vertices, which can be overcome by changing the methodology of the subdivision. Instead of using cubes, tetrahedrons were used to subdivide the grid, without creating nodes in the middle of the edges [14]. This method recursively subdivides the space into tetrahedrons.

The previous methodologies increment the number of cells of the grid in order to achieve more resolution in the regions of interest. Balmelli [15] presented an algorithm based on the warping of the grid to a defined region of interest. The warping of the vertices is performed in a hierarchical procedure, the volume is considered as a single cell of the grid, and then, the central point of the grid is warped in the direction of the *ROI*. Then, this cell is divide then in eight cells and the process is repeated until the number of selected cells is achieved. The result is a new grid with the same number of cells, but with higher resolution near to the *ROI*. The algorithm was tested with discrete datasets, and the *ROI* is created by the user or defined by a crossing edges criteria.

The presented method generates a similar warping grid as Balmelli does, but we avoid the use of hierarchical procedures and our region of interest is automatically generated based in the input implicit function, obtaining dense distribution of vertices near the iso-surface. (see Figure 2)

3   Methodology

The presented algorithm in this work is an extension of the MC algorithm. The main goal is to generate a more accurate representations of the given implicit surfaces with the same grid resolution.

Applying a calculated displacement to the vertices of the grid, the algorithm reconfigure the position of the vertices of the grid to obtain more accurate representations of the iso-surface. In order to avoid self-intersections and to preserve the topological structure of the grid, the vertices are translated inside the cells of the neighbor of the vertex. The displacement to be applied to all the vertices are calculated iteratively until a stop condition is satisfied.

Let be Θ a rectangular prism tessellated as a cubical honeycomb, W the vertices of Θ [Eq. 1], B the boundary vertices of Θ [Eq. 2], and V the inner vertices of Θ [Eq. 3]. For each vertex $v_i \in V$, a N_i set is defined as the 26 *adjacent* vertices to v_i, denoting each adjacent vertex as $n_{i,j}$ [Eq. 4]. (see Figure 3). $f(w)$ is the value of the function in the position w and A is the scale value for the attraction force for the displacement of the vertices.

$$W = \{w_i / w_i \in \Theta\} \tag{1}$$

$$B = \{b_i / b_i \in \delta\Theta\} \tag{2}$$

$$V = W - B \tag{3}$$

$$N_i = \{n_{i,j} / n_{i,j} \text{ is } j\text{th neighborhood of } v_i\} \tag{4}$$

The proposed algorithm is an iterative process. In each iteration, each vertex v_i of the grid Θ is translated by a d_i displacement vector [Eq. 6], obtaining a new configuration of Θ, where *i)* the topological connections of the grid are preserved, *ii)* cells containing patches of f are a more accurate representation of the surface, and *iii)* the total displacement [Eq. 7] of the grid is lower and is used as the stop condition of the algorithm when it reach a value Δ(see Figure 3).

The distance vector d_i is calculated as shown in [Eq. 6] and it can be seen as the resultant force of each neighboring vertex scaled by the value of f at the position of each vertex and the attraction value A. In order to limit the maximum displacement of the vertices and to guarantee the topological order of Θ, the distance vector d_i is clamped in the interval expressed in [Eq. 5]

The attraction value A is empirical value which scale the value of the function in all the grid. This value control the attraction factor of the vertices of the grid to the iso-surface, values between 0 and 1 produces a grid avoids the iso-surface, values lesser than 0 generate incorrect behavior of the function. The recommended and useful values

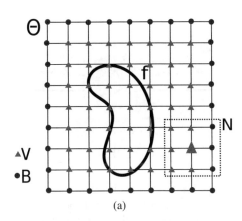
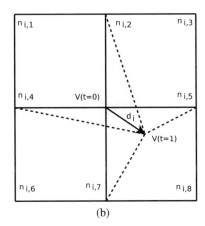

(a)   (b)

Fig. 3. (a) Grid nomenclature, Θ cubical grid, $f(x, y, z) = 0$ implicit function, N vertex neighborhood, V vertices inside the grid, B vertices at the boundary of the grid. (b) Two consecutive iterations are show where the vertex v is moved between the iterations $t = 0$ and $t = 1$. The new configuration of the grid is shown as dotted lines.

are equal or greater than 1, very high values of A could generate problems for the grid, produces big stepping factors for the displacement vectors d_i and then some characteristics of the iso-surface could be lost. The A value is highly related to the value of the distance of the bounding box of the grid, and the size of the objects inside the grid.

$$0 \leq |d_i| \leq \text{MIN} \left(\frac{|n_{i,j} - v_i|}{2} \right) \tag{5}$$

$$d_i = \frac{1}{26} \sum_{n_{i,j}} \frac{n_{i,j} - v_i}{1 + A|f(n_{i,j}) + f(v_i)|} \tag{6}$$

$$\sum_{v_i} |d_i| \geq \Delta \tag{7}$$

The algorithm stops when the sum of the distances added to all the vertices in the previous iteration is less that a given threshold Δ [Eq. 7] (see Algorithm 1).

---

repeat
  s := 0;
  foreach *Vertex v_i* **do**
    $d_i := \frac{1}{26} \sum_{n_{i,j}} \frac{n_{i,j} - v_i}{1 + A|f(n_{i,j}) + f(v_i)|}$;
    $\text{mindist} := \text{MIN} \left(\frac{|n_{i,j} - v_i|}{2} \right)$;
    $d_i := \bar{d}_i \text{CLAMP} (|d_i|, 0.0, \text{mindist})$;
    $v_i := v_i + d_i$;
    s := s + $|d_i|$;
  end
until s $\geq \Delta$;

Algorithm 1: Vertex Displacement Pseudo-algorithm. $|x|$ represents the magnitude of x, $\bar{v}$ represents the normalised vector of v.

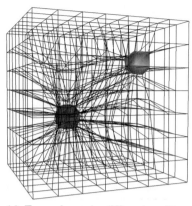 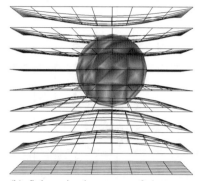

(a) Two spheres in different positions with a scalar function as the distance transform, representing the behavior of the algorithm with different objects in the space.

(b) Sphere in the center of the space with a scalar function as the distance transform. The slides shows the different warping of the grid in the different positions.

Fig. 4. Implicit function of spheres as distance transforms

4   Results

The proposed algorithm was tested with a set of implicit functions as distance transforms (see Figure 4) of a set of spheres, the spheres are define as a point in the space with their radius. The result of the sphere data set (4(b),5(a),6(a)) and the two-sphere data set (4(a),5(b),6(b)) are presented, but the algorithm also has been tested with datasets composed of more than 1000 spheres (see Figure 1). The algorithm has been tested also with other non-distance transform implicit functions, but the generation of false *ROI* in the grid degenerates the structure of the grid resulting in bad representations of the iso-surface. For demonstration purposes, the number of cells has been chosen to enhance visual perception of the improvements produced by the algorithm. For the visualization process we use Marching Tetrahedra[16] because it produces correct topological representation of the iso-surface, and allows the identification of the topological correctness of the algorithm.

The obtained results of the algorithm are visually noticeable, as shown in Figure 2. Without using the algorithm, the two spheres model is perceived as a single object (see Figure 2). In an intermediate state the spheres are still joined, but their shapes are more rounded. In the final state, when the algorithm converges, both spheres are separated correctly, each one being rendered as a near-perfect sphere. Thus, using the same grid resolution and the proposed algorithm, the resolution of the results has been increased and also topological errors of the original explicit representation were considerably reduce with the algorithm.

Accuracy of the explicit representations of the algorithm were measured using the methodology of De Bruin [17] which is based on the Hausdorff distance explain by Dubuisson [18]. The figures 5 and 6 shows the behavior of the algorithm where, in

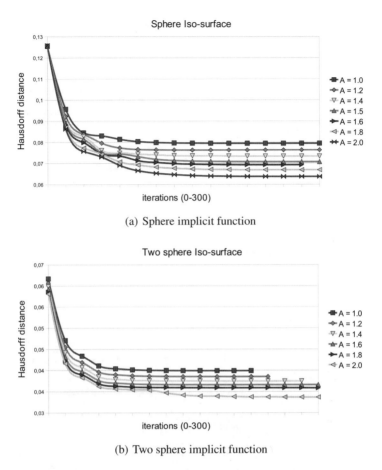

(a) Sphere implicit function

(b) Two sphere implicit function

Fig. 5. Hausdorff distance of the explicit representations of the figures in each iteration of the algorithm with different attraction values

almost all the iterations, the Hausdorff distance between the implicit iso-surface and the explicit surface are decreasing. The iterations where there is an increment of the distance, could represent a point where the configuration of the grid is not suitable for optimization and then the algorithm needs to modify the grid looking for suitable configurations.

Figure 5 presents the results of the algorithm with the same implicit surfaces but with different attraction factor values (A). As the results show the accuracy of the iso-surface is highly related with the (A) value, because the allowed warping of the grid is bigger obtaining a dense grid near to the iso-surface, but this over-fit of the grid can be dangerous if the grid is going to be used for other implicit functions, like time varying functions, because the grid need more iterations to adapt to the new iso-surface.

Figure 6 shows the behavior of the algorithm with different grid sizes. The accuracy of the final explicit representation of the iso-surfaces shows an improvement of the accuracy of the representation. Then it is possible with the algorithm to represent

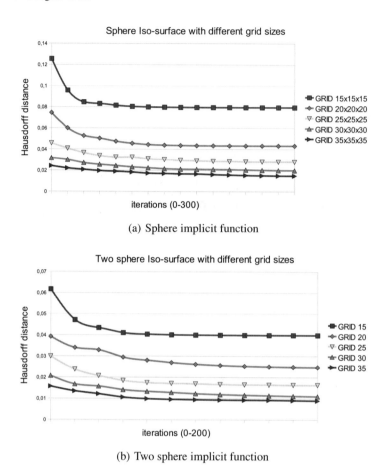

(a) Sphere implicit function

(b) Two sphere implicit function

Fig. 6. Hausdorff distance of the explicit representations of the figures in each iteration of the algorithm with different grid sizes

iso-surfaces with good accuracy and quality without increasing grid sizes. This characteristic allow us to use smaller grids for the representation without loss of accuracy or quality in the representation and saving computational resources.

5   Conclusions and Future Work

Our proposed iterative algorithm has shown significant advantages in the representation of distance transform functions. With the same grid size, it allows a better resolution by displacing the vertices of the cube grids towards the surface, increasing the number of cells containing the surface. The algorithm was tested with algebraic functions, representing distance transforms of the models. The generated scalar field has been selected to avoid the creation of regions of false interest [19], which are for static images in which these regions are not used.

The number of iterations is directly related to the chosen value Δ as it is the stop condition. The algorithm will continuously displace the cube vertices until the accumulated displacement in a single iteration is less than Δ. The accumulated distance converges quickly to the desired value. This behavior is very convenient to represent time varying scalar functions like 3D videos, where the function itself is continuously changing. In this context, the algorithm will iterate until a good representation of the surface is obtained. If the surface varies smoothly, the cube grid will be continuously and quickly re-adapted by running a few iterations of the presented algorithm. Whenever the surface changes can be considered no be small, the number of iterations until a new final condition is reached will be low. Then the obtained results will be a better real-time surface representation using a coarser cube grid.

The value Δ is sensitive to the grid size, so a better stop condition should be evaluated which represent the state of the quality of the representation and reduce the number of iteration which are unnecessary. The model used in this algorithm is close to a physics spring model, a close comparison of the proposed algorithm with the spring model could be done.

Acknowledgements. This work has been partially supported by the Spanish Administration agency CDTI, under project CENIT-VISION 2007-1007. CAD/CAM/CAE Laboratory - EAFIT University and the Colombian Council for Science and Technology -Colciencias-. The bunny model is courtesy of the Stanford Computer Graphics Laboratory.

References

1. Krek, P.: Flow reduction marching cubes algorithm. In: Proceedings of ICCVG 2004, pp. 100–106. Springer, Heidelberg (2005)
2. Ruiz, O.E., Miguel Granados, C.C.: Fea-driven geometric modelling for meshless methods. In: Virtual Concept 2005, pp. 1–8 (2005)
3. Carr, J.C., Beatson, R.K., Cherrie, J.B., Mitchell, T.J., Fright, W.R., McCallum, B.C., Evans, T.R.: Reconstruction and representation of 3d objects with radial basis functions. In: SIGGRAPH 2001: Proceedings of the 28th annual conference on Computer graphics and interactive techniques, pp. 67–76. ACM, New York (2001)
4. Morse, B.S., Yoo, T.S., Rheingans, P., Chen, D.T., Subramanian, K.R.: Interpolating implicit surfaces from scattered surface data using compactly supported radial basis functions. In: SIGGRAPH 2005: ACM SIGGRAPH 2005 Courses, p. 78. ACM, New York (2005)
5. Frisken, S.F., Perry, R.N., Rockwood, A.P., Jones, T.R.: Adaptively sampled distance fields: a general representation of shape for computer graphics. In: SIGGRAPH 2000: Proceedings of the 27th annual conference on Computer graphics and interactive techniques, pp. 249–254. ACM Press/Addison-Wesley Publishing Co., New York (2000)
6. Lorensen, W.E., Cline, H.E.: Marching cubes: A high resolution 3d surface construction algorithm. SIGGRAPH Comput. Graph. 21(4), 169–169 (1987)
7. Newman, T.S., Yi, H.: A survey of the marching cubes algorithm. Computers & Graphics 30(5), 854–879 (2006)
8. Chernyaev, E.: Marching cubes 33: Construction of topologically correct isosurfaces. Technical report, Technical Report CERN CN 95-17 (1995)

9. Lewiner, T., Lopes, H., Vieira, A., Tavares, G.: Efficient implementation of marching cubes' cases with topological guarantees. Journal of Graphics Tools 8(2), 1–15 (2003)
10. Weber, G.H., Kreylos, O., Ligocki, T.J., Shalf, J.M., Hamann, B., Joy, K.I.: Extraction of crack-free isosurfaces from adaptive mesh refinement data. In: Data Visualization 2001 (Proceedings of VisSym 2001), pp. 25–34. Springer, Heidelberg (2001)
11. Shekhar, R., Fayyad, E., Yagel, R., Cornhill, J.F.: Octree-based decimation of marching cubes surfaces. In: VIS 1996: Proceedings of the 7th conference on Visualization 1996, p. 335. IEEE Computer Society Press, Los Alamitos (1996)
12. Schaefer, S., Warren, J.: Dual marching cubes: Primal contouring of dual grids. In: PG 2004: Proceedings of the Computer Graphics and Applications, 12th Pacific Conference, pp. 70–76. IEEE Computer Society, Los Alamitos (2004)
13. Paiva, A., Lopes, H., Lewiner, T., de Figueiredo, L.H.: Robust adaptive meshes for implicit surfaces. SIBGRAPI, 205–212 (2006)
14. Kimura, A., Takama, Y., Yamazoe, Y., Tanaka, S., Tanaka, H.T.: Parallel volume segmentation with tetrahedral adaptive grid. ICPR 02, 281–286 (2004)
15. Balmelli, L., Morris, C.J., Taubin, G., Bernardini, F.: Volume warping for adaptive isosurface extraction. In: Proceedings of the conference on Visualization 2002, pp. 467–474. IEEE Computer Society, Los Alamitos (2002)
16. Carneiroz, B.P., Silva, C.T.Y., Kaufman, A.E.: Tetra-cubes: An algorithm to generate 3d isosurfaces based upon tetrahedra. In: IX Brazilian symposium on computer, graphics, image processing and vision (SIBGRAPI 1996), pp. 205–210 (1996)
17. Vos, D.B., Bruin, P.W.D., Vos, F.M., Post, F.H., Frisken-gibson, S.F., Vossepoel, A.M.: Improving triangle mesh quality with surfacenets. In: Delp, S.L., DiGoia, A.M., Jaramaz, B. (eds.) MICCAI 2000. LNCS, vol. 1935, pp. 804–813. Springer, Heidelberg (2000)
18. Dubuisson, M.P., Jain, A.K.: A modified hausdorff distance for object matching. In: Proceedings of the 12th IAPR International Conference on Pattern Recognition, Conference A: Computer Vision & Image Processing, vol. 1, pp. 566–568 (1994)
19. Congote, J., Moreno, A., Barandiaran, I., Barandiaran, J., Ruiz, O.: Adaptative cubical grid for isosurface extraction. In: 4th International Conference on Computer Graphics Theory and Applications GRAPP 2009, Lisbon, Portugal, February 5-8, pp. 21–26 (2009)

High-Quality Non-planar Projections Using Real-Time Piecewise Perspective Projections

Haik Lorenz and Jürgen Döllner

Hasso-Plattner-Institute, University of Potsdam, Germany
{haik.lorenz,doellner}@hpi.uni-potsdam.de

Abstract. This paper presents an approach to real-time rendering of non-planar projections with a single center and straight projection rays. Its goal is to provide the same optimal and consistent image quality GPUs deliver for perspective projections. It therefor renders the result directly without image resampling. In contrast to most object-space approaches, it does not evaluate non-linear functions on the GPU, but approximates the projection itself by a set of perspective projection pieces. Within each piece, graphics hardware can provide optimal image quality. The result is a coherent and crisp rendering. Procedural textures and stylization effects greatly benefit from our method as they usually rely on screen-space operations. The real-time implementation runs entirely on GPU. It replicates input primitives on demand and renders them into all relevant projection pieces. The method is independent of the input mesh density and is not restricted to static meshes. Thus, it is well suited for interactive applications. We demonstrate an analytic and a freely designed projection based on our method.

Keywords: Non-planar projections, Geometry shaders, Geometry amplification, Non-photorealistic rendering.

1 Introduction

Automatic depiction of three-dimensional worlds, being real or virtual, requires a camera. What is the construction and inner workings of a real camera becomes the camera model and projection for the virtual camera. From all possible models, the pinhole camera model is the most widely used model. Today's graphics hardware is tailored to the underlying projection types: planar perspective or orthographic projections. Nonetheless, numerous applications in computer graphics require other, non-pinhole projection types:

- Non-planar displays, such as cylindrical or spherical walls, require non-linear projections to compensate for distortions [1].
- Some natural phenomena, such as caustics, reflections, or refractions off curved surfaces, can be described by projections [2].
- Visualizations benefit from adapted projections, such as increased field of view, lens effects, or reduced panorama distortions [3,4,5]. Such deliberate distortions can provide improved perception of a virtual environment.
- Arts and non-photorealism achieve dramatic effects using irregular projections [6,7,8,9].

A. Ranchordas et al. (Eds.): VISIGRAPP 2009, CCIS 68, pp. 45–58, 2010.

Fig. 1. A 360° cylindrical view of a city rendered using a piecewise perspective projection. The city model contains 35,000 triangles. The projection uses 160 pieces. At a resolution of 1600 × 1200, an NVidia 8800GTS achieves 55 fps with 16x anisotropic texture filtering and 16x antialiasing. Our technique enables the use of screen-space-dependent rendering effects such as solid wireframe [16] or pen-and-ink style [17].

- Images of particular projection types serve as storage for parts of the plenoptic function [10]. Most commonly, these are cubical, spherical, or paraboloidal images used for rendering reflections or refractions in real-time [11,12].

Non-pinhole projections have been discussed extensively in literature, resulting in various camera models, e.g., [4,13,14]. They cannot be rendered directly with today's graphics hardware. Instead, ray-tracing is commonly used [13]. A large body of work exists on implementing ray-tracing on GPU for various phenomena and scene conditions. Wei et al. [2] and Popov et al. [15] present recent approaches and good surveys of related methods. Mostly, they use the GPU as powerful stream processor instead of as rasterization device and thus rarely benefit from built-in capabilities such as anisotropic texture filtering, perspective-correct interpolation, or screen-space derivatives.

1.1 Real-Time Non-pinhole Projections on GPU without Raytracing

A straightforward and efficient approach is the implementation as *image-based* post-processing effect [18,19]. The rendering consists of two steps: First, a perspective projection is rendered into an offscreen buffer. Second, this buffer is used as texture for rendering a deformed mesh. The offscreen buffer can contain a cube map to enable 360° views. This approach is capable of rendering projections with a single center and straight projection rays (Single Center Of Projection – SCOP) only. It is image-based since the actual deformation happens after, not during, rendering the scene. Its advantages are easy implementation and good support by graphics hardware. The major drawback is image quality. The resampling in the second step inevitably introduces blurring artifacts that especially degrade edges, detailed geometry, procedural textures, and stylization effects. Today's hardware capability of antialiasing through multi-sampling does not improve image quality substantially as it applies before resampling.

Object-space approaches do not suffer from image resampling artifacts and are not limited to SCOP effects as they render the image directly. A simple solution is applying the non-pinhole projection in the vertex shader [20]. Then, a triangle's vertices are projected correctly, but the interior and edges are rasterized incorrectly in a linear fashion. This is acceptable as long as a triangle's size on screen and thus the rasterization error is limited. To ensure this property, interactive environments require dynamic refinement. Approaches include precomputed static levels of detail [21], progressive meshes [22], adaptive mesh refinement [23,24], render-to-vertex-buffer [25], dynamic mesh refinement [26], or hardware tessellation units [27,28]. They vary in the distribution of computation between CPU and GPU. The rendered mesh must be free of T-junctions to prevent artifacts due to correct vertex location but incorrect edge rasterization. Even with refinement, the incorrect rasterization greatly amplifies Z-Buffer artifacts, such as inaccurate near plane clipping and interpenetrations of parallel triangles. A solution is emitting correct depth values in the fragment shader. This reduces depth test performance and increases fragment processing overhead due to a disabled early z-test [29].

A more sophisticated solution is using *non-linear rasterization*. Since the rasterizer uses hardwired linear interpolation, Hou et al. [30] and Gascuel et al. [31] replace each primitive by a bounding shape and use ray intersection in a fragment shader to compute the actual fragments and all their attributes under non-pinhole projections within that shape. As a consequence, these methods cannot benefit from high quality screen-space-dependent operations built into modern graphics hardware, such as mipmapping, anisotropic filtering, or screen-space derivatives.

This paper focuses on enabling these high quality rasterization capabilities of current GPUs for non-pinhole projections. Our approach achieves a significantly improved and consistent image quality regardless of the input mesh while maintaining real-time performance (Fig. 1). We enable the rasterization hardware to work under perspective projections exclusively and, hence, obtain optimal image quality. As a result, procedural textures and stylization effects can be used instantly regardless of the actual projection.

1.2 Piecewise Perspective Projection Overview

Piecewise perspective projections use an idea proposed in [30]: approximate a complex projection by a set of simpler projections. We refer to these simpler projections as *projection pieces*. The pieces' projection frusta are connected but disjoint with their union approximating the original projection volume. Hou et al. [30] rely on *triangle cameras*, simple non-pinhole projections, which make this method capable of rendering multi-perspective views but prevent it from exploiting hardware functionality. We restrict the projection pieces to using perspective projections exclusively, which limits our technique to SCOP effects.

Key advantage of our construction compared to other object-space approaches is the absence of non-linearities during rasterization. All non-linear aspects of the non-pinhole projection are encoded into the layout of the piecewise approximation. Consequently, rasterization and all high quality screen-space-dependent operations work with optimal quality within each piece. Similarly, existing shaders, particularly procedural textures and stylization effects, can be used instantly. The resulting images do not exhibit blurring artifacts and capture the non-pinhole projection regardless of the input mesh and rendering effect. There is no need for refinement. In addition, Z-buffer artifacts are not amplified.

The increase in image quality comes at the cost of increased geometry processing overhead. Each primitive needs to be rendered into each projection piece it is visible in. Hence, it needs to be processed multiple times per frame. Depending on the number of pieces in an approximation, this can result in a substantial overhead.

The remaining paper is organized as follows: the next section provides an in-depth discussion of the idea of piecewise perspective projections, devises a real-time implementation using geometry shaders, and gives an implementation outline for future GPUs. Sec. 3 provides two example applications. Sec. 4 provides experimental results and compares them to alternative approaches. Sec. 5 concludes.

2 Piecewise Perspective Projection

The key idea of piecewise perspective projections is the approximation of a non-pinhole projection volume by a set of connected but disjoint perspective projection frusta, so-called projection pieces. Each projection piece uses a regular perspective projection clipped to the piece's boundaries for image formation. Thus, the rendering encounters no non-linearities and hardware rasterization generates a correct image at optimal quality for each piece. The combination of all piece images creates an approximation of the desired non-pinhole projection. The number of pieces defines the approximation quality.

Our method can reproduce the same projection effects as the image-based approach of [18]. Their intermediate rendering uses a perspective projection described by a matrix M_P. The triangle mesh used for deforming this rendering implicitly defines an affine transformation $M(t)$ from the source area of each triangle t to the screen. An equivalent piecewise perspective projection can be constructed of triangular pieces by clipping a perspective projection $M(t) * M_P$ to the deformed triangle's boundaries for all t.

For implementing this idea, three challenges need to be addressed:

1. Approximation of the non-pinhole projection with projection pieces,
2. Rendering of a primitive in all projection pieces it is visible in, and
3. Clipping of a primitive's rendering to the projection piece's boundaries.

Approximation. An artifact-free approximation is only possible for SCOP effects, as other projections lead to overlapping piece frusta. In general, each projection piece p uses an individual projection matrix $M_P(p)$, such that neighboring pieces produce matching renderings at their shared boundary. Matrix computation depends on the particular projection and happens once in a preprocessing step. Two typical approaches are exemplified in Section 3.

Rendering. A simple implementation renders the whole model for each projection piece with the respective projection matrix and clipping in effect. Rendering should use additional culling to account for a projection piece's small screen area but does not require any changes to shaders or meshes to deal with a non-pinhole projection.

Clipping. Clipping can rely on viewport clipping if all pieces are rectangular or on user clip planes for convex pieces. Since both possibilities are performed by the rasterization hardware, no explicit clipping needs to be implemented in a shader. The resulting piece images are non-overlapping and thus they can be rendered directly to the framebuffer without the need for a dedicated composition step.

Due to additional culling and a large number of draw calls, this straight-forward implementation suffers from increased CPU load. At the same time, GPU efficiency is reduced as each draw call renders to a small screen portion only. Thus, rendering becomes CPU-bound and real-time performance is limited to projection approximations with very small piece counts.

2.1   Real-Time Implementation

Our real-time implementation reverses the rendering approach to make it GPU-friendly. Instead of determining all primitives for a projection piece through culling, we determine all relevant, i.e., covered, pieces for a primitive. We can then render the final image in a single draw call by replicating each primitive to all its relevant pieces. Projection matrices are stored in buffer textures for shader access. User clip planes cannot be updated by a shader. The alternative is to define a standard clip space with fixed clip planes and provide a transformation from camera space to clip space for each projection piece.

Since a primitive can fill the whole screen, the maximum replication count is the projection piece count. Hence, a straight forward replication using geometry shaders, which are currently limited to at most 128 output vertices, is not possible. In [26] a solution to a similar problem has been described. They use a fixed three-pass scheme for per-primitive view-dependent tessellation on GPU and achieve arbitrary and unbounded geometry amplification without CPU intervention. Core of their scheme is a continuously updated intermediate mesh of barycentric subtriangles. This transforms the geometry shader's output limit from a mesh size limit to a per-frame growth limit. Since we only require replicated, not tessellated, primitives, we replace their intermediate mesh with a primitive index and accompanying replication numbers. Both are stored in separate ping-pong buffers. The primitive index works similar to a traditional vertex index. The accompanying replication number consecutively numbers all a single primitive's occurences in the index. Together, they enable indexed access to a primitive's vertex attributes in the vertex shader (e.g., by passing all 3 positions for a triangle at once) but also allow for distinguishing replications of a single primitive in the geometry shader.

In the following, we provide a brief description of the rendering process (Fig. 2). For details, refer to [26]. In the first pass, all original primitives are processed by a geometry shader to determine the number of covered projection pieces. This information is stored in a buffer using transform feedback. The second pass takes the previous frame's primitive index and produces a new primitive index and matching replication numbers, such that each primitive is replicated according to the counts calculated in pass 1. Pass 3 finally renders all replicated primitives. It uses the primitive index to fetch all a primitive's vertex attributes from vertex buffers and the replication number to select the projection piece with projection and clip matrix. Additional vertex,

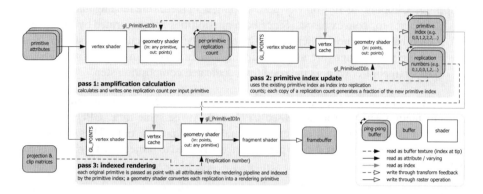

Fig. 2. Primitive replication algorithm overview and data flow. Pass 3 can implement any rendering effect.

geometry and fragment processing can implement any effect as if no piecewise perspective projection was in effect. Thus, existing shaders are easily incorporated.

This scheme applies to arbitrary "primitive soups" since no connectivity information or topological restriction is assumed. Key for rendering is the determination of covered projection pieces (pass 1) and their enumeration (pass 3). Both depend on the desired non-pinhole projection. Two aspects need to be considered: First, while rendering primitives to irrelevant pieces does not influence image quality, it degrades performance since additional replications are created and processed only to become clipped again. Thus, the determination is not required to be exact. Nevertheless, poor estimation reduces performance. Second, given a primitive and its replication number, the target projection piece needs to be identified in $O(1)$ time in a shader (function f(replicationnumber) in Fig. 2). The mapping can be supported by additional information generated in pass 1. In Sec. 3, we present two approaches.

2.2 Single-Pass Implementation with a Configurable Tessellator Unit

The next generation of GPUs will include a configurable tessellator unit [28]. In conjuction with two new shader stages, hull and domain shaders, it becomes possible to generate up to 8192 triangles for a single input primitive. This unit is expected to provide much better performance regarding geometry amplification than geometry shaders. In this section, we outline an implementation of piecewise perspective projections based on the tessellator unit in Direct3D 11 (Fig. 3). As there is no supporting hardware available so far, the implementation has been tested using the Microsoft reference rasterizer. Thus, it should be considered a proof-of-concept and a starting point for optimizations.

Basic implementation idea is the mapping of all computations found in Fig. 2 to the new pipeline stages. Amplification calculation is handled by the hull shader, which determines the number of covered projection pieces. It then selects corresponding tessellation factors for each primitive, such that the tessellator creates the required number of subtriangles. Since Direct3D 11 does not guarantee specific tessellation rules so far, we use a table that contains tessellation factors for each possible subtriangle count. This

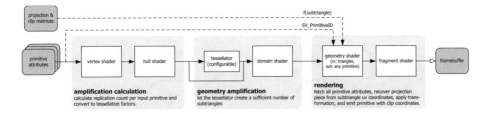

Fig. 3. Single-pass piecewise perspective projections based on Direct3D 11. The three passes from Fig. 2 clearly map to Direct3D 11's extended graphics pipeline. This figure uses the same notation as Fig. 2.

table is filled in advance. The domain shader computes vertices of these subtriangles. Since we use the tessellator to replicate the input primitive, not to create a contiguous mesh, the domain shader only passes the produced uv-coordinates to the geometry shader. The geometry shader loads the primitive's attributes from a buffer texture using the primitive id and determines the projection and clip matrices using the uv-coordinates. The geometry shader cannot rely on a replication number (pass 3 in Fig. 2) as it is not provided by the tessellator. After transformation the replicated triangle is emitted. The pixel shader, again, is not influenced by our method and can implement any rendering style without taking into account the non-pinhole projection.

A pitfall in this implementation is the limitation to 8192 replications per primitive. If the projection approximation uses more than 8192 pieces, a primitive could exceed this limitation if it fills the whole screen. As a workaround, the geometry shader can emit multiple replications per subtriangle to retain the single-pass scheme.

Compared to the implementation from Sec. 2.1, the tessellator-based implementation has various advantages: It can cull primitives early by specifying negative tessellation factors. It does not require intermediate buffers and overflow control. Finally, it does not require ping-pong buffers and thus has no interframe dependencies. As a result, this implementation is much better suited for integration in existing graphics frameworks and for use in multi-GPU environments.

3   Applications

Our real-time implementation involves two application-dependent parts: projection piece definition and projection piece coverage determination/enumeration. We demonstrate the use for two typical applications: a horizontal cylindrical projection, which can be described analytically, and a texture-based view deformation, which improves the camera texture technique of [20].

3.1   Cylindrical Projection

A horizontal cylindrical projection uses a perspective projection in the vertical direction but a non-planar projection horizontally. Thus, it suffices to limit the horizontal edge length to control an approximation's quality. The piecewise perspective projection then

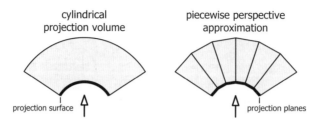

Fig. 4. Top-down view of the cylindrical projection volume and its approximation with perspective projections

splits the curved projection volume into narrow rectangular slices. Figure 4 sketches this setting.

Projection piece coverage determination and enumeration for rendering is rather simple as a single primitive normally covers a consecutive range of projection pieces. It suffices to find the leftmost and rightmost point of the primitive's projection and render it to all pieces in between. Wrap-arounds require special care. A special case occurs when cylinder axis and primitive intersect. In that case, the primitive is potentially visible in all projection pieces. Finally, pass 1 outputs both start piece index (which can be to the right of the end index) and piece count. Pass 3 uses a primitive's replication number plus the start index modulo n – the number of projection pieces – as target projection piece.

The projection matrix M of a piece p can be described by a series of transformations:

$$M(p) = M_{tx}(p) * M_{sx} * M_P * M_{ry}(p) \tag{1}$$

M_{ry} rotates the center axis of a projection piece about the y axis onto the negative z axis. M_P is a perspective projection matrix with a horizontal field of view $\varphi_p = \varphi_c/n$, where φ_c denotes the cylindrical field of view. M_{sx} scales the standard postprojective space to fit the piece's width on the screen. M_{tx} finally moves the piece's projection from the screen center to its actual location on screen.

Clipping requires a standard clip space to enable fixed clip planes. The following transformation leads to such a space:

$$M_{clip}(p) = M_s(M_{P_{11}}; M_{P_{22}}; 1) * M_{ry}(p) \tag{2}$$

M_s is a scaling operation that uses the first ($M_{P_{11}}$) and second ($M_{P_{22}}$) value from the projection matrix's diagonal. The complete transformation effectively transforms into the normalized space used for perspective division. The corresponding four clip planes define an infinite pyramid with the tip being located in the origin and the opening pointing down the negative z axis with an opening angle of 90° both vertically and horizontally.

Fig. 5 depicts a sample image with highlighted piece boundaries and primitive edges. For clarity, it uses only 32 pieces with a width of 50 pixels. Experiments show, that pieces of width 10-20 pixels provide a good approximation. The average replication count in that case is less than 2, while the maximum replication is the total piece count n.

Fig. 5. Rendering of a piecewise perspective 360° cylindrical projection with an overlayed thick white wireframe. Piece borders are marked with thin black lines.

3.2   Texture-Based View Deformation

View deformation [19] uses one or more standard perspective views (e.g., a cube map) and distorts them to create the final image. The distortion is either analytical, such as a paraboloid mapping, or freely defined, such as camera textures [20]. Both approaches use a rectangular two-dimensional grid in the perspective view(s) and map it to a deformed mesh on the screen. The construction of a piecewise perspective projection follows the description in Section 2. In the following, we provide details for an improved implementation of camera textures. They encode the distortion as offset vectors in a 2D texture (Fig. 6). A point's deformed projection is found by using its perspective projection for texture lookup and adding the resulting offset vector to that perspective projection. In contrast to the original implementation, ours is independent of mesh density. Regardless of a primitive's projected size, all details of the distortion are captured in the primitive's interior.

Piecewise perspective projections require splitting the rectangular grid into triangles. Even though it is possible to specify a projective mapping from a two-dimensional rectangle to an arbitrary quadrangle, it is not possible to guarantee a matching mapping for shared edges. This property would require a bilinear transformation [32] current rasterizers cannot deal with. Splitting the rectangle into two triangles leads to two affine transformations and a continuous approximation. Nevertheless, considering pairs of triangluar projection pieces as one cell is benefical regarding coverage determination and enumeration. It enables operating on a simple rectangular grid in pass 1. View deformation is irrelevant to pass 1 as it does not change visibility. Pass 2 replicates primitives for cells. Pass 3 finally emits each primitive twice – once for each triangle in a cell – with the respective transformation matrices in effect.

A simple solution for determining the coverage of a primitive is using its bounding box in the undistorted projection plane. All cells intersected by the bounding box are considered as being covered. Thus, the output of pass 1 is the position of the lower left cell c_{ll} and width w and height h of the bounding box in cell units. For efficient

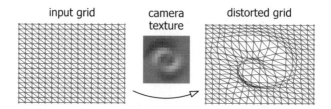

Fig. 6. Projection plane splitting and subsequent distortion using a 16×16 pixel camera texture. The model is rendered directly into the distorted grid.

storage, all four values use 16-bit integers and are packed into two 32-bit integers. Pass 3 can map the replication number r to a cell at position $(c_{ll}.x + r \bmod w; c_{ll}.y + \lfloor r/w \rfloor)$. This two-dimensional index can be used for lookup in a texture containing the affine transformation matrices for both projection pieces in this cell. Since the bounding box coverage determination is very conservative, we added culling to pass 3 to discard invisible primitives before rasterization setup.

The derivation of affine transformation matrices can be found in [32]. During rendering, it is applied subsequent to the original model-view-projection matrix. Clipping uses an approach similar to the cylindrical projection. Here, only three clip planes are in effect which form a triangular pyramid. To clip both pieces of one cell to the same clip planes, one piece's clip coordinates are rotated about the z axis by 180°.

Fig. 7 shows a 64×64 camera texture (similar to Fig. 6) applied to a view of a city model. A thin black wireframe indicates the triangular projection cells, thick white lines highlight primitive edges. Our implementation of texture-based view deformation allows for animating the deformation effect, as this only involves updating the matrices.

4 Results

We compare piecewise perspective projections with image-based implementations for both applications presented in Section 3. The implementations use native OpenGL 2.0 with relevant extensions. All measurements have been taken on a desktop PC running Windows XP with an AMD Athlon 64 X2 4200+ processor, 2GB RAM, and an NVidia GeForce 8800 GTS with 640 MB RAM. The tests use a path through the textured city model data shown in Figures 5 and 7. It consists of 35,000 triangles in 14 state groups. The viewport resolution is 1600×1200. In contrast to [26], no latency hiding has been used since it showed no improvements. Besides the frame rate, we provide the number of triangles used for rendering (av. tri. count), their replication ratio to the original triangle count (av. repl. ratio), and the total size of all vertex buffers used for rendering (Vbuf.). High quality (HQ) measurements use 16x anisotropic texture filtering and 16xQ antialiasing.

The image-based implementation of the 360° cylindrical camera uses a dynamic 2048×2048 cubemap that is created in a single pass through layered rendering. It implements frustum and backface culling in the geometry shader [29] which explains the replication count less than 1. The piecewise perspective projection uses strips of

Table 1. Rendering statistics. Our piecewise perspective projection (PPP) outperforms the image-based implementation (IB) for the 360° cylindrical camera. For view deformation, IB provides higher frame rates. In terms of image quality, PPP is always superior (Fig. 8).

Impl	360° cylindrical camera (160 pieces)				view deformation (9,322 pieces)			
	Fps	Av. tri. count	Av. repl. ratio	Vbuf. (kB)	Fps	Av. tri. count	Av. repl. ratio	Vbuf. (kB)
IB	41.7	21,151	0.61	1,081	206.2	34,596	1	1,081
PPP	84.7	67,675	1.96	2,672	22.1	351,954	10.17	7,661
IB HQ	33.8	21,151	0.61	1,081	95.8	34,596	1	1,081
PPP HQ	54.8	67,675	1.96	2,672	20.9	351,954	10.17	7,661

Fig. 7. Rendering using the camera texture shown in Fig. 6 at a resolution of 64 × 64. Thin black lines indicate projection pieces. Thick white lines highlight primitive edges.

10 pixels, i.e., 160 pieces, for approximation. On average, each triangle is visible in only two strips. The increased memory footprint results from the intermediate mesh, which requires 16 bytes per rendered primitive. In total, our method outperforms the image-based approach while providing higher image quality (Fig. 8). Even for smaller cubemaps, the image-based approach does not overtake ours, but image quality further degrades.

For the texture-based view deformation, the image-based technique uses only a 2D texture, no cubemap. Therefor, it achieves higher frame rates than for the cylindrical projection. In contrast, our method needs to render a significantly higher amount of triangles, which translates to a reduced speed. Each input triangle spans on average about 10 of the 9,322 projection pieces. While delivering interactive frame rates, the vertex processing overhead is substantial. The bottleneck here is pass 3. Primitive replication performed in pass 1 and 2 accounts for less than 10% of the total workload.

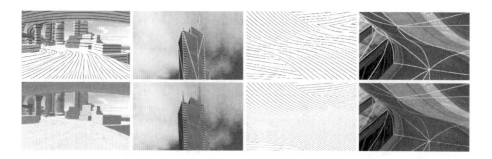

Fig. 8. Comparision of image quality. Closeups of screen shots for PPP (top) and IB (bottom). Left to right: cylindrical camera pen-and-ink style, cylindrical camera solid wireframe, view deformation pen-and-ink style, view deformation solid wireframe.

Consequently, a more aggressive coverage determination than the bounding box test could significantly improve performance. In addition, a projection piece size of 20×20 pixels suffices for good approximations, i.e., the camera texture resolution should be adapted to the viewport resolution. In our example, we use a 80×60 camera texture. For a 128×128 camera texture, the replication ratio jumps from 10 to about 21 (i.e., about 725,000 triangles per frame) and the frame rate drops to 8.2 fps.

Figure 8 shows the difference in image quality. The image-based implementation cannot produce a consistent result due to the separate image resampling. Accordingly, stroke width for the solid wireframe and stroke distance for the pen-and-ink style vary across the image. Our piecewise perspective projection, in contrast, delivers consistent results even in highly distorted areas without the effect being "aware" of the non-pinhole projection.

A supplemental demo of the texture-based view deformation is available online [33]. It uses OpenGL 2.1 and requires Windows XP or later and a NVidia GPU 8000 series or better.

5   Conclusions

This paper has presented a novel approach to rendering non-pinhole projections with a single projection center. The piecewise perspective projection technique removes non-linearities from rendering by approximating a projection with a set of perspective projections. The distorted image is formed directly on screen without intermediate rendering steps. As a result, all image quality optimizations provided by modern graphics hardware that assume a perspective projection continue to operate with regular precision. Particularly, antialiasing, procedural textures, and stylization effects profit from our technique. It can be implemented on any graphics hardware but requires Direct3D 10 features for real-time performance. Core is on-demand replication of primitives on the GPU using geometry shaders and transform feedback, such that a primitive is rendered only into projection pieces it actually covers. A demo is available online [33].

The technique's drawback is a high geometry processing overhead. Primitive replication itself is rather efficient. The major bottleneck is vertex processing in pass 3 since a rendered primitive covers at most a single projection piece. In the future, we seek to improve the performance of pass 3 by better coverage determination. A second direction of research is evaluating applicability to other types of projections, such as slit or pushbroom cameras. The rendering scheme might also prove useful for other algorithms, e.g., [30]. Finally, we need to verify and tune our tessellator-based single-pass implementation (Sec. 2.2) as soon as respective GPUs become available.

Acknowledgements. This work has been funded by the German Federal Ministry of Education and Research (BMBF) as part of the InnoProfile research group "3D Geoinformation" (www.3dgi.de).

References

1. Jo, K., Minamizawa, K., Nii, H., Kawakami, N., Tachi, S.: A GPU-based real-time rendering method for immersive stereoscopic displays. In: ACM SIGGRAPH 2008 posters, p. 1. ACM, New York (2008)
2. Wei, L.Y., Liu, B., Yang, X., Ma, C., Xu, Y.Q., Guo, B.: Nonlinear beam tracing on a GPU. Technical report, Microsoft, MSR-TR-2007-168 (2007)
3. Popescu, V., Aliaga, D.G.: The depth discontinuity occlusion camera. In: SI3D, pp. 139–143. ACM, New York (2006)
4. Brosz, J., Samavati, F.F., Sheelagh, M.T.C., Sousa, M.C.: Single camera flexible projection. In: Proc. of NPAR 2007, pp. 33–42. ACM, New York (2007)
5. Kopf, J., Lischinski, D., Deussen, O., Cohen-Or, D., Cohen, M.: Locally Adapted Projections to Reduce Panorama Distortions. Computer Graphics Forum (Proceedings of EGSR 2009) 28 (to appear, 2009)
6. Wood, D.N., Finkelstein, A., Hughes, J.F., Thayer, C.E., Salesin, D.H.: Multiperspective panoramas for cel animation. In: Proc. of ACM SIGGRAPH 1997, pp. 243–250. ACM Press/Addison-Wesley Publishing Co., New York (1997)
7. Agrawala, M., Zorin, D., Munzner, T.: Artistic multiprojection rendering. In: Proc. of the Eurographics Workshop on Rendering Techniques 2000, pp. 125–136. Springer, Heidelberg (2000)
8. Glassner, A.S.: Digital cubism. IEEE Computer Graphics and Applications 24, 82–90 (2004)
9. Glassner, A.S.: Digital cubism, part 2. IEEE Computer Graphics and Applications 24, 84–95 (2004)
10. Rademacher, P., Bishop, G.: Multiple-center-of-projection images. In: SIGGRAPH, pp. 199–206 (1998)
11. Heidrich, W., Seidel, H.P.: View-independent environment maps. In: HWWS 1998: ACM SIGGRAPH/EUROGRAPHICS workshop on Graphics hardware, pp. 39–45. ACM, New York (1998)
12. Wan, L., Wong, T.T., Leung, C.S.: Isocube: Exploiting the cubemap hardware. IEEE Trans. on Vis. and Comp. Graphics 13, 720–731 (2007)
13. Löffelmann, H., Gröller, E.: Ray tracing with extended cameras. Journal of Visualization and Computer Animation 7, 211–227 (1996)
14. Yu, J., McMillan, L.: General linear cameras. In: Pajdla, T., Matas, J.G. (eds.) ECCV 2004. LNCS, vol. 3022, pp. 14–27. Springer, Heidelberg (2004)
15. Popov, S., Gunther, J., Seidel, H.P., Slusallek, P.: Stackless kd-tree traversal for high performance gpu ray tracing. Computer Graphics Forum 26, 415–424 (2007)

16. Bærentzen, A., Nielsen, S.L., Gjøl, M., Larsen, B.D., Christensen, N.J.: Single-pass wireframe rendering. In: ACM SIGGRAPH 2006, Sketches, p. 149. ACM, New York (2006)
17. Freudenberg, B., Masuch, M., Strothotte, T.: Walk-through illustrations: Frame-coherent pen-and-ink in game engine. In: Proc. of Eurographics 2001, pp. 184–191 (2001)
18. Yang, Y., Chen, J.X., Beheshti, M.: Nonlinear perspective projections and magic lenses: 3d view deformation. IEEE Comput. Graph. Appl. 25, 76–84 (2005)
19. Trapp, M., Döllner, J.: A generalization approach for 3d viewing deformations of single-center projections. In: Proc. of GRAPP 2008, pp. 162–170. INSTICC Press (2008)
20. Spindler, M., Bubke, M., Germer, T., Strothotte, T.: Camera textures. In: Proc. of the 4th GRAPHITE, pp. 295–302. ACM, New York (2006)
21. Sander, P.V., Mitchell, J.L.: Progressive Buffers: View-dependent Geometry and Texture for LOD Rendering. In: Symposium on Geometry Processing, pp. 129–138. Eurographics Association (2005)
22. Hoppe, H.: Progressive meshes. In: Proc. of SIGGRAPH 1996, pp. 99–108. ACM, New York (1996)
23. Boubekeur, T., Schlick, C.: A flexible kernel for adaptive mesh refinement on GPU. Computer Graphics Forum 27, 102–114 (2008)
24. Tatarinov, A.: Instanced tessellation in DirectX10. In: GDC 2008: Game Developers' Conference 2008 (2008)
25. Yu, X., Yu, J., McMillan, L.: Towards multi-perspective rasterization. Vis. Comput. 25, 549–557 (2009)
26. Lorenz, H., Döllner, J.: Dynamic mesh refinement on GPU using geometry shaders. In: Proc. of the 16th WSCG (2008)
27. Tatarchuk, N.: Real-time tessellation on GPU. In: Course 28: Advanced Real-Time Rendering in 3D Graphics and Games. ACM SIGGRAPH 2007 (2007)
28. Castaño, I.: Tesselation of displaced subdivision surfaces in DX11. In: XNA Gamefest 2008 (2008)
29. Persson, E.: ATI radeon HD2000 programming guide. Technical report, AMD, Inc. (2007)
30. Hou, X., Wei, L.Y., Shum, H.Y., Guo, B.: Real-time multi-perspective rendering on graphics hardware. In: EUROGRAPHICS Symposium on Rendering. Blackwell Publishing, Malden (2006)
31. Gascuel, J.D., Holzschuch, N., Fournier, G., Péroche, B.: Fast non-linear projections using graphics hardware. In: Symposium on Interactive 3D graphics and games, SI3D 2008, pp. 107–114. ACM, New York (2008)
32. Heckbert, P.S.: Fundamentals of texture mapping and image warping. Technical report, University of California at Berkeley, Berkeley, CA, USA (1989)
33. Lorenz, H.: PPP demo (2009),
    http://www.haik-lorenz.de/geometryshaders.html

An Interactive Fluid Model of Jellyfish for Animation

Dave Rudolf[1,2] and David Mould[1,3]

[1] Department of Computer Science, University of Saskatchewan, Saskatoon, Canada
[2] PhaseSpace Motion Capture Inc., San Leandro, U.S.A.
[3] School of Computer Science, Carleton University, Ottawa, Canada
dave.rudolf@usask.ca, mould@scs.carleton.ca

Abstract. We present an automatic animation system for jellyfish that is based on a physical simulation. We model the thrust of an adult jellyfish, and the organism's morphology in its most active mode of locomotion. We reduce our model by considering only species that are axially symmetric so that we can approximate the full 3D geometry of a jellyfish with a 2D simulation. We simulate the organism's elastic volume with a spring-mass system, and the surrounding sea water using the semi-Lagrangian method. We couple the two representations with the immersed boundary method. We propose a simple open-loop controller to contract the swimming muscles of the jellyfish. A 3D rendering model is extrapolated from our 2D simulation. We add variation to the extrapolated 3D geometry, which is inspired by empirical observations of real jellyfish. The resulting animation system is efficient with an acceptable compromise in physical accuracy.

1 Introduction

As the field of computer graphics progresses, physics-based animation techniques are increasingly used to both improve realism and relieve animators of lower-level tasks. To this end, we propose a method of animating jellyfish locomotion that makes relies on computational fluid dynamics. We are interested in the unique mode of locomotion exhibited by jellyfish: namely, jet propulsion. Physiologically, jellyfish are not overly complex creatures: they are invertebrates with no significant cranial capacity [2]. However, their style of motion is largely not understood either by computer scientists or by marine biologists. As Beer et al. [3] discuss, we can learn much about motion and control systems by studying natural systems in the world around us. A general model of jellyfish would be difficult to attain because of differences in species of jellyfish, and even between individuals within the same species. In this paper, we seek to develop a means of generating animations of jellyfish that would be convincing to the general population. Figure 1 illustrates the kind of motion that we aspire to animate.

The combination of a jellyfish's elastic body and the surrounding incompressible fluids are difficult to simulate. Numerical methods for such coupled systems are quite computationally expensive [28]. We use simulation not for accuracy reasons, but so that our virtual jellyfish can physically interact with its environment, especially the water. Our simulations use a spring-mass model [30] to represent the elastic body of the jellyfish, and a semi-Lagrangian fluid solver [27] for the surrounding sea water. The two representations are coupled using the immersed boundary method [19].

A. Ranchordas et al. (Eds.): VISIGRAPP 2009, CCIS 68, pp. 59–72, 2010.

Fig. 1. Captured footage of a jellyfish swimming, as filmed by Cummins [4]

To animate jellyfish at interactive rates, we must simplify our simulation model. We simulate the jellyfish whose umbrella is axially symmetric in a coarse 2D plane, and extrapolate the results to higher resolutions and to 3D space. The result is a model whose motions are qualitatively similar to that of real jellyfish. However, if we naïvely extrapolate our simulations to a 3D model, the surface will lack the geometric complexity seen in real jellyfish. We propose a means of adding variation back to the 3D geometry of our model, based on observations from the biology community [10,25].

A further challenge in animating jellyfish is determining motor controls for the model. Jellyfish have only a small number of muscles, but those muscles are used in complex ways, and in manners that are not well studied. In this paper, we give one possible approach to a motor control for jellyfish, based on empirical observation of the organism. The resulting animations are appealing to a general audience, but may not be accurate enough for use by marine biologists.

2   Previous Work

Interactive animation techniques have been developed for a variety of characters, including snakes and worms [15], fish [31] and other marine vertebrates [9], as well as legged mammals [21]. Legged locomotion has also been studied by the robotics community [3]. A large amount of research has been aimed at animating various aspects of human motion [13]. However, little has been done to model marine invertebrates. Jellyfish have previously been animated with key-framing techniques [20], though without regard for the interaction between the organism and its environment.

To simulate elastic bodies like that of our jellyfish, particle-based approaches such as spring-mass systems [30] are commonly used. One might then be tempted to use a particle-based fluid representation, such as *smoothed particle hydrodynamics* [8,16], to simulate the sea water around our jellyfish. However, SPH systems approximate incompressibility with large pressure gradient forces, which makes the simulation numerically stiff, and thus computationally expensive. Grid-based fluid simulators are better suited for incompressible fluids. Classical grid methods are very accurate but slow because of stability restrictions [11]. As a compromise, the semi-Lagrangian method [27] is unconditionally stable, though it adds numerical dampening. To couple grid-based fluids with particle-based solids, the graphics community typically uses pressure gradients across fluid-solid interfaces. However, much care must be taken to ensure that fluid does not leak across thin solid regions [12]. An alternative is the immersed boundary method [19], which allows a minimal amount of leakage across solid boundaries [28]. A challenge in all simulation-based animation techniques is that we need to automatically control the bodies that are in motion. An adaptive method, such as a PID controller [7], is feasible; however, choosing the goal state of the system and tuning the controller's parameters are not trivial tasks.

The biology community has a fair body of literature on jellyfish. Megill [14] categorizes different gaits that jellyfish exhibit. Dabiri and Gharib [5] provide empirical data of a jellyfish's position and shape as it swims. Gladfelter [10] describes how the jellyfish will deform as it contracts. Aria [2], Gladfelter [10], and Megill [14] discuss the organism's elastic properties, and its distribution of muscles fibres. Megill [14] theorizes about how jellyfish achieve optimal thrust in several gaits. Sullivan et al. [29] provide data on the mechanics behind jellyfish movement and the reaction of the sea water surrounding the organism. Daniel [6] devised a differential equation for the organism's swimming thrust. However, Dabiri and Gharib [5] show that Daniel's equation is too sensitive to its parameters to be a good general model. Megill [14] determined the approximate resonant frequencies of the organism. However, Dabiri and Gharib [5] observed different resonant frequencies than those of Megill's theoretical predictions.

Dabiri and Gharib [5] exploit axial symmetry in a manner similar us, except that they rotate only one half of the lateral slice about the axis of symmetry. To add variation to our 3D volume, we take inspiration from Rasmussen et al. [22], who animated 3D explosions with 2D simulation and a cyclical 3D noise spectrum. Perlin [18] provides a continuous noise field which we find more suitable to our application.

3   A Numerical Model of Jellyfish

Jellyfish are essentially elastic volumes that activate muscles in order to contract their umbrellas, creating a jet of fluid that propels the organism. We build a model of jellyfish that accounts for the elastic flesh of the organism and the sea water that surrounds it.

3.1   Jellyfish Physiology

Jellyfish deflate their umbrella by contracting muscles that spread across the umbrella hull. The left side of Figure 2 highlights the anatomy of the organism that plays a role in locomotion. The right side of Figure 2 shows the muscular structure for one species of jellyfish. The left side of Figure 2 illustrates the different types of tissue within the umbrella itself. The chief muscle involved in locomotion is the circumferential muscle that lines the subumbrellar wall. This muscle contracts to pull the umbrella wall inward and creating a fluid jet at the aperture. The circumferential muscle has no opposing muscle, unlike muscles that rotate skeletal joints in other species. When the circumferential muscle relaxes, the umbrella is pushed outward by the elastic properties of the surrounding tissue [14] shows The organism also has tentacles along the aperture of the umbrella, which are passive, but cause additional drag.

Aside from muscles, the remainder of the umbrella is loosely categorized into two types of tissue: the *bell mesoglea* and the *joint mesoglea*. These mesogleae are essentially passive. However, the bell mesoglea does contain some sparsely placed *radial muscle fibres*, oriented normal the umbrella's surface. Megill [14] states that these radial muscles changes the symmetry of the umbrella when contracted, and so are used to

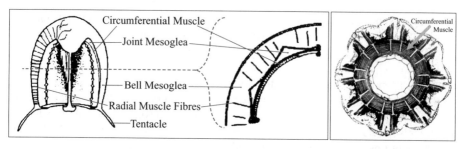

Fig. 2. Left: Cross-sections of an umbrella [10]. Right: Muscles in the umbrella [2].

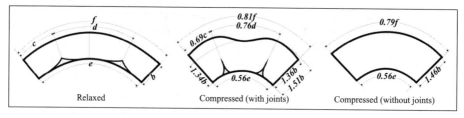

Fig. 3. Horizontal cross-sections of umbrella deformation [10]. Left: the umbrella at its rest configuration. Centre: a contracted umbrella, and the deformation that occurs because of joint mesoglea. Right: the deformation that would occur if the entire umbrella was bell mesoglea.

reorient the organism as it swims. The joint mesoglea is so-called because it is much less elastically stiff than the bell mesoglea. When the umbrella contracts, the joint mesoglea deforms into sharp ridges or "joints", as is illustrated in Figure 3. Because of the joint mesoglea, the stress-strain curve for the umbrella is not linear. Megill [14] shows empirically that the elastic response of the mesoglea is essentially linear except for extremely large stresses, where the mesoglea becomes more stiff and thus compresses less. Thus, we ignore this non-linearity and assume linear springs. Lastly, the compression pattern given in Figure 3 suggests that a jellyfish has eight waves around its aperture. However, a survey of Canadian Atlantic species [25] shows that, some species commonly have different numbers and shapes of these segments.

Spencer [26] noted that the entire circumferential muscle is not completely synchronized. The neuronal impulses that tell the muscle to contract must travel across the nervous system of the organism, and a tiny delay is incurred at each neuronal synapse. The effect of this synaptic delay is that fibres which are further away from neuronal sources will receive the impulses at a slightly later time. However, in practice, we find that this delay pattern actually has little effect on the results of our model.

Many species of jellyfish are approximately axially symmetric, where the axis of symmetry runs from the apex of the umbrella through the centre of its aperture. Shih [25] lists a large number of jellyfish species, ranging in physical configuration, many of which are not axially symmetric. In this work, we only deal with the jellyfish that do have axial symmetry. We choose our simulation slice plane such that the organism's axis of symmetry lies on the plane.

3.2   2D Simulation Model

We want to model three aspects of the jellyfish's anatomy: the umbrella's mesoglea, the tentacles, and the circumferential muscle. The jellyfish will be a mass-spring system, and a grid-based fluid simulation will represent the fluids around the organism. We represent the subumbrellar surface of the mesoglea with a chain of Hookean springs, and further enforce the structure of the umbrella with angular springs. Instead of angular springs, one might be tempted to create small networks of Hookean springs to enforce relative orientations of the surface points, similar to the work of Miller[15] or Tu and Terzopoulos [31]. However, we found experimentally that the large number of short springs (relative to the resolution of our fluid grid) made the system more numerically stiff. Figure 4 shows the configuration of springs that we chose to use. We represent the tentacles in the same manner as the subumbrellar surface, with the same elastic modulus, but with a volume $1/100^{th}$ that of the umbrella springs.

The circumferential muscle is represented by linear springs going longitudinally across the umbrella, as shown in Figure 4. We contract the umbrella by reducing the rest lengths of these springs. Megill [14] measured the elastic strength of the bell mesoglea (including muscle fibres), finding that the mesoglea has an elastic modulus of approximately 1186 Pa, and that the joint mesoglea has an elastic modulus of 130 Pa. The modulus for the muscle fibres is significantly higher, at around 400,000 Pa.

We model sea water using the incompressible Navier-Stokes equations:

$$\frac{\partial u}{\partial t} = \nu\nabla^2 u - u \cdot \nabla u - \frac{\nabla p}{\rho} + F, \qquad \nabla \cdot u = 0, \tag{1}$$

where u is a vector field that represents the fluid's velocity, p is a scalar field for pressure, ρ is the density of the fluid, ν is the coefficient of kinetic viscosity, and F is a vector field for external forces that act on the fluid. The symbols ∇ and ∇^2 are spatial gradient and Laplacian operators, respectively. Griebel et al. [11] give an in-depth description of Equation 1. We integrate these equations numerically over time.

Of particular interest to our work with jellyfish, the second part of Equation 1 enforces constant density and incompressibility. Jellyfish exert large forces on the fluid within its subumbrellar cavity, and the high thrust achieved by the organism depends greatly on the fact that sea water is essentially incompressible. We choose the grid-based semi-Lagrangian method to simulate our fluids because it strictly upholds incompressibility. We immerse our spring-mass model in a square fluid volume that is ten times the jellyfish's diameter, and give the fluid cavity free-slip boundary conditions [11].

We use Peskin's immersed boundary method [19] to combine the particle-based spring-mass model with the grid-based semi-Lagrangian solver. In Peskin's method, the elastic point-masses are advected along the flow field of the fluid grid, and the elastic forces of the Hookean springs are applied to the fluid grid using the force term F in Equation 1. We diverge slightly from Peskin's method of distributing the elastic forces onto the fluid grid. Peskin uses a smoothing kernel to distribute the forces to several, possibly dozens, of grid cells near the point-mass. Doing so increases the cost of simulation, and effectively puts an upper limit on the frequency at which the force profile can vary over the fluid grid. Since we use relatively coarse grids (i.e., 50×50 or 100×100 cells), the frequency limitation of Peskin's smoothing kernel can make the fluid appear artificially viscous. We instead distribute the elastic force of a point-mass onto its four closest grid cells with bilinear interpolation.

Peskin's method is known to be numerically stiff, and so can be slow if done naïvely. Semi-implicit integration schemes gain us approximately an order of magnitude in efficiency [28]. However, we find experimentally that we gain two orders of magnitude in speed-up simply by using Stam's semi-Lagrangian method [27] instead of an explicit scheme. Note, though, that Stam's method does not gain us larger time-steps, but rather decreases the cost of each step. Stam's method may be unconditionally stable when simulating fluids by themselves, but the elastic body can still introduce instabilities into the system when time-steps are too large. We are unaware of any stability conditions that we can apply to our model to determine an adaptive time-step. Even the commonly used *Courant-Friedrichs-Lewy* condition [11] does not control the stability of the elastic body. In the end, we use this CFL condition, but with a safety factor of 0.001.

For our 2D simulation, we use a Cartesian formulation of the Navier-Stokes equation over a plane. One may be tempted to use a cylindrical formulation [1], given that we are modeling a system with axial symmetry. However, the jellyfish may tilt itself and change the axis of symmetry. When this occurs (potentially on every frame), we would have to resample the fluid grid so that the axis of symmetry aligns itself with the grid lines. This effectively blurs the flow field across the grid, as well as adding to the cost of simulation. Thus, we use a Cartesian formulation, though at the cost of rigorous physical accuracy.

3.3   Muscle Activation

Megill [14] describes several jellyfish gaits. The majority of the biology research is on the *resonant gait*. We also limit our discussion to this gait. It is characterized by the organism contracting at (or near) the resonant frequency of itself and its surrounding sea water, giving the jellyfish optimal thrust during swimming. We simulate muscle contractions by modifying the rest lengths of the subumbrellar springs. Biology literature does not provide evidence that the organism uses closed-loop controllers such as those described by Dean [7] to induce muscle contractions. Instead, we suspect that jellyfish contractions are governed by a cyclical pattern that is quite predictable [26,14,5]. We thus define a function that describes the rest length of the springs over time. Specifically, we created a curve based on Hermite splines. We then normalize the contraction function to be between 1 and 0.56, since a jellyfish may contract to 56% of its maximum diameter when contracting, as seen in Figure 3.

When the jellyfish contracts, it will propel itself forward. However, when it expands, it also pulls itself backward. For a jellyfish to achieve a net positive movement over the course of a contraction cycle, the organism must incur less drag in the expansion phase of the cycle than it does in the contraction phase. This is analogous to how a human swimmer's arm must push more water during its downstroke than it does during its upstroke. We are unaware of any biology literature that details how jellyfish achieve this drag reduction. We suspect that jellyfish make themselves more flat to achieve higher drag, and more rounded to reduce their drag. To support our hypothesis, see Figure 1, which is a short image sequence of an actual jellyfish that expands, and then contracts. In the first three images, the jellyfish is expanding, and its umbrella's shape is relatively

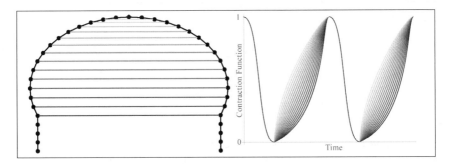

Fig. 4. Our spring-mass network for a jellyfish slice, and the corresponding contraction functions that we use. The subumbrellar springs in the left image are colour-coded to correspond with the contraction function for that spring in the graph on the right.

curved. However, in the fourth frame of Figure 1, the jellyfish is contracting, and the umbrella appears less curved and resembles a cone shape. This conic resemblance is especially striking toward the aperture of the umbrella.

In order to achieve the sort of morphology that we see in Figure 1, we have to slow the expansion of springs that are at the bottom of the umbrella, relative to those at the top. We give each subumbrellar spring a unique contraction function so that springs close to the aperture expand more slowly than those closer to the apex of the umbrella. Figure 4 shows our spring-mass model of the jellyfish, but with the corresponding contraction functions for each spring. By using this staggered expansion mechanism, our jellyfish travels approximately 68% farther with each stroke than it did when all springs expanded in unison. Interestingly, the jellyfish still did have some positive net thrust when all springs moved in unison.

The frequency of the jellyfish's contractions has a direct effect on the thrust that is achieved by the organism, as well as the morphology of the organism. The resonant frequency of the system depends on the diameter of its umbrella. Megill [14] derives an approximate analytical model of the jellyfish, though his findings differ from empirical data [5]. Without further confirmation of either result, we experimented with different contraction frequencies to determine which ones were optimal for our model. Figure 5 shows the translational motion of our simulated jellyfish with different contraction frequencies. As seen in the right side of Figure 5, we get a large maximum for a frequency of 0.7 Hz, which agrees with data measured by Dabiri and Gharib [5].

3.4 2D Rendering Model

Our physics model is quite coarse, and we want to be able to resample it to a resolution appropriate for the rendering configuration. We also need a way to account for the thickness of the umbrella and the tentacles, since we are modeling both as piecewise linear curves. We first add a finite thickness to our model of the umbrella. In our simulation model that involved both linear and angular springs, the point-masses of the umbrella represent the subumbrellar surface. We can generate the exumbrellar side by computing

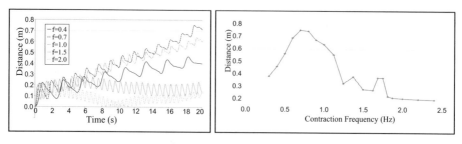

Fig. 5. Left: Trajectories of several simulated organisms with different frequencies of contraction. Right: Distance traveled with different frequencies of contraction. All results were simulated with a 4 *cm* organism, and the elastic modulus of the jellyfish's umbrella is $\lambda = 1186\ Pa$.

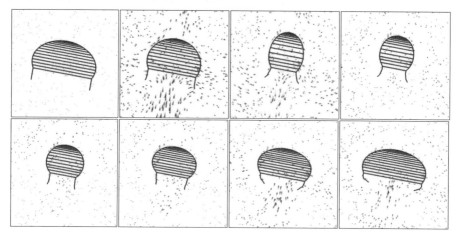

Fig. 6. Simulation of a contraction cycle. Trace particles show the fluid flow around the jellyfish.

surface normals at each point-mass, and then projecting backward through the thickness of the umbrella. Figure 3 provides us with suitable thickness values. We can then generate an arbitrary resolution model for rendering by interpolating a cubic spline through the original point-masses and then the newly generated exumbrellar points.

3.5 3D Extrapolation

We must extrapolate our 2D rendering model to a 3D volume. However, our 2D slice may not be symmetric itself (i.e., the two sides of the umbrella may be different). Thus, we cannot merely rotate the results of the 2D slice about a single axis of symmetry. Our 3D interpolation proceeds by considering each pair of points x_i and x_j opposite to each other on the umbrella. On our simulation model in Section 3.2, these opposing points would be joined by a subumbrellar spring. However, since we have resampled our model for rendering, we use opposing pairs from the rendering model. We define an axis of rotation for each pair, which goes orthogonally through the centre of the line segment between the two points x_i and x_j. Note that each pair of points will potentially have

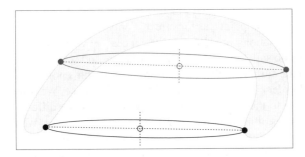

Fig. 7. Example point pairs along the 2D umbrella slice that have been extrapolated to 3D discs

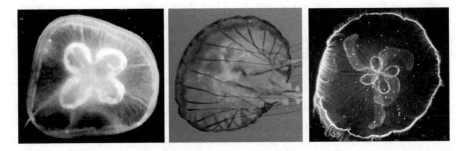

Fig. 8. Jellyfish that are only approximately axially symmetric. Left: courtesy of Mark Eramian. Centre: taken by the authors. Right: taken by the Florida Keys National Marine Sanctuary [24].

a different axis of symmetry. Figure 7 illustrates our process of extrapolating circular area from pairs of points in our 2D model. We use the same disc extrapolation scheme for generating tentacles along the 3D aperture of the umbrella.

The volume that will result from our disc-based extrapolation will be artificially smooth and perfect. Although a jellyfish may be roughly symmetric, they are not exactly so. Figure 8 shows example individuals whose umbrellas are approximately symmetric, but with some small-scale asymmetries. To add variation to our rendering model, we perturb each point $z_{i,j}$ on the surface by some scalar distance $c_{i,j}$ in the direction of its surface normal $n_{i,j}$. We use an two subscripts in our notation for the points because we are now dealing with points on two different axes (i.e., latitude and longitude).

Several factors can cause small-scale asymmetries in jellyfish. For one, a particular species may exhibit periodic structures in their umbrella's geometry [25]. For these structural patterns, we define simple functions to generate the desired appearance, such as $\alpha^{str} sin(f\sigma_j)$ or $\alpha^{str}|sin(f\sigma_j)|$, where α^{str} is a scale factor, f is the artistically chosen frequency that suits the target species, and σ_j is the longitudinal angle of points $x_{i,j}$ for all values of i.

Another type of variation, seen in Figure 3, is caused by the nonuniform elastic properties of the jellyfish's mesoglea, which cause ripples across the umbrella as it contracts. This variation is roughly sinusoidal. We achieve the desired effect by normalizing the function $sin(f\sigma_j)$ to be between 0 and 1, and scale the result by a factor that linearly interpolates between 0 and $(1.51 - 1.36)\vartheta$ as each umbrella spring moves from being fully expanded to fully contracted. For this variation due to compression, we do not modify the subumbrellar points, as the effect is only seen on the exumbrellar surface.

Lastly, some variations are due to differences between individuals of the same species. We have no suitable model for this variation, and so we mimic it artistically by adding noise to the surface of the umbrella. We use Perlin's noise function [18], which yields a second-order continuous scalar field over a 3D space. We control the frequency of each parameter to the noise function independently, since different species display different frequencies of noise in the lateral and longitudinal axes. We chose parameters to qualitatively approximate the look of a target species. We also attenuate the amplitude of the noise function for points that are near the apex of the umbrella. This is partially done because the umbrella is thicker near the apex, and thus will ripple less. Also, the discs that we extrapolate from our slice data are smaller near the peak of the umbrella than the discs that are closer to the aperture. Thus, the noise function appears to have a higher frequency on the discs with smaller radii. By attenuating the noise function near the top of the umbrella, we remove these artifacts. Our expression for the displacement of the umbrella points due to non-periodic variation is as follows:

$$c_{i,j}^{unstructured} = \alpha^{unstr} d_i * Q_P(2d_i, 8d_j, 0.01t), \tag{2}$$

where (d_i, d_j) is a normalized latitude-longitude coordinate for each surface point, t is the simulation time, Q_P is the Perlin noise field, and α^{unstr} is again a scaling factor. We apply this displacement to both umbrella points, and also tentacle points, so that the tentacles themselves exhibit some variation.

4   Results

Figure 10 shows a series of frames from our system, rendered with a simple Lambertian surface lighting model. We find the motion of our jellyfish to be quite satisfactory and convincing. The model's movement is more closely tied to the contraction of the organism than previous animations of jellyfish such as in Disney's "Finding Nemo" [20]. Also, our model's morphology, motion, and resonant frequency shown in Figures 5 and 11 are similar to empirical results [5].

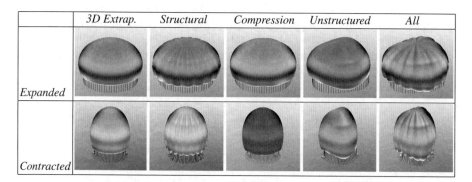

Fig. 9. The results of naïve 3D extrapolation for both an expanded (rest) and contracted state, and the three types of variation that we apply to the umbrella, as well as the combined variation

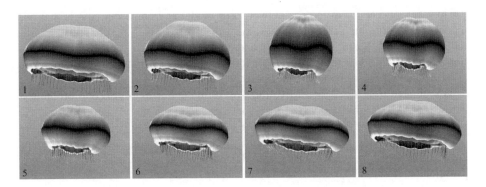

Fig. 10. A single contraction-expansion cycle for our virtual jellyfish, fully rendered

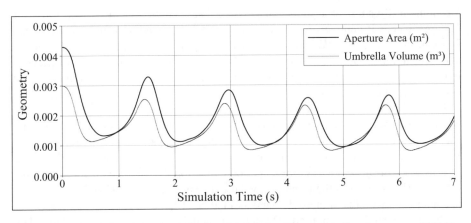

Fig. 11. The morphology of a 4 *cm* simulated jellyfish with a contraction frequency of 0.7 Hz. All other simulation parameters were the same as Figure 5.

Parameter	Value
Fluid Grid Height/Width (n)	100
Fluid Viscosity (ν)	1.304×10^{-3}
Fluid Density (ρ)	1
Safety Factor for Integration Step Size	0.001
Jellyfish Contraction Frequency	$0.7 Hz$
Jellyfish Diameter	$40mm$
Jellyfish Height	$28mm$
Jellyfish Thickness (ϑ)	$4mm$
Hookean Elastic Modulus (λ)	$1186 Pa$
Angular Elastic Stiffness	$1.186 \ N \cdot m/rad$
Tentacle Cross-sectional Area Factor	$1/100$
Structural Variation Scale (α^{str})	$0.375 \cdot \vartheta$
Unstructured Variation Scale (α^{unstr})	$2.25 \cdot \vartheta$

Fig. 12. Parameters of our animation system

However, one major difference between our model and empirical data is that our model yields more high-frequency movement than is seen with real jellyfish. Essentially, our model's position oscillates up and down more, relative to its overall translational motion. Thus, our model is suitable for entertainment purposes, but would not be accurate enough for the biology community.

We are able to achieve interactive rates of 30 to 40 frames per second on modest hardware (AMD Turion 1.6 GHz processor), depending on the resolution of our 2D simulation and of our 3D extrapolation. We experimentally find that time-steps of the order of 0.01 seconds begin to hit the stability limits of the system, and so several steps are taken between frames. Of course, the 3D extrapolation process is done only once per rendered frame.

5   Conclusions and Future Work

We numerically simulate a model of jellyfish that accounts for the elastic forces of the organism as it contracts its muscles, as well as the reaction of the sea water that surrounds the organism. We choose simulation as our animation technique because it allows us to model the interaction of the jellyfish and its environment. We restrict our model to species that are axially symmetric, so that we only need to simulate a 2D vertical slice of the organism. We also concentrate on the resonant gait of adult jellyfish.

In our simulations, we represent the jellyfish's flesh as a spring-mass system that consists of a combination of linear and angular springs. The muscles that line the under part of the umbrella are modeled as linear springs that span the subumbrellar cavity. We mimic the contraction of these muscles by shortening the subumbrellar springs' rest lengths based on an artistically chosen periodic function. To simulate the reaction of the sea water that surrounds the organism, we use a semi-Lagrangian [27] fluid simulator in conjunction with the immersed boundary method [19].

We generate a high resolution 2D rendering model by threading a cubic interpolant around the point-masses of our coarse simulation model. With this higher resolution slice model, we extrapolate to a 3D surface by defining discs that go through both sides of the 2D umbrella curve. We add several forms of variation to the resulting 3D surface. First, parabolic patterns are added, which run vertically down the surface of the umbrella. These patterns are specific to certain species of jellyfish. Second, vertically sinusoidal ridges are introduced as the organism contracts, due to its non-linear elastic properties. The amplitude of these ridges depend on the contraction of the umbrella. Lastly, we add continuous noise to the umbrella's surface to give each individual jellyfish a unique shape, artistically defined for lack of a concrete model of this variation.

Further work with respect to jellyfish animation could be done. We would like to remove the restriction of axial symmetry, possibly by simulating multiple 2D slices and interpolating between them. One challenge with this approach is to reconcile the simulated slices where they intersect. Rendering could be improved by considering translucency and bioluminescence. We are unaware of any literature that describes a jellyfish's optical properties. Similarly, one could model the venous structures that are present in some species, though again we are unaware of any relevant biology literature.

We still know little about how jellyfish control their muscles to achieve jet propulsion. Much work in this regard could be carried out by the biology community, but we could also make use of work in the field of computer animation. Specifically, we could experiment with different muscle control schemes in a manner similar to *sensor actuator networks* [17]. Also, jellyfish are capable of other locomotion modes besides the common resonant gait, and so these other modes could be investigated.

In our work, we have not discussed how some species of jellyfish are able to reorient themselves. Megill [14] states that jellyfish use sparsely placed radial muscle fibres in the bell mesoglea to change the symmetry of the umbrella and thus affect a course change for the organism as it swims. The exact process is not well understood. So far, we were not able to reproduce this phenomenon within our model.

With relation to fluid dynamics, there are a number of improvements that could be made to numerical techniques. Stability criteria could be derived for the immersed boundary method. Also, the numerical stiffness of SPH techniques for incompressible flows could be improved. Recently, Robinson-Mosher et al. [23] have introduced pressure-based elastic-fluid methods that are unconditionally stable, though we have not investigated these new results.

References

1. Acheson, D.J.: Elementary Fluid Dynamics. Oxford University Press, Oxford (1990)
2. Arai, M.N.: A Functional Biology of Scyphozoa. Chapman and Hall, London (1997)
3. Beer, R.D., Quinn, R.D., Chiel, H.J., Ritzmann, R.E.: Biologically inspired approaches to robotics: what can we learn from insects? Commun. ACM 40(3), 30–38 (1997)
4. Cummins, R.H.: My best pictures and movies from marine ecology (1999), `http://www.junglewalk.com/popup.asp?type=v&AnimalVideoID=759`
5. Dabiri, J.O., Gharib, M.: Sensitivity analysis of kinematic approximations in dynamic medusan swimming models. Journal of Experimental Biology 206, 3675–3680 (2003)
6. Daniel, T.L.: Mechanics and energetics of medusan jet propulsion. Canadian Journal of Zoology 61, 1406–1420 (1983)
7. Dean, T., Wellman, M.: Planning and Control. Morgan Kaufmann Publishers, San Francisco (1991)
8. Desbrun, M., Gascuel, M.P.: Smoothed particles: a new paradigm for animating highly deformable bodies. In: Proceedings of the Eurographics workshop on Computer animation and simulation 1996, pp. 61–76. Springer, New York (1996)
9. Fröhlich, T.: The virtual oceanarium. Commun. ACM 43(7), 94–101 (2000)
10. Gladfelter, W.B.: Structure and function of the locomotory system of polyorchis montereyensis (cnidaria, hydrozoa). Helgolaender Wiss. Meeresunters 23, 38–79 (1972)
11. Griebel, M., Dornseifer, T., Neunhoeffer, T.: Numerical Simulation in Fluid Dynamics: a practical introduction. Society for Industrial and Applied Mathematics, Philadelphia (1998)
12. Guendelman, E., Selle, A., Losasso, F., Fedkiw, R.: Coupling water and smoke to thin deformable and rigid shells. In: SIGGRAPH 2005: ACM SIGGRAPH 2005 Papers, pp. 973–981. ACM, New York (2005)
13. Hodgins, J.K., Wooten, W.L., Brogan, D.C., O'Brien, J.F.: Animating human athletics. In: Proceedings of SIGGRAPH 1995, pp. 71–78. ACM Press, New York (1995)
14. Megill, W.M.: The biomechanics of jellyfish swimming, Ph.D. Dissertation, Department of Zoology, University of British Columbia (2002)
15. Miller, G.S.P.: The motion dynamics of snakes and worms. In: Proceedings of SIGGRAPH 1988, pp. 169–173. ACM Press, New York (1988)

16. Müller, M., Schirm, S., Teschner, M., Heidelberger, B., Gross, M.: Interaction of fluids with deformable solids: Research articles. Comput. Animat. Virtual Worlds 15(3-4), 159–171 (2004)
17. Michiel van de Panne, E.F.: Sensor-actuator networks. In: Proceedings of SIGGRAPH 1993, pp. 335–342. ACM Press, New York (1993)
18. Perlin, K.: Improving noise. In: Proceedings of SIGGRAPH 2002, pp. 681–682. ACM Press, New York (2002)
19. Peskin, C.: The immersed boundary method. Acta Numerica 11, 479–517 (2002)
20. Pixar Animation Studios, W.D.P.: Finding Nemo motion picture. DVD (2003)
21. Raibert, M.H., Hodgins, J.K.: Animation of dynamic legged locomotion. In: Proceedings of SIGGRAPH 1991, pp. 349–358. ACM Press, New York (1991)
22. Rasmussen, N., Nguyen, D.Q., Geiger, W., Fedkiw, R.: Smoke simulation for large scale phenomena. ACM Trans. Graph. 22(3), 703–707 (2003)
23. Robinson-Mosher, A., Shinar, T., Gretarsson, J., Su, J., Fedkiw, R.: Two-way coupling of fluids to rigid and deformable solids and shells. In: SIGGRAPH 2008: ACM SIGGRAPH 2008 papers, pp. 1–9. ACM, New York (2008)
24. Sanctuary, F.K.N.M.: NOAA's Coral Kingdom Collection: reef2547 (2007), http://www.photolib.noaa.gov/htmls/reef2547.htm
25. Shih, C.T.: A Guide to the Jellyfish of Canadian Atlantic Waters. No. 5, National Museum of Natural Sciences, Ottawa, Canada (1977)
26. Spencer, A.N.: The physiology of a coelenterate neuromuscular synapse. Journal of Comparative Physiology 148, 353–363 (1982)
27. Stam, J.: Stable fluids. In: Proceedings of SIGGRAPH 1999, pp. 121–128. ACM Press/Addison-Wesley Publishing Co., New York (1999)
28. Stockie, J.M., Wetton, B.R.: Analysis of stiffness in the immersed boundary method and implications for time-stepping schemes (1999)
29. Sullivan, B.K., Suchman, C.L., Costello, J.H.: Mechanics of prey selection by ephyrae of the scyphomedusa aurelia aurita. Marine Biology 130(2), 213–222 (1997)
30. Terzopoulos, D., Platt, J., Barr, A., Fleischer, K.: Elastically deformable models. In: Proceedings of SIGGRAPH 1987, pp. 205–214. ACM Press, New York (1987)
31. Tu, X., Terzopoulos, D.: Artificial fishes: Physics, locomotion, perception, behavior. Computer Graphics 28, 43–50 (1994), http://citeseer.nj.nec.com/tu94artificial.html

Unbiased Closed-Form Solutions for Center of Rotation

Jonathan Kipling Knight[1] and Sudhanshu Kumar Semwal[2]

[1] ITT, Colorado Springs CO, U.S.A.
[2] Dept of Computer Science, University of Colorado, Colorado Springs CO, U.S.A.
semwal@eas.uccs.edu, Kip.Knight@itt.com

Abstract. We present a fast closed form solution for estimating the exact joint locations inside the human body from motion capture data. The closed-form solution is robust, fast and unbiased. For example, the formulae are as much as 100 times faster than the traditional non-linear Maximum Likelihood Estimator and about 10 times faster than linear least squares methods. The methods are proven to be statistically efficient when measurement error is smaller than the joint-marker distance. Unbiased Generalized Delogne-Kása (UGDK), multiple radii solution (MGDK), and incrementally improved GDK (IGDK) are important contributions of our research providing closed form fast solutions for skeleton extraction from motion capture data. Skeletal animation sequences are generated using the CMU Graphics Lab motion capture database.

1 Introduction

Skeleton extraction methods use temporal marker positions from motion capture data to predict the joint locations. These predicted joint locations then define the skeleton. Skeleton extraction methods therefore are different than those methods where a fixed, predetermined skeleton is best fit to any motion capture data. The motion of the marker looks like it remains on the surface of a sphere when it is analyzed relative one of the two segments involved. Recently, O'Brien, et al., in 2000 [13] and with Kirk in 2005 [9] have produced a fast method for skeleton extraction using a linear least squares method assuming there is a relatively stationary point between two segments, and then solving for that point, which is essentially the rotation point. Some years ago, Leendert de Witte [20], in 1960, found a solution for a circle in $3D$ space. He used spherical trigonometry to solve the minimized distance from the best great circle path. He used approximations that are convenient for large radii and had to choose from three solutions to get the correct one. The Maximum Likelihood Estimator (MLE) was the first solution for finding the sphere parameters. In 1961 Stephen Robinson [16] presented the iterative method of solving the sphere and developed a closed form solution for the radius estimator but not for the center estimator. In 1972, Paul Delogne [5] presented a method for solving a circle for the purposes of determining reflection measurements on transmission lines. Delogne's solution to the circle involves the inverse of a 3×3 matrix. István Kása did more analysis in 1976 [8]. He was the first to recognize the bias in the answer and produced better error analysis. Vaughan Pratt [14] in 1987 produced a very generic linear least squares method for algebraic surfaces. His solution was slower for spheres due to the need to extract the eigenvectors. Gander, et. al. in 1994 [6] produced the linear least-squares method for circle fitting. Samuel Thomas and Y. Chan in 1995 [19] created a

A. Ranchordas et al. (Eds.): VISIGRAPP 2009, CCIS 68, pp. 73–88, 2010.

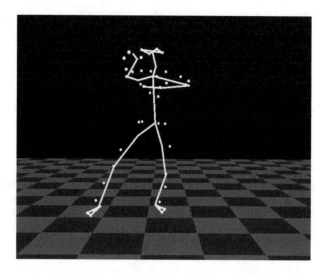

Fig. 1. Skeleton Extraction of Motion Capture Data

formula for the Cramér-Rao Lower Bound for the circle estimation. In 1997, Lukács, et. al. [12], produced some improvements on non-linear minimization for spheres. Corral, et. al. [4] in 1998 analyzed the Kása formula in more detail and a way to reject the answer if the confinement angle got too small. A paper in nuclear physics [18] describes a method in 2000 to produce the circular arc of a particle traveling in a cloud chamber. In that paper, Strandlie, et. al. [18] transformed a Riemann sphere into a plane and fit the plane using standard methods involving the eigenvalues of the sample covariance matrix. Zelniker in 2003 [21] reformulated the circle equation to solve directly for the center using the pseudo-inverse $(^{\#})$ of a $D \times N$ matrix. Michael Burr, et. al. [2] in 2004 created a geometric inversion technique which far surpassed the complexity needed to solve for a hypersphere. It was a non-linear approach and they failed to recognize there were simpler linear solutions to what they were solving. In 2007, Knight et al. [10], published the initial results from the research for this research in which a skeleton was formed from a closed-form solution of generic motion capture data.

2   Skeleton Extraction Techniques

Producing a skeleton involves finding the centers of joint rotations, the hierarchy of segmentation, and the orientation of each segment. The hierarchy of segmentation is known ahead of time such as in human animation. The orientation of a segment is determined by one of two methods. Either it is given in the raw data, e.g. magnetic trackers, or it is calculated by the fastest technique known. The fastest way to calculate the orientation of a segment from positional information of markers is quite intuitive and has been in use for a long time. One of the earliest uses found in motion capture were published in 2000 by Herda, et al. [7]. Fortunately, this speedy method of orienting the segment can also be used to calculate the entire skeleton. The most common approach to calculating a skeleton from motion capture data is through minimization until the skeleton fits where the rotation points have been approximated. The minimization involves squishing segments and moving joints until all joints are nearest to the calculated rotation points. O'Brien, et al. [13] uses a linear least-squares minimization that produces the rotation points from a collection of time frames. Their method relies on the constraint that two connected segments have a common point between them during rotation. Their solution calculates a point from the knowledge of the orientation of both the parent and the child segments and calculates the best fit point that remains the most still relative to the two segments. The solution involves the Singular Value Decomposition of a $3N \times 6$ matrix to produce the common point that is the rotation point. If the solution fails to come up with an answer, as in the case of no motion or planar motion, then the closest point between the two coordinate systems is used. This technique relies heavily on orientation information that is not always available. In their study, magnetic motion tracking devices are used which contain both position and orientation. This is akin to solving for the best-fit sphere around a center. $3D$ marker trajectories are also analyzed in [1].

3 Spherical Curve-Fitting Approaches

There are three techniques in use today: iterative; least squares; and algebraic best fits. They each have their advantages and disadvantages. Iterative techniques are good for accuracy, least squares are faster than iterative but slower than algebraic, and algebraic techniques are good for speed.

3.1 Monte-Carlo Experiments

In order to compare the methods, a Monte-Carlo experiment was run using 1000 trials, each of which had anywhere from 4 to 10^6 samples. The runs took over a week of computational effort to collect. Each trial had a fixed standard deviation of the samples from the sphere with values ranging from 10^{-13} to 10^{14}. Each trial was further varied by a limiting angle from some random point on a sphere. The limiting angle varied from 0 to 180°, where 180° means full sphere coverage. It is important to have a limiting angle in this experiment because all sphere-fit algorithms are error-prone when this angle gets smaller. The sample must be confined to be within an angle from a fixed point on the sphere. This experiment allows for the in-depth analysis of the error in the answer from four different estimators. The four techniques are Maximum-Likelihood Estimator (MLE), Linear Least-Squares (LLS), Generalized Delogne-Kása Estimator (GDKE), and the new Unbiased Generalized Delogne-Kása estimator (UGDK). The first three are established formulae and has been used for two hundred years (MLE [17]) to as young as three years (GDKE [21]). UGDK is new method proposed in this paper. The following graph (Figure 2) shows the errors in the estimators compared to the standard deviation of the samples indicating that UGDK performs closest to CRLB. The graph shows that the relative error versus relative standard deviation is a line for each of these methods. The error is thus proportional to the standard deviation on a log-log display showing a power law. What is also clear from the graph is the comparison. The outliers on the graph have been circled. The obvious differences between the estimators show up in the graph by deviations from the straight line when error equals standard

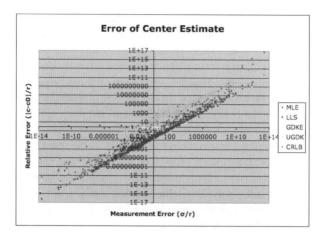

Fig. 2. Relative error comparison

deviation. From the graph, it appears that there is a common limitation to the error in the estimator. This common limitation is named the Cramér-Rao Lower Bound to the covariance of an estimator. The following sections discuss the limit to all estimators for this particular problem. The MLE has outliers when the error equals the radius. This is due to multiple solutions when the error equals the radius. The LLS has outliers when the standard deviation is below about 10^{-6} times the radius and greater than 10^{10} times the radius. These are due to numerical instability during the extremes of using finite representation of decimal numbers. The GDKE seems to be on par with the MLE except for the MLE outliers. The UGDK is consistently close to the CRLB indicating that it is more accurate than other methods.

3.2   Cramér-Rao Lower Bound

The Cramér-Rao Lower Bound (CRLB) is the proven lower bound for any estimator's covariance. It is equal to the inverse of the Fisher Information. It is an important measure when dealing with any estimator because it is the best error that an estimator can achieve. All estimators will have at best an error of the CRLB.

3.3   Non-linear Maximum Likelihood Estimator

According to the National Institute of Standards and Technology (NIST) [17], the best way to find the center of a sphere is through non-linear minimization of the variance of the radius. This is also called the Maximum-Likelihood Estimator (MLE) for the center $\hat{c}$ and radius $\hat{r}$. The minimization is usually carried out by iterative methods like the Levenberg-Marquardt Method [17] and cannot be solved directly. One disadvantage of the iterative technique is the need to produce an initial guess. When we compared MLE to CRLB, the outliers are present and correspond to when the error equals the radius. This is the case when the coverage angle is small and the MLE converges to the middle of the points instead of nearer to the center. An angle of 180 means full coverage of the sphere, whereas an angle of 0 means all points confined to a single spot on the sphere. The outliers occur at low angles and indicate that the Levenberg-Marquardt technique converged on an answer that was embedded in the set of points that reside on the sphere.

3.4   Linear Least Square Method

The next best thing to the very slow MLE method is through linear least-squares solution. This is usually an over-constrained problem since there are N equations and four (i.e. $D + 1$) unknowns. The N equations can be put into a single matrix equation to solve with standard linear algebra techniques. When LLS and CRLB are compared, once again, the outlier cases show that the answer erroneously lies on the sphere. For the most part, the answer error is proportional to the square root of the CRLB. The next fastest algorithm is the linear least squares method which has been analyzed in floating point operations ($FLOPs$) in [11] as

$$FLOP = N \left(14D^2 + 32D + 14\right) + \frac{1}{3}\left(13D^3 + 102D^2 + 245D + 123\right) \quad (1)$$

$$FLOP\left(3\right) = 236N + 709 \quad (2)$$

In the next section, we start with an exposition of Generalized Delogne-Kása method which provides basis of discussion in this paper. The method is fast and produced similar results when GDK is compared with CRLB. However, this method is not fully accepted because it is a biased estimator. An estimator of a parameter is considered biased if it is expected to be a little off of the real answer. Zelniker [21] has shown that the bias of the GDKE is on the order of the measurement standard deviation. Our statistical

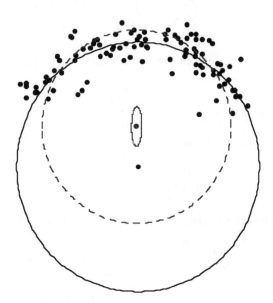

Fig. 3. GDKE Solution with Error Ellipse

analysis has shown that there are cases when the bias is quite significant and does not disappear even when more samples are taken. The dashed bar in Figure 3 show that the true center is not anywhere within the error ellipsoid of the estimate. This is due solely to the bias in the estimator. This is a good example of why the GDKE has not been adopted as much as the others.

4   Generalized Delogne-Kása Exposition

The Generalized Delogne-Kása (GDK) estimator [21] is the starting basis for our new formulae. This estimator is a general solution for finding the best-fit hypersphere from measurements on the surface. However until now the estimator has limited uses as the estimator is biased and can produce significantly different answers from the solution. The GDK estimator provides a good estimate if the data is evenly distributed over the entire surface of the hypersphere. The estimate falls farther away as the data gets clumped to one side. The GDK estimator is derived from surface measurements x_i and their deviation from a fixed distance from the center. The deviation for N measurements is written as

$$s^2_{GDKE}\left(\hat{c}, \hat{r}\right) = \frac{1}{N-1} \sum_{i=1}^{N} \left[(x_i - \hat{c})^T (x_i - \hat{c}) - \hat{r}^2 \right]^2. \tag{3}$$

The minimization of this [11] produces estimations for the center and the radius

$$\hat{c} = \bar{x} + \frac{1}{2} \mathbf{C}^{-1} \mathbf{S} \tag{4}$$

$$\hat{r}^2 = \frac{1}{N} \sum_{i=1}^{N} (x_i - \hat{c})^T (x_i - \hat{c}). \tag{5}$$

where the intermediate quantities include the arithmetic vector mean

$$\bar{x} = \frac{1}{N} \sum_{i=1}^{N} x_i \tag{6}$$

and the variance-covariance matrix

$$\mathbf{C} = \frac{1}{N-1} \sum_{i=1}^{N} (x_i - \bar{x})(x_i - \bar{x})^T. \tag{7}$$

and the third central vector moment

$$\mathbf{S} = \frac{1}{N-1} \sum_{i=1}^{N} (x_i - \bar{x})(x_i - \bar{x})^T (x_i - \bar{x}). \tag{8}$$

These two estimators are proven [11] to be the absolute minimum for equation 3. This estimation of the hypersphere is very fast due to the Cholesky inverse since equation 7 is positive-semidefinite. The floating point operations for a D-dimensional hypersphere can be counted as

$$FLOP = N\left(D^2 + 6D - 1\right) + \frac{1}{3}D\left(D + 1\right)\left(D + 8\right) + 1 \tag{9}$$

which, for the sphere, is

$$FLOP = N26 + 45 \tag{10}$$

This estimator is about as fast as you can get for this problem but it has one fatal flaw. The estimator has been shown to be biased providing an answer that is offset even under fairly normal conditions. The bias is proportional to the variance of the data [22] but analysis here shows the multiplication factor can outweigh an accurate measurement. The bias comes from the fact that one of the variables in the center equation is biased. We consider a measurement system that has a consistent error for each measurement on the surface of the sphere. The measurement is expected to be on the surface but varies from it by the multi-dimensional Gaussian distribution thus

$$x_i \sim Gaussian_D\left(\mu_i, \mathbf{\Sigma}\right) \tag{11}$$

The covariance matrix is then expected to be

$$E\left(\mathbf{C}\right) = \mathbf{C}_0 + \mathbf{\Sigma} \tag{12}$$

where

$$\mathbf{C}_0 = \frac{1}{N-1}\sum_{i=1}^{N}\left(\mu_i - \bar{\mu}\right)\left(\mu_i - \bar{\mu}\right)^T. \tag{13}$$

Similarly, the third central vector moment is expected to be

$$E\left(\mathbf{S}\right) = \mathbf{S}_0 \tag{14}$$

where

$$\mathbf{S}_0 = \frac{1}{N-1}\sum_{i=1}^{N}\left(\mu_i - \bar{\mu}\right)\left(\mu_i - \bar{\mu}\right)^T\left(\mu_i - \bar{\mu}\right). \tag{15}$$

The bias of the GDKE can be seen as the number of samples get large.

$$\lim_{N\to\infty} E\left(\hat{c}\right) = c_0 + \frac{1}{2}\left(\left(\mathbf{C}_0 + \mathbf{\Sigma}\right)^{-1} - \mathbf{C}_0^{-1}\right)\mathbf{S}_0 \tag{16}$$

5   Unbiased Generalized Delogne-Kása Estimator

Unbiased Generalized Delogne-Kása Estimator (UGDK) provides a quick method to draw a skeleton from motion capture data. The main contribution to the state of the art is that the estimator explained below is asymptotically unbiased. Asymptotically unbiased is defined as an inversely proportional relationship with the sample count: $E\left(\hat{q}\right) = q_0 + O\left(1/N\right)$ where q_0 is the parameter that the estimator is trying to estimate. This basically says that the estimator is expected to get closer to the true answer if more samples are taken. It is shown in [11] that the GDKE estimators for center and radius do not satisfy this requirement. Our algorithm uses a simple substitution that turns the GDKE into one with a diminishing bias. It involves the use of an a-priori estimate of the measurement error in the samples. This is very reasonable since most systems of measurement have some kind of estimate to the measurement error. Since the sample covariance matrix $\mathbf{C}$ is the only biased term in the equation for the GDKE center, this is what will be altered.

$$\mathbf{C}_u = \mathbf{C} - \hat{\boldsymbol{\Sigma}} \tag{17}$$

The bias of this new covariance is expected to disappear if the estimation of the covariance is close to the real noise inherent in the system. The expected covariance now becomes

$$E\left(\mathbf{C}_u\right) = \mathbf{C}_0 + \boldsymbol{\Sigma} - \hat{\boldsymbol{\Sigma}} . \tag{18}$$

This leads to the fastest, asymptotically unbiased estimator of a hypersphere [11] as

$$\hat{c}_u = \bar{x} + \frac{1}{2}\mathbf{C}_u^{-1}\mathbf{S} \tag{19}$$

$$\hat{r}_u^2 = \frac{1}{N}\sum_{i=1}^{N} \left(x_i - \hat{c}_u\right)^T \left(x_i - \hat{c}_u\right) . \tag{20}$$

Removing the bias can significant improve the answer but leaves the question of where to come up with this estimation of the system noise. Most systems of measurement (e.g. motion marker systems) have a predetermined measurement error which can be leveraged. In the case where it is not known, a calibration must be performed to determine

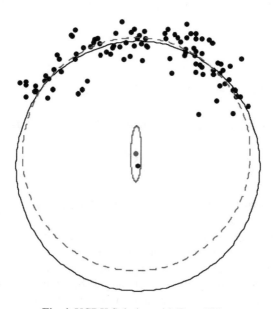

Fig. 4. UGDK Solution with Error Ellipse

the noise of the system. In this case, an estimation of the trace of the measurement noise matrix can be achieved from measurements on the surface of a known sphere with

$$Tr\left(\hat{\Sigma}\right) = \frac{1}{N}\sum_{i=1}^{N}\left(x_i - c_0\right)^T\left(x_i - c_0\right) - r_0^2 . \tag{21}$$

A typical use of these new estimators can be displayed using Mathematica, with exactly the same data as used for displayed for the GDKE. The true center is within the error ellipsoid (Figure 4). This data contains 100 points generated with a diagonal measurement covariance with all diagonals equal to 0.05^2. The Leontief condition (i.e. largest absolute eigenvalue of $\mathbf{C}$ less than one) is satisfied with the spectral radius in question equal to 0.557238. These equations show that there still is a bias, but it is asymptotically unbiased. We implemented (results in Figure 7) a Monte-Carlo run that explicitly shows the $1/\sqrt{N}$ dependency. The error in the estimate is compared with how many points were analyzed for a particular joint in given motion capture data. An example analysis using MLE, UGDK and GDKE is presented in Figure 5. The figure clearly shows the improvement over the GDKE with same $FLOP$ count for UGDK as GDKE. The figure shows the bias is removed using the UGDK and results produced by UGDK are close to MLE. The $FLOP$ counts for UGDK remains same as GDK [11]. Our analysis in [11] also shows that there is a case when all methods have troubles in estimating the joint location this is the case when measurement error is actually bigger than the item being measured. This situation is a bit impractical, as no one wants such a system of measurement.

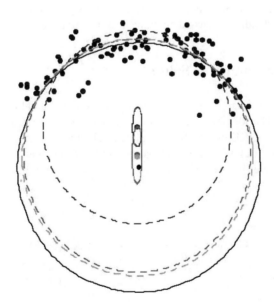

Fig. 5. One hundred sample comparison of MLE(green), GDKE (blue) and UGDK (red)

6   Multiple Radii Solution

For multiple markers going around the same center of rotation, another formula can be achieved by the same analysis of least squares. This technique is good to use when more than one marker is available. It has the ability to average out errors when one marker is too close to the rotation point or has other systematic problems. Excluding the derivation, we have the following equations for center and radius estimates where M is the number of markers and subscript p indicates values that utilize the single marker's positions:

$$\hat{c}_m = \left(\sum_{p=1}^{M} \mathbf{C}_p \right)^{-1} \sum_{p=1}^{M} \left(\mathbf{C}_p \bar{x}_p + \frac{1}{2} \mathbf{S}_p \right) \tag{22}$$

$$\hat{r}_p^2 = \frac{1}{N} \sum_{i=1}^{N} (x_{ip} - \hat{c}_m)^T (x_{ip} - \hat{c}_m). \tag{23}$$

The matrix that is to be inversed here is still a positive-definite matrix since positive-definite matrices added together still produce a positive-definite matrix. This allows for the speedier Cholesky decomposition and the singular values can be excluded. An example of the MGDK method is presented in Figure 6. This example shows what happens when the individual circles are compared to that when combined in the MGDK. The outer circle solution is drawn in red; the inner circle solution is drawn in blue, and the MGDK solution is drawn in green. The example shows a dramatic improvement over both of the individual circle calculations. FLOP count analysis is in [11].

7   Incremental Improved Solution

A more refined answer can be achieved when using a incremental improvement GDK (IGDK) formula. The idea here is a group of samples are collected and an answer is retrieved from the GDKE or UGDK formulae. Excluding the derivation, we have the following equations. Below are the final equations for the center and radius. The advantage is that no new matrix inverse is needed and the storage requirements are of constant order.

$$\bar{x}_{n+1} = \bar{x}_n + \frac{x_{n+1} - \bar{x}_n}{n+1} \tag{24}$$

$$\mathbf{C}_{n+1} = \frac{n-1}{n} \mathbf{C}_n + \frac{1}{(n+1)^2} \mathbf{\Delta} \; where \tag{25}$$

$$\mathbf{\Delta} = (x_{n+1} - \bar{x}_n)(x_{n+1} - \bar{x}_n)^T \tag{26}$$

The unbiased covariance matrix can be similarly improved by

$$\mathbf{C}_{u,\,n+1} = \frac{n-1}{n} \mathbf{C}_{u,\,n} + \frac{1}{(n+1)^2} \mathbf{\Delta} - \frac{1}{n} \hat{\mathbf{\Sigma}} \tag{27}$$

The interesting thing about the IGDK solution is that the matrix inverse does not need to be recomputed for every new point added. The matrix inverse itself has a recursive relationship

$$\mathbf{C}_{n+1}^{-1} = \frac{n}{n-1}\mathbf{C}_n^{-1}\left(\mathbf{I} + \frac{\mathbf{B}}{\frac{n(n-1)}{n+1} + Tr\,(\mathbf{B})}\right) \quad where \tag{28}$$

$$\mathbf{B} = \frac{n^2}{(n+1)^2}\boldsymbol{\Delta}\mathbf{C}_n^{-1} \tag{29}$$

The third central vector moment has the following recursive relationship

$$\mathbf{S}_{n+1} = \frac{n-1}{n}\mathbf{S}_n + \frac{1}{n+1}\left(-2\mathbf{C}_{n+1} - Tr\,(\mathbf{C}_{n+1}) + \frac{n+2}{n+1}\boldsymbol{\Delta}\right)(x_{n+1} - \bar{x}_n) \tag{30}$$

These recursions will then plug into the hypersphere solution

$$\hat{c}_{n+1} = \bar{x}_{n+1} + \frac{1}{2}\mathbf{C}_{n+1}^{-1}\mathbf{S}_{n+1} \tag{31}$$

$$\hat{r}_{n+1}^2 = \frac{n}{n+1}Tr\,(\mathbf{C}_{n+1}) + (\bar{x}_{n+1} - \hat{c}_{n+1})^T(\bar{x}_{n+1} - \hat{c}_{n+1}) \tag{32}$$

When compared to the FLOPs for the GDKE method, this incremental approach is about four times slower. This makes the incremental approach faster than linear least squares solution but slower than GDKE. The IGDK solution has the distinct advantage of constant memory requirements no matter how many points are analyzed. This makes the IGDK the perfect solution for embedded firmware applications like optical recognition.

8   Results

8.1   Case Study CMU Data

The Carnegie Mellon University Graphics Lab produced a one minute long motion capture data-set of a salsa dance in 60-08. The data file contains 3421 time slices for 41 markers on two figures. This case study will concentrate on analyzing the performance of the UGDK in determining the rotation points in the female subject. Four data sets were created by removing random samples from the CMU data sets. 400 rotation points were collected. The calculated constants are the relative rotation points as referenced in each segment's parent's coordinate system. The 400 calculations were averaged and the standard deviations were calculated as well. Details results are analyzed in [11] Most of the standard deviations are less than one centimeter, but there are some significant outliers like the right ankle. Further analysis of the calculated points for the ankles and elbows shows that the four runs produced two answers due to different orientations of the parent's reference frame. As can be readily seen from the above graph, a statistically significant amount of calculations are within one centimeter of accuracy when analyzing more than about 200 samples. The accuracy gets better on average with a power law close to $1/\sqrt{N}$ (Figure 7). Skeletal animation of our results is provided in mpeg files.

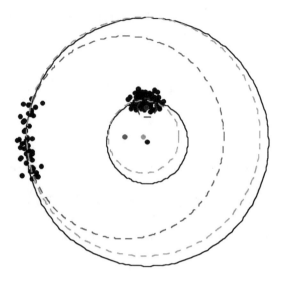

Fig. 6. MGDK example: outer UGDK(red), inner UGDK(blue), MGDK(green)

8.2 Case Study of Eric Camper's ACCAD Data

The motion capture data in the ericcamper.c3d [3] was analyzed to produce a skeleton. The subject did various martial arts maneuvers that moved every joint involved in drawing. One time frame is presented in the following figure. We show a frame of animation in Figure 1 which shows what appears to be a natural pose for all joints during a karate exercise.

9   Comparison

The Table 1 provides a succinct view of all of the methods studied in our research. It provides the positive and negative aspects of the methods. This table makes it easier to choose which solution is right for a particular situation. A Monte-Carlo experiment was set up to determine the speed of the various sphere-fit algorithms. Up to a million samples were chosen on a sphere with varying measurement error, confinement angle,

Table 1. Comparison of Center Estimators

Method	Advantages	Disadvantages
MLE	best accepted theory	slow, initial guess, may not converge
LLS	semi-fast $O(236N)$, no guess	loss of significant figures
GDKE	fast $O(26N)$, no guess	biased, $O(\sigma)$
UGDK	fast $O(26N)$, no guess, unbiased	asymptotically unbiased, $O(\sigma/\sqrt{N})$
MGDK	multiple markers, averages better	asymptotically unbiased, $O(\sigma/\sqrt{N})$
IGDK	space $O(1)$, time $O(123N)$	uses GDK first

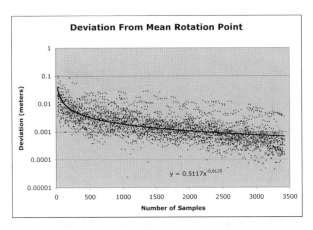

Fig. 7. Inverse Power Law for Rotation Point Calculation

sphere-center and sphere-radius. The measurement error varied from 1×10^{-11} to 1×10^{12}. The confinement angle varied from 0 to $180°$. The sphere center varied as much as 2 around the origin. The radius varied 0 to 37. The linear algebra algorithms were all implemented from well-accepted implementations presented in Numerical Recipes in C [15]. The code was compiled optimized for a PowerPC G4 processor and run on a 1GHz Apple PowerBook 12".

As can be seen (Figure 8), the GDKE, and therefore UGDK, is always faster with FLOP count as $26N$ [10]. The GDKE or UGDK speed is 2.17 times faster than IGDK on average. Based on FLOP counts as explained in [11] in detail, the GDKE or UGDK is 11.05 times faster than the LLS method and about 80 times faster than the MLE when the measurement error is less than the radius. The FLOP count predicts this closely with $LLS = 236/26 = 9.07$ and $IGDK = 123/26 = 4.73$. The differences between the FLOP count and implementation results can be accounted for in the hardware and software overhead that FLOP count never accounts for.

9.1   Summary of Important Results

Three new closed-form methods have been presented to find rotation points of a skeleton from motion capture data. A generic skeleton can be directly extracted from noisy data with no previous knowledge of skeleton measurements. The new methods are ten times faster than the next fastest and a hundred times faster than the most widely accepted method. Two phases are used to produce an accurate skeleton of the captured data. The first phase, fitting the skeleton, is robust even with noisy motion capture data. As explained earlier, the formulae use an asymptotically unbiased version of the Generalized Delogne-Kása (GDKE) Hyperspherical Estimation (i.e UGDK). The second estimator takes advantage of multiple markers located at different distances from the rotation point (MGDK) thereby increasing accuracy. The third estimator incrementally improves an answer and has advantages of constant memory requirements suitable for firmware applications (IGDK). The UGDK produces the answer faster than any previous algorithm and with the same efficiency with respect to the Cramér-Rao Lower

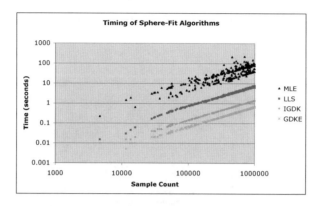

Fig. 8. Timing of Algorithms – note that GDKE and UGDK has the same complexity

Bound for fitting spheres and circles. The UGDK method significantly reduces the amount of work needed for calculating rotation points by only requiring $26N$ flops for each joint. The next fastest method, Linear Least-Squares requires $236N$ flops. In-depth statistical analysis shows the UGDK method converges to the actual rotation point with an error of $O(\sigma/\sqrt{N})$ improving on the GDKE's biased answer of $O(\sigma)$. The second phase is a real-time algorithm to draw the skeleton at each time frame with as little as one point on a segment. This speedy method, on the order of the number of segments, aids the realism of motion data animation by allowing for the subtle nuances of each time frame to be displayed. Flexibility of motion is displayed in detail as the figure follows the captured motion more closely. With the reduced time complexity, multiple figures, even crowds can be animated. In addition, calculations can be reused for the same actor and marker-set allowing different data sets to be blended.

10   Conclusions and Further Research

In our effort to try to speed up skeleton extraction from motion capture date we discovered a new asymptotically unbiased GDK (UGDK) formulation which fills the vital low-level hole and makes GDK formulation practical. This paper presents the fastest known general method for calculating the rotation points and can be as much as ten times faster than the next fastest method available as explained in [11]. The UGDK method has further impact in a vast collection of fields as diverse as character recognition to nuclear physics where an algorithm is needed for the speedy recovery of the center of a circle or sphere. The UGDK is expected to play a vital role in the process of determining a skeleton from motion capture data. The MGDK adds robustness to the equations allowing to use every bit of available data. The IGDK further has the application of being an ideal algorithm to burn into a silicon chip whose memory requirements are constrained. The UGDK estimators are an improvement on existing science but they are strictly dependent on a-priori knowledge of the measurement error. It has been shown that the measurement error trace can itself be estimated but not the whole measurement covariance matrix. An estimator for the whole matrix would be most ideal but was not found in the course of this study and should be a topic of future research. The main contributions are the new unbiased center formulae; the full statistical analysis of this new formula; and the analysis of when the best measurement conditions are to initiate the formula. The research further establishes the application of these new formulae to motion capture to produce a real-time method of drawing skeletons of arbitrary articulated figures.

Acknowledgements. We are grateful to the Carnegie-Mellon University Graphics Lab for providing a wealth of motion capture data free on the Internet at mocap.cs.cmu.edu. The database was created with funding from NSF EIA-0196217.

References

1. de Aguilar, E., Theobalt, C., Seidal, H.: Automatic learning of articulated Skeletons from 3D marker Trajectories. In: Bebis, G., Boyle, R., Parvin, B., Koracin, D., Remagnino, P., Nefian, A., Meenakshisundaram, G., Pascucci, V., Zara, J., Molineros, J., Theisel, H., Malzbender, T. (eds.) ISVC 2006. LNCS, vol. 4291, pp. 485–494. Springer, Heidelberg (2006)
2. Burr, M., Cheng, A., Coleman, R., Souvaine, D.: Transformations and Algorithms for Least Sum of Squares Hypersphere Fitting. In: 16th Canadian Conference on Computational Geometry, pp. 104–107 (2004)
3. Camper, E.: Motion Capture Data at accad.osu.edu
4. Corral, C., Lindquist, C.: On implementing Kása's circle fit procedure. IEEE Transactions on Instrumentation and Measurement 47(3), 789–795 (1998)
5. Delogne, P.: Computer Optimization of Deschamps' Method and Error Cancellation in Reflectometry. In: Proceedings of the IMEKO Symposium on Microwave Measurements, Budapest, Hungary, May 1972, pp. 117–129 (1972)
6. Gander, W., Golub, G., Strebel, R.: Least-Squares Fitting of Circles and Ellipses. BIT Numerical Mathematics 34, 558–578 (1994)
7. Herda, L., Fua, P., Plankers, R., Boulic, R., Thalmann, D.: Skeleton-based motion capture for robust reconstruction of Human Motion. In: Computer Animation, Philadelphia, PA, May 2000, p. 77 (2000)
8. Kása, I.: A circle fitting procedure and its error analysis. IEEE Transactions on Instrumentation and Measurement 25, 8–14 (1976)
9. Kirk, A.G., O'Brien, J., Forsyth, D.A.: Skeletal parameter estimation from optical motion capture data. In: IEEE Conf. on Computer Vision and Pattern Recognition (CVPR). IEEE, Los Alamitos (2005)
10. Knight, J., Semwal, S.: Fast Skeleton Estimation from Motion Captured using Genralized Delogne-Kása Method. In: 15th International Conference in Central Europe on Computer Graphics, Visualization and Computer Vision, WSCG Conference Proceedings, Plzen, CZ, February 2007, pp. 225–232 (2007) ISBN 978-80-86943-98-5
11. Knight, J.K.: Rotation Points from Motion Capture Data using a Closed Form Solution. PhD Thesis, University of Colorado at Colorado Springs, Advisor Professor Semwal, S.K., pp. 1–152 (2008)
12. Lukács, G., Marshall, A., Martin, R.: Geometric Least-Squares Fitting of Spheres, Cylinders, Cones, and Tori. RECCAD Deliverable Documents 2 and 3 Copernicus Project No. 1068 Reports on basic geometry and geometric model creation; Martin, Dr.R.R., Varady, Dr.T.: Report GML 1997/5. Computer and Automation Institute, Hungarian Academy of Sciences, Budapest (1997)

13. O'Brien, J.F., Bodenheimer Jr, R.E., Brostow, G.J., Hodgins, J.K.: Automatic Joint Parameter Estimation from Magnetic Motion Capture Data, Montreal, Quebec, Canada, May 15-17, pp. 53–60. Graphics Interface (2000)
14. Pratt, V.: Direct least-squares fitting of algebraic surfaces. Computer Graphics 21(4), 145–152 (1987)
15. Press, W., Teukolsky, T., Vetterling, W., Flannery, B.: Numerical Recipes in C: The Art of Scientific Computing, 2nd edn. Cambridge University Press, Cambridge (1992)
16. Robinson, S.: Fitting Spheres by the Method of Least Squares. Communications of the ACM 4(11), 491 (1967)
17. Shakarji, C.: Least-Squares Fitting Algorithms of the NIST Algorithm Testing System. J. of Research of the National Institute of Standards and Technology 103(6), 633 (1998)
18. Strandlie, A., Wroldsen, J., Frühwirth, R., Lillekjendlie, B.: Track Fitting on the Riemann Sphere. In: International Conference on Computing in High Energy and Nuclear Physics, Padova, Italy (February 2000)
19. Thomas, S., Chan, Y.: Cramer-Rao Lower Bounds for Estimation of a Circular Arc Center and Its' Radius. CVGIP: Graphics Model and Image Processing 57(6), 527–532 (1995)
20. de Witte, L.: Least Squares Fitting of a Great Circle Through Points on a Sphere. Communications of the ACM 3(11), 611–613 (1960)
21. Zelniker, E., Clarkson, I.: A Statistical Analysis Least-Squares Circle-Centre Estimation. In: IEEE International Symposium on Signal Processing and Information Technology, Darmstadt, Germany, December 2003, pp. 114–117 (2003)
22. Zelniker, E., Clarkson, I.: A Generalisation of the Delogne-Kása Method for Fitting Hyperspheres. In: Thirty-Eighth Asiomar Conference on Signals, Systems and Computers, Pacific Grove, California (November 2004)

A Visualization Paradigm for 3D Map-Based Mobile Services

Mário Freitas[1], A. Augusto Sousa[1,2], and António Coelho[1,2]

[1] FEUP, Rua Dr. Roberto Frias, s/n 4200-465 Porto, Portugal
[2] INESC Porto, Campus da FEUP, Rua Dr. Roberto Frias, s/n 4200-465 Porto, Portugal

Abstract. Nowadays, there is a wide range of commercial LBMS (Location-Based Mobile Services) available in the market, and a trend towards the display of 3D maps can be clearly observed. Given the complete disparity of ideas and a visible commercial orientation in the industry, the study of the visualization aspects that influence user performance and experience in the exploration of urban environments, using 3D maps, becomes an important issue. Based on a proposed conceptual framework, an online questionnaire was developed and administered in order to measure the real impact of each element. Combining the experimental results with the current state-of-the-art, a new visualization paradigm is defined in a dual specification: "layers" providing relevant visual content to the map, and "functions" providing the necessary functionality.

1 Introduction

The LBMS technology, namely in the form of GPS-based navigation systems, has just recently reached a state of technological maturity, enabling the development of 3D map-based graphical interfaces. By looking at the variety of visualization paradigms being proposed, one can clearly notice a great disparity of ideas without a clear notion of its usefulness. Provided the non-existence of an objective state-of-the-art generalizing theory capable of unifying and evaluating all the visualization elements and properties, the main motivation of this work is to study the most relevant of these features and how to adjust them appropriately, by defining a new visualization paradigm in order to maximize the usability of mobile maps and to improve the navigation experience, in accordance with the following objectives:

1. Elicit and assess the state-of-the-art contributions on visualization paradigms of 3D maps, with particular interest on mobile services and devices;
2. Develop a methodology for evaluating the different issues that influence user experience and performance when exploring an urban environment with mobile maps;
3. Define a new visualization paradigm of 3D maps for urban environments.

In this section we present fundamental concepts, regarding visual perception of realism and user tasks, and a list of LBMS that have been analyzed. Section 2 introduces a conceptual framework for evaluating visual elements, section 3 presents the methodology used for the experimental work and section 4 discusses the results obtained. Finally,

A. Ranchordas et al. (Eds.): VISIGRAPP 2009, CCIS 68, pp. 89–103, 2010.

section 5 presents the proposed visualization paradigm and section 6 presents some conclusions and future work.

Map-based mobile services depend upon image to display orientation information, although audio is also used for specific instructions. The concept of *Image Realism* is thus fundamental to the understanding of how maps are visually perceived, and so we need to measure its effectiveness. The results from several experiments [1,2] demonstrate that the variable that most contributed to the sense of realism was – by far – the high-resolution orthophotographic imagery, immediately followed by texture-mapping. In other works like [3], the importance of perception-based image quality metrics is studied, such as the ones given by the VDP (Visible Differences Predictor) and the VDM (Visual Discrimination Metric). The VDP quality metric takes two images as input and generates a *difference map* that predicts the probability of the human eye to find differences between the two pictures, as demonstrated in [4].A simplification of the VDM quality metric was provided by finding a *just noticeable difference map* corresponding to a 75% probability of a person detecting a difference between the two images [3]. Because of some controversy and no agreed-upon standards for measuring realism in computer-generated imagery, a conceptual framework for measuring image realism and evaluating its usefulness was proposed in [5]. The framework distinguishes three different varieties of realism: *physical realism*, *photo-realism* and *functional realism*. However, this framework does not seem to be enough to encompass the extents to which reality or virtuality can be "augmented". Accounting for such circumstances, the concept of *Virtuality Continuum* was introduced in [6].

Map-based mobile services are used for specific navigation tasks. The underlying basic equation that can help us to find the "perfect" balance in map-based mobile services is what could be called of *Mobility Equation*. This equation was first formulated by Leonard and Durrant-Whyte for mobile robot navigation [7] but can be equally extended to human navigation. In [8], user tasks are classified into 4 different groups that have a strong relationship with these questions, as described in Table 1.

Table 1. High level user tasks [8]

Task	Description
Locator	Identification of the user's own position and other objects. Answers 'Where am I?' questions.
Proximity	Inform the users of nearby facilities. Implied by 'Where am I going?' questions.
Navigation	The most tangible example is routing from one location to another. Answers 'How do I get there?' questions.
Event	Time/Location dependent objects, allowing the users to know what is happening and when/where. Answers 'And now what?' questions.

In this work we have analyzed and studied several state-of-the-art contributions on LBMS which provide a wide variety of visualization paradigms, in order to understand the current tendencies in the industry and to formulate hypothesis regarding their validity and usefulness. The contributions range from pilot studies to commercial

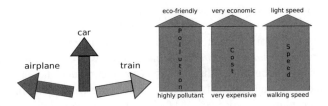

Fig. 1. A possible feature vector for "Transportation"

products, within the scope of road and pedestrian maps, as follows: TellMaris, m-LOMA, LAMP3D, TomTom, Navigon, NDrive, iGO, Google Earth, INSTAR, Virtual Cable™, and Enkin.

2   Conceptual Framework

The generic evaluation framework already proposed in [9] will be used for evaluating the most relevant visualization elements that influence user performance and experience in 3D map-based mobile-services. This framework defines the concept of *feature vectors* comprising *orientations* and *magnitudes*. The *orientation* defines the idea or concept that the visualization paradigm represents, and *magnitude* the degree or level to which the paradigm "amplifies" the vector. An example can be seen in Fig. 1 to describe a possible feature vector for transportation. An orientation of this feature vector is the mode of transport, while pollution, cost and speed are magnitudes.

The framework is composed by six feature vectors as shown in table 2 and described in the following text.

Table 2. Structure of the proposed evaluation framework

Feature Vector	Orientations	Magnitudes
Image Realism	3D Buildings, Map Vectors, Surface Model	Physical Realism, Mixed Realism, Photo-Realism, Functional Realism
Object Labeling	Perspective-Adaptive, Positioning (Point, Line, Area, General)	Static / Dynamic Selection / Placement
Visual-Spatial Abstraction	Ground Level, Local-Area Level, Wide-Area Level	Adaptive Level, Adaptive Orientation
Route Indication	Arrows, Cords, Way points, Carpet	Instructive, Simulative
Landmark Symbology	Shops (referenced by name), Shops (referenced by type), Buildings (with unique name / function), Buildings (with unique visual properties)	Abstractness (Words, Sign, Icon, Sketch, Drawing, Image), Adaptive Zoom, Adaptive Complexity
Contextual Awareness	Reconstructional, Recreational, Fictional	Active Awareness, Passive Awareness

Image Realism is the feature vector that is concerned with how real, i.e., free from any idealizations or abstractions, is the image of the map presented to the user. The suggested *magnitudes* for this vector will be based on the framework proposed in [5] and the concepts on *virtuality continuum* defined in [6], with a few modifications.

Object Labeling encompasses the kind of visual techniques and strategies that are followed to label map elements such as rivers, streets, cities, and so on. In [10] and other studies, the importance of two types of labeling, namely *static labeling* and *dynamic labeling*, is discussed.

Visual-Spatial Abstraction measures the complexity of mental operations that are required to perform the visual matching of the real environment that can be observed and the one on the screen. We define *Adaptive Level* and *Adaptive Orientation* when the camera adapts to the user's movement (according to some variable like speed), and whether it adapts to his looking direction, respectively.

Route Indication provides a classification of the visual techniques and strategies for showing the itinerary path in road maps, and the kind of maneuver indicators or way points that are presented in the display. The proposed *orientations* for this vector, can be regarded as the visual indicators that are generally used by the majority of the contributions to display the route: *Arrows*, *Cords*, *Way Points* and *Carpet*-like shapes. These indicators can be used with different "immersion" levels which are considered the proposed *magnitudes* for *Route Indication*, namely *Instructive* (when just indicating what to do) and *Simulative* (when they resemble real world indicators).

Landmark Symbology evaluates the cartographic symbology that is used to portray the world using a pictorial language, represented by "map symbols". The *orientations* for this vector will reflect the kind of buildings represented by symbols, based on the design guidelines proposed in [11], and the first *magnitude* (*Abstractness*) defines the levels of abstractions for landmarks also proposed in this work. To avoid problems such as *congestion*, *coalescence*, and *imperceptibility*, the proposed *magnitudes* consist of *Adaptive Zoom* and *Adaptive Complexity*, respectively, whether the abstraction level of landmarks adapts to the current zoom level, and whether they change with the varying complexity of features.

Contextual Awareness measures the extent to which a visualization paradigm is applied to get additional information on a contextual or situational basis. Based on three groups of application areas in which virtual urban environments can be valuable, the proposed orientations are *Reconstructional* (reconstruction of urban environments that were totally or partially lost), *Recreational* (urban design, urban planning, etc.) and *Fictional* (creation of imaginary realities). The proposed *magnitudes* for this vector will reflect the different autonomy levels of "contextual awareness" an application can demonstrate in different contexts and tasks, as previously denoted by [12], specifically *Active Awareness* (without the need of user intervention) and *Passive Awareness* (when the user shows interest for getting context-based information).

3   Evaluation of *Feature Vectors*

In order to formulate a visualization paradigm for 3D map-based mobile services, several hypotheses were formulated in order to assess the real impact of each visualization feature. Since some of these hypotheses could not be directly demonstrated from the analysis of current state-of-the-art (regarding their impact and relevance), an interactive online questionnaire was developed. Due to the intrinsic limitations of the proposed questionnaire and to make it simple to understand, only four feature vectures were evaluated: *Image Realism*, *Object Labeling*, *Route Indication* and *Landmark Symbology*. Following this structure, the questionnaire was divided into 3 parts. In the first part, the exercises were mainly based on the *pointing task paradigm* as previously performed in other studies [13]. In the second part, a similar approach was followed, but instead of evaluating the matching of the two realities, the main objective was to measure how well users perform a given task. In the last part, users were asked about their preferences regarding the visualization of map elements such as landmarks.

3.1 Image Realism

All *Image Realism orientations* were tested along with the various degrees of *magnitudes*, in accordance with the vector instances (*orientations* and *magnitudes* combined) found in the state-of-the-art contributions. These instances were considered eligible for the evaluation through the questionnaire, since there are few or no indications, with regards to their impact:

- *Simple Textured Buildings* (i.e. 3D building shaded with color or texture of the material) versus *Photo Textured Buildings* (i.e. 3D building textured with images of the façades)
- *Colored Map* versus *Orthophotomap*
- *Flat Model* versus *Terrain Model*

It was hypothesized that, in the absence of *Simple Textured Buildings*, test subjects will have to rely on their ability to match the 3D geometry of the real building with the geometry of the 2D polygon representation on the map. At the same time, it is supposed that, by providing the three-dimensional (yet simple) geometry of the whole building, test subjects make fewer mistakes and, as a consequence, will require less time matching both realities (see Fig. 2: images 1 and 2). In the case of the *Photo Textured Buildings* component (see Fig. 2: images 3 and 4), it was hypothesized that, by simultaneously providing the 3D geometry of a building along with photographic façades, test subjects will be able to detect features (e.g. windows, doors, unique wall patterns, etc.) more accurately and faster than in the case of *Simple Textured Buildings*.

Regarding *Map Vectors*, it is assumed that an *Orthophotomap* can provide subjects a much more enriching visualization experience than the one provided by a *Colored Map*

Fig. 2. The 4 images supporting the questions that evaluate Simple vs. Photo Textured Buildings

Fig. 3. The 4 images supporting the questions that evaluate Colored vs. Orthophoto Maps and Flat vs. Terrain Models

(see Fig. 3: images 1 and 2). The hypothesis rests on the belief that an *Orthophotomap* component can be easier for users to discern the true features of the map's surface, by giving a realistic view rather than a rough generalization. There are many situations were colored vector polygons are not enough to represent features like a tiled pavement; a group of trees arranged in a special and unique way; and several "static" features like public benches, zebra crossings, and many others that are impossible to find in a colored vector map. In terms of *Surface Model*, it was hypothesized that, by using a *Terrain Model* rather than a *Flat Model* component, users will be able to perform the spatial matching of both reality and virtuality in a much more immersive and natural way (see Fig. 3: images 3 and 4). It is expected that by providing the *Terrain Model* component, users will be able to use elevated reference points, and to understand and visualize occlusions caused by the varying landscape elevation.

This feature vector is evaluated in the first part of the questionnaire by presenting 10 questions, each one displaying one of these images (see figures 2 and 3) with a symbol locating and directing the observer, and 4 pictures of the real site. The user has to select the correct picture in the minimum time possible.

3.2   Object Labeling

With respect to *Object Labeling*, it was hypothesized that, when users are analyzing labels (e.g. of streets, rivers, cities, and so on) which are not oriented towards the current viewing direction depicted in the device, they feel much more difficult in reading the words, due to the decreased visibility, especially when looking in a direction which is parallel to the map's surface (see Fig. 4: images 1 and 2). In such case, users will not be able to read labels as fast, and will pan the map closer to the camera so it becomes easier to read. Particularly in the case of labels which are almost parallel to the camera's viewing direction, some users will wish to skip words, if they find them "too difficult" to read.

Evaluation of this feature vector is done by measuring the time taken by users to read a sequence of labels with and without *Perspective-Adaptive Labelling*.

3.3   Route Indication

In terms of *Route Indication*, it was hypothesized that, when a user is presented with an image which looks more familiar to him, given the current context, he will be able to perform his task with lesser effort (see Fig. 4: images 3 and 4).

Fig. 4. The tasks that evaluate Perspective-Adaptive Labeling and Instructive vs. Simulative route indications

For this feature vector the evaluation was done by presenting four images with either *instructive* or *simulative* route indication. The user had to select the image showing the correct directions to a specific location, in the minimum time possible.

3.4 Landmark Symbology

For this feature vector, it was hypothesized that users require *Adaptive Zoom* functionality, i.e., that the majority of them choose an abstract landmark representation of a given building, in a map which is zoomed out far from the ground, but a more concrete representation when at close range.

Following this hypothesis the questionnaire evaluated the users preferences based on images displaying two types of landmark symbology at distinct zoom levels (see Fig. 5).

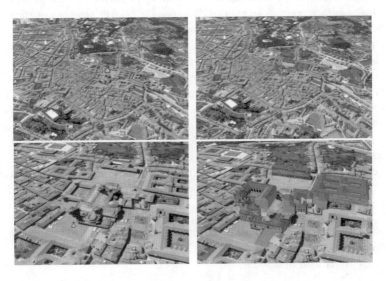

Fig. 5. The preferences that evaluates the users' need for an Adaptive Zoom approach, when a map which is zoomed out far / zoomed in close to the ground is used.

4   Discussion of the Results

In total, 149 test subjects answered the questionnaire, mostly from a student population in Computer Science and Informatics: 89% were male and 78% were in the 18 to 25 age group. In general, prior to answering the questionnaire, subjects considered themselves fairly capable of using both maps and GPS navigators, given the approximate 50-50 ratio shared between "average" and "experienced" users. Only 3% of the participants reported they were unfamiliar with either maps or GPS navigators.

4.1   Image Realism

The results of the questionnaire shows that the presence of *Simple Textured Buildings* can benefit user experience, as 91% of the users answered correctly, while only 77% correct answers were obtained with its absence. In the case of *Photo Textured Buildings* component there were 88% correct answers, while only 30% users could get the correct answer without 3D buildings. Despite the amplitude difference between both questions, the number of correct answers in the presence of *Photo Textured Buildings* was almost the same as in the case of *Simple Textured Buildings*. In terms of answering time, 95% of the subjects had already answered before the first 21s in the presence of *Photo Textured Buildings*, about 4.4s faster than in the presence of *Simple Textured Buildings*. This demonstrates that *Photo Textured Buildings* are more efficient than *Simple Textured Buildings* and more effective than the absence of 3D buildings.

In the presence of a *Colored Map*, the number of participants who were unable to answer the question right was quite high (81%: 67% wrong and 14% clueless). Nevertheless, subjects had no apparent difficulty in finding the correct answer, in the presence of the *Orthophotomap* component, as 92% chose the correct answer in similar conditions. Besides being more effective, the *Orthophotomap* proved also to be more efficient as subjects took an average time of 9.3s (s.d. 18.4s) to answer the question, considerably faster compared to the 23.5s (s.d. 16.8s) in the case of the *Colored Map*.

In terms of *Surface Model*, there was just a 5% difference in the number of correct answers between both cases, with advantage to the *Terrain Model*. However, the *Terrain Model* was much more efficient, as the average response time was 7.5s (s.d. 5s), compared to the 15.3s (s.d. 13.8s) obtained with the *Flat Model*. These results point out that image realism can improve the task of matching the 3D map with reality, both maximizing effectiveness (lesser mistakes) and effectiveness (lesser time).

These results of the questionnaire clearly identified the three best approaches, by means of identifying instances (combining orientation and magnitude) of *Image Realism*:

– *Photo* rather than *Simple Textured Buildings*;
– *Orthophoto* rather than *Colored Map*;
– *Terrain* rather than *Flat Model*.

It is safe to assume that *Mixed Realism* or *Photo-Realism* cannot be used interchangeably at any time, i.e, it cannot be affirmed that their use does not affect users performance nor is limited by any restriction. *Virtuality*, if used alone, it is enough to allow a user to perform every task, although not as immersive as the experience provided by an *Augmented Reality* (AR). This kind of paradigm is ideal when the user is driving a car, i.e., performing a navigation task [14]. The problem arises when the user tries to apply this paradigm outside the limited visibility range provided by the live imagery, like when planning an itinerary, or to get a route overview. Therefore, it is believed that the merging of both paradigms could prove to be the best choice. In general, it is believed that the combination of both, *Photo-Realism* and *Mixed Realism* magnitudes, will provide the best results.

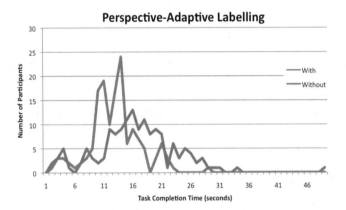

Fig. 6. Answer times in the presence and absence of Perspective-Adaptive Labeling component

4.2 Object Labeling

With respect to *Object Labeling*, when labels were oriented towards the camera, the subjects took lesser time to perform the task (avg. 11.8s, s.d. 5.2s) than when labels were not oriented according to the camera (avg. 15s, s.d. 6.4s), as shown in Fig. 6. This demonstrates that a *Perspective-Adaptive Labeling* approach, i.e. labels oriented towards the current perspective, results in faster responsiveness from the users.

Based on the study of the state-of-the-art contributions, it can be observed that the current tendency in this feature orientation is towards the adoption of *General Positioning* algorithms. Rivers and other polygonal chains are best described using a *Line Positioning* approach; countries and other polygonal features are more easily recognized using an *Area Positioning*; and finally, cities and municipalities are better perceived if they are indicated with a *Point Positioning* approach. the *General Positioning* algorithms, being the combination of the 3 strategies seems to be the most appropriate choice. Regarding the proposed magnitudes for object labeling (*Static / Dynamic Selection / Placement*), the desiderata described in [10] should be taken into account when creating dynamic maps, otherwise it would be very difficult for users to perform the matching of labels with the corresponding point, line or polygonal features of the map.

4.3 Visual-Spatial Abstraction

There are already several directions provided by the state-of-the-art contributions regarding *Visual-Spatial Abstraction* and thus no results were obtained from the questionnaire. First of all, there is an evident tendency towards the use of all the camera level orientations in mobile map applications (*Ground Level*, *Local-Area Level* and *Wide-Area Level*). Due to the nature of the *Ground Level* perspective, one can argue that the walking view mode is among the best choices for *Locator Tasks*. In the top view mode, since there is a lower occlusion of other buildings, it becomes easier to search for nearby facilities, which is the purpose of *Proximity Tasks*. On the other hand, both flying and top view modes can be used for orientation purposes, as the users are able to get a better overview of the surroundings.

Most AR-based prototypes and experimental studies [15] not only demonstrated that the 3D maps provided shorter completion times, but also that the worst problematic misalignments between the 2D and the 3D maps could be found at the conditions of 90 degrees. Provided that misalignments and the wide range of possible viewing directions can pose a big problem to the success and effectiveness of a user task, it is believed that an *Adaptive Orientation* approach is an important requirement. Regarding the *Adaptive Level* magnitude, there are already some options available that take contextual variables into account. For instance, when a driver accelerates, the automotive navigation system should generally adapt to this situation by increasing the camera altitude, providing a better overview of what is ahead.

4.4   Route Indication

With respect to the *Route Indication* there was no relevant difference in terms of answer correctness between *Instructive* or *Simulative* components. In terms of average answer time, the *Instructive* component resulted in 11.8s (s.d. 7.9s) against 8.6s (s.d. 5.9s). Provided with the *Simulative* approach, 95% of the participants had already found the matching route indication, after about 19.8s, compared to 26.6s in the opposite case. Although both techniques can achieve similar levels of correctness, the *Simulative* approach can speed-up the task of matching reality with the 3D map. This can be of great importance when supporting activities that demand short response times, such as driving.

4.5   Landmark Symbology

The main question regarding this feature vector is how and when should each building be represented. To answer this question, the *Adaptiveness* magnitude for this vector should be taken into account. According to the experience in practical use of maps, all the various abstraction levels are considered relevant, depending on the type of building, as demonstrated by [11].

A vast majority of participants (87%) answered they would more easily identify and recognize the presence of a given distant landmark, when an abstract representation of that landmark was used. Approximately 86% of them indicated their preference towards the use of concrete landmarks at close range. Different zoom levels over 3D maps will encompass also different levels of visual complexity, and as such, *Adaptive Zoom* functionality is of great importance for maximizing readability. Regarding *Adaptive Complexity* and looking at a typical view of a map provided by Google Earth there is a huge amount of icons and signs overlapping mutually and filling the whole map. Because of this it can be easily argued that the task of decoding all the represented

Fig. 7. Adaptive Complexity

information is very difficult and time-consuming. *Adaptive Complexity* is the key to solve this problem, by grouping or merging similar symbols (see Fig. 7).

4.6 Contextual Awareness

The proposed orientations for *Contextual Awareness* (*Reconstructional*, *Recreational*, and *Fictional*) should be chosen according to the context and scope of the mobile application. For instance, a mobile guide that aims to rebuild the ancient city of Atlantis will provide a strong reconstructional approach rather than the other two orientations, because it is related to the scope of the application. Similar examples can be given for the other two orientations.

In terms of magnitudes, there is an *Active Awareness* variable that is common to all mobile map applications (or they wouldnt be called 'mobile'), i.e. the location context. Apart from this, the other contexts can be 'processed' in a passive (when the user asks for more information) or in an active way (i.e., automatically) by adapting to the detected context. In some studies it is argued that an *Active Awareness* approach can become very obtrusive, especially when the detected context does not correspond to the real context and, thus, opposes the users expectations. Nevertheless, it is believed that every mobile map application should leverage the awareness levels appropriately, depending on whether the information is considered relevant or not, and hopefully provide means to toggle back and forth between both *Active Awareness* and *Passive Awareness* modes.

5   A Visualization Paradigm for 3D Map-Based Mobile Services

The analysis in the previous section delivered a set of recommendations for each feature vector, as summarized in Table 3. Based on these analysis, a visualization paradigm was developed for 3D map-based mobile services, taking into account the interactions between feature vector components as well as eventual conflicts that may arise.

We present this paradigm as a dual specification:

- Visualization layers that can be turned on or off in order to add or remove features to the image being visualized;
- Visualization functions that should be provided to improve the effectiveness of the user interaction.

Table 3. Set of *feature vector* components that individually maximise user experience and performance with mobile 3D maps

Feature Vector	Orientations	Magnitudes
Image Realism	3D Buildings, Map Vectors, Surface Model	Mixed Realism, Photo-Realism
Object Labeling	Perspective-Adaptive, General Positioning	Dynamic Selection and Dynamic Placement
Visual-Spatial Abstraction	Ground Level, Local-Area Level, Wide-Area Level	Adaptive Level, Adaptive Orientation
Route Indication	Arrows, Cords, Carpet, Way Points	Simulative
Landmark Symbology	Shops (referenced by name), Shops (referenced by type), Buildings (with unique name / function), Buildings (with unique visual properties)	Abstractness (Words, Sign, Icon, Sketch, Drawing, Image), Adaptive Zoom, Adaptive Complexity
Contextual Awareness	Reconstructional, Recreational, Fictional	Active Awareness, Passive Awareness

5.1   Visualization Layers

The first part of the visualization paradigm specification is outlined in this section, regarding the multiple layers of visualization elements, that were depicted from the analysis of current state-of-the-art. These layers, as the name implies, can be turned on or off to compose the final image presented on a device. For each of these layers we identify the most relevant feature vectors and magnitudes and how to adjust and combine them to get a better user experience:

Roads is a layer of major importance for a mobile 3D map, especially for car driving assistance. Other polygonal features, comprising urban, water and vegetation features, often represented by polygons, allow us to identify and recognize the surrounding environment, while comparing it to the image presented on a device. For these two elements, and following the results in section 4.1, the best approach consists on using aerial image component, since it allows a faster and more reliable identification of the ground features that surrounds the users. However, when using the *Orthophotomap* component, it may be more difficult to visualize the road network. One possible solution consists on coloring the vectors with a translucent color, over the aerial images. Following section 4.2, the labels of the roads should be, as much as possible, oriented towards the camera (*Perspective-Adaptive Labeling*) for higher readability. Roads and polygonal features should be labeled using a *General Positioning* approach.

Buildings is also an important map layer, since they often correspond to the source and destination in a navigation task. For a better user responsiveness in identification tasks, the buildings should be depicted as *Photo Textured Buildings* or, if not possible, *Simple Textured Buildings*, according to section 4.1. The questionnaire proved that, by providing the third dimension (even with simple textured or colored façades) there is an improvement on the user performance. However there are cases where 3D buildings can cause occlusions along the route, making the navigation task more difficult. One solution for this can include rendering buildings near a maneuver point, in a translucent way, so that the route becomes visible, while keeping the presence of such buildings perceptible to the human eye.

Results pointed out in section 4.1 recommend the use of a *Terrain Model*, which should be combined with the aerial image, for a higher degree of *Photo-Realism*. When this layer is turned on, it will be possible to see a clear distinction between the altitude of rivers and the altitude of the peaks of mountains. In certain circumstances, especially when the user is in a mountain place, many occlusions may block him/her from observing whats ahead. Because of these restrictions, the ability to turn on and off the *Terrain Model* component may become an advantage for the user.

Points of Interest, also known as landmarks, refer to buildings with historical, cultural or social significance or other prominent objects in a given landscape. Users must be able to find all kinds of Points of Interest, including shops referenced by name or type, and buildings with unique name, function or visual properties. For many specifications of a mobile map, it may be difficult to provide all the possible abstraction levels, as pointed out in section 4.5. Nevertheless, at least 2 or 3 levels of abstraction should be used:

1. *Sign*, *Icon* or *Sketch* for the most abstract representations;
2. *Drawing* or *Image* for the most concrete representations;
3. *Words* as an addition, especially in the case of landmarks referenced by their unique names.

5.2   Visualization Functions

The second part of the specification addresses the high-level visualization functions that should be considered as a requirement for the great majority of 3D map-based mobile services, regardless of the layers involved:

It should be possible to pan the map around and see the labels in a continuous way (*Dynamic Placement*), as stated in section 4.2. The user should not be confused with visual artifacts of labels popping in or out, especially in the limits of the screen.

Under monotonic zoom, the labels of the map should appear also in a continuous way (*Dynamic Selection*). This implies that, for example, when zooming in, labels that are visible should not suddenly "vanish" but instead slide out of the view area [10]. The same reasoning can be used in the opposite circumstance. The size of labels should be decided as a function of zoom level.

When displaying POIs, some care should be taken regarding the choice of the represented abstraction level. The *Adaptive Zoom* component can help the visualization paradigm selecting the appropriate abstraction level of a landmark as a function of zoom, as seen in section 4.5. At far distances, there are cases where the number of overlapping POIs becomes so high that is impossible to recognize what is where. For this reason, the visualization paradigm should be capable of aggregating close or overlapping POIs into abstract clouds representative of the group of POI s that were aggregated. This "clouds" will be broken into smaller clouds as we *zoom in* the map, since the number of POIs will be reduced along with the size of the view area.

Active Awareness approach should be used, especially in an automotive navigation experience, to provide users route indication instructions, as stated in section 4.6. In terms of *Route Indication*, and following section 4.3, it can be argued that a *Cord* or a *Carpet* may not provide enough visual information, when used alone. Since it is a continuous visual cue, it does not give a clear indication for maneuvers, i.e. if you are driving a car you must know precisely if you are turning or changing direction in an intersection. Thus, for navigation tasks, other visual indicators, like arrows, should be used to describe discreet events such as maneuvers.

When coming closer to a major interchange, drivers will be able to read (on the device) life-like signposts with destinations written on them, along with maneuver indicators provided by a *Simulative Route Indication* approach, allowing them to identify much faster and accurately the correct way to follow. The previous example also introduces another issue, which was addressed in section 4.2: when a user is driving fast, it should be possible to see "more ahead", in order to properly anticipate maneuvers. On the other hand, in a pedestrian navigation, users will be interested: in a *Ground Level* perspective that allows an easy identification of the buildings around them; in a *Wide-Area* perspective for acquiring an overview or planning their itinerary; and in an intermediate *Local-Area* Level perspective for confirming the presence of a landmark in the surroundings. Ideally, the map should perform this change automatically, i.e., it should provide an *Adaptive Level* camera. In a pedestrian navigation experience, it should be of extreme importance that the visualization adapts to match the same orientation than in reality, i.e., that it supports *Adaptive Orientation*.

6   Conclusions and Future Work

In this study, we have presented a visual paradigm to support the development of 3D map-based mobile services. This specification contemplates visual contents in the form of visualization layers and required functionality as visualization functions. This definition was based on a comprehensive analysis on current state-of-the-art and on an experiment made by using an online questionnaire. This analysis was directed by a conceptual framework developed to focus the study on the most relevant visualization elements (*feature vectors*) that influence user performance and experience.

Since there were several limitations on the kind of measurements that could be performed with the proposed questionnaire in order to evaluate *feature vectors*, it would be interesting to perform other kinds of tests, with particular focus on dynamic experiments, to get more information about other vectors such as *Visual-Spatial Abstraction* and *Contextual Awareness* which were not evaluated. An example of these experiments would include using a driving simulator to test the participants' reflexes, given a situation where they are approaching a maneuver, and deciding which way to go. Given that the proposed visualization paradigm still has a lot of empirical knowledge within itself, the future research would focus on studying the interactions between feature vectors, to understand eventual conflicts that may arise, and how can they be combined to maximize usability and user experience.

References

1. Rademacher, P., Lengyel, J., Cutrell, E., Whitted, T.: Measuring the perception of visual realism in images. In: Proceedings of the 12th Eurographics Workshop on Rendering Techniques, London, UK, pp. 235–248. Springer, Heidelberg (2001)
2. Lange, E., Ri, Z.C.: The degree of realism of GIS-based virtual landscapes: Implications for spatial planning. In: Fritsch, D., Spiller, R. (eds.) Photogrammetric Week 1999, November 28, pp. 367–374 (2003)
3. McNamara, A., Chalmers, A., Trocianko, T.: Visual perception in realistic image synthesis. In: Coquillart, S., Duke, D. (eds.) STAR Proceedings of Eurographics 2000, Interlaken, Switzerland, August 2000, pp. 315–322. Eurographics Association (2000)
4. Bolin, M.R., Meyer, G.W.: A visual difference metric for realistic image synthesis. In: Proc. SPIE, pp. 106–120 (1999)
5. Ferwerda, J.A.: Three varieties of realism in computer graphics. In: Proceedings SPIE Human Vision and Electronic Imaging 2003, pp. 290–297 (2003)
6. Milgram, P., Kishino, F.: A taxonomy of mixed reality visual displays. IEICE Transactions on Information Systems E77-D(12), 1321–1329 (1994)
7. Borenstein, J., Everett, H.R., Feng, L.: "Where am I?" – Sensors and Methods for Mobile Robot Positioning. The University of Michigan (April 1996)
8. Hunolstein, S.V., Zipf, A.: Towards task oriented map-based mobile guides. In: Workshop "HCI in Mobile Guides" at Mobile HCI 2003. 5th International Symp. on HCI with Mobile Devices and Services, July 29 (2003)
9. Freitas, M., Sousa, A., Coelho, A.: Evaluation of visualization features in three-dimensional location-based mobile services. In: Proceedings of GRAPP 2009, pp. 328–336. Springer, Heidelberg (2009)
10. Been, K., Daiches, E., Yap, C.: Dynamic map labeling. IEEE Transactions on Visualization and Computer Graphics 12(5), 773–780 (2006)
11. Elias, B., Paelke, V., Kuhnt, S.: Concepts for the cartographic visualization of landmarks. In: Proceedings of Symposium 2005 Location Based Services & TeleCartography, pp. 149–155 (2005)
12. Chen, G., Kotz, D.: A survey of context-aware mobile computing research. Technical Report TR2000-381, Dept. of Computer Science, Dartmouth College (November 2000)
13. Nurminen, A.: The m-loma mobile 3d map project website (2006), http://www.init.hut.fi/research%26projects/m-loma/ (Last Checked: November 2008)
14. Narzt, W., Pomberger, G., Ferscha, A., Kolb, D., Muller, R., Wieghardt, J., Hortner, H., Lindinger, C.: Augmented reality navigation systems. Universal Access in the Information Society 4(3), 177–187 (2006)
15. Oulasvirta, A., Nurminen, A., Nivala, A.M.: Interacting with 3d and 2d mobile maps: An exploratory study. Technical report, Helsinki Institute for Information Technology (HIIT); Finnish Geodetic Institute (April 2007)

New Augmented Reality Techniques for Product Design: The Flip-Flop Menu

Mickael Naud, Paul Richard, and Jean-Louis Ferrier

Laboratoire d'Ingnirie des Systmes Automatiss (LISA) - EA 4094,
Universit d'Angers, 62 Avenue Notre-Dame du Lac 49000 Angers, France

Abstract. This paper presents two bimanual augmented reality (AR) interaction techniques for product design. The first technique allows the user to visualize 3D virtual object in his/her non-dominant hand while being able to map different textures on it using his/her dominant hand. The second technique is based on nine fiducial markers placed on a desk in front of the user. Two experiments were carried out using the second technique to compare four different markers arrangements and four viewing conditions. In these experiments, subjects were instructed to perform nine actions such as rotate the object, apply a texture on it, etc. Results of the first experiment revealed that a V-shape configuration was the best. Results of the second experiment revealed that camera placed behind the user was the more efficient condition.

Keywords: Augmented reality, 3D interaction techniques, product design, user evaluation.

1 Introduction

Virtual Reality (VR) allows a user to experience both immersion and real-time interactions that may involve visual feedback, 3D sound, haptics, smell and taste. Instead, Augmented Reality (AR) or Mixed Reality (MR) propose to interact with virtual objects in the real world. In this sense, AR/MR techniques seem to be more interesting for application such as product design because it allows the designer or the end-user to both visualize and interact with the virtual mockup of the product in the real world.

AR/MR systems usually require see-through head-mounted displays (HMD) in which the real images are obtained through a video camera mounted on the HMD and aligned with the direction of the users eyes. This configuration can produce a naturally combined imagery. However, in many cases, due to operational reasons (e.g. cost, maintenance problems), the use of HMD may not be viable. In addition, if the task is confined to a small area, thus requiring only limited head turning, one can resort to using a desktop monitor instead.

Although several compelling AR/MR systems have been demonstrated [1], many serve merely as information browsers, allowing users to see or hear virtual data embedded in the physical world. Thus, very little work has been done on designing effective AR/MR interaction techniques.

In order to make AR/MR fully effective, simple and efficient 3D interaction techniques need to be developed and validated through user studies. Moreover, inherent

A. Ranchordas et al. (Eds.): VISIGRAPP 2009, CCIS 68, pp. 104–115, 2010.

drawbacks of AR techniques such as real/virtual image discrepancy, system calibration (markerless AR/MR), or ergonomic problems related to head-mounted displays have to be overcome.

In this paper, we present the design of bimanual augmented reality (AR) interaction techniques. The first technique allows the user to visualize a 3D virtual object in his/her non-dominant hand while being able to map different textures on it using his/her dominant hand. The second interaction technique is based on nine fiducial markers [4] placed on a desk in front of the user. Two experiments were carried out with the second interaction technique to compare four different markers arrangements and four viewing conditions. We measured the subjects task performance and surveyed for perceived usability and preference.

The remainder of this paper is organized as follows. In section 2, we give an overview of the related work. In section 3 we describe the first bimanual interaction technique called "jumping". In section 4 we present the second interaction technique called "Flip-flop" and propose four arrangements for the fiducial markers. Section 5 is dedicated to the experiment that compare the proposed arrangements. In section 6, we describe the experimental study that was carried out to compare different viewing conditions. The paper ends by a conclusion and give some tracks for future work.

2   Related Work

Most AR/MR applications of design work developed up to present are limited to large-scale objects that the designers are not able to grasp and move. In these examples, the information provided was limited to visual information, lacking physical interactions between the observer and the object. For example Fata Morgana project [9], designers were able to walk around a newly designed virtual car for inspection and comparisons with others.

In this context, Lee et al. proposed to bring the users hand into the VE using a Mixed Reality platform [10]. The hand region was separated and inserted into Virtual Environment (VE) to enhance reality.

Regenbrecht et al. developed a Magic Pen that uses ray-casting techniques for selection and manipulation of virtual objects [13]. Camera-based tracking was performed using ARToolkit, a software library that supports tangible user interaction with fiducial markers [8]. Two or more light emitting diodes (LEDs) were mounted on a real pen barrel. A camera was used to track the position of the pen, using the LEDs as position markers. Direct manipulation was performed with the end of the pen, or a virtual ray can be cast in the direction that the pen is pointing. This provides a cable-less interaction device for AR environments.

Dias et al. have developed a series of tools based on ARToolkit : the *Paddle* and the *Magic Ring* [3]. They both have a specific marker attached. As a visual aid, when a marker is recognized by the system, a virtual paddle or virtual blue circle is displayed on top of it. The Magic Ring (a small marker attached to a finger, by means of a ring) is used in several interaction tasks, such as object picking, moving and dropping, object scaling and rotation, menu manipulation, menu items browsing and selection, and for all various types of commands given to the system. A similar AR/VR unified user interface was proposed by Piekarsky and Thomas . This interface called the Tinmith-Hand is based on the flexible Tinmith-evo5 software system [11]. Using some modeling techniques, based on constructive solid geometry, tracked input gloves, image plane techniques, and a menu control system, it is possible to build applications that can be used to construct complex 3D models of objects in both indoor and outdoor settings.

Buchmann et al have proposed a technique for natural, fingertip-based interaction with virtual objects in Augmented Reality (AR) environments [2]. They use image processing software and finger- and hand-based fiducial markers to track gestures from the user, stencil buffering to enable the user to see their fingers at all times, and fingertip-based haptic feedback devices to enable the user to feel virtual objects. This approach allows users to interact with virtual content using natural hand gestures. It was successfully applied in an urban planning AR application. Besides more traditional AR interaction techniques, like mouse raycast, MagicBook, and models-on-marker e.g. [13] some techniques were proposed by Regenbrecht and Wagner [12]. The main one, called *cake platter* uses a turnable, plate-shaped device functions as the central location for shared 3D objects. The objects or models can be placed on the platter using different interaction techniques, e.g. by triggering the transfer from a 2D application or by using transfer devices brought close to the *cake platter*.

Few AR/MR applications use desktop displays as its major display by design. It is suspected that using desktop displays (upright) is implicitly regarded non-ideal compared to HMDs most probably due to the viewpoint mismatch. Field et al. used an upright rear projection screen and a camera looking toward the user and the interaction space in their Augmented Chemistry application. However, they did not specify in details why such a display was used other that it was meant to give the feeling of a mirror image of the interaction space [5]. The term "Desktop AR" is in fact more commonly used to indicate that the desktop is used as the interaction space.

Kraut et al. compared different display configurations for video based remote collaboration. The authors compared the level of collaboration with displays, for instance, coming from the collaborators head mounted camera (giving a small view of the interaction space), a fixed camera located a step back of the collaborator (to give a wider view), or both. Not much difference in performances was found among the test conditions in this study [6].

Jeon et al. [7] have compared the task performance and usability among three different viewing configurations of AR system that uses a desktop monitor instead of a head mounted display. Their results indicated that mounting a camera on the users head and placing a fixed camera in the back of the user was the best option in terms of task performance, user perceived performance and easiness of setting up the environment. They are also showed that there was not statistically significant advantage of mirrored+warped configuration. The mirrored-only configuration resulted in marginally faster task completion time.

3 "Jumping" Interaction Technique

The "jumping" interaction technique, illustrated in figure 1, is based on an intuitive metaphor which consists of approaching an object to another one to transfer information between them.

Fig. 1. Illustration of the "jumping" interaction technique

Two fiducial markers each sticked on rigid supports are manipulated by the user. For right-handed users, textures are mapped on the right-hand fiducial marker while a 3D virtual object to be decorated (a doll in figure 1) is displayed on the left-hand fiducial marker.

A 15 centimeters threshold distance between the two fiducial markers has been experimentally determined. When the actual distance between the markers is less than this threshold, then the texture displayed on the right-hand marker is automatically mapped onto the virtual object. When the distance between the markers goes beyond the threshold, a new texture appears on the right-hand marker, and so on. Thus, the user can successively apply textures on the 3D object. Moreover, the 3D object may be easily changed by simply masking the associated fiducial marker.

This interaction technique was evaluated through a preliminary experiment (subjective evaluation only). Ten subject aged from 18 to 22 participated in the experiment. They were instructed to successively map ten textures on a virtual doll. Both results from questionnaires and observations during the experiment reveals that this technique is very attractive and intuitive. However, the technique was found a little repetitive and limited in terms of interaction possibilities. This led us to design the "flip-flop" interaction technique, presented in the next section.

4   Flip-Flop Interaction Technique

Augmented reality techniques may involve different configurations : (1) immersive configurations in which the users are equipped with either an optical see-through or a video see-through head-mounted display, (2) desk-top configurations that may be based on a large screen placed in front of the users, and (3) embedded configurations that involve mobile devices such as PDAs.

In the context of virtual prototyping, desktop configurations may be interesting because the user could see himself/herself on the screen, manipulating a virtual product. In such a configuration, the video camera has to be placed in front of the user. Then the images on the screen may be reversed. This interaction technique was developed with the aim to reach a large panel of users. Therefore, it is relatively simple to use.

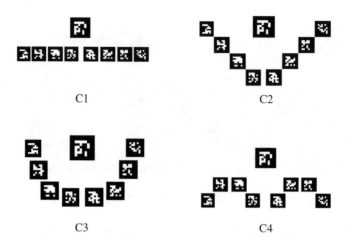

Fig. 2. Possible arrangements for the fiducial markers : (C1) Line-shaped, (C2) V-shaped, (C3) U-shaped, (C4) M-shaped

4.1 Description

The flip-flop interaction technique uses 9 Artag fiducial markers arranged on a table. Fiducial markers were placed on the table in different arrangements as illustrated in figure 2. The main (central) fiducial marker is used to display 3D virtual objects. Side parts of the menu are made-up of 4 Artag fiducial markers. The left part of the menu (*master sub-menu*) allows to activate different functionalities of the right part of the menu (*slave sub-menu*). The *slave sub-menu* is used to interact with the 3D model (figure 3).

The specific number of the fiducial markers was determined by technical and ergonomic considerations. Firstly, the size of the markers has to be large enough to facilitate the interaction technique. Secondly, all the markers have to be permanently viewed and recognized. The number of markers was also determined by the number of menu options required.

This interaction technique was called "flip-flop" because of the multiple back-and-forth movements that the user must do between the *master sub-menu* and the *slave sub-menu* in order to interact with the virtual objects. The figure 4 illustrates the functionalities activated by masking fiducial markers of the *master sub-menu*. These functionalities are the following :

- **Colors exploration.** Exploration of the colors palettes. The change of palette is automatically done each 800ms,
- **Model Animation.** Activation of functionalities allowing to (1) reduce or (2) increase the size of the doll and (3) to make the doll rotate or (4) to stop it in a specific position,
- **Texture Database Exploration.** Exploration of the different preset texture sets. The display of a new texture sets is done automatically each 800ms,
- **Materials Exploration.** Activation of functionalities allowing to change the material that simulate the fabric visual aspect.

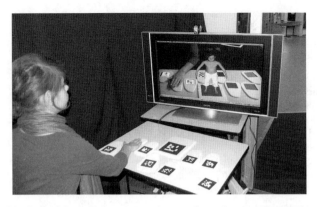

Fig. 3. Subject participate at marker configuration experimentation

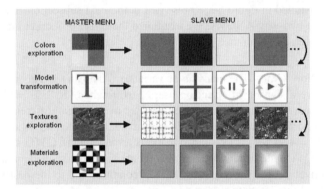

Fig. 4. Illustration of the functionalities of the *slave sub-menu* activated from the *master sub-menu*

5   Experiment 1: Effect of Marker Arrangement

5.1   Aim

In previous section, four marker arrangements have been proposed (see fig. 2). This experiment aimed to investigate user performance and preference associated with the pattern configurations in order to determine the best one.

5.2   Experimental Protocol

A total of 40 right-handed volunteer aged from 12 to 31 years, participated in the experiment. They were divided in 4 groups (G1,G2,G3,G4). Each group has to perform the task in the conditions C1,C2,C3,C4 (fig. 2). Experimental conditions were counterbalanced to avoid any training transfer.

5.3   Task

The task was split into 9 sub-tasks that the subject have to perform in a sequential predefined order. These sub-tasks are the following:

1. Scroll all textures (5 sets of 4 textures),
2. Scroll colors and select the red set,
3. Apply the clearest red color on the 3D model,
4. Scroll colors and select the blue set,
5. Apply the darkest blue color on the 3D model,
6. Select transformations,
7. Shrink the character (five steps),
8. Enlarge the character (three step),
9. Rotate the character and stop it (one turn).

5.4   Results

The results illustrated in figure 5 are presented in the next subsection. They were analyzed through a two-way ANOVA. We examined the effect of marker arrangement on user performance and preference.

Task Completion Time. The analysis of variance (ANOVA) reveals that marker arrangements have a significant effect on users performance $(F(3,9) = 146.13, P < 0.005)$. We observed that marker arrangements led to statistical different task completion time. User performance was about 55 sec (std = 3.3), 61 sec (std = 4.6), 74 sec (std = 3.8), 85 sec (std = 4.9), for C2 (V-shaped markers arrangement), C3 (U-shaped markers arrangement), C4 (M-shaped markers arrangement), C1 (Line-shaped markers arrangement), respectively. Thus we observed that C2 condition led to the best performance and that C1 condition led to the worst performance.

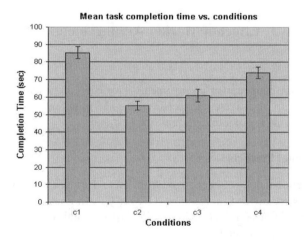

Fig. 5. Mean task completion time vs. experimental conditions

User Preference. User preference was analyzed using questionnaires and observations during the experiment. We observed that all the users were very enthusiastic while performing the task. Most of them preferred the V-shaped markers arrangement. Some users had difficulties with the other marker arrangements because they used their right hand to mask patterns of the *master sub-menu* as illustrated in figure 3. Therefore the bi-manual aspect of the technique was not fully achieved. This resulted in time loss. Moreover we observed in this three markers arrangements that the user masked two markers at the same times, resulting in malfunctioning of the application.

6 Experiment 2: Effect of Viewing Condition

Results of the first experiment showed that the V-shaped arrangement for the fiducial markers was the best. Therefore, this configuration was used for the second experiment.

6.1 Aim

The objective of this experiment is to investigate the effect of desktop viewing condition on user performance and system usability. The video camera is placed either in front or behind the user (fig. 6). The image reversal was also tested.

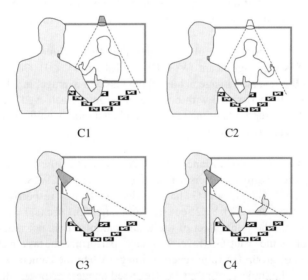

Fig. 6. Experimental configurations for viewing conditions

6.2 Experimental Protocol

A total of 40 volunteers subjects (20 males and 20 females) right-handed, aged from 15 to 35 years, participated in the experiment. They never used augmented reality techniques before. The subjects were divided in 4 groups (G1,G2,G3,G4). Each group has to perform the task in the following conditions :

- C1 : the webcam was placed in front of the user, and the image was reversed,
- C2 : the webcam was placed in front of the user, and the image was not reversed,
- C3 : the webcam was placed behind the user, and the image was reversed,
- C4 : the webcam was placed behind the user, and the image was not reversed.

The task was the same as the previous experiment. It has to be repeated 5 times by each subject. A 2 minutes rest period was given between each trial. Completion time was measured for each trial.

6.3   Results

The results illustrated in figure 7 are presented in the next three subsections. They were analyzed through a two-way ANOVA. We firstly examine the effect of camera position on subjects performance. Data from groups G1 and G2 were compared to the data from groups G3 and G4. Then, the effect of image reversion on subjects performance was examined. Therefore, data from groups G1 and G3 were compared to the data from groups G2 and G4. Finally we looked at the joint effect of the studied parameters.

Effect of Camera Position. We observed that the effect of camera position on task completion time is statistically significant $(F(1, 19) = 17.7, P < 0.005)$. Subjects that have the camera in front of them performed the task, on average in 71.5 sec (std = 5.2) while those whose camera was placed behind achieved the task in 67.7 sec (std = 4.6).

Effect of Image Reversion. We observed that the effect of image reversion on task completion time is very significant $(F(1, 19) = 790.26, P < 0.005)$. Subjects who performed with the reversed image achieved the task, on average, in 84.55 sec (std = 6.4) while those who performed with none reversed image achieved the task in 54.7 sec (std = 3.4). We observed that image reversion had a more significant effect on user performance than camera position.

Joint Effect. The analysis of variance (ANOVA) reveals that the experimental conditions have a significant effect on users performance $(F(3, 9) = 298.8, P < 0.005)$. The subjects of Group G1, G2, G3, and G4 have carried out the task respectively in 86.9 sec (std = 6.6), 56.2 sec (std = 3.8), 82.2 sec (std = 6.2), and 53.1 sec (std = 2.9).

Results show that the joint effect of the tested parameters is not much significant. Thus, the subjects of the group G3 (reversed image) performed the task in 29.1 sec faster than the subjects of group G4 (non-reversed image) when the camera was positioned behind. Similarly, the subjects of group G1 (reversed image) performed the task in 30.7 sec faster than the subjects of group G2 (non-reversed image).

Learning Process. Learning is defined here by the improvement of subjects performance during task repetition. We asked subjects to repeat 5 times the previously defined task. The results show that the subjects of group G1 achieved the task in 102.5 sec (std = 9.6) during the first trial and in 65.7 sec (std = 6.5) during the last trial. Subjects of groups G2, G3 and G4, achieved the task respectively in 69.5 sec (std = 6.2), 95.5 sec (std = 9.0) and 67.4 sec (std = 4.4) during the first trial and 49.1 sec (std = 2.6), 64.8

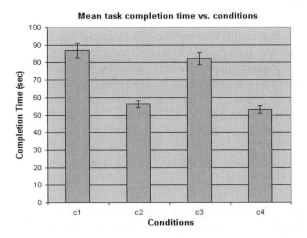

Fig. 7. Mean task completion time vs. experimental conditions

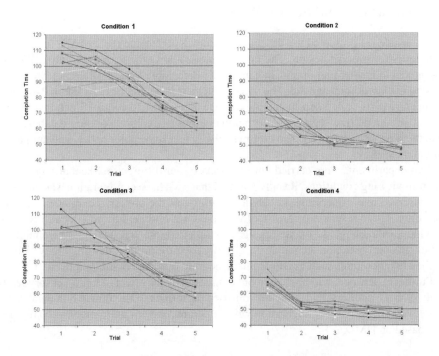

Fig. 8. Learning curves for the 4 conditions

sec (std = 5.9) and 47.5 sec (std = 2.2) during the last trial. This result in performance improvement percentage of 34%, 29%, 32% and 30% respectively for groups G1, G2, G3 and G4. Figures 8(a), 8(b), 8(c) and 8(d) show learning curves of each subject. We observed that for configurations in which the image is reversed, learning is slower.

7   Discussion

Results of the first experiment revealed that the V-shaped arrangement of the fiducial markers led to the best performance and was the users preferred configuration. We observed that this arrangement is more convenient for bimanual interaction. The line-shaped arrangement was found the worst because it does not provide a clear indication concerning the separation between the master and slave sub-menus and thus led to a non efficient bimanual interaction. Moreover, this arrangement do not take advantage of the users workspace and constraints the fiducial marker to be very closer, increasing possible mistakes. The C2 and C3 configuration gives approximatively the same results. This is not very surprising since the markers placement are not very different.

As observed by Jeon et al. [7], our results revealed that the best viewing condition is when the camera was placed behind the users and the image was reversed. However, we observed a significant difference in the performance between reversed and non-reversed image. This can be explained by the fact that in our experiment, the task is bimanual and requires intermittent uses of the left and the right sub-menus.

8   Conclusions and Future Work

In this article we presented the design of bimanual augmented reality (AR) interaction techniques for product design. The first technique allows the user to visualize 3D virtual model in his/her non-dominant hand while being able to map different textures on it using his/her dominant hand. The second interaction technique is based on two complementary parts : a left sub-menu (the master) that allows to control functionalities of a right sub-menu (the slave). The technique allows to explore a texture database and map them on virtual clothes. The user may also select some color pallets and animate a virtual mannequin.

Two experiments were carried out to compare four different markers arrangements and four viewing conditions. Results revealed that a V-shape configuration was the best. We observed that camera placed behind the user was the preferred and more efficient condition. These results are consistent with the ones observed by Jeon et al. [7] They provide a valuable guide for designing desktop AR bimanual interaction techniques. Although our interaction technique is currently used for product design, it may also be applied to other fields such as edutainment, cognitive/motor rehabilitation, etc.

Further experiment will be carried out to investigate the effect of multi-sensory feedback such as auditory and olfactory on user performance in similar bimanual task. Moreover, our desktop configuration will be compared with an immersive configuration based on HMD.

References

1. Bimber, O., Ramesh, R.: Spatial Augmented Reality, p. 383. A K Peters, ISBN: 978156881
2. Buchmann, V., Violich, S., Billinghurst, M., Cockburn, A.: FingARtips: gesture based direct manipulation in Augmented Reality. In: GRAPHITE 2004: Proceedings of the 2nd international conference on Computer graphics and interactive techniques in Australasia and South East Asia, Singapore, pp. 212–221. ACM, New York (2004)

3. Dias, J.M.S., Santos, P., Bastos, R.: Gesturing with tangible interfaces for mixed reality. In: Camurri, A., Volpe, G. (eds.) GW 2003. LNCS (LNAI), vol. 2915, pp. 399–408. Springer, Heidelberg (2004)
4. Fiala, M.: ARTag, An Improved Marker System Based on ARToolkit in NRC Publication Number: NRC 47166 (July 2004)
5. Fjeld, M., Voegtli, B.: Augmented Chemistry: An Interactive Educational Workbench. In: The video program of the International Symposium on Mixed and Augmented Reality, IS-MAR (2002)
6. Fussell, S.R., Setlock, L.D., Kraut, R.E.: Effects of Head-Mounted and Scene-Oriented Video Systems on Remote Collaboration on Physical Tasks. Presented at CHI 2003: Proceedings of the Conference on Human Factors in Computing Systems (2003)
7. Seokhee, J., Hyeongseop, S., Gerard, J.K.: Viewpoint Usability for Desktop Augmented Reality. The International Journal of Virtual Reality 5(3), 33–39 (2006)
8. Kato, H., Billinghurst, M.: Marker tracking and HMD calibration for a video-based augmented reality conferencing system. In: 2nd IEEE and ACM International Workshop on Augmented Reality, pp. 84–94 (1999)
9. Klinker, G., Dutoit, A.H., Bauer, M., Bayer, J., Novak, V., Matzke, D.: Fata Morgana - A Presentation System for Product Design. In: ISMAR 2002, pp. 76–85 (2002)
10. Lee, S., Chen, T., Kim, J., Kim, G.J., Han, S., Pan, Z.: Using Virtual Reality for Affective Properties of Product Design. In: Proc. of IEEE Intl. Conf. on Virtual Reality, pp. 207–214 (2004)
11. Piekarski, W., Thomas, B.H.: Unifying augmented reality and virtual reality user interfaces (2002)
12. Regenbrecht, H.T., Wagner, M.T.: Interaction in a collaborative augmented reality environment. In: CHI 2002 (2002)
13. Regenbrecht, H., Baratoff, G., Poupyrev, I., Billinghurst, M.: A cable-less interaction device for ar and vr environnement. In: Proc. ISMR, pp. 151–152 (2001)

Part II
Imaging Theory and Applications
(IMAGAPP)

Analytical Imaging of Traditional Japanese Paintings Using Multispectral Images

Jay Arre Toque, Masateru Komori, Yusuke Murayama, and Ari Ide-Ektessabi

Advanced Imaging Technology Laboratory, Graudate School of Engineering,
Kyoto Univeristy, Yoshida-honmachi, Sakyo-ku, 606-8501, Kyoto, Japan
jayarre81@gmail.com,
masateru-komori@t0407.mbox.media.kyoto-u.ac.jp,
soundscope3@gmail.com, h51167@sakura.kudpc.kyoto-u.ac.jp

Abstract. In this study, the influence of lighting conditions on the reconstruction of spectral reflectance and image stitching was explored. Pigment estimation using the reconstructed spectral reflectance was also discussed. Spectral reflectance was estimated using pseudoinverse model from multispectral images of a traditional Japanese painting. It was observed that the accuracy of the estimation is greatly influenced by lighting conditions. High specular reflection on the target yielded large amount of estimation errors. On the other hand, it was observed that in addition to specular reflection, the distribution of light highly affects image stitching. Image stitching is important especially when acquiring images of large objects. Finally, pigments used on the painting were estimated using spectral curve matching of the reconstructed spectral reflectance compared to a pigment database. It was shown that multispectral images could be used for the analytical imaging of artworks.

Keywords: Multispectral imaging, analytical imaging, spectral reflectance, image stitching, pigment identification.

1 Introduction

Multispectral imaging finds wide array of applications in the field of medicine, remote sensing, satellite imaging and cultural heritage analysis [1-3]. This involves taking images at different wavelengths to capture spectral features that cannot be detected by the naked human eye. The spectral characteristics can be regarded as signatures, which can help in analyzing the object being imaged. In a way, multispectral imaging is different from "conventional" imaging techniques.

Conventional imaging is carried out in the visible region of the electromagnetic spectrum. This region covers wavelengths from 400-700nm, which corresponds to frequencies from 428-750 THz. This is called visible region because the human eyes are only sensitive within this range [4]. Normally, this involves images with tristimulus values corresponding to red, green and blue colors (RGB). In applications such as display and visualization, this imaging technique is more than sufficient. The information that can be extracted from an image depends on the quality and the amount of data it contains. For a typical image with tristimulus values, its information is limited

A. Ranchordas et al. (Eds.): VISIGRAPP 2009, CCIS 68, pp. 119–132, 2010.

to color as perceived by the human's visual capability. However, if images are to be used for analytical imaging, conventional imaging might not be enough because of the limited amount of data.

Analytical imaging refers to techniques, which provides useful information about an object being imaged beyond its "conventional" visual content. In conventional imaging, normally, "what you see is what you get". This is based on the paradigm using three variables to characterize an image [5]. With analytical imaging, it is desired that images provide more information, which may include material characteristics, surface and topographic information and spectroscopic data just to name a few. It is based on the assumption that similar to other electromagnetic spectrum (e.g x-ray, microwave, etc.); material interaction within the visible light-near infrared (VL-NIR) range can be quantified. However, this interaction is quite complex. In order to perform sufficient analysis at VL-NIR range; the amount of data an image contains should be increased. This may be accomplished using multispectral imaging [6].

In this study, multispectral images were captured from 380-850 nm using image filters with different spectral transmittances. The images obtained contain information from the visible up to the near infrared range. The study focused on how the lighting conditions affect the reconstruction of spectral reflectance of Japanese paintings. Paintings were chosen as target because it normally requires non-destructive and non-invasive analysis. This is especially true if it is a cultural heritage [7]. Since paintings vary in sizes, it may sometimes not be possible to acquire the image of the whole painting at once if high-resolution images are desired. This will require image stitching. In this case, the influence of lighting is also of particular interest.

This study defines lighting condition as the cumulative effect of the various illumination factors affecting the perceived image. This includes intensity, type of light and angle of incidence. In reality, the factors affecting the lighting condition are not limited to the three mentioned. Since we are interested in the perceived image as detected by the image-capturing device, the factors can also include the distance of the light source to the target, surface property of the target and many more others. As the number of factors increase, the complexity of the interaction also increase. In this study, the factors are limited to the main light source characteristics mentioned previously.

Moreover, the reconstructed spectral reflectance was used for pigment identification. This was achieved using spectral curve matching to identify the pigments from a database of almost 100 commonly used Japanese pigments.

2 Experiment

Multispectral images were captured using a monochromatic CCD camera with spectral sensitivity from 350-1000 nm, which peaks at around 520 nm. The distance of the camera to the target was approximately 480 mm. The images were acquired using four types of filters {i.e. band pass filter (BPB), special purpose (SP) filter, sharp cut (SC) filter and infrared filter (IR)}. A total of seven filters were used (BPB-50, BPB-55, BPB-60, SP-9, SC-64, SC-70 and IR-76). These filters have different peak sensitivities, which enable the images to contain more information from specific wavelength range. In some cases, an IR-cut filter was used, specifically BPB and SP

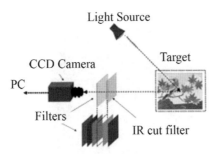

Fig. 1. Schematic representation of the multispectral imaging set-up

filters, because they have unwanted sensitivities at the near infrared region which could affect the accuracy of the spectral reflectance reconstruction. The sharp cut and IR filters were used for obtaining information at longer wavelengths. The schematic representation of the multispectral imaging system is shown in Figure 1.

In order to investigate the effects on spectral reflectance reconstruction and image stitching of lighting conditions, images were acquired using four variations summarized in Table 1. Three parameters were selected, such as type of light source, light source angle and intensity. These parameters were found to greatly affect the quality of the image and the corresponding information it contains.

Table 1. Lighting conditions used in acquiring the multispectral images. Note: E1 corresponds to experiment 1 and so on.

Parameters	E1	E2	E3	E4
Type	Halogen	Halogen	Halogen	Fluorescent
Angle (°)	30	30	60	N.A.
Intensity (%)	100	30	80	N.A.

2.1 Image Acquisition

In order to facilitate spectral reflectance reconstruction and image stitching, the target was imaged using the orientation shown in Figure 2. A total of three targets were used; a white background, a learning sample and a Japanese painting. The white background is used to calibrate the uneven distribution of light when imaging the learning sample and the Japanese painting. The learning sample, which was composed of conventionally used Japanese mineral pigments, was employed as the basis for the calculation of the conversion matrix used for reconstructing the spectral reflectance. A Japanese painting was chosen as the main target because of the technical challenges it presents (e.g. non-invasive, non-destructive, etc.). There exist other more advanced analytical technique for studying paintings, which are commonly x-ray-based [8]. However, x-ray-based technique is relatively non-destructive but not entirely non-invasive. Usually, a small piece of the sample is required. For paintings with high cultural value, taking even a minute sample is often unacceptable.

Fig. 2. Orientation of the target during image acquisition

2.2 Spectral Reflectance Reconstruction, Image Calibration and Pigment Identification

The effect of the lighting condition during imaging was evaluated based on the accuracy of the spectral reflectance reconstruction and the quality of image stitching. Before reconstructing the spectral reflectances, the images were calibrated using a white background to compensate for the effect of the uneven distribution of light shone on the surface of the target. This helps facilitate better image stitching. The pixel values of the images were adjusted using Eq.1

$$T_i' = T_i \left(\frac{\overline{X}_{pv}}{B_i} \right) \qquad (1)$$

where T_i corresponds to the ith pixel value of the uncompensated target image, $\overline{X}_{pv}$ is the average pixel value of the white background, B_i is the ith pixel value of the white background and T_i' *is the new* i^{th} pixel value of the white background-adjusted target.

After the images were adjusted using the white background, the spectral reflectance was estimated. In general, the spectral characteristic of an image is described by Eq.2 [9]:

$$\mathbf{p} = \mathbf{CLr} + \mathbf{e} \qquad (2)$$

where, $\mathbf{p}$ is the pixel value of the image captured at a certain band, C is the spectral sensitivity of the capturing device, L is the spectral power distribution of the light source, $\mathbf{r}$ is the spectral reflectance and $\mathbf{e}$ is an additive noise corresponding to the measurement errors of the spectral characteristics of the sensors, illumination and reflectances. All of the quantities in Eq.2 are functions of the wavelength. In this case, in order to estimate the spectral reflectance, the spectral characteristic of the camera and light source should be known. However, this information is often unavailable. Using pseudoinverse model, the spectral reflectance can be estimated without prior knowledge of the spectral characteristics of the camera and light source.

The pseudoinverse model is a modification of the Wiener estimation by regression analysis [9]. In this model, a matrix W is derived by minimizing $\|R - WP\|$ from a known spectral reflectance of a learning sample, R, and the corresponding pixel values, P, captured at a certain band. The matrix W is given by Eq.3

$$W = RP^+ \tag{3}$$

Where P^+ represents the pseudoinverse matrix of P. By applying the derived matrix W to the pixel value of the target image, $\mathbf{p}$, the spectral reflectance $\hat{\mathbf{r}}$ can be estimated using Eq.4

$$\hat{\mathbf{r}} = W\mathbf{p} \tag{4}$$

The size of the matrices used in Eq.3 and Eq.4 is a function of the number of learning sample k, number of multispectral bands M and number of spectral reflectances N measured at 10nm interval from 380-850 nm. In this study, k is 98, M is 7 and N is 48. The learning sample used in this study is a collection of 98 commonly used Japanese pigments and the spectral reflectance is measured using a spectrometer.

Reconstruction of the spectral reflectance was carried out using multispectral images because it can contain both spectroscopic and spatial information. With the conventional spectrometers, the data acquired are only spectroscopic in nature. The information

Fig. 3. Image of the Japanese painting used as target to evaluate the effect of lighting condition. The spectral reflectances are estimated from three regions on the painting.

Fig. 4. Areas on the painting selected to demonstrate pigment identification using the multispectral images

is confined to reflectance, transmittance and absorbance. However, by manipulating some image acquisition parameters (e.g. lighting angle, camera position, etc.) in multis-pectral imaging, it is possible to get spatial information about the object such as surface features, topography and other physical aspects of the material's surface.

In order to evaluate how the lighting condition affects the spectral reflectance esti-mation, three regions on the Japanese painting were selected namely Region 1, 2 and 3 as depicted by Figure 3.

Finally, to demonstrate the practical merits of this study, the reconstructed spectral reflectance was used for pigment identification. Different areas on the painting were selected as shown in Figure 4. This was achieved by calculating the root mean square error (RMSE) of the reconstructed spectral reflectances compared with measured reflectance of the learning sample. The pigment with the least RSME value was cho-sen as the most likely match. The reference spectral reflectance values were measured using a spectrometer.

3   Results and Discussion

3.1   Reconstruction of Spectral Reflectance

In this study, three regions on the painting were selected where the spectral reflectances were reconstructed. The three areas possess distinct charateristics which was the reason for its selection. For example, Region 1 is the area on the Japanese painting that experienced high specular reflection. This region has gold foil laid on the surface. Using gold foils in painting is a common practice in Japanese art. Since the region has metallic constituent, it explains why it has high specular reflection. This significantly affected the estimated spectral reflectance as shown in Figure 5. The figure shows five reflectance values, four from the different lighting conditions and one for the spectral reflectance measured using a spectrometer, which acts as the reference spectral reflectance. It could be observed that the reconstructed spectral reflectances of the multispectral images on Region 1 is quite poor. This might be due to the reflectance characteristics of the gold foil in the region. Specular reflection was not observed in all experiments, when this was the case, Region 1 appeared to be dark. This results to very low spectral reflectance but still not close to the measured reflectance. Unfortunately, the lighting parameters used in the experiment were not optimum. However, the main aim of the study is to observe how the lighting condition affects the estimation. Based on the phenomena observed, it can be concluded that the issue on specular reflection needs to be addressed in order to achieve better reconstruction.

On the other hand, Region 2 was selected because it did not show any specular reflection in all the experiments. It was painted with an orange mineral pigment resembling atumn leaves. The reconstructed spectral reflectance is depicted by Figure 6. Compared to Region 1, the reconstructed spectral reflectance is close to the measured reflectance up to wavelengths of 600 nm. Between 600-700 nm however, the estimation was relatively poor except for E4. The estimated spectral reflectance of E4 was close to the measured one up to 700 nm. At the near infrared region, no

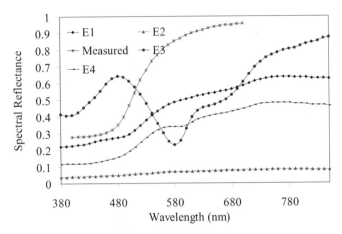

Fig. 5. Reconstructed spectral reflectance from multispectral images on Region 1 of the Japanese painting

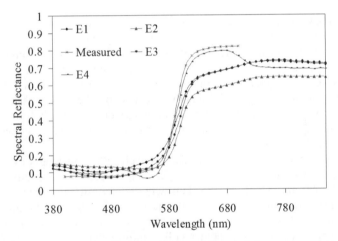

Fig. 6. Reconstructed spectral reflectance from multispectral images on Region 2 of the Japanese painting

comparison could be made because the data from the spectrometer is only available from 400-700 nm.

Finally, Region 3 was selected because it yielded multispectral images with and without specular reflection across the different parameters. What is unique in this region is that it has both mineral and metallic pigment. The metal consitituents in this case are traces of silver particle instead of gold foil. Figure 7 shows the reconstructed spectral reflectance. The estimation is still not as accurate as it should be but it is better compared to Region 1. Again, the poor reconstruction may be attributed to specular reflection. In this case since the metallic constituents are in particle form, the effect on the multispectral images is not as severe when compared to the gold foil since the relative exposed area is smaller.

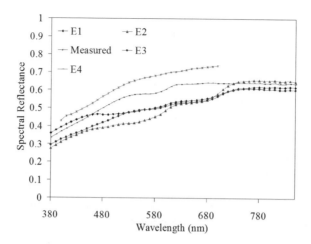

Fig. 7. Reconstructed spectral reflectance from multispectral images on Region 1 of the Japanese painting

The accuracy of the spectral reflectance reconstruction may also be explained by the characteristics of the filters used to capture multispectral images. In order to get a good estimation result, the filters should be able to get significant amount of data. Figure 8 shows the spectral characteristics of the seven filters used, along with the measured spectral reflectances of the selected regions. Among the selected regions, Region 2 has the most number of filters that are able to collect spectral information. A total of four filters were able to collect the necessary data especially between 420-580 nm. This can explain why the accuracy of the estimation is relatively better if compared to the other wavelengths.

On the other hand, the filters with short wavelengths and long wavelengths collected the data from Region 3. No filter was able to collect any useful information between 480-680 nm, which may explain why the reconstructed spectral reflectance within this range deviated from that of the measured. Finally as for Region 1, on top of the severe effect of specular reflection of the gold-laden surface, it could be observed that only two filters were able to collect information.

In addition, it is interesting to note how well the estimated spectral reflectances above 700 nm were convergent except for Region 1. Evidently, the influence of high specular reflection also affected the reconstructed reflectance at that wavelength. It is difficult to ascertain its accuracy because the measured data only goes up to 700 nm but it may be assumed that it might be good enough. Filter selection plays an important role in the accuracy of the reconstruction. In this study, only seven filters were used. However, similar study has shown that the optimum number of filter is eight. The optimum filter selection was explored and reported elsewhere [10].

Why is important to reconstruct the spectral reflectance above the visible range? This is because previous studies have shown that some materials have unique spectral features at the near infrared range [11]. In addition, acquiring images beyond the visible range can help increase the amount of information available from the image.

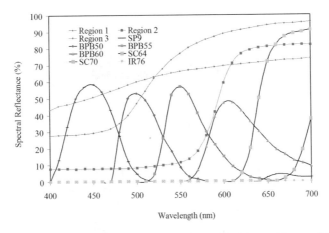

Fig 8. Spectral characteristics of the filters used in capturing the multispectral images along with the measured spectral reflectance of the three selected regions

Fig. 9. Stitched image of a Japanese painting using uncalibrated images

3.2 Image Stitching

Image stitching is important in acquiring images of large objects that cannot be captured entirely at once. In principle, as long as the object is in the line of sight of the capturing device, the size of the image that can be acquired is virtually unlimited. This can be accomplished by increasing the distance between the camera and the target object. However, as the distance increases, the resolution of the image could also decrease. This affects the quality of data the image contains. It is possible to solve this issue by performing some processing on the image but it is usually better to use the image with as little alteration as possible in order to preserve the information it holds.

In this study, the influence of lighting condition on image stitching was investigated. Since the lighting was varied several times, it is to be expected to get images with different characteristics. Figure 9 shows an example of a stitched image acquired using IR 76 filter. The stitching line is very obvious which is a result of uneven light distribution. Figure 10 depicts a 3D representation the said distribution. It can be seen that a portion of the target receives more intense light as compared to the other parts especially towards the edges of the target. As a result, some area appears to be

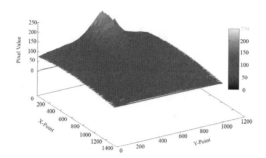

Fig. 10. 3D representation of the distribution of light as reflected by the white background. The pixel values of the 1360x1024 image were used to create this 3D impression.

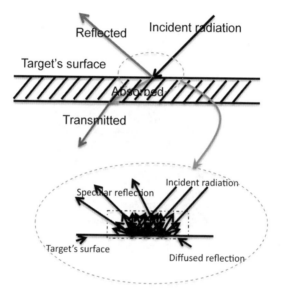

Fig. 11. Simple interaction model when a material is subjected to radiation

brighter than the other. In addition to the obvious stitching line, some specular reflection can also be seen.

Generally, when an object is subjected to a radiation, three common interaction occurs. The incident radiation may be reflected, absorbed and transmitted as illutrated by Figure 11. It can be a mixture of any of the three. Depending on the characteristics of the material and the energy of the radiation, this interaction can be more complex. However, radiation in the form of visible light, the three mentioned is likely to occur. In imaging, the reflected portion of the radiation is more significant. This is the quantity that the camera sensors use to form the images. As shown in the simplified model (Figure 11), the reflected light is further classified into specular and diffused reflection [12]. Specular reflection is the potion of the reflected light that is also known as a mirror reflection. This results to saturation of the image in some areas of the target painting. Once the image is saturated, little information can be extracted from it and worse it obscure the stitching of the images.

Fig. 12. Stitched image of the Japanese painting calibrated using a white background

In order to solve the issues brought by the uneven light distribution, the images were calibrated using a white background. The details of the calibration process were described in the previous section. The images were acquired using various position in order to have a specular reflection-free image. Figure 12 shows an example of the final stitched image. After calibration and removal of regions with high specular reflections, the stitching line is barely visible. It is believed that the quality of the stitching can be further improved by using more sophisticated calibration techniques. In this study, only a simple technique was implemented. It was discovered that this method is only effective within a certain threshold. If the standard deviation of the average pixel values of the white standard is less than 20 pixels, then method employed here is sufficieint. If it goes beyond the 20 pixels threshold, stitching lines eventually become visible. Therefore there is a need to improve the white background calibration by using other techniques [13-16].

3.3 Pigment Estimation

Pigment identification is an important aspect of artworks analysis. The pigments used to create the artwork may be indicative of the style, era and historical footprint of the object. For famous works such as those by Da Vinci, Michael Angelo and Carravagio just to name a few, detailed records may be available. However, for lesser-known works but with good cultural value, information might be scarce. Techniques used for pigment identification includes X-ray fluorescence, energy dispersive x-ray detection, Raman spectroscopy, color spectroscopy, etc. These techniques have been proven to be sufficient but non-invasive at times. For instance, X-ray-based techniques require a sampling a small piece of the object for the analysis. For normal type of samples, this might be acceptable. However, for objects with high cultural values, this is unacceptable. A way to address this concern is by using digital images of the artworks for the analysis.

In this study, multispectral images were used for pigment identification. The spectral reflectance of the painting reconstructed from the multispectral images is compared to a reference database. Multispectral images were used as supposed to conventional RGB images because it contains more spectroscopic information since it has more spectral channels. In the case of RGB images, three spectral channels are available. On the other hand, for multispectral images, the number varies depending on the number of filters used where in this study was seven. As demonstrated and

Table 2. Pigment estimation results based on the reconstructed spectral reflectance

Point	Actual Pigments		Estimated Pigments		Estimation Result
	Japanese Name	English Name	Japanese Name	English Name	
A	*Ryokusho*	Malachite	*Ryokusho*	Malachite	O
B	*Touou*	Fuji yellow	*Touou*	Fuji yellow	O
C	*Tan*	Minium	*Irozumi*	Vermilion	X
D	*Shinsha*	Cinnabar	*Shinsha*	Cinnabar	O
E	*Gofun*	Chalk	*Hakudo*	Clay	X
F	*Taisha*	Hematite	*Taisha*	Hematite	O
G	*Syoenboku*	Pine Ink	*Syoenboku*	Pine Ink	O

discussed in the previous section, the number of filters and its spectral characteristics affects the accuracy of the reconstruction of the spectral reflectance.

After choosing the areas of interest (Figure 4), the algorithm for spectral reflectance reconstruction was employed. The result was run through the reference database of about a hundred of commonly used Japanese pigments. The estimation result is found in Table 2. Based on the result it could infer that the identification algorithm was sufficient but could still be improved. This could be achieved by including colorimetric information on the selection algorithm. For example, Point C, which was painted with minium, it was falsely identified as vermilion. This would not be the case if color information were included since minium is orange while vermilion is red. In addition, increasing the range of spectral reflectance reconstruction might also help since some pigments have similar profile within the visible light spectrum but could be distinguished by its profile in the near infrared range. This might have been the case for Point E. Even though the reconstruction was performed between 380-850 nm, the reference database was only measured between 400-700 nm due to the physical limits of the instrument used. The database may be improved by addressing this problem. All in all, the estimation result was fairly accurate.

The estimation technique employed in this study has the advantage of being more versatile than the conventional techniques presently being used for the analysis of artworks. For example, spectrometers used for measuring spectral reflectance require a large area (~1 cm^2) to be able to produce accurate results. It also often needs to be in contact with the target. This is unacceptable especially for samples with high cultural value. Using the technique employed in this study, if a high-resolution image is captured, the estimation could be performed at micron level without touching the sample [10].

4 Conclusions

In this study, the influence of lighting condition on image stitching and spectral reflectance reconstruction was explored. Using multispectral images, spectral reflectance of a traditional Japanese painting was estimated by the pseudoinverse method. Results show that specular reflection, which is influenced by illumination, significantly affects the accuracy of the reconstruction. It was also observed that the spectral features of the filters used play an important role. According to the comparison of spectral reflectance curves, the estimation is more accurate between 420-580 nm especially for Region 2 because at least four filters were able to collect information within that range. On the other hand, it was shown that image stitching was greatly influenced by the light distribution on the target and its surface reflection characteristics. Stitching lines were highly visible when specular reflection is severe. It is also observed that the calibration technique was only effective within a 20-pixel standard deviation-threshold. Beyond this, more advanced calibration technique is necessary. In addition, pigment estimation using the reconstructed spectral reflectances was presented. It was shown that the method used for estimation produced relatively accurate results. The technique presented in this study could be a good alternative for the conventionally used techniques (e.g. spectrometers, XRF, XRD, etc.) in analyzing artworks because of its versatility, accuracy and simplicity.

Acknowledgements. This work has been done as part of the project "An Integrated System for Secure and Dynamic Display of Cultural Heritage" sponsored by Japan Science and Technology Agency, Regional Resources Development Program. This collaborative project was organized by Kyoto University Graduate School of Engineering, S-tennine Kyoto (Ltd) and Kyushu National Museum. The Authors would like to express their thanks to Imazu Setsuo of Kyushu National Museum and other staff of the museum and, Oshima of S-tennine Kyoto and his group for supporting this work. The authors are also grateful to Mr. Yuji Sakatoku and Ms. Julia Anders for their valuable contribution for the success of this project.

References

1. Elaksher, A.: Fusion of hyperspectral images and lidar-based dems for coastal mapping. Optics and Lasers in Engineering 46(7), 493–498 (2008)
2. Lane, G.R., Martin, C., Pirard, E.: Techniques and applications for predictive metallurgy and ore characterization using optical image analysis. Minerals Engineering 21(7), 568–577 (2008)
3. Biehl, L., Landgrebe, D.: MultiSpec—a tool for multispectral–hyperspectral image data analysis. Computers & Geosciences 28(10), 1153–1159 (2002)
4. Lee, H.-C.: Introduction to color imaging science. Cambridge University Press, Cambridge (2005)
5. MacAdam, D.: Selected Papers on Colorimetry- Fundamentals. Milestone Series, vol. 77. SPIE Optical Engineering Press, Bellingham (1993)
6. Conde, J., Haneisihi, H., Yamaguchi, M., Ohyama, N., Baez, J.: Spectral reflectance estimation of ancient Mexican codices, multispectral images approach. Revisita Mexhicana De Fisica 50(5), 484–489 (2004)
7. Balas, C., Papadakis, V., Papadakis, N., Papadakis, A., Vazgiouraki, E., Themelis, G.: A novel hyper-spectral imaging apparatus for the non-destructive analsyis of objects of artistic and historic values. Journal of Cultural Heritage 4, 330–337 (2003)
8. Marengo, E., Liparota, M.C., Robotti, E., Bobba, M.: Multivariate calibration applied to the field of cultural heritage: analysis of pigments on the surface of a painting. Analytica Chimica Acta 553, 111–122 (2005)
9. Shimano, N., Terai, K., Hironaga, M.: Recovery of spectral reflectance of objects being imaged by multispectral cameras. Journal of Optical Society of America A 24(10), 3211–3219 (2007)

10. Sakatoku, Y., Toque, J.A., Ide-Ektessabi, A.: Reconstruction of hyperspetral image from multispectral image based on regression analysis: optimum regression model and channel selection. In: Proceedings on the International Joint Conference on Computer Vision, Imaging and Computer Graphics Theory and Applications. Lisbon, Portugal (2009)
11. Anderson, J.A.: The diffuse reflectance of paints in the near-infrared. Journal of the Optical Society of America 37(10), 771–777 (1947)
12. Vargas, W., Amador, A., Niklasson, G.: Diffuse reflectance of TiO_2 pigmented paints: spectral dependence of the average pathlength parameter and forward scattering ratio. Optics Communication 261, 71–78 (2006)
13. Pajdla, T., Matas, J. (eds.): ECCV 2004. LNCS, vol. 3024, pp. 377–389. Springer, Heidelberg (2004)
14. Solina, F., Leonardis, A. (eds.): CAIP 1999. LNCS, vol. 1689, pp. 615–622. Springer, Heidelberg (1999)
15. Brown, M., Lowe, D.: Automatic panoramic image stitching using invariant features. International Journal of Computer Vision 74(1), 59–73 (2007)
16. Zomet, A., Levin, A., Peleg, Shmuel, Weiss, Y.: IEEE Transactions on Image Processing 15(4), 969–977 (2006)

Stereo Analysis of Archaelogical Scenes Using Monogenic Signal Representation

Manthos Alifragis and Costas S. Tzafestas

National Technical University of Athens
School of Electrical and Computer Engineering
Division of Signals, Control, and Robotics
Zographou Campus, 15773 Athens, Greece
manthos@central.ntua.gr, ktzaf@softlab.ntua.gr

Abstract. This paper presents the results of an experimental study regarding the application of recent stereo analysis theories in the frequency domain, particularly the phase congruency and monogenic filtering methods. The initial approach to the stereo matching problem employed feature based correlation methods. However, the requirement for more dense depth-map output led us to the development of disparity map estimation methods, minimizing a matching cost function between image regions or pixels. The cost function consists of a newly proposed similarity measure function, based on the geometrical properties of the monogenic signal. Our goal was to examine the performance of these methods in a stereo matching problem setting, on photos of complicated scenes. Two objects were used for this purpose: (i) a scene from an ancient Greek temple of Acropolis and (ii) the outside scene of the gate of an ancient theatre. Due to the complex structure of the photographed objects, classic techniques used for stereo matching give poor results. On the contrary, the three-dimensional models and disparity map of the scene computed when applying the proposed method, are much more detailed and consistent.

Keywords: Monogenic signal, Phase domain, Phase congruency, 3D reconstruction, Disparity map, Graph cuts.

1 Introduction

The problems of stereo matching and depth estimation have, in recent years, become the focus of considerable research in the field of computer vision. Reliable edge or feature detection techniques constitute the precursors of three dimensional structure or scene reconstruction methods. Throughout the years, there has been a significant progress in the development of image correspondence analysis and feature detection methods. As far as feature (edge or corner) detection is concerned, the traditional approach endorsed in most of the applications, is the one applying gradient-based methods, such as those developed by Canny [3], and Marr & Hildreth [18]. These methods have the drawbacks of sensitivity in image illumination, contrast, blurring and magnification. Another disadvantage when using these methods is the non-automatic determination of the appropriate thresholds for feature detection. More recently, Fleck [8] used an a-priori knowledge

A. Ranchordas et al. (Eds.): VISIGRAPP 2009, CCIS 68, pp. 133–145, 2010.

of the noise characteristics of the camera, in order to set feature detection thresholds. A remarkable study on the detection of image features invariant to image scale and rotation has been made by Lowe [17]. This specific approach has been named Scale Invariant Feature Transform (SIFT). This approach imposes a local image descriptor which is highly distinctive and invariant to image scale-space variations and changes in illuminations or 3D viewpoint. In the feature matching approach presented in this paper, we apply Fourier transformations of the images, and Gabor filtering, together with the phase congruency method proposed by Kovesi [16]. This method utilizes the local frequency spread and uses this information to weigh the phase congruency measure of the image. Concerning the image correspondence of the extracted features, we extend the approach proposed in [15], using monogenic filtering with a new correlation measure in the frequency domain. This approach is enriched by a normalized expression of the correlation measure, as well as by the additional information of line detection results and an approximately known camera motion. The combination of the above methods led us to the development and implementation of a filter in the frequency domain, which has been experimentally applied in a stereo matching problem.

An alternative approach is the disparity map computation. The term disparity describes the 2D vector between the positions of corresponding features of stereo pair images. It is inversely proportional to depth, at a specific position of the image plane. A major stage of the disparity map estimation is the detection of similar pixels or regions of the stereo pair. Classic methods assume only pixels brightness similarity. In this study, we propose the use of a new pixel similarity function, additionally enriched by the structural and geometrical properties of the monogenic signal, described in [19]. The stereo correspondence process is based on local matching methods. Such algorithms seek a smooth disparity function that minimize matching cost functions. Such functions, satisfy the requirements for image region similarity and smoothness. There exists a variety of different approaches in minimization procedure, e.g. simulated annealing [12][2], probabilistic diffusion [22] or graph cuts [25]. Regarding the work presented in this paper, the graph cut method was implemented in order to minimize the cost function that arose from the use of the proposed pixel similarity function.

The rest of the paper is organized as follows: Section 2.1 presents the computational methodology applied in the frequency domain for image processing and edge detection. Section 2.2 presents the new stereo-matching approach that is based on the application of monogenic filtering. Section 3 presents the proposed similarity function and briefly discusses global optimization issues. Finally, an evaluation of all the above mentioned methods in comparison with the traditional approaches as applied to the problem of stereo matching and depth estimation for 3D scene reconstruction and dense disparity maps computation, is presented in Section 4.

2   Phase Domain Methods

2.1   Feature Extraction Using Phase Congruency

The first stage in a stereo analysis problem is the extraction of useful information from the images. This stage consists of detecting edges or other geometrical structures of interest in the images. In the approach followed in this paper, we use complex Gabor functions (sine and cosine functions modulated over gaussian). In order to measure the amplitude and the phase, on a specific location of the signal, we can apply two linear phase filters in quadrature as Gabor complex filters, for a specific scale and frequency. The Gabor filter is composed of two main components, the complex sinusoidal carrier, and a gaussian envelope. Alternatively, log-Gabor filters can be applied as proposed by Field [7]. The log-Gabor filter has a gaussian transfer function and allows the construction of large bandwidth filters with odd symmetry and DC component equal to zero. The zero DC component cannot be kept in Gabor filters with bandwidth greater than one octave. The log Gabor function has a frequency response described by:

$$G(f) = e^{-[log(f/f_0)]^2/2[log(\sigma/f_0)]^2} \tag{1}$$

The frequency response of a log-Gabor filter is a Gaussian on a log frequency axis, where f_0 defines the center frequency of the sinusoid, representing the scaling factor of the filter, and σ is a scaling factor of the bandwidth. In order to maintain constant shape ratio filters, the ratio of σ/f_0 should be maintained constant. The equation for 2-D phase congruency in a two-dimensional signal analysis, like in images, can be obtained at each two-dimensional image location x, as follows:

$$PC_2 = \frac{\sum_o \sum_n W_o(x) \lfloor A_{no} \triangle \phi_{no}(x) - T \rfloor}{\sum_o \sum_n A_{no}(x) + \varepsilon} \tag{2}$$

where $\triangle \phi_{no}(x) = \cos(\varphi_{no}(x) - \overline{\varphi}(x)) - |\sin(\varphi_{no}(x) - \overline{\varphi}(x))|$, and o, n refer to the filter's orientation and scale, respectively. It must be also noted that when the amount between the symbols $\lfloor . \rfloor$ is non-positive, then the outcome becomes zero. The numerator of the above fraction represents the total energy of the 2D signal at a local point of the image. This amount of energy is an approximation of the local energy function defined for an analytical signal, according to Venkatesh and Owens [24]. The term $W_o(x)$ weighs the frequency spread. Kovesi made use of $W_o(x)$ as a component to cope with the lack of reliability of phase congruency measures in image areas with less frequency spread (e.g. smoothed images). The role of ε is to avoid division by zero. Finally, only the values which are above a threshold T (the expected influence of noise) are used to calculate the final result. The appropriate threshold T for the noise is set experimentally, according to the response of the smallest scale filter on each image.

It must be also noted here that the type of image feature detected, such as a line or a corner corresponding to maximum phase congruency value, needs to be classified accordingly. Towards this end, the phase congruency feature maps were calculated, according to [14].

2.2 Feature Matching on the Phase Domain

The image correspondence problem has been excessively studied as a fundamental problem of low-level computer vision. In order to track correspondent points through images, intensity correlation processes can be applied. However, the apparent complexity of the images used in our experiments, dictated the use of a different approach in order to address this issue. In the work presented in this paper, we employ an approach based on two-dimensional analytic signal theory and monogenic signal theory, inspired by the work of Sommer and Ferlsberg in [6].

The two dimensional analytic signal is based on a two dimensional generalization of Hilbert transformation, also known as Rietz transformation. The expression of the Rietz-transformed signal $F(\mathbf{u})$ in the frequency domain is:

$$F_R(\mathbf{u}) = i\frac{\mathbf{u}}{|\mathbf{u}|}F(\mathbf{u})$$

where $\mathbf{u}$ denotes the two dimensional frequency vector (u_1, u_2), and $|\mathbf{u}| = \sqrt{u_1^2 + u_2^2}$. The Fourier transformation of each image I_F needs to be computed at first. The next stage is the introduction of a log-Gabor filter (see Eq.(1)), which contributes to the construction of bandpass expressions of the signal $\mathbf{F}_R$ in the frequency domain:

$$\mathbf{H}_{R_s} = \mathbf{F}_R G(f) \tag{3}$$

where $\mathbf{H}_{R_s} = \left(H_{R_s}^1 \ H_{R_s}^2 \right)^{\mathrm{T}}$. The above image filters are applied in the frequency domain, and after the application of an inverse Fourier transformation, the real part of the consequent signals is obtained as follows:

$$I_{F_s} = Re\left[F^{-1}\left\{ I_F G(f) \right\} \right] \tag{4}$$

$$H_{F_s}^1 = Re\left[F^{-1}\left\{ I_F H_{R_s}^1 \right\} \right] \tag{5}$$

$$H_{F_s}^2 = Re\left[F^{-1}\left\{ I_F H_{R_s}^2 \right\} \right] \tag{6}$$

This leads to a generalized complex 2D analytic signal expression, which has as real part the signal I_{F_s} (4) and complex part the mathematical expression of its Rietz transformation, as described in Ferlsberg and Sommer [6]. Therefore, the complex part of the 2D analytic signal consists of two signals, the signal $H_{F_s}^1$ (5) and the signal $H_{F_s}^2$ (6). Consequently, at each point of the image (x, y), at a specific scale and orientation, we have a 3D vector $\mathbf{x}(x, y)$ consisting of the three above signals (4), (5) and (6). In addition, the measure of the amplitude of the energy is given by:

$$A = \sqrt{(H_{F_s}^1)^2 + (H_{F_s}^2)^2 + (I_{F_s})^2} \tag{7}$$

The geometrical information extraction from the monogenic signal follows. The orientation angle is given by the argument computation of the signal's complex part.

$$\theta = arctan(H_{F_s}^2, H_{F_s}^1) \tag{8}$$

The phase angle is proportional to an elevation angle between the monogenic signal's three-dimensional representation and the plane $H_{F_s}^1 - H_{F_s}^2$, which ranges from $-\frac{\pi}{2}$ to $\frac{\pi}{2}$.

$$\phi = arctan(I_{F_s}, \sqrt{(H_{F_s}^1)^2 + (H_{F_s}^2)^2}) \tag{9}$$

Given two locations (x_1, y_1) and (x_2, y_2) in the first and second image (Im_1 and Im_2) respectively, the correlation measure is then given by:

$$C_{12}(\mathbf{x}_1^{Im_1}, \mathbf{x}_2^{Im_2}) = \frac{\sum_{m=-k}^{+k} \sum_{n=-l}^{+l} \mathbf{x}_1^{Im_1}(x_1 + m, y_1 + n) \ \mathbf{x}_2^{Im_2}(x_2 + m, y_2 + n)}{\sum_{m=-k}^{+k} \sum_{n=-l}^{+l} A^{Im_1}(x_1 + m, y_1 + n) \ A^{Im_2}(x_2 + m, y_2 + n)} \quad (10)$$

where $\mathbf{x}_1^{Im_1}$ and $\mathbf{x}_1^{Im_2}$ are the three dimensional monogenic filter responses vectors of candidate points (x_1, y_1) and (x_2, y_2) for matching. The correlation measure, in Eq.(10) was computed by the dot product of above vectors with window $-l$ to l and $-k$ to k in the two-dimensional image plane. In addition, this measure was normalized by the sum of the amplitude responses, according to Eq.(7). The matching is considered successful for the pairs of points where the above correlation measure is maximized (i.e. $argmax|C_{12}(\mathbf{x}_1^{Im_1}, \mathbf{x}_2^{Im_2})|)$. Examining the performance of the above correlation measure in image areas beyond these where the phase conqruency is maximized, confirmed the poor matching results.

Modern applications such as image based rendering require depth estimation in all image regions even those textureless or occluded. Thus, the requirement for dense disparity estimation emerges as an inverse depth computation technique. The disparity map computation of stereo set images is based on energy models. Those models are based on energy function minimization methods for solving the correspondence problem. The energy function is equivalent to the sum of a pixel-wise matching cost. Such global stereo methods aggregate the sum of squared differences over appropriately formed feature vectors.

3   Dense Disparity Computation

3.1   Similarity Function

Disparity in stereo vision refers to the absolute difference in image location of a pair of correspondent pixels. The estimated disparity value is an inverse depth measure at the same position of the disparity map. The expansion of the feature based stereo matching methods to dense disparity map estimation was based on the frequency analysis of the stereo pair of images. We based our analysis on the fundamental property of the monogenic signal: the *identity splitting*, which is a signal decomposition in its energetic information (possibility of structure presence), in its orientation θ, and in its contrast transition expressed by the phase ϕ. The extracted features correspond to the local energy maximum of the image. The phase value ϕ represents the amount of the contrast transition needed to get an energy maximum. The concept of direction measure arises when this information is compromised with the orientation of an edge in a local area. Using Eq. (8) and Eq. (9) we compute the local values of phase p and direction d ($p = \phi$ if $d = \theta$ and $p = -\phi$ if $d = \theta + \pi$) [19]. The extracted geometrical, structural and intensity information form a new feature vector at each local area of the image plane: $\mathbf{e} = (d, p, \mathbf{c}, m))$. The elements $(\mathbf{c}, m)$ represent two basic parts of the local information. In this work, the vector of color information $\mathbf{c}$ is one-dimensional, due to the grayscale mode of the experimental images, while m represents the amplitude of the monogenic signal $f_M(\mathbf{x})$ on location $\mathbf{x}$ of the two dimensional signal (see Eq. (7)).

The energy function, in the case of a stereo matching problem, is proportional to the Euclidean distance of the correspondent feature vectors $\mathbf{e}^l, \mathbf{e}^r$. Therefore the similarity equation becomes:

$$\mathcal{D}(\mathbf{e}^l, \mathbf{e}^r) = (\triangle d)^2 + (\triangle p)^2 + (\triangle c)^2 + (\triangle m)^2 \tag{11}$$

where $\triangle d$ is the variation of the direction and $\triangle p$ is the phase variation, as have been defined in [19]. The quantity $\triangle c$ represents the intensity difference between the comparing pixels. Finally, $\triangle m$ represents the local amplitude variation of the monogenic signal. Moreover, an arithmetic smoothness is essential for the monogenic phase, amplitude and intensity, due to their different range of values. A normalization procedure has been applied with common mean and standard deviation, to obtain values ranging within $[0, 1]$. The traditional expression of the classic energy function, based exclusively on the intensity values of a local image neighborhood, is thus enriched to encompass structural and local geometric information contained in the image.

3.2 Optimization

The correspondence algorithm follows an energy function minimization formulation. The computed disparity function d minimizes the following global energy function [23]:

$$E(d) = E_{data}(d) + \lambda E_{smooth}(d) \tag{12}$$

The data term $E_{data}(d)$ represents the matching cost, which is computed by the similarity function of Eq. (11). Consequently, the new form of data energy is expressed by the sum of a quadratic cost:

$$E_{data}(d) = \sum_p D(\mathbf{e}^l, \mathbf{e}^r)(d) \tag{13}$$

Eq. (13) represents the sum of the matching cost over all correspondent pixels p with disparity values obtained by the function d. More specifically, the cost function D in (13) is the squared difference of the feature vectors $\mathbf{e}^l$ and $\mathbf{e}^r$, at left and right pixels of stereo image pair, respectively, as defined in Eq. (11). The minimization of D corresponds to a successful pixel matching. The minimization procedure followed to find the optimal disparity function d, was based on a graph cuts method introduced in [25].

The smoothness term E_{smooth} incorporates any assumptions made by the optimization algorithm, regarding the smoothness of the disparity function d. The measurements needed for the computation of the smoothness term are conducted in a neighborhood of the candidate matching pixels. The smoothness cost consists of the sum of the disparity value over a window around the examined pixel at (x, y):

$$E_{smooth}(d) = \sum_{x,y} f(d(x, y) - d(x + 1, y)) + f(d(x, y) - d(x, y + 1)) \tag{14}$$

The choice of an appropriate function f has been the focus of considerable research in recent years. Using a disparity function d that is smooth everywhere can lead to poor results regarding object boundaries. For this reason, energy functions have been

Fig. 1. Successive photos, in grayscale, of a temple in Acropolis and the gate of an ancient theatre, captured with a camera moving on a straight line

adopted that preserve the discontinuity in image areas [23]. Geman and Geman in [9] have proposed a Bayesian representation of energy functions based on Markov Random Fields (MRFs). An interesting special case of the energy equation (12) arises when E_{smooth} consists of the Potts model [21]. Geman et al. [4] were the pioneers of applying the Potts model in the field of computer vision. This model constitutes the simplest form of discontinuity preservation.

4   Implementation - Results

4.1   Feature Detection - Matching

The camera used for the experiments was a Nikon D70s 18-74mm. The camera was calibrated using the algorithm presented by Zhang in [26] with planar patterns. Regarding the camera model, it was assumed that there was no skew. The image rectification transformation used to place the epipolar lines in parallel, simplifying the matching problem, was based on the above assumptions concerning the camera intrinsic parameters, according to Hartley [10], Hartley and Zisserman [11], and Koch et al. [13]. The metric information of the scene was recovered using the camera calibration matrix by implementing Zhang's method [26]. Depth estimation for each matching pair of points was performed by point triangulation, and was further refined by minimizing the reprojection error using the Levenberg-Marquadt method [5].

Successive photographs of the side views of the two subjects (namely, a temple in Acropolis of Athens and the outside scene of an ancient theatre's gate) were used as experimental data, with the camera sliding on an almost straight line. A short displacement was used to avoid having large occluded areas. All the images were transformed in grayscale, and color information was not used for depth estimation. The photos captured and used for the experiments are shown in Fig.1.

The initial phase in a stereo matching process is feature detection for each image frame. The main approaches for feature detection that were experimentally evaluated and compared are presented in detail in [1]. The feature detection results for phase congruency approach are shown in Fig. 2. In [1], the accuracy of the those results has

Fig. 2. Edge detection results for the two photos. Application of phase congruency methods.

been confirmed as compared to traditional approaches of the problem [3], [17]. For the task of edge detection based on phase congruency concepts, log-Gabor functions were used, with Gaussian transfer functions on a logarithmic frequency scale. This filter was applied in six orientations and at four scales, with a constant one octave bandwidth, according to equations (2) and (1), and following the analysis presented in [7].

The next stage in depth estimation is the process of matching corresponding points of detected features between successive images, an ill-conditioned problem in low-level vision. The quality of the solution of the matching problem has a direct impact on the quality of the scene reconstruction. The feature based matching process was performed based on a comparison of the three following methods: (a) The first approach used Canny filtering for feature detection and a typical intensity-based correlation method for the matching process. (b) The second approach consisted of SIFT keypoint detections, based on image gradient amplitudes and orientation measurements, the construction of invariant keypoint descriptors for each image of the stereo pair and, finally, the matching process which was based on these descriptors' correspondence, through Euclidean distance measurements. (c) Finally, the third approach followed in this paper was based on the application of monogenic filters, as has been described in section 2.2.

The application of energy functions minimization was also evaluated, as an expansion step of the feature based matching. These functions have been formed by the monogenic signal representations of the stereo images. In the first phase of the evaluation process, typical experimental stereo data sets from the computer vision community were used. The quality evaluation of the estimated disparity maps was based on the percentage of the non-reliable disparity values, as compared to the already known values from ground truth maps. The reliable disparity values have specific disparity mean squared error tolerance (1-4 units). The results are presented in Table 1, for a set of representative stereo image pairs, obtained from the literature [20].

Table 1 is organised into four columns. The first column contains the names of the experimental stereo pair images. The second column consists of the different disparity range for each set. The third and fourth column show the % percentage of pixels with disparity values that exceed a predefined error threshold, as compared to their ideal values depicted on ground truth maps. Those pixels are considered as non-reliable pixels. The third column corresponds to an intensity-based similarity function, while the fourth column presents results obtained with the proposed similarity function. Taking into account the promising results of the proposed similarity function in the stereo matching problem, complex archaeological scenes were used to extract dense disparity maps. Two

Table 1. % percentage of pixels with non-acceptable disparity values, as compared to their ground truth values, for typical stereo image sets. First column: Name of stereo image set [20]. Second column: the range of estimated disparity values according to ground truth data. Third column: Percentage of non-reliable disparity values obtained by intensity-based similarity function. Fourth column: Percentage of non-reliable disparity values obtained by the proposed similarity function, based on monogenic signal properties.

experimental stereo set	disparity range (pixels)	%percentage bad pixels intensity-based similarity	%percentage bad pixels monogenic-based similarity
Tsukuba	16	1.33	1.19
Venus	20	11.57	10.49
Teddy	60	18.52	13.66
Sawtooth	16	14.45	8.65
Map	20	15.71	11.82
Aloe	60	8,94	8.12

approaches were applied comparatively, in order to estimate the quality of the obtained disparity maps: (a) the minimization of the energy function, by using as data energy function a typical one based on the similarity between the intensity values, and (b) the use of a data energy function enriched by the structural and geometric features of the monogenic signal.

4.2   3D Reconstruction Results

The first approach to the stereo matching problem, detects matching pairs of image points based on either the correlation of image intensity values, or the correlating values in the phase domain. The second approach expands the previous one to achieve a dense output of depth reconstruction. This was based on the minimization of the new proposed similarity function (described in Section 3).

Comparative results for the three different feature-based matching methods are presented in Figures 3(a) and 3(b). The first row of both these subfigures presents the results obtained when applying classic methods both for feature detection and point matching (that is, Canny edge detection and intensity-based correlation techniques). For the results depicted in the second row, the difference of Gaussian filter was applied for SIFT keypoint detection. The approach used for the matching process for image points was based on the construction of local image descriptors. Local image region descriptors assign the gradient magnitude and orientation to each keypoint according to [17]. The best candidate match was found by identifying that point on the other image of the stereo pair, with minimum Euclidean distance for the invariant keypoint descriptor vector. In the third row, the results are obtained by using both the phase congruency method for edge detection, and the monogenic filtering approach for point correlation.

The results presented in Fig. 3(a) and 3(b), are also organized into three columns. The first column of each subfigure shows the 3D scene reconstruction results, for the three methods mentioned above, while the second column depicts the same reconstructed scenes but rotated by a small angle (approximately 20 degrees, to better illustrate the estimated scene depth). Finally, the third column presents a coloured illustration of the

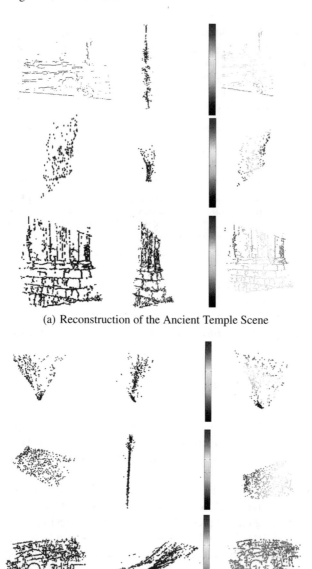

(a) Reconstruction of the Ancient Temple Scene

(b) Reconstruction of the Ancient Theatre Gate Scene

Fig. 3. Scene reconstruction results obtained from two experimental stereo pairs. The organization of the results in rows and columns is the same for both subfigures. First row: classic techniques applied using only the intensity values of each image. Second row: scene reconstruction results using gradient measurements for edge detection and SIFT keypoints matching for scene reconstruction. Third row: computations conducted solely in the phase domain. First Column: scene reconstruction results using different edge detection and matching methods. Second column: reconstruction results rotated by a small angle. Third column: colored illustration of the scene depth, with red being the color of the nearest and blue the color of the most distant points.

(a) Disparity map for the Temple scene, based on intensity similarity

(b) Disparity map for the Temple scene, using monogenic phase similarity

(c) Disparity map for the Theatre scene, based on intensity similarity

(d) Disparity map for the Theatre scene, using monogenic phase similarity

Fig. 4. Application of the new proposed energy function on experimental images of the two archaeological outdoor scenes. First column: disparity maps with the use of energy function based exclusively on intensity similarities. Second column: disparity maps computed with the use of graph cuts, both with local information retrieved by the monogenic filters.

scene depth, with red being the colour of the nearest points and blue the colour of the most distant ones (with linear colour to distance variation). By observing these experimental results, it can be seen that a more dense and accurate representation of the scene structure is obtained when all computations are conducted in the phase domain (third row in Fig. 3(a) and 3(b)). In addition, we observe that a better variance of the depth values is obtained when the matching process is implemented in the phase domain. This observation becomes more evident when the reconstructed scene is rotated, as shown in the second column of Figures 3(a) and 3(b). The classic methods give results that are evidently non-satisfactory in this case, regarding the structure and depth estimation of the scene.

The second approach presented in Section 3 has also been evaluated using the same experimental data of the complex images (archaeological scenes) shown in Fig.1. In the first stage of this experimental evaluation, the disparity map computation was based exclusively on the intensity values, in accordance to the classical approach of this problem. This process assumes brightness constancy for similar pixels. The consequent disparity maps, as presented in Fig. 4(a) and Fig. 4(c), include wide areas of unspecified depth. On the contrary, the disparity map restoration resulting from the implementation of the proposed similarity measure, with the consequent energy function, is more detailed, with a more reliable values variation. This proposed implementation establishes more structural elements, for example in temple pillars with less areas of noisy or unspecified disparity values, Fig.4(b) and Fig.4(d). The accuracy of the phase-domain methods for pixel-wise disparity estimation was also confirmed. The independence of these methods' performance from image contrast and image illumination variations in the outdoor scenes, like those examined in this study, is evident. It must be also noted that the repeatable geometry of the temple's columns and the uniform distribution of the intensity values in the image of the theatre's gate, result in very similar energy values, with the existence of nearby local minima as a direct consequence. This is a common problem in the depth restoration of similar images, which results in the loss of structural information and the existence of noisy image areas with unspecified disparity values.

5   Conclusions and Future Work

This paper presents an approach for dense depth estimation and scene reconstruction using phase domain methods, based on concepts that involve local representation of image features. Recent ideas of local energy models were implemented for each stage of the 3D reconstruction process, utilising mainly the tasks of feature detection and image correspondence. Additionally, global minimization techniques were applied in order to achieve a dense output of the disparity. For the task of detecting edges as image features, the phase congruency method was applied, as introduced by Kovesi [16], whereas for the image correspondence task, a new version of a correlation measure, based on monogenic filtering, was implemented. The task of dense disparity map estimation was based on the minimization of specific cost functions, expressed as a distance minimization process between appropriate feature vectors. These vectors combine both intensity values and structural and geometric information, extracted by the monogenic signal representation.

   In conclusion, the proposed approach leads to more reliable results, producing a more accurate metric information of the scene and a more dense structure regarding the outcome of the 3D scene reconstruction process. The good behaviour of such phase-domain models was confirmed, which seem to present a choice of preference for the task of image-based 3D reconstruction of complex sceneries, such as the archaeological site or an outside scene used in the experimental study of this work. Proposed future studies include extending the approach presented in this paper to a comparative study for dense disparity maps extraction from multiple camera views, integrated within probabilistic frameworks.

Acknowledgements. This work was supported by grant ΠENEΔ-2003-EΔ865 [co-financed by E.U.-European Social Fund (80%) and the Greek Ministry of Development-GSRT (20%)].

References

1. Alifragis, M., Tzafestas, C.S.: Stereo pair matching of archaeological scenes using phase domain methods. In: Proceedings VISIGRAPP 2009, Lisbon (2009)
2. Barnard, S.T.: Stochastic stereo matching over scale. International Journal of Computer Vision 3(1), 17–32 (1989)

3. Canny, F.: A computational approach to edge detection. IEEE Trans. Pattern Analysis and Machine Intelligence 8, 112–131 (1986)
4. Geman, D., Geman, S., Graffigne, C., Dong, P.: Boundary detection by constrained optimization. IEEE Transactions on Pattern Analysis and Machine Intelligence 12(7), 609–628 (1990)
5. Faugeras, O.: Three-dimensional computer vision: A geometric viewpoint (1993)
6. Felsberg, M., Sommer, G.: The monogenic signal. IEEE Transactions on Signal Processing 49(12) (December 2001)
7. Field, D.J.: Relations between the statistics of natural images and the response properties of cortical cells. Journal of The Optical Society of America A 4(12), 2379–2394 (1987)
8. Fleck, M.M.: Multiple widths yield reliable finite differences. IEEE Transactions on Pattern Analysis and Machine Intelligence 14(3), 337–345 (1992)
9. Geman, S., Geman, D.: Stochastic relaxation, gibbs distributions, and the bayesian restoration of images. IEEE Transactions on Pattern Analysis and Machine Intelligence 6, 721–741 (1984)
10. Hartley, R.: In defence of the eight-point algorithm. IEEE Transactions on Pattern Analysis and Machine Intelligence 19(6), 580–593 (1997)
11. Hartley, R., Zisserman, A.: Multiview Geometry in Computer Vision. Cambridge University Press, Cambridge (2000)
12. Marroquin, J., Mitter, S., Poggio, T.: Probabilistic solution of ill-posed problems in computational vision. Journal of the American Statistical Association 82(397), 76–89 (1987)
13. Koch, R., Pollefeys, M., Gool, L.V.: Automatic 3d model acquisition from uncalibrated image. In: Proceedings Computer Graphics International, Hannover, pp. 597–604 (1998)
14. Kovesi, P.D.: Matlab and octave functions for computer vision and image processing, http://www.csse.uwa.edu.au/~pk/research/matlabfns
15. Kovesi, P.D.: Image correlation from local frequency information. In: The Australian Pattern Recognition Society Conference: DICTA 1995, Brisbane, pp. 336–341 (1995)
16. Kovesi, P.D.: Image features from phase congruency. Videre: A Journal of Computer Vision Research (1999)
17. Lowe, D.: Distinctive image features from scale-invariant keypoints. International Journal of Computer Vision 60(2), 91–110 (2004)
18. Marr, D., Hildreth, E.C.: Theory of edge detection. Proceedings of the Royal Society, London B, 187–217 (1980)
19. Krüger, N., Felsberg, M., Gebken, C.: An explicit and compact coding of geometric and structural information applied to stereo processing. In: Vision, Modeling, and Visualization, Erlangen (2002)
20. Middlebury stereo website, http://www.middlebury.edu/stereo
21. Potts, R.: Some generalized order-disorder transformation. Proceedings of the Cambridge Philosophical Society 48, 106–109 (1952)
22. Scharstein, D., Szeliski, R.: Stereo matching with nonlinear diffusion. International Journal of Computer Vision 28(2), 155–174 (1998)
23. Terzopoulos, D.: Regularization of inverse visual problems involving discontinuities. IEEE Transactions on Pattern Analysis and Machine Intelligence 8(4), 413–424 (1986)
24. Venkatesh, S., Owens, R.: An energy feature detection scheme. In: International Conference on Image Processing, Singapore, pp. 553–557 (1989)
25. Boykov, Y., Veksler, O., Zabih, R.: Fast approximate energy minimization via graph cuts. IEEE Transactions on Pattern Analysis & Machine Intelligence 23(11), 1222–1239 (2001)
26. Zhang, Z.: A flexible new technique for camera calibration. In: International Conference on Computer Vision, Kerkyra, Greece (1999)

Imaging of the Vocal Tract Based on Magnetic Resonance Techniques

Sandra Ventura[1], Diamantino Freitas[2], and João Manuel R.S. Tavares[2]

[1] Área Científico-pedagógica da Radiologia, School of Allied Health Science – IPP
Rua Valente Perfeito 322, 4400-330 Vila Nova de Gaia, Portugal
[2] FEUP – Faculty of Engineering of University of Porto
Rua Dr. Roberto Frias, s/n 4200-465 Porto, Portugal
`smr@estsp.ipp.pt, {dfreitas,tavares}@fe.up.pt`

Abstract. Magnetic resonance (MR) imaging has been used to analyze and evaluate the vocal tract shape through different techniques and with promising results in several application fields. Our main purpose is to demonstrate the relevance of MR and techniques of image processing in the analysis of vocal tract. The extraction of contours of the air cavities from 2D images (slices) allowed the built of several 3D reconstruction image stacks by the combination of orthogonally oriented sets of slices for each articulatory gesture, as a new approach to solve the expected spatial under sampling of the imaging process. In result, these computational models provide valuable information for the enhanced visualization of morphologic and anatomical aspects and are useful for partial measurements of the vocal tract shape in different situations. Potential use of this information can be found in Medical and therapeutic applications as well as in acoustic articulatory speech modeling.

Keywords: Image processing and analysis, Contours extraction, 3D modeling, Speech production, Portuguese language.

1 Introduction

Magnetic Resonance (MR) improvements, accomplished in the past decades, allow the imaging of the vocal tract with suitable quality, making it one of the most powerful and promising tools in several research domains, in particularly, in speech production analysis.

Speech is the most important apparatus in human communication and interaction. Nevertheless, the knowledge about its production is far from being completed or even sufficient to describe the most relevant acoustic phenomena that are conditioned at morphological and dynamic levels. The anatomic and physiologic aspects of the vocal tract are claimed to be essential for a better understanding of this essential process. The quality and resolution of the soft-tissues and the use of non-ionizing radiation are some of the most important advantages of MR imaging for that understanding [1, 2].

Up to now, several approaches have been considered for the analysis of the vocal tract based on MR images. Since the first study proposed by [3], many MR techniques

A. Ranchordas et al. (Eds.): VISIGRAPP 2009, CCIS 68, pp. 146–157, 2010.

have been used (from static to dynamic studies, and more recently even in real-time studies), starting by studies on vowel production [4, 5], followed on consonant production [6, 7], for different languages, such as French [8, 9], German [10, 11] and Japanese [12, 13].

The work presented in this paper, consisting basically in the static analysis of the vocal tract shape during sustained vowels and consonants and in the dynamic description of some syllables, is the first to consider the application of MR imaging for the characterization of European Portuguese (EP) language. This study started in 2004, having attained initial series of results, been some of them published in 2006 [14] and in 2009 [15]. Our approach can be seen as a contribution to the wide area of articultory speech modeling since, it provides geometrical data to the acoustic modeling phase or research.

MR imaging is a reference technique allowing the simultaneous study of the whole vocal tract extension and the airway area and volume can be directly estimated. Even so, the currently available information to understand speech production can be considered as insufficient or even nonexisting, particularly for EP sounds [16].

In the articulatory speech research on EP language, a few studies of nasal vowels have been carried through at the acoustic production and perceptual levels based on acoustic analysis and electromagnetic articulography [17-19]. More recently, another MR study on EP language presents some results relative to oral and nasal vowels exploring the extraction of contours from 2D images, articulatory measures and area functions [20].

In former works, vocal tract modeling has been limited to the midsagittal plane [13, 21], but the improvements undergone by the MR imaging equipments allowed the growth of research and made possible the accomplishment of three-dimensional (3D) models [22]. The more realistic models of the vocal tract shape that are possible to obtain currently, are hugely demanded in further research towards the development of improved speech synthesis algorithms and the definition of more efficient speech rehabilitation processes. Recently, [23] provides the first application of "accelerated" MR acquisition, performed on a 3.0 Tesla scanner, to obtain valuable 3D vocal tract information during sustained production of some English language sounds.

The main purpose of this paper is to present 3D models of the vocal tract built from the MR data of some relevant sustained articulations of EP language in a static study. From the point of view of image processing an analysis, a new approach for 3D modeling by the combination of orthogonal stacks, to describe the vocal tract shape in different articulatory positions is presented. We also demonstrate a MR technique to acquire useful image sequences during speech production (dynamic analysis). In addition, some preliminary results of the dynamic analysis done are presented.

The remaining of this paper is organized as follows: Next section is dedicated to the methods considered and describes the equipment, corpus and subjects, as well as the procedures used for the speech study done, namely for morphologic and dynamic imaging of the vocal tract. The experimental results are included in the following section, through presenting some of the three-dimensional models built of the vocal tract and an image sequence acquired during speech production. Finally, the main conclusions of the work described are addressed.

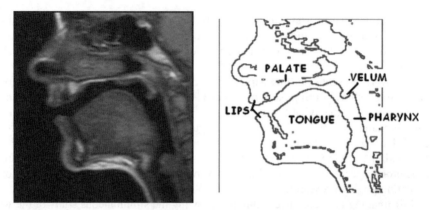

Fig. 1. A sagittal MR image of vocal tract. It should be noted that the signal intensity of the teeth is equal to signal intensity of the air presented in the cavities formed by the vocal tract organs (represented in black). Thus, during speech production, these articulators cannot be distinguished from the air cavities.

1.1 MR Imaging of the Vocal Tract

The anatomic and physiological characteristics of the human vocal tract represent an important challenge for imaging techniques; mainly, due to its non-regular shape and considerable length, and the number of moving articulators involved in speech production. Thus, it is crucial the use of faster and accurate techniques and multiplanar imaging to achieve useful data.

Magnetic resonance is a very complete medical imaging technique for this purpose that has commonly been successfully used in speech research. Despite the several advantages of MR, the speech research has some particularly constrains related with the performance of this imaging technique, specifically the limited temporal resolution and MR acoustic noise.

Vocal tract organs include the lips, the teeth, the tongue, the palate and pharynx. These soft tissues and air cavities are clearly visualized by MR imaging, except the teeth because of their lack of hydrogen protons, Figure 1.

In medical practice, magnetic resonance imaging is applied for several diagnoses, especially for tumor assessment, and considering almost organs. However, for the study of the vocal tract, no specific-protocol is followed, and it varies according to the main purpose of desired analysis.

2 Methods

This study was performed in two main phases: 1) exploration of MR techniques applied to the vocal tract imaging; 2) the use of image processing and analysis techniques that can aid the study of vocal tract.

2.1 Equipment, Corpus and Subjects

A MR Siemens Magneton Symphony 1.5 Tesla system and a head array coil were used, with subjects in supine position. The image data were acquired from two subjects (one male and one female) for the static study, and from four subjects for the dynamic study, all subjects without any speech disorder.

The corpus of the static study consisted in twenty five sounds of the EP language: oral and nasal vowels, and consonants. For the dynamic study, the subjects produced several repetitions of sequences of three consonant-vowel syllables (/tu/, /ma/, /pa/) during the acquisition.

Due to the MR acoustic noise produced during the imaging acquisition process, the acoustic recording of the produced speech was not yet possible.

2.2 Techniques

According to the safety procedures for MR, subjects were previously informed about the exam involved and instructed about the procedures to be followed during the acquisition processes. A consent informed was obtained from each subject involved.

Furthermore, the training of the subjects was performed to ensure the proper production of the intended sounds for the static study, and to achieve good speech-acquisition synchronization for the dynamic one.

2.2.1 Static Study

A set of MR WT1-images using Turbo Spin-Echo (TSE) sequences was acquired in sagittal and coronal orientations. The subjects sustained the articulation during 9 seconds for the acquisition of three sagittal slices and 9.9 seconds for the four coronal slices. The acquisition time was a compromise between image resolution and the duration of the sustained articulation allowed by the subject.

Initially, a single midsagittal T1-weighted image was acquired with subjects instructed to rest with mouth close and the tongue in full contact with the teeth. This reference image was used for teeth space identification and contour extraction, Figure 2.

The used imaging acquisition protocol includes the parameters shown in Table 1.

Table 1. MR protocol followed for vocal tract imaging

Image acquisition parameters	
Sagittal slices	Coronal slices
Repetition time (TR) = 443 ms	TR = 470 ms
Echo time (TE) = 17 ms	TE = 15 ms
Echo Train Length (ETL) = 7	ETL = 7
Signal to Noise Ratio (SNR) = 1	SNR = 1.03
5 mm thickness	6 mm thickness and 10 mm gap
3 slice images	4 slice images
Matrix size 128 x 128 pixels	
Resolution = 0.853 px/mm	
Field of View (FOV) = 150 mm	

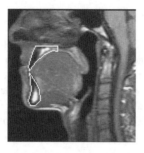

Fig. 2. Midsagittal reference image for teeth identification and contours extraction

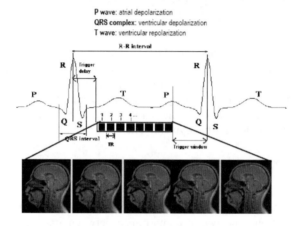

Fig. 3. Diagram of the dynamic MR acquisition performed based on ECG monitoring and synchronization

2.2.2 Dynamic Study

The dynamic study was performed following the same principle of MR cardiac analysis, with the modification of a FLASH-2D sequence using the subjects' heart beat as a trigger signal, a 300 mm Field of View (FOV) and the acquisition parameters: Repetition time (TR) = 60 ms and Echo time (TE) = 4.4 ms. The subjects tried to synchronize the utterance of the syllables to their own cardiac rhythm by the acoustic monitoring of their own simple electrocardiogram (ECG) through a synchronous sound emission conveyed to them by an earphone device.

Each set of images from a single-slice (midsagittal) of 6 mm thickness was collected during 12 to 22 seconds. For each sequence, a variable number of images (4-6 images) were acquired with a regularly increasing shift in synchrony from the start of the cardiac cycle, Figure 3.

The RR interval is the time duration between two consecutive R waves (in ECG graph), and it is usually the reference interval for programming the slice acquisitions. It should be noted that depicted the images were acquired in a single cardiac cycle for the sake of representation, this is an under-sampling method, assuming that the phenomenon is stationary, which is quite good in cardiac analysis but not so in repeated speech production. In fact, the images were collected distributed along the time with a period as short as possible, but always longer than a cardiac cycle due to imaging system limitations.

2.2.3 Image Processing and Analysis

Few segmentation methods have been described in speech studies to extract contours of the vocal tract from MR images. Briefly, those methods are based on manual definition and edition of curves, such as Bezier curves, and threshold based binarizations [24-26]. In the study proposed in [27], the authors compared different approaches on the same data in order to assess the accuracy of some manual segmentation methods, and concluded that the considered methods accomplish comparable results and that the threshold based binarization method is the one that presents minor dispersion.

Here, image processing and analysis and 3D reconstruction of models were accomplished in two main stages:

- Image segmentation using the *Segmenting Assistant*, a 3D editing plug-in of *Image J* (Image Processing and Analysis in Java), the image processing software developed by the National Institute of Health (USA), and subsequent 3D reconstruction;
- Graphic representation and combination of orthogonal stacks using the *Blender* software (Blender Foundation, The Netherlands) for 3D graphics creation.

The histogram-derived threshold technique was chosen for the segmentation of the airway of its surrounding tissues. The extraction of the contours of the vocal tract was then performed by following this sequence of procedures:

a) Identification and closure of the vocal tract area of interest, mandatory closure of the mouth, larynx, vertebral column and velum, through the manual superimposition of opaque objects;
b) Manual overlapping of teeth image (only done on the sagittal stacks), after extraction of the teeth contours from the initially acquired sagittal anatomic reference image;
c) Extraction of the contours of the vocal tract, for each image of 2D slices using the *Image J* semi-automatic threshold technique.

Figure 4 depicts the image segmentation procedure used in sagittal and coronal slices during a sustained nasal vowel. The closure of the vocal tract area was necessary to avoid the leakage of the contours and complicate the segmentation task.

The contour extraction process resulted in a total of 175 2D contours (maximally 7 contours for each sound).

Outlines were subsequently used to generate a 3D surface, after importing the contours in *.shapes* format, into the *Blender* software.

For each articulatory position, the next phase was the combination of sagittal and coronal outlines (2D curves). To make this possible, it was required that the outline curves be well aligned – this process is usually known as image registration. In Computational Vision, the term image registration means the process of transforming the different sets of images into one common coordinate system. Thus, this transformation was here necessary in order to be able the integration and comparison of data obtained from distinct measurement systems.

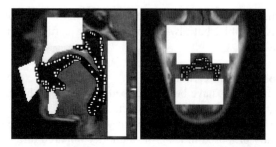

Fig. 4. Contours extraction from sagittal (right) and coronal (left) slices after closure of the vocal tract area and manual overlapping of the teeth

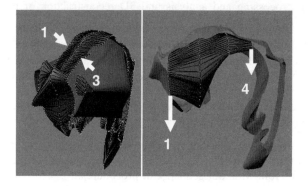

Fig. 5. Surfaces representations for the 3D model of the vowel [u] (two views)

3   Results and Discussion

The static study was designed to obtain the morphologic data of most of the range of the articulators' positions aiming the imaging characterization of Portuguese sounds. A variable number of images was obtained by dynamic MR, according to the cardiac cycle of each subject, followed by the assembly of all images for sequence visualization.

3.1.1 3D Models
The images of Figure 5 represent two different views of the 3D model built for the vowel [u]. In the same images, the blue surface represents the union of the three outlines extracted from the sagittal stack. Additionally, the red surface represents the union of the four outlines extracted from the coronal stack.

Figure 6 depicts two 3D models built of vowels corresponding to an oral sound (top) and to a nasal sound (bottom). The images shown permit the identification of the velum lowering, and especially the verification of partial closure of the oral cavity comparatively to the oral sound. In the EP language, there is a special interest on nasal sounds due to their frequent use in common speech.

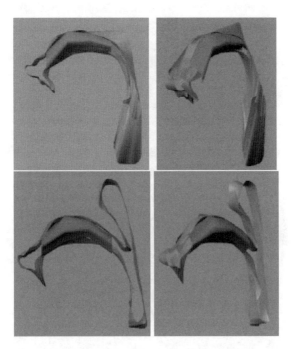

Fig. 6. Three-dimensional models built for the oral (top) and nasal (bottom) vowel [a] of the EP language (two views for each case)

In the 3D models built, some differences in the vertical lengths between sagittal and coronal stacks were observed for some sounds resulting in some registration errors. This could reflect the specific variability of the speaker in sound production, due in this case, to the fact that acquisitions of different orientations were separately accomplished (first sagittal images, and subsequently coronal images), to minimize the subjects' effort needed for an extra long utterance. Moreover, the segmentation process used had also some implications on the determination of the vocal tract area contour.

Furthermore, the coronal data is important for 3D modelling of the vocal tract, because some articulatory situations lead to occlusions in the midsagittal plane, while lateral channels are maintained open (e.g. lateral consonants, nasals vowels). The models shown in Figure 7 intend to demonstrate the relevance of coronal stacks for the characterization of lateral consonants of the EP language.

Although the 3D models built are not completely closed, it can be observed several essential features needed for the articulatory description of speech production.

3.1.2 Image Sequence during Speech

A variable number of images (sagittal slices) were obtained from dynamic studies, according to the cardiac cycle (heart frequency) of each subject, followed by the assembly of all images to visualize the image sequences. The best image features were obtained for the syllable /tu/, as illustrate in Figure 8, because, when compared with the other syllables, the articulatory positions are very different between single sounds.

When considering the differences verified by image comparison among the subjects analyzed, the dynamic studies demonstrated the actual variability in the

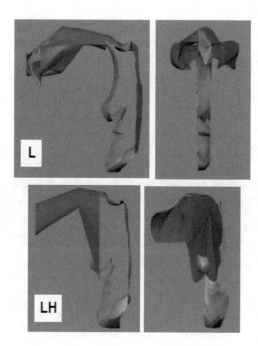

Fig. 7. Three-dimensional models built of the laterals consonants [l] and [lh] of EP language (two views)

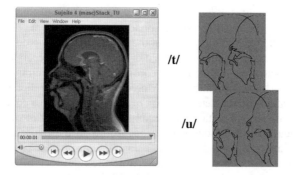

Fig. 8. Contours extracted (on the right) from midsagittal images obtained from a dynamic study by the repetition of the sequence /tu/ (on the left)

production of sounds between subjects, not only due to anatomical differences, but also because each subject uses different strategies in motion control and articulation.

4 Conclusions and Future Work

In our study, a considerable number and diversity of images were acquired aiming at not only morphological but also a dynamic characterization, by exploring various MR techniques. Thus, it was tried to acquire a number of images with enough anatomical resolution, maximum vocal tract extension of representative speech gestures, minimizing speaker effort (reducing hyperarticulation). The image data was analyzed and processed resulting in the reconstruction of 3D models for the entire corpus (3D geometrical database).

For most 3D models built for European Portuguese language sounds, the morphologic data showed that both orientation slices (sagittal and coronal) are useful for the knowledge of the vocal tract shape during speech production. Articulators positions are better demonstrated in sagittal images, and the coronal images allow the observation of the lateral dimension of oral cavity.

The completion of the construction of the surfaces for the hybrid models made from sagittal and coronal stacks is the next step in the way to obtain a complete 3D anatomical model of the vocal tract, prepared for the subsequent prediction of the acoustic output.

The extension of the dynamic sequences obtained to other sequences is also important in terms of coverage of the study, and will be done soon.

Other problems verified related with the image registration step and with the acoustic recording of speech during the image acquisition process are being investigated until now, aiming to solve them in a near future.

The new imaging progresses in MR acquisitions and the wider application of 3.0 Tesla scanners are promising advances expected for enhanced vocal tract imaging and analysis. Therefore, the study of the vocal track from those image sequences is expected to be addressed in the near future using the approach here presented.

Acknowledgements. The images considered were acquired at the Radiology Department of Hospital S. João, Porto, with the collaboration of Isabel Ramos (Professor at Faculdade de Medicina da Universidade do Porto and Department Director) and the technical staff, which are gratefully acknowledged.

References

1. Avila-García, M.S., Carter, J.N., Damper, R.I.: Extracting Tongue Shape Dynamics from Magnetic Resonance Image Sequences. In: Transactions on Engineering, Computing and Technology V2, December 2004, pp. 288–291 (2004)
2. Engwall, O.: A revisit to the Application of MRI to the Analysis of Speech Production - Testing our assumptions. In: 6th Int. Seminar on Speech Production, Sydney, pp. 43-48 (2003)
3. Baer, T., Gore, J.C., Gracco, L.C., Nye, P.W.: Analysis of Vocal Tract Shape and Dimensions using Magnetic Resonance Imaging: Vowels. J. Acoust. Soc. Am. 90, 799–828 (1991)
4. Badin, P., Bailly, G., Raybaudi, M., Segebarth, C.: A three-dimensional linear articulatory model based on MRI data. In: 3rd ESCA / COCOSDA Int. Workshop on Speech Synthesis, Australia, pp. 249–254 (1998)
5. Demolin, D., Metens, T., Soquet, A.: Real time MRI and articulatory coordinations in vowels. In: 5th Speech Production Seminar, Germany, pp. 86-93 (2000)

6. Engwall, O.: Are static MRI representative of dynamic speech? Results from a comparative study using MRI, EPG and EMA. In: 6th Int. Conf. on Spoken Language Processing (ICSLP), China, pp. 17–20 (2000)
7. Narayanan, S., Nayak, K., Lee, S., Sethy, A., Byrd, D.: An Approach to Real-time Magnetic Resonance Imaging for Speech Production. Journal Acoustical Society of America 115(4), 1771–1776 (2004)
8. Demolin, D., Metens, T., Soquet, A.: Three-dimensional Measurement of the Vocal Tract by MRI. In: 4th Int. Conf. on Spoken Language Processing (ICSLP 1996), USA, pp. 272–275 (1996)
9. Serrurier, A., Badin, P.: A Three-dimensional Linear Articulatory Model of Velum based on MRI data. In: Interspeech 2005: Eurospeech, 9th Europ. Conf. on Speech Communication and Technology, Portugal, pp. 2161–2164 (2005)
10. Behrends, J., Wismuller, A.: A Segmentation and Analysis Method for MRI data of the Human Vocal Tract, FIPKM-37, pp. 179–189 (2001)
11. Mády, K., Sader, R., Zimmermann, A., Hoole, P., Beer, A., Zeilhofe, H., Hannig, C.: Use of real-time MRI in assessment of consonant articulation before and after tongue surgery and tongue reconstruction. In: 4th Int. Speech Motor Conf., Netherlands, pp. 142–145 (2001)
12. Kitamura, T., Takemoto, H., Honda, K., Shimada, Y., Fujimoto, I., Syakudo, Y., Masaki, S., Kuroda, K., Oku-uchi, N., Senda, M.: Difference in vocal tract shape between upright and supine postures: Observations by an open-type MRI scanner. Acoustical Science and Technology 26(5), 465–468 (2005)
13. Takemoto, H., Honda, K.: Measurement of Temporal Changes in Vocal Tract Area Function during a continuous vowel sequence using a 3D Cine-MRI Technique. In: 6th Int. Seminar on Speech Production, Australia, pp. 284–289 (2003)
14. Rua, S.M., Freitas, D.R.: Morphological Dynamic Imaging of Human Vocal Tract. In: Computational Modelling of Objects Represented in Images: Fundamentals, Methods and Applications (CompIMAGE), Portugal, pp. 381–386 (2006)
15. Ventura, S.R., Freitas, D.R., Tavares, J.M.: Magnetic Resonance Imaging of the Vocal Tract: Techniques and Applications. In: International Conference on Imaging Theory and Applications (IMAGAPP 2009), Portugal, pp. 105–110 (2009)
16. Ventura, S.R., Freitas, D.R., Tavares, J.M.: Application of MRI and biomedical engineering in speech production study. Computer Methods in Biomechanics and Biomedical Engineering 12(6), 671–681 (2009)
17. Teixeira, A., Vaz, F.: European Portuguese Nasal Vowels: An EMMA Study. In: Eurospeech 2001, Aveiro, Portugal, pp. 1483–1486 (2001)
18. Teixeira, A., et al.: SAPWindows – Towards a Versatile Modular Articulatory Synthesizer. In: Proceedings of 2002 IEEE Workshop on Speech Synthesis, Portugal, pp. 31–34 (2002)
19. Teixeira, A., Moutinho, L.C., Coimbra, R.L.: Production, Acoustic and Perceptual Studies on European Portuguese Vowels Height. In: 15th Int. Congress of Phonetic Sciences, Spain, pp. 3033–3036 (2003)
20. Martins, P., Carbone, I.C., Pinto, A., Silva, A., Teixeira, A.J.: European Portuguese MRI based speech production studies. Speech Communication 50, 925–952 (2008)
21. Engwall, O.: A 3D Tongue Model based on MRI data. In: 6th Int. Conf. on Spoken Language Processing (ICSLP), China, pp. 901–904 (2000)
22. Badin, P., Serrurier, A.: Three-dimensional Modeling of Speech Organs: Articulatory Data and Models. In: IEICE Technical Committee on Speech, Japan, pp. 29–34 (2006)

23. Kim, Y.-C., Narayanan, S., Nayak, K.: Accelerated 3D MRI of vocal tract shaping using compressed sensing and parallel imaging. In: ICASSP 2009 IEEE International Conference on Acoustics, Speech and Signal Processing, Taiwan, pp. 389–392 (2009)
24. Badin, P., Borel, P., Bailly, G., Revéret, L., Baciu, M., Segebarth, C.: Towards an audio-visual virtual talking head: 3D articulatory modeling of tongue, lips and face based on MRI and video images. In: 5th Speech Production Seminar, Germany, pp. 261–264 (2000)
25. Engwall, O.: From real-time MRI to 3D tongue movements. In: ICSLP 2004, Korea, October 2004, vol. II, pp. 1109–1112 (2004)
26. Soquet, A., Lecuit, V., Metens, T., Demolin, D.: Mid-sagittal cut to area function transformations: Direct measurements of mid-sagittal distance and area with MRI. Speech Communication 36, 169–180 (2002)
27. Soquet, A., Lecuit, V., Metens, T., Nazarian, B., Demolin, D.: Segmentation of the Airway from the Surrounding Tissues on Magnetic Resonance Images: A comparative study. In: ICSLP, Sydney, pp. 3083–3086 (1998)

SRAD, Optical Flow and Primitive Prior Based Active Contours for Echocardiography

Ali K. Hamou and Mahmoud R. El-Sakka

Computer Science Department, The University of Western Ontario
London, Ontario, N6A 5B7, Canada
{ahamou,elsakka}@csd.uwo.ca

Abstract. Accurate delineation of object borders is highly desirable in echocardiography, especially the left ventricle. Among other model-based techniques, active contours (or snakes) provide a unique and powerful approach to image analysis. In this work, we propose the use of a novel external energy for a gradient vector flow (GVF) snake. This energy consists of optical flow estimates of heart sequences along with the use of a speckle reducing anisotropic diffusion (SRAD) operator. This energy provides more information to the active contour model garnering adequate results for noisy moving sequences. Furthermore, an automatic primitive shape prior algorithm was employed to further improve the results and regularity of the snake, when dealing with especially speckle laden echocardiographic images. Results were compared with expert-defined segmentations yielding better sensitivity, precision rate and overlap ratio than the standard GVF model.

Keywords: Image segmentation, active contours, gradient vector flow, optical flow, shape priors, curve fitting, echocardiography, speckle reducing anisotropic diffusion, instantaneous coefficient of variation.

1 Introduction

The assessment of cardiac function has been a major area of interest in the medical field. Normal heart function consists of pumping chambers (known as ventricles) which regulate the systemic and pulmonary circulation systems by delivering blood to the proper areas. Detection of non-normal heart function in the *left ventricle* (LV), for instance, can cause systolic dysfunction, being the reduction in the ability to contract, or diastolic dysfunction, being the inability to fill efficiently. Various heart structures may also fail causing cardiomyopathies, endangering the life of the host individual. Fortunately, many myopathies are treatable (with medication, implanted pacemakers, defibrillators, or ventricular assist devices) given early detection. Echocardiography, imaging the heart using ultrasound waves, facilitates the ability to do so.

The advent of real time ultrasonography provides the ability to image an entire LV and surrounding anatomy within one cardiac cycle (approximately one second). However, depending on the patient's 'photogenicity' (impacting factors include surrounding fatty tissues, calcifications, gender), these images are most likely marred by speckle artifacts. Many computer vision techniques attempt to reduce such speckle

A. Ranchordas et al. (Eds.): VISIGRAPP 2009, CCIS 68, pp. 158–171, 2010.
© Springer-Verlag Berlin Heidelberg 2010

noise by means of filtering [16] or incorporating the speckle effect directly into their algorithms [22]. Normally, these ultrasound images are analyzed for area and volume assessment by trapezoidal estimation. Such techniques introduce a large user bias into the calculations and are quite time consuming on the clinicians behalf. The advent of boundary detection techniques can help to automate this task. Boundary detection techniques are employed in order to segment the wanted regions for analyses on the heart structures, such as endocardial borders [4], stress and strain of the septum wall [17], and wall motility [1] to name a few.

Kass el al. [12] first proposed the original active contour model (commonly known as a snake or a deformable model). In their formulation, image segmentation was posed as an energy minimization problem.

Active contours treat the surface of an object as an elastic sheet that stretches and deforms when external and internal forces are applied to it. These models are physically-based, since their behaviour is designed to mimic the physical laws that govern real-world objects [5]. Since this approach relied on variational calculus to find a solution, time complexity was one of the main drawbacks of this original model. *Amini et al.* [2] proposed an algorithm for using dynamic programming, in order to incorporate soft and hard constraints into the formulation, improving time complexity and results. Further improvements to time complexity were proposed by *Williams et al.* [23], by using a greedy algorithm while incorporating a simple curvature approximation. Issues with large capture ranges and concavities are solved by other advances, which include inflation forces [6], probabilistic models [15], oriented particles [21], and gradient vector flows [24]. For the purposes of this study, focus will be placed on those advances best suited for echocardiographic images.

Since the LV represents one of the most important heart functions, many semi-automatic techniques attempt to segment this region from surrounding tissues [4][7][18]. Yet, no universally accepted standard exists for segmenting echocardiographic images.

Papademetris et al. [18] took advantage of a b-splines parameterized deformable model for segmenting cardiac regions. The external energy consisted of the standard intensity term and a texture-based *markov random field* (MRF) term. The MRF is based on a combination of gradient, regional and curvature data computed from the original image. Initial contours are manually placed for each 2D plane and are passed to a shape tracking algorithm. Displacements are probabilistically computed using a confidence measurement for the entire set. Final displacements are fed into an anisotropic linear elastic model which is computed vis-à-vis a Bayesian estimation framework. The manual placement of the contours makes this technique quite labour intensive.

Felix-Gonzalez et al. [7] proposed a segmentation technique for echocardiographic images using an *active surface model* (ASM). The ASM is made up of cubic splines and is based on a gradient descent procedure. When using gradient descent, the empirical setting of parameters is required based on the quality and types of images used. This makes this proposed technique extremely sensitive to its input. Furthermore, *Felix-Gonzalez et al.*'s work was only tested on two limited datasets.

Leung et al. [13] proposed the use of an *active appearance model* (AAM) and intensity based registration for segmenting multiple 2D image slices. An AAM uses all the information in an image region covered by the target object, rather than just that near modeled edges. An AAM involves the principal component analysis of the various shapes and textures from several manually segmented 2D slices for training. The AAM makes use of the training set to converge the initial set mesh to the best textures on the image. However, this trained set required several manual segmentations of the 2D image slices to tune it to the medium being used.

The *gradient vector flow* (GVF) [24] snake was introduced as a modification to the original snake model in order to overcome the capture range and curve concavity issues. However, using the GVF snake directly on echocardiograms will not provide an adequate solution due to the complication of speckle noise and the existence of valves within the heart cavity, inhibiting a proper segmentation.

Zhou et al. [27] proposed the segmentation of MRI cardiac sequences using a generalized *fuzzy gradient vector flow* (FGVF) map along with a relative optical flow field. Optical flow measurements are computed on the cardiac sequence being considered and a *maximum a posteriori probability* (MAP) was used as a window for the movement of the curve. The use of optical flow with GVF provides promising results, however this technique is used exclusively on clear MRI data, and hence the presence of speckle noise on echocardiographic images would require modifications of this technique. Both GVF and optical flow measurements will be used in the proposed technique.

The proposed segmentation algorithm differs from previous works mainly in that it combines the benefits of multiple data sources within echocardiographic video cines. This includes the collection of motion data (helping to solve the static noise problem), localized detail data (helping to solve the inherent speckle noise problem), and structural data (helping to solve the occluded borders problem), which are represented by the optical flow module, the *speckle reducing anisotropic diffusion* (SRAD) edge map and the primitive priori knowledge module respectively.

The rest of this paper is organized as follows. In Section 2, the proposed scheme will be introduced. Results and discussion will be presented in Section 3, and Section 4 will contain conclusions.

2   System and Methods

In this study, we utilize and improve our previous preliminary works [8][9][10]. The proposed scheme will contain a fusion of knowledge about the image in order to improve the automation and inter-variable efficiency of left ventricular segmentation methods. The system will incorporate three distinct elements into the external energy of the active contour. These elements are SRAD measurements, optical flow estimates and priori knowledge measurements on contour points.

2.1   Parametric Active Contour Review

A snake is an energy minimization problem. Its energy is represented by two forces (internal energy, E_{in}, and external energy, E_{ex}) which work against each other. The total energy should converge to a local minimum – in the perfect case – at the desired boundary. The snake is defined as $v(s) = [x(s), y(s)]^T$, where s belongs to the interval [0,1]. Hence, the total energy to be minimized, E_{AC}, to give the best fit between a snake and a desired object shape is:

$$E_{AC} = \int_0^1 E_{in}(v(s)) + E_{ex}(v(s)) \, ds \qquad (1)$$

The internal energy decreases as the curve becomes smooth (by incorporating both elasticity and stiffness); whereas the external energy decreases as approaching the features of interest, such as image structures or edges.

The internal energy of the active contour formulation is further defined as:

$$E_{in}(v(s)) = \alpha(s) \left| \frac{dv(s)}{ds} \right|^2 + \beta(s) \left| \frac{d^2 v(s)}{ds^2} \right|^2 \qquad (2)$$

where $\alpha(s)$ and $\beta(s)$ are weighting factors of elasticity and stiffness terms, respectively. The first order term makes the snake's surface act like a membrane. The weight $\alpha(s)$ controls the tension along the spine (stretching a balloon or elastic band). The second order term makes the snake act like a thin plate. The weight $\beta(s)$ controls the rigidity of the spine (bending a thin plate or wire).

A typical external energy formulation to identify edges for a given image, $I(x,y)$, is:

$$E_{ex}(x, y) = -|\nabla I(x, y)|^2 \qquad (3)$$

where ∇ denotes the gradient operator. In the case of a noisier image the edges are further smoothed:

$$E_{ex}(x, y) = -|\nabla(G_\sigma(x, y) * I(x, y))|^2 \qquad (4)$$

where $G_\sigma(x,y)$ is a two-dimensional Gaussian function with standard deviation σ, and $*$ denotes a convolution operator. Since the contour may get trapped by the noisy areas of the image, σ must be large enough to compensate for the image noise that would interfere with the active contour's capture range. The standard snake algorithm also suffers from poor capture range due to initialization and the inability to capture concavities. These problems are largely solved by the advent of the GVF snake [24].

The concavity problem exists since the gradient vectors in an image generally have large magnitudes only in the immediate vicinity of the boundary, and are nearly zero at points further away from the boundary. As such, the capture range of the snake will be quite small. In order to resolve this, the gradient map is extended to points away from boundaries using a computational diffusion process. The GVF field is used as an external energy in the active contour and is characterized by the vector field $z(x,y)=[u(x,y),v(x,y)]^T$ that minimizes the energy functional [24]:

$$E_{GVF} = \iint \mu \, (|\nabla u|^2 + |\nabla v|^2) + |\nabla f|^2 \, |z - \nabla f|^2 \, dxdy \qquad (5)$$

where f is an edge map derived from the image, μ is the degree of smoothness of the field, u and v characterize the direction and strength of the field. Hence, when $|\nabla f|$ is small the energy will be dominated by the partial derivates, yielding a slow field. Alternatively, when $|\nabla f|$ is large, the latter term dominates and the function is minimized by setting $z = \nabla f$.

The external energy for the proposed scheme will be generated using a *virtual electric field* (VEF) [19] of f over the traditional GVF technique. Traditional GVF field generation is performed by optimizing the cost function represented as the different partials shown in (5), which is quite a time consuming process. The VEF is defined by considering each edge pixel as a point charge within an electric field. This can be accomplished by convolving the edge map with the following two masks:

$$g_x(x, y) = \frac{-c \cdot x}{(x^2 + y^2)^{3/2}}$$

(6)

$$g_y(x, y) = \frac{-c \cdot y}{(x^2 + y^2)^{3/2}}$$

(7)

where $c = (4\pi\varepsilon)^{-1}$ and ε is sufficiently small constant. The resulting field yields a vector flow identical to a GVF field; given the masks are of sufficient size. A smaller mask size would ignore outlying edges that would have little impact on the interested features since their range is quite far. However, since echoardiographic images contain many features throughout the image, quantizing any part of the edge map is not an option.

According to *Park et al.* [19], an area of radius 32 around the feature should provide adequate flow vectors to accurately recreate a GVF field, without suffering from the high computational cost associated with vector flow generation. Fig. 1(b) shows an example of a vector flow field on the standard U-Image, shown in Fig. 1(a), using 65×65 masks generated from (6) and (7), which is identical to the original GVF field.

2.2 SRAD Measurements

Diffusion is a process that equalizes differing concentrations without creating or destroying an object's mass. Simple diffusion can be defined as

$$\frac{\partial p'}{\partial t} = div\left(D \cdot \nabla p'\right)$$

(8)

where *div* is the divergence operator, D is the diffusivity tensor, and p refers to the diffused image at time point t. In *Perona and Malik's* anisotropic diffusion model [20], they defind D for smoothing image data as

$$D = g\left(\left\|\nabla p'\right\|\right) = \frac{1}{1 + \left(\frac{\left\|\nabla p'\right\|}{\lambda}\right)^2}$$

(9)

where λ is the edge magnitude parameter. Hence, $g(.)$ will yield low values (near zero) for gradient values much greater than λ inhibiting diffusion near edges. Using (9) as the diffusivity coefficient of (8), the model sharpens edges if their gradient value is larger than the edge magnitude parameter λ by inhibiting diffusion. In other words, $g(.)$ acts as a means to standardize edge response across homogeneous regions and non-homogeneous regions.

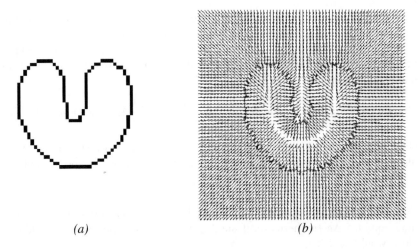

(a)   (b)

Fig. 1. Example of gradient vector forces; (a) standard U-Image, and (b) Gradient Vector Flow of U-Image

Yu et al. [25] introduced the *instantaneous coefficient of variation* (ICOV) as a noise-estimating operator. The ICOV operator is defined by

$$ICOV(p^t) = \frac{\sqrt{\left|1/2 \cdot \left\|\nabla p^t\right\|^2 - 1/16 \cdot \left(\nabla^2 p^t\right)^2\right|}}{\left(p^t + 1/4 \cdot \nabla^2 p^t\right)} \tag{10}$$

where ∇^2 is the Laplacian operator. By combining the anisotropic diffusion model with the ICOV operator, *Yu et al.* [25] yielded a partial differential equation called the *speckle reducing anisotropic diffusion* (SRAD).

$$SRAD(p^t) = p^{t+\Delta t} = p^t + \frac{\Delta t}{|\eta|} \cdot div\big(g\big(ICOV(p^t)\big) \cdot \nabla p^t\big) \tag{11}$$

where, $|\eta|$ is the number of pixels in the neighbourhood of pixel x (usually taken to be equal four). *Yu et al.* [26] showed that using (11) provided better results at detecting real borders when faced with high levels of speckle noise.

Applying SRAD on the echocardiograms will help to reduce much of the speckle that impedes the accurate calculation of optical flow, which will be incorporated into the external energy. SRAD edge-maps will also be fed as the gradient estimates for the snake.

2.3 Optical Flow Estimates

Optical flow approximates the apparent motion of an object over a series of images (or time). The relationship between the optical flow in the image plane and the velocities of objects in the three dimensional world is not necessarily obvious [3]. For the sake of convenience, most optical flow techniques consider a particularly simple world where the apparent velocity of brightness patterns can be directly identified with the movement of surfaces in the scene. This implies that objects maintaining structure but changing intensity would break this assumption.

Consider an image intensity, $I(x,y,t)$ at time t. Time, in this instance, implies that next frame in an image cine. Assuming that at a small distance away, and some time later the given intensity is:

$$I(x+\Delta x, y+\Delta y, t+\Delta t) = I(x, y, t) + \frac{\partial I}{\partial x}\Delta x + \frac{\partial I}{\partial y}\Delta y + \frac{\partial I}{\partial t}\Delta t + higher\ order\ terms \quad (12)$$

Given that the object started at position (x,y) at time t, and that it moved by a small distance of $(\Delta x, \Delta y)$ over a period of time Δt, the following assumption can be made:

$$I(x+\Delta x, y+\Delta y, t+\Delta t) = I(x, y, t) \quad (13)$$

The assumption in (13) would only be true if the intensity of our object is the same at time t and $t + \Delta t$. Furthermore, if our Δx, Δy and Δt are very small, our higher order terms would vanish, i.e.,

$$\frac{\partial I}{\partial x}\Delta x + \frac{\partial I}{\partial y}\Delta y + \frac{\partial I}{\partial t}\Delta t = 0 \quad (14)$$

Dividing (14) by Δt will yield:

$$-\frac{\partial I}{\partial t} = \frac{\partial I}{\partial x}\frac{\Delta x}{\Delta t} + \frac{\partial I}{\partial y}\frac{\Delta y}{\Delta t} \quad (15)$$

$$-I_t = \frac{\partial I}{\partial x}u + \frac{\partial I}{\partial y}v, \quad \text{where } u = \frac{\Delta x}{\Delta t} \text{ and } v = \frac{\Delta y}{\Delta t}. \quad (16)$$

Equation (16) is known as the optical flow constraint equation, where I_t at a particular pixel location, (x,y), is how fast its intensity at this location is changing with respect to time, u and v are the spatial rates of change for any given pixel (i.e., how fast an intensity is moving across an image). However, effectively estimating the component of the flow (along with intensity values) cannot directly be solved in this form since it will yield one equation per pixel for every two unknowns, u and v. In order to do so, additional constraints must be applied to this equation.

Lucas-Kanade [14] and *Horn-Schunck* [11] introduced two common methods for solving this problem using partial derivatives. The former assumes that the flow field is locally smooth (for a given static window size) and then solves (16) by means of a least squares approximation technique. The latter uses a global regularization parameter which assumes that images consist of objects undergoing rigid motion, resulting in a smooth optical flow over a relatively large area. Fig. 2 depicts a visual representation of the optical flow of a simple Rubik's cube. Notice that the greyscale image has few shadows, helping to maintain consistency in the luminance of each pixel, hence yielding accurate results.

When dealing with noisy echocardiograms, a global regularization parameter will deal with the speckle better than the static window. This is due to the speckle noise remaining relatively static, lacking fluidity, throughout an image. Hence, the speckle will be 'filtered', since the optical flow calculations will fail to realize it within the frames.

Optical flow magnitudes will be combined with the SRAD edge maps (see Section 2.5), in order to generate the external energy in (1) of the GVF snake. This will help to reduce artifacts due to static speckle noise, while also providing more information for the contour points to track (i.e., the movement of the tissue mass).

2.4 Primitive Shape Measurements on Contour Points

Since we are dealing with structures that have known shapes and sizes, and many real world models have been already measured, prior knowledge information can be directly used to increase the performance of a segmentation algorithm. Priors based on shape statistical models require modifications to the standard active contour model. An iterative solution can be incorporated directly into any optimization model by using the proposed framework.

Since it is desirable to incorporate shape priors without directly involving the user for training, automatic shape detection takes place on the set of discrete snake points, $v(s)$. This is achieved by first generating the least squares fit polynomial(s) of the current $v(s)$ points. For our left ventricle application, snake points were divided into an upper region and a lower region representing two separate third-order hyperbolas, which will better suit the shape of the left ventricle during both systole and diastole, though any shape prior can be represented by means of simple primitives. Least squares fitting technique is utilized to estimate the two hyperbolas coefficients. The axis separating the two regions is computed by taking the two-thirds upper and one-third lower bounds on all snake points and computing their division. This division can be tuned by shifting it upwards or downwards (either manually by the user or automatically by the system) in order to minimize the distance between the fitted hyperbolas and snake points.

Priors are then generated by joining the fitted primitives to form one solid shape. Primitives are bounded by the furthest easterly and westerly points by the snake points, in order to prevent the possibility of a non-connecting shape.

Once priors have been generated, its GVF field is computed. This new field will replace the existing external energy of the GVF snake for this specific snake iteration. Fig. 3 portrays the process of generating a primitive prior for the left ventricle of the 4-chamber view image, where two intersecting hyperbolas are used (default shape for our left ventricle application).

The fitting of a primitive shape (or a series of primitives as needed for the left ventricle) to the snake points, $v(s)$, will help compensate for the noise that inhibits the snake from migrating past a certain point. It will also help retract the snake towards the primitive prior when an occluded border exists; common in many echocardiographic images. The user can control the number of cycles between any two consecutive prior calculation cycles (prior step parameter). This allows for the increase or decrease in the inherent effect of the prior knowledge to the snake's convergence cycle.

This primitive prior module is useful in the medical arena where the specialist or clinician has a clear understanding of the underlying structure being detected, such as a liver, an artery, or a heart. They can choose their desired primitive shape (or series of shapes) before curve evolution takes place.

Fig. 2. An example of an optical flow field on a Rubik's cube rotated image; (a) cube at time t, (b) cube at time $t+\Delta t$, and (c) Optical flow of image (a) to (b) using Lucas-Kanade method (originally published in *Barron et al.* [3]).

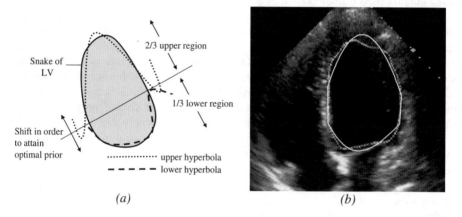

Fig. 3. Left ventricle primitive shape fitting; (a) primitive shape fitting algorithm using two hyperbolas, and (b) echocardiogram with segmentation overlay; solid line represents primitive whereas X-line represents active contour.

2.5 Fusion Characteristics

The proposed external energy is a fusion of SRAD gradient edge-map information and the optical flow estimates. Fig. 4 illustrates a top-level block diagram of the proposed system. It starts by calculating the SRAD edge map of the image cines (as explained in Section 2.2). The edge maps optical flows are then extracted (as explained in Section 2.3). The estimated optical flow is median filtered and are added to the SRAD image edge map following normalization. This result is used to generate the GVF for the snake's external energy. GVF snake evolution (as explained in Section 2.1) iterates to further minimize the energy function until a prior cycle condition is satisfied (as explained in Section 2.4), at which, the prior cycle is initiated. During the prior cycle, a GVF is generated from the desired primitive and a single optimization evolution of the snake is executed before returning to the original non-primitive snake iterations. This process is repeated until the snake is optimized and equilibrium is achieved.

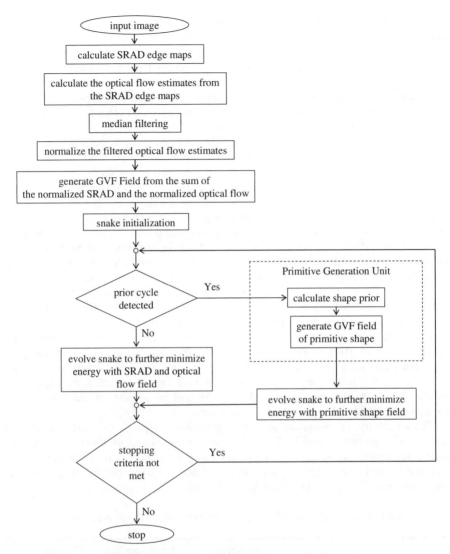

Fig. 4. Top level block diagram of proposed scheme

3 Results and Discussion

For this study, a series of B-mode echocardiogram cross-sectional videos of the heart have been used to investigate the proposed snake algorithm. These videos were acquired using a SONOS 5500 by Philips Medical System. The transducer frequency was set at 2.5 MHz in order to insure adequate penetration of tissue, while maintaining image quality with the existing speckle noise. Longitudinal views of the heart, which visualize the left ventricle, were acquired in order to verify the prior knowledge algorithm using more than one primitive shape.

The videos were parsed into image cines and each frame was considered with its direct neighbouring frame. Optical flow calculations for the edge map were completed using the Horn-Schunck technique with a regularization constraint of 0.2 in order to compensate for the general speckle throughout the US images. The initial contour placement was set to a small circle which was placed by the user within the left ventricle of the heart and the prior step parameter was set to 5 cycles.

Overall, experiments were run on eight complete cardiac cycles from different patients. The performance of the proposed system was measured by comparing 130 indexed segmented image cines from the eight cardiac cycles to the manually delineated segmentations by an expert radiologist, representing the gold standard used. Since the images at hand were mainly small-segmented foregrounds (left ventricular surface area) against vast backgrounds, the system performance would best be measured by means of its sensitivity, precision rate and overlap ratio. Let us consider the following metrics; a true positive pixel is a pixel that is considered part of the left ventricle by both of the proposed method and the gold standard. A false positive pixel is a pixel that is considered part of the left ventricle by the proposed method but it is not considered as such on the gold standard. A false negative pixel is a pixel that is not considered as part of the left ventricle by the proposed method, yet it is considered to be part of the ventricle according to the gold standard. The sensitivity is the percentage of the number of true positive pixels divided by the sum of the number of true positive pixels and false negative pixels. In other words, it classifies how well a binary classification test correctly identifies a condition. Precision rate is the percentage of the number of true positive pixels divided by the sum of the number of true positive pixels and false positive pixels. In other words, it classifies how accurate the results of the test when the results are positive. Overlap ratio is the percentage of the number of true positive pixels divided by the sum of the number of true positive pixels, false positive pixels and false negative pixels.

The sensitivity, precision rate and overlap ratio of the proposed system on the 130 segmented cines are shown in Table 1. This was generated by combining the total metric aggregates across all 130 cines, and calculating the sensitivity, precision rate and overlap ratio measures. Examination of Table 1 shows that the proposed technique outranks the standard GVF snake in all of the metrics shown.

Table 1. Sensitivity, precision rate and overlap ratio of the proposed system

	Sensitivity	Precision Rate	Overlap Ratio
Standard GVF Snake	90.4%	70.2%	65.3%
GVF Snake with SRAD Optical flow and priors	92.9%	77.4%	73.0%

An example of segmentation results is exhibited in Fig. 5, where Fig 5(b) reveals the SRAD contours used in the external energy of the proposed scheme, Fig(c) shows the expert manually traced delineation of the left ventricle, (d) shows the segmentation results when utilizing GVF only, and Fig 5(e) reveals the segmentation results when utilizing the proposed scheme. As seen in Fig(e), the shape priors improve regularity by allowing the snake to overcome various noise artifacts. This allows for proper delineation of the left ventricular endocardial lining. Furthermore,

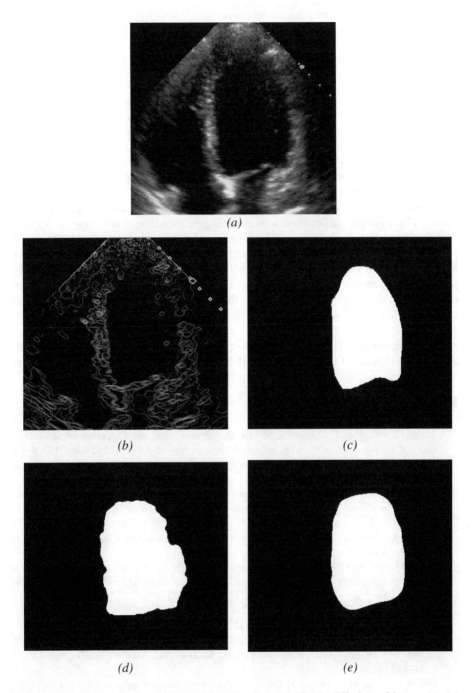

Fig. 5. Segmentation results; (a) LV echocardiogram, (b) SRAD diffusion of image (a), (c) manual expert delineation of image (a), (d) and (e) segmentations when utilizing GVF only and when utilizing the proposed scheme, respectively

the motion information (optical flow) is used as structural information in the external energy of the snake.

4 Conclusions

In this work, we have shown that the use of optical flow estimations and SRAD diffusion techniques perform well when integrated with a GVF active contour. This scheme helped alleviate the inherent difficulties in segmenting echocardiograms, such as considering speckle noise and contour bleeding. Furthermore, it strengthens the principle that tissue movement should be considered within segmentation techniques, where the data facilitates it.

Contour regularity and accuracy were further improved by using primitive shapes priors. The inherent difficulties in segmenting echocardiographic images, such as avoiding speckle noise and valve interference were also overcome by the primitive priors. Results were validated against a gold standard, which was manually segmented by a clinician and yielded stronger results than the standard GVF snake in sensitivity, precision rate and overlap ratios. Such segmentations would improve the calculation of various clinical measures by reducing the inconsistencies and variability between clinicians while simultaneously reducing the time for clinician interaction.

Acknowledgements. This research is partially funded by the Natural Sciences and Engineering Research Council of Canada (NSERC). This support is greatly appreciated.

References

1. Amini, A., Radeva, P., Elayyadi, M., Li, D.: Measurement of 3D motion of myocardial material points from explicit B-surface reconstruction of tagged MRI data. In: Wells, W.M., Colchester, A.C.F., Delp, S.L. (eds.) MICCAI 1998. LNCS, vol. 1496, pp. 110–118. Springer, Heidelberg (1998)
2. Amini, A., Weymouth, T., Jain, R.: Using dynamic programming for solving variational problems in vision. IEEE Trans. on Pattern Analysis in Machine Intelligence 12(9), 855–866 (1990)
3. Barron, J., Fleet, D., Beauchemin, D.: Performance of optical flow techniques. Int. J. of Computer Vision 12(1), 43–77 (1994)
4. Choy, M., Jin, J.: Morphological image analysis of left ventricular endocardial borders in 2D echocardiograms. In: SPIE Proceedings on Medical Imaging, vol. 2710, pp. 852–864 (1996)
5. Cohen, L.: On active contour models and balloons. Computer Vision, Graphics, and Image Processing: Image Understanding 53(2), 211–218 (1991)
6. Cohen, L., Cohen, I.: Finite-element methods for active contour models and balloons for 2-D and 3-D images. IEEE Trans. on Pattern Analysis and Machine Intelligence 15(11), 1131–1147 (1993)
7. Felix-Gonzalez, N., Valdes-Cristerna, R.: 3D echocardiographic segmentation using the mean-shift algorithm and an active surface model. In: Medical Imaging. SPIE, vol. 6144, pp. 147–151 (2006)

8. Hamou, A., El-Sakka, M.: An SRAD and optical flow based external energy for echocar-diograms. In: Int. Conf. of Image Processing (2009)
9. Hamou, A., El-Sakka, M.: Active contours with Optical Flow and Primitive Shape Priors for echocardiographic Imagery. In: Int. Conf. of Imaging Theory and Applications, pp. 111–118 (2009)
10. Hamou, A., Osman, S., El-Sakka, M.: Carotid ultrasound segmentation using DP active contours. In: Kamel, M.S., Campilho, A. (eds.) ICIAR 2007. LNCS, vol. 4633, pp. 961–971. Springer, Heidelberg (2007)
11. Horn, B., Schunck, B.: Determining optical flow. Artificial Intelligence 17, 185–203 (1981)
12. Kass, M., Witkin, A., Terzopoulos, D.: Snakes: active contour models. Int. J. of Computer Vision 1(4), 321–331 (1987)
13. Leung, K., van Stralen, M., van Burken, G., Voormolen, M., Nemes, A., ten Cate, F., de Jong, N., van der Steen, A., Reiber, J., Bosch, J.: Sparse appearance model based registra-tion of 3D ultrasound images. In: Yang, G.-Z., Jiang, T.-Z., Shen, D., Gu, L., Yang, J. (eds.) MIAR 2006. LNCS, vol. 4091, pp. 236–243. Springer, Heidelberg (2006)
14. Lucas, B., Kanade, T.: An iterative image registration technique with an application to ste-reo vision. In: Proceedings of Imaging Understanding Workshop, pp. 121–130 (1981)
15. Mallouche, H., de Guise, J., Goussard, Y.: Probabilistic model of multiple dynamic curve matching for a semitransparent scene. In: Vision Geometry IV, vol. 2573, pp. 148–157 (1995)
16. Mazumdar, B., Mediratta, A., Bhattacharyya, J., Banerjee, S.: A real time speckle noise cleaning filter for ultrasound images. In: IEEE Symposium on Computer-Based Medical Systems, pp. 341–346 (2006)
17. Montagnat, J., Delingette, H.: Space and time shape constrained deformable surfaces for 4D medical image segmentation. In: Delp, S.L., DiGoia, A.M., Jaramaz, B. (eds.) MICCAI 2000. LNCS, vol. 1935, pp. 196–205. Springer, Heidelberg (2000)
18. Papademetris, X., Sinusas, A., Dione, D., Duncan, J.: 3D cardiac deformation from ultra-sound images. In: Taylor, C., Colchester, A. (eds.) MICCAI 1999. LNCS, vol. 1679, pp. 420–429. Springer, Heidelberg (1999)
19. Park, H., Chung, M.: A new external force for active contour model: virtual electric field. In: Int. Conf. on Visualization, Imaging and Image Processing, pp. 103–106 (2002)
20. Perona, P., Malik, J.: Scale space and edge detection using anisotropic diffusion. IEEE Trans. Pattern Analysis Machine Intelligence 12(7), 629–639 (1990)
21. Szeliski, R., Tonnesen, D.: Surface modeling with oriented particle systems. SIGGRAPH: Computer Graphics 26(2), 185–194 (1992)
22. Tauber, C., Batatia, H., Ayache, A.: Robust B-spline snakes for ultrasound image segmen-tation. J. of Signal Processing Systems 54(1), 159–169 (2009)
23. Williams, D., Shah, M.: A fast algorithm for active contours and curvature estimation. Computer Vision Graphics and Image Processing: Image Understanding 55(1), 14–26 (1992)
24. Xu, C., Prince, J.: Snakes, shapes, and gradient vector flow. IEEE Trans. on Image Proc-essing 7(3), 359–369 (1998)
25. Yu, Y., Acton, S.: Speckle reducing anisotropic diffusion. IEEE Trans. on Image Process-ing 11(11), 1260–1270 (2002)
26. Yu, Y., Acton, S.: Edge detection in ultrasound imagery using the instantaneous coeffi-cient of variation. IEEE Trans. on Image Processing 13(12), 1640–1655 (2004)
27. Zhou, S., Liangbin, C.W.: A new method for robust contour tracking in cardiac image se-quences. In: IEEE Int. Symposium on Biomedical Imaging: Nano to Macro, vol. 1, pp. 181–184 (2004)

Part III
Computer Vision Theory and Applications (VISAPP)

Scene Segmentation from 3D Motion and Category-Specific Information

Alexander Bachmann and Irina Lulcheva

Department for Measurement and Control
University of Karlsruhe (TH), 76 131 Karlsruhe, Germany
{bachmann,lulcheva}@mrt.uka.de

Abstract. In this paper we address the problem of detecting objects from a moving camera by jointly considering low-level image features and high-level object information. The proposed method partitions an image sequence into independently moving regions with similar 3-dimensional (3D) motion and distance to the observer. In the recognition stage, category-specific information is integrated into the partitioning process. An object category is represented by a set of descriptors expressing the local appearance of salient object parts. To account for the geometric relationships among object parts, a structural prior over part configurations is designed. This prior structure expresses the spatial dependencies of object parts observed in a training data set. To achieve global consistency in the recognition process, information about the scene is extracted from the entire image based on a set of global image features. These features are used to predict the scene context of the image from which characteristic spatial distributions and properties of an object category are derived. The scene context helps to resolve local ambiguities and achieves locally and globally consistent image segmentation. Segmentation results are presented based on real image sequences.

1 Introduction

One of the cornerstones in the development of automotive driver assistance systems is the comprehensive perception and understanding of the environment in the vicinity of the vehicle. Especially for applications in the road traffic domain the robust and reliable detection of close-by traffic participants is of major interest. In this context, vision sensors provide a rich and versatile source of information [16], [15]. Visual object detectors are expected to cope with a wide range of intra-class characteristics, i.e. variations in the visual appearance of an object due to changes in orientation, lighting conditions, scale, etc.. At the same time, these methods must retain enough specificity to yield a minimum amount of misclassifications. Here, most of the approaches developed in the last decades can be partitioned into either: (i) methods based on classification, which constrain the detection process to a very specific representation of an object learned from a reference data set or (ii) methods performing object detection by employing local object characteristics on a low level of abstraction using image-based criteria to describe coherent groups of image points as e.g. grey level similarity, texture or motion uniformity of image regions. A major drawback of these methods is the fact that the grouping criteria mostly ignore object-specific properties with the consequence of misdetection rates in cluttered real world scenes that are still prohibitive for most driver

A. Ranchordas et al. (Eds.): VISIGRAPP 2009, CCIS 68, pp. 175–187, 2010.

assistance applications. This limitation can be weakened by classification methods that have proven to detect a large portion of typical objects at moderate computational cost.

In our approach, object detection is performed based on the *relative motion* of textured objects and the observer. The expectation of spatial compactness for most real world objects is expressed by its *position* relative to the observer. To obtain a dense representation of the observed scene, object detection is formulated as an image segmentation task. Here, each image point is tested for consistency with a set of possible hypothesis, each defined by a 3D motion and position. The set of object parameters that best explains the measured quantities of the image point is assigned to the image point.

To further increase the quality of the segmentation result, we incorporate information about the objects to be recognised by the system. The integration of object-specific information for driving image segmentation methods has recently developed into a field of active research and seems to be a promising way to incorporate more information into existing low-level object detection methods, see e.g. [13,5]. Our work is inspired by recent research results in human vision, as e.g. [14], indicating that the recognition and segmentation of a scene is a heavily interweaved process in human perception. Following this biological model, our segmentation method is based on low-level features but guided and supported by category-specific information. The question of how to describe this knowledge is very challenging because there is no formal definition of what constitutes an object category. Though most people agree on the choice of a certain object category, there is still much discussion on the choice of an appropriate object descriptor. In our approach the high-level information comprises the appearance of a set of characteristic object parts and its arrangement relative to each other and in the scene. Though good for modeling local object information, it fails to capture global consistency in the recognition process, as e.g. the detection of a car in a tree high above the road. We establish global consistency by exploiting the close relationships of certain object categories to the scene of the image. The method characterises a scene by global image features and derives the predicted category likelihood and distribution of an object for a particular scene. We argue that the incorporation of category-specific scene context into our scene segmentation framework can drastically improve the process as (i) insufficient intrinsic object information can be augmented with and (ii) local ambiguities can be better resolved from a global perspective. Figure 1 shows the principle of our probabilistic image segmentation framework.

The remainder of the paper is organised as follows. Section 2 recalls some of the theoretical background that is needed to understand image segmentation as presented here. It is shown how object-specific information can be incorporated into the existing probabilistic framework by means of a sparse object model and category-specific scene information. Section 3 presents the experimental results before conclusions are drawn in Section 4.

2 Scene Segmentation Using MRFs

This section outlines the mechanism that evaluates the local and global properties of image points and separates the image accordingly. Notably there are two issues to be addressed in this task: (i) how to encourage the segmentation to consider local properties in the image on a low abstraction level and (ii) how to enforce the process to incorporate category-specific information into the segregation of the image.

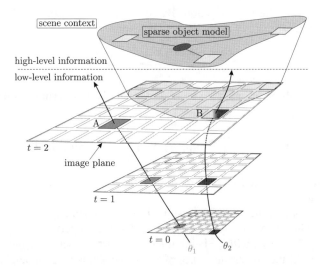

Fig. 1. Principle of the combined segmentation process. Image segmentation is performed by a Bayesian maximum a posteriori estimator assigning the most probable object hypothesis to each image point. In the example, image points are assigned to either object hypothesis A (expressed by θ_1) or object hypothesis B (expressed by θ_2).

First, a number of constraints are formulated that specify an acceptable solution to the problem. In computer vision, commonly the data and prior knowledge are used as constraints. The data constraint restricts a desired solution to be close to the observed data and the prior constraint confines the desired solution to have a form agreeable with the *a priori* knowledge.

The challenging task is the estimation of object parameters $\theta = \{\theta^1, .., \theta^K\}$, given an observation set $\mathbf{Y}$ which has been generated by an unknown and constantly changing number of objects K. Within our framework we solved this by formally expressing the scene segmentation process as *labeling problem*: Let a set of sites (or units) $\mathrm{P} = \{\mathrm{p}_1, .., \mathrm{p}_N\}$, $\mathrm{p}_i \in \mathbb{R}^2$ and a set of possible labels $\mathbf{L}$ be given with one label l_i for each site p_i specifying the process which generated the data. l_i is a binary vector such that $l_i^j = 1$ if object j generated the data at site p_i. The desired labeling is then a mapping $l : \mathrm{P} \mapsto \mathbf{L}$ that assigns a unique label to each site. The labeling $l = (l(\mathrm{p}_1), .., l(\mathrm{p}_N)) = (l_1, .., l_N)$ shall ascertain that (i) the data of all sites with identical label exhibit similarity w.r.t. some measure and that (ii) the labeling conforms with the *a priori* knowledge.

Taking a Bayesian perspective, the posterior probability of a labeling l can be formulated

$$P(l|\mathbf{Y}, \theta) = \frac{P(\mathbf{Y}|l, \theta)P(l|\theta)}{P(\mathbf{Y}, \theta)} \quad , \tag{1}$$

where we try to find the labeling l which maximises $P(l|\mathbf{Y}, \theta)$. Here, $P(\mathbf{Y}|l, \theta)$ states the data constraint parametrised by object parameter vector θ. $P(l|\theta)$ states the prior term. Obviously, $P(\mathbf{Y})$ in Equation (1) does not depend on the labeling l and can thus be discarded during the maximisation. By rearranging Equation (1) the *maximum a posteriori* (MAP) estimate of a labeling can be expressed

$$\widehat{1} = \arg\max_{1} \underbrace{P(\mathbf{Y}|1,\theta)}_{\text{data term}} \underbrace{P(1|\theta)}_{\text{prior term}} .$$

(2)

Assuming the observations $\mathbf{Y}$ to be i.i.d. normal, the first term in Equation (2) can be written

$$P(\mathbf{Y}|1,\theta) = \prod_{i=1}^{N} P(y_i|1_i,\theta) \propto \prod_{i=1}^{N} \exp(-E_i(y_i|1_i,\theta)).$$

(3)

E_i denotes an energy functional, rating observation y_i given label vector 1_i and object parameter vector θ.

Within the scope of this work we assume 1 to be independent of θ and model prior expectations on 1 using MRFs. An MRF is defined by the property $P(1_i | 1_1, ..., 1_{i-1}, 1_{i+1}, 1_N) = P(1_i | 1_j, \forall_j \in \mathcal{G}_i)$, with $\mathcal{G}_i$ being the neighbourhood set of image point p_i. The system must fulfill the constraints (i) $p_i \notin \mathcal{G}_i \forall 1_i$, no site is its own neighbour and (ii) $p_i \in \mathcal{G}_i \Leftrightarrow p_j \in \mathcal{G}_i$, if p_i is a neighbour of p_j, then p_j is also a neighbour of p_i. Due to the equivalence of MRF and Gibbs distributions, see e.g. [4], an MRF may be written as $P(1) = \mathbf{Z}^{-1} \exp(-V_k(1))$, where $V_k(1) \in \mathbb{R}$ is referred to as clique potential which only depends on those labels of 1 whose sites are elements of clique k. A clique $k \subseteq P$ is any set of sites such that any of its pairs are neighbours. We model the clique potential for 2-element cliques $k = \{p_i, p_j\}$ with $|p_i - p_j| = 1$ using an extension of the generalised Potts model ([10])

$$V_{\{i,j\}}(1_i, 1_j) = \begin{cases} \lambda & if \ 1_i \neq 1_j \\ 0 & \text{otherwise} \end{cases} ,$$

(4)

favouring identical labels at neighbouring sites. The coefficient λ modulates the effect of the prior term and therefore the degree of label smoothness in the segmentation result. The generalised Potts model is a natural and simple way to define a clique potential function that describes the smoothness of neighbouring points. With Equation (3)–(4), Equation (2) evolves to

$$\widehat{1} = \arg\min_{1} \sum_{i=1}^{N} E_i(y_i|1_i,\theta) + \sum_{j\in k} V_{\{i,j\}}(1_i, 1_j) = \arg\min_{1} \Psi(E, 1, \theta) .$$

(5)

2.1   Low-Level Information

Concerning the data term, in [3] good results have been achieved using the property *object motion*. Here, objects are specified by a 6-degree-of-freedom (dof) parametric motion model, representing the motion of an image region by parameter vector $\mathbf{v}$. The similarity between expected and observed object motion is expressed by evaluating the similarity between expected image texture $G_{t-1}(p_i; \mathbf{r}; \mathbf{v})$ derived from motion profile $\mathbf{v}$ and observed image texture $G_t(p_i; \mathbf{r})$ within a block of size B centered around image point p_i

$$E_i(\varepsilon_i^{\mathbf{v}}|1_i, \mathbf{v}) = \sum_{r\in B} \left(G_t(p_i; \mathbf{r}) - G_{t-1}(p_i; \mathbf{r}; \mathbf{v}) \right)^2 ,$$

(6)

with $\varepsilon_i^{\mathbf{v}}$ stating the residual at image position p_i.

This object model has been further extended by the object position ξ relative to the own vehicle, i.e. $\theta = (\mathbf{v}, \xi)$. The relative object position is expressed by the mean distance of an image segment assigned to one specific label (based on the stereoscopic scene reconstruction). The assignment energy of image point p_i (with depth value z_i), given an object label, then is

$$E_i(\varepsilon_i^\xi | l_i, \xi) = \frac{(z_i - \xi)^2}{2\sigma_\xi^2} \,. \tag{7}$$

σ_ξ states the extension of the object in terms of the depth variation of the respective label. This model allows to segregate an image sequence into K regions with each region being defined as homogenously moving object at a certain distance to the observer, i.e. $\mathbf{L} = \{\texttt{background}, \texttt{object 2}, .., \texttt{object K}\}$. Image regions that are moving static relative to the observer (as e.g. trees, buildings, etc.) are labeled $\{\texttt{background}\}$. A scheme that recursively estimates the object parameters for a set of object hypotheses independently is presented in [1].

With the intention to classify every image point into a meaningful semantic category and due to the well-known limitations of motion-based segmentation methods (as e.g. the aperture problem or poorly textured image regions) the next step is to incorporate category-specific information into the segmentation process.

2.2 Category-Specific Information

Therefore we extend our algorithm to perform interleaved object recognition and segmentation. To achieve this, the object parameter vector θ is extended by model parameter Φ, expressing the configuration of an object of a certain category c_O. An image point is either assigned to one of the defined object categories $\{\texttt{car}, \texttt{bicycle}, \texttt{pedestrian}\}$ $\in c_O$ or, if none of the categories adequately describes the image point, $\{\texttt{obstacle}\} \in c_O$. To incorporate object categories into our segmentation scheme, Equation (5) is extended to

$$\Psi(E, \mathbf{l}, \theta) = \underbrace{\Psi(E, \mathbf{l}, \mathbf{v}, \xi)}_{\text{object motion \& position}} + \underbrace{\Psi(E, \mathbf{l}, \Phi)}_{\text{object category}}, \tag{8}$$

with

$$\Psi(E, \mathbf{l}, \Phi) = \sum_{i=1}^{N} E_i(\varepsilon_i^\Phi | l_i, \Phi) \,. \tag{9}$$

The function $E_i(\varepsilon_i^\Phi | l_i, \Phi)$ ascertains that image points falling close to a given object description would more likely carry the object category label and vice versa. The energy functional has the form

$$E_i(\varepsilon_i^\Phi | l_i, \Phi) = -\log P(\varepsilon_i^\Phi | l_i, \Phi) \,. \tag{10}$$

For this work $P(\varepsilon_i^\Phi | l_i, \Phi)$ is defined as

$$P(\varepsilon_i^\Phi | l_i^j = 1, \Phi) = \frac{1}{1 + d(p_i, \Phi^j)} \,, \tag{11}$$

with $d(p_i, \Phi^j)$ expressing the distance from image point p_i to the object that is parametrised by Φ^j.

An object category is characterised by the local appearance of a set of n salient parts $\Phi = (\phi_1, ..., \phi_n)$, with $\phi_i = (x_i, y_i, z_i, \varrho_i)$ stating the location of the i-th part in 3D space and ϱ_i being the scale factor. Depth z_i is obtained from a calibrated stereo camera setup. The structural arrangement of the parts comprising an object is expressed by the spatial configuration of Φ. Spatial relationships between parts in the sparse object model are captured by parameter s. The local appearance of each part is characterised by parameter a. The pair $M = (s, a)$ parameterises an object category. Using Bayes' rule, the probability of an object being at a particular location, given fixed model parameters, can be written

$$P_M(\Phi|Y) \propto P_M(Y|\Phi)P_M(\Phi). \tag{12}$$

Above, $P_M(Y|\Phi)$ is the likelihood of the feature points depicting an object for a certain configuration of the object parts. The second term in Equation (12) is the prior probability that the object obeys the spatial configuration Φ. Assuming the object is present in an image, the location that is most likely its true position is the one with maximum posterior probability

$$\hat{\Phi} \propto \quad \arg\max_{\Phi} P_M(Y|\Phi)P_M(\Phi). \tag{13}$$

Local Appearance. The image evidence $P_M(Y|\Phi)$ of the individual parts in the sparse object model is modelled by its local appearance. The part appearance a_i, characterising the i-th part of a certain object model, is extracted from an image patch centered at $\Pi(\phi_i)$, where $\Pi(\cdot)$ symbolises the projection of a scene point onto the image plane. The object-characteristic appearance of each image patch $i \in (1, .., n)$ has been learned from a set of labeled training images. In this work three types of appearance measures $a_i = \{a_i^1; a_i^2; a_i^3\}$ have been used to describe an object:

- **Texture information** a_i^1, the magnitude of each pixel within the patch is stacked into a histogramm vector to express the texture.
- **Shape information** a_i^2, the Euclidean distance transform of the edge map within the patch expresses the shape.
- **Height information** a_i^3, the characteristic height of ϕ_i above the estimated road plane expresses the relative location in the scene.

The resulting patch responses constitute a vector of local identifiers for each object category. The model parameters have been learned from a set of labeled training images in order to generate a representative description of the local appearance of an object category. Prominent regions have been extracted from the image using the Harris interest point detector [11] and a corner detector based on curvature scale space technique as described in [12]. For object part ϕ_i and observation vector Y follows the model likelihood

$$P_M(Y|\Phi) = \prod_{i=1}^{n} P_M(Y|\phi_i). \tag{14}$$

The likelihood function measures the probability of observing Y in an image, given a particular configuration Φ. Intuitively, the likelihood should be high when the appearance of the parts agree with the image data at the positions they are placed, and low otherwise. Figure 2 shows the sparse object model of object category car.

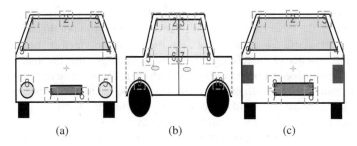

(a)   (b)   (c)

Fig. 2. Sparse representation of object category car: **(a)** front view, **(b)** side view, **(c)** rear view. The parts used in the training stage are marked with green rectangles containing the part-ID. The yellow star indicates the reference point for the individual parts.

Structural Prior. What remains is to encode the assumed spatial relationships among object parts. As presented in [3], the assumption can be made that the part locations are independent, i.e.

$$P_{\mathbf{M}}(\Phi) = \prod_{i=1}^{n} P_{\mathbf{M}}(\phi_i) \,. \tag{15}$$

Here, only the metric height above the estimated road plane has been used as structural information. Maximising $P_{\mathbf{M}}(\Phi|\mathbf{Y})$ is easy as $P_{\mathbf{M}}(\mathbf{Y}|\Phi)P_{\mathbf{M}}(\Phi)$ can be solved independently for each ϕ_i. For n parts and N possible locations in the image this can be done in $O(nN)$ time. A major drawback of this method is that it encodes only weak spatial information and is unable to accurately represent objects composed of various parts.

The most obvious approach to represent multi-part objects is to make no independence assumption on the locations of different parts. Though theoretically appealing the question of how to efficiently perform inference on this spatial prior is not trivial.

A balance between the inadequate independence assumption and the strong but hard to implement full dependency between object parts is assumed by maintaining certain conditional independence assumptions. These assumptions can be elegantly represented using an MRF, where the location of part ϕ_i is independent of the values of all other parts ϕ_j, $j \neq i$, conditioned on the values of the neighbours $\mathcal{G}_i$ of ϕ_i in an undirected graph $G(\Phi, E)$. The structural prior is characterised by pairwise only dependencies between parts.

Sparse Object Model. The spatial prior is modeled as a star graph with the location of the object parts being conditioned on the location of reference point ϕ_R. For a better understanding, ϕ_R can be interpreted as center of mass of the object (see Figure 2). All object parts arranged around ϕ_R are independent of one another. A similar model is used by e.g. [6], [9]. Let $G = (\Phi, E)$ be a star graph with central node ϕ_R. Graphical models with a star structure have a straight forward interpretation in terms of the conditional distribution

$$P_{\mathbf{M}}(\Phi) = P(\phi_R) \prod_{i=1}^{n} P_{\mathbf{M}}(\phi_i|\phi_R) \,. \tag{16}$$

Reference point ϕ_R acts as the anchor point for all neighbouring parts. The positions of all other parts in the model are evaluated relative to the position of this reference point. In this work we chose ϕ_R to be virtual, i.e. there exists no measurable quantity that indicates the existence of the reference point itself. We argue that this makes the model insensitive to partial object occlusion and, therefore, to the absence of reference points. $P_M(\Phi)$ is modelled using Mixture of Gaussians (MoG). The model parameter subset $\mathbf{M} = (\mathbf{s}, \cdot)$, with mean $\mu_{i,R}$ and covariance $\sigma_{i,R}$, stating the location of ϕ_i relative to the reference point ϕ_R, has been determined in a training stage.

A specific object part configuration can be written in terms of observing an object at a particular spatial configuration $\Phi = (\phi_1, .., \phi_n)$, given the observations $\mathbf{Y}$ in the image. With the likelihood function of seing object part i at position ϕ_i (given by Equation (14)) and the structural prior in Equation (16) this can be formulated as

$$P_M(\Phi|\mathbf{Y}) \propto P(\phi_R)\Gamma(\phi_R|\mathbf{Y}), \tag{17}$$

where the quality of the reference point ϕ_R relative to all parts ϕ_i within the object definition is written

$$\Gamma(\phi_R|\mathbf{Y}) = \max_{\phi} \prod_{i=1}^{n} P_M(\phi_i|\phi_R)P_M(\mathbf{Y}|\phi_i). \tag{18}$$

What we are interested in, is finding the best configuration for all n parts of the object model relative to ϕ_R. To reduce computational costs, only points with a likelihood $P_M(\mathbf{Y}|\phi_i) > T$ are further processed. T states the acceptance threshold for the object hypothesis to be true. This results in a number of candidates m for each object part i. As this is computationally infeasible ($O(m^n)$) for large growing n, we propose a greedy search algorithm to maximise $P_M(\Phi|\mathbf{Y})$ over all possible configurations $\{\phi_i^j : i = 1, .., n; j = 1, .., m\}$ as outlined in Table 1.

2.3   Context Information

The MRF presented above efficiently models local image information consisting of low-level features enriched by high-level category-specific information.

However, context information capturing the overall global consistency of the segmentation result has been ignored so far. By introducing a set of semantic categories into

Table 1. Iterative search algorithm

1. Compute candidates $\phi^j, j = (1, .., m)$ for which $P_M(\mathbf{Y}|\phi_i^j) > T$
2. WHILE $j < m$ ...
   (a) Initialise $\phi_i^j, j \in (1, .., m)$ with $i = 1$; set $\mathbf{k} = i$; WHILE $i < n$ ...
       i. ...vote for reference point ϕ_R^j based on part location ϕ_i
       ii. ...set $i = i + 1$ and $\mathbf{k} = [\mathbf{k}; i]$
       iii. ...back-project ϕ_i from ϕ_R^j and compute $P_M(\Phi^*|\mathbf{Y})$, with $\Phi^* = (\phi_\mathbf{k})$
   (b) IF $P_M(\Phi^*|\mathbf{Y}) > T$: accept hypotheses
       i. delete j's from candidate list
       ii. go back to (a)
3. Fuse hypotheses according to Euclidean distance measure

the segmentation process, it is now possible to derive category-specific object character-istics not only on a local, object-intrinsic level but also on a global scale, expressing the relationships between labels and global image features. Based on the work presented in [2], we exploit the relation between the expected distribution of a certain object category and the scene. The scene-based information is formally introduced into our framework by extending Equation (5) with a context-aware object prior

$$\Psi(E,\mathbf{l},\theta) = \underbrace{\Psi(E,\mathbf{l},\mathbf{v},\xi,\Phi)}_{\text{local information}} + \underbrace{\sum_{i=1}^{N} G_i\left(\mathbf{l}_i|\mathbf{Y}\right)}_{\text{context information}}. \tag{19}$$

The category context potential

$$G_i\left(\mathbf{l}_i|\mathbf{Y}\right) = \log P(\mathbf{l}_i|\mathbf{M}_C), \tag{20}$$

predicts the label $\mathbf{l}_i$ from a global perspective using global image features $\mathbf{M}_C$. The global features characterise the entire image in terms of magnitude and orientation of edges in different image resolutions. For this work we defined a set of scene categories $c_S = \{\texttt{open}, \texttt{semi-open}, \texttt{closed}\}$, each expressed by a unique feature vector $\mathbf{M}_C$, describing the *openness* of the scene. This information is used to derive the dis-tribution of category labels and category probability in the image. The feature vector $\mathbf{M}_C$ for each specific scene has been calculated from a training data set and is formally expressed by a mixture of Gaussian model. The relationships between the contextual features and a specific object category c_O has been learned in a training stage. Given an input image, the prior probability of an object category c_O at each pixel position is expressed as its marginal distribution over all scene categories c_S. A more detailed description can be found in [2].

3   Experimental Results

This section presents the experimental evaluation of the object detection approach de-veloped in the previous sections. The results are based on image sequences of typical urban traffic scenarios. The algorithm is initialised automatically by scanning for the ac-tual number of dominant motions in the scene. Concerning the motion of the observer, the road plane is determined at the beginning of the image sequence as described in [8]. Thus, the motion profile of the observer can be determined by sampling feature points exclusively from the region that is labeled as road plane and therefore static relative to the observer. During the segmentation process, the motion profiles are refined and updated continuously with the motion tracker scheme described in [1]. Regarding the relative importance of data and smoothness term in the segmentation process, the regu-larisation factor was adapted empirically to values between $\lambda = (0.05, .., 0.5)$.

   The confidence of an image point to be part of an object hypothesis, i.e. label, is calculated based on its relative motion, its position and similarity to the defined object categories. The image point is assigned to the label with highest confidence. The train-ing data for object category car as presented here was extracted from an image data base of 160 images.

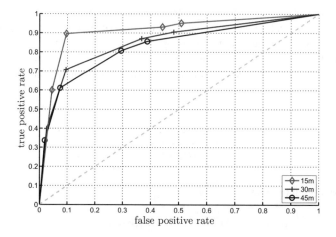

Fig. 3. ROC-curve for rear view of object category `car` as a function of the distance from the observer (for $T = 0.6$)

Fig. 4. Detection results (threshold value $T = 0.5$) for object category `car`. The figure on the bottom right shows a false positive.

Figure 3 shows that a threshold value of $T = 0.6$ yields a good compromise between a reasonable true positive rate and a false positive rate at relative low values. Figure 4 shows some of the detection results for object category `car`. The model was learned from labeled data. The patch-size of the extracted interest points was scale-normalised based on a predefined reference scale.

Figure 5 shows the classification results for detected objects solely based on scene context. No local category information has been integrated. It can be seen that the integration of global information is useful as a first process of image recognition. The joint use of a local object detector together with category-specific scene context improves the recognition accuracy as shown in Figure 6. Here, the object detection and segmentation results for different traffic scenes are depicted. As in this work only object category

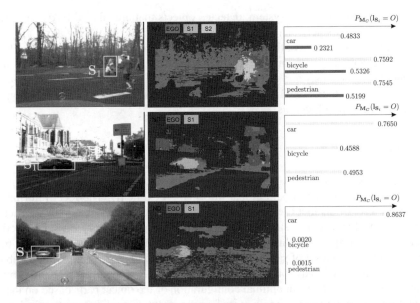

Fig. 5. Left: Detected objects based on the local object properties *motion similarity* and *position*. **Middle:** Segmentation map. Image points coloured red could not be assigned uniquely to one of the existing object hypotheses. **Right:** Prior probability $P_{\mathrm{M}_C}(\mathbf{ls}_i = O)$ of image region $\mathbf{S}_i$ to belong to object category $O = \{\texttt{car}, \texttt{bicycle}, \texttt{pedestrian}\}$ solely based on scene context information.

Fig. 6. Left: Scenes with a variable number of moving objects. The 6–dof motion for each object is determined based on a set of interest points extracted from the respective object. Coloured markers indicate the tracked points. **Middle:** The resulting segmentation map. Each image point is assigned the label containing the most probable motion profile and position. Each object label is assigned a different colour. **Right:** The segmented image. Image points assigned to an object label are highlighted.

car is known locally to the system, detected objects that are labeled bicyclist or pedestrian rely solely on the global context of the image. In the initialisation phase of the segmentation process, the motion estimates for the labels are inaccurate. Therefore the segmentation is mainly driven by the appearance-based confidence measure. With increasing accuracy and distinctiveness of the labels motion profile, the influence of the motion cue increases. In most cases, it takes less than 3 frames to partition the image into meaningful regions.

4   Conclusions

This paper has presented an approach for pixel-accurate object recognition that models local object information and global information explicitly. The local information consists of a set of distinct 6-dof motion profiles, positions and - on a high abstraction level - the local appearance similarity to the trained object category car. Distinctive, local object descriptors and a structural prior on the object-parts configuration have been extracted from a set of sample images. The structural relationships among object parts has been modelled as sparse structural prior. Object recognition is realised by an iterative method that finds an optimal configuration of the object parts based on the local appearance in the image and its spatial arrangement. Global information is derived from scene-based information generated according to the scene of the input image. As the occurrence of object categories is closely related to the scene of the image, scene context is exploited to derive characteristic category distributions and probabilities. It has been shown that the joint use of a local object detector and scene context improves the recognition accuracy. Under the assumption of motion and category homogeneity within the boundaries of an object, spatial consistency has been modelled through a Markov Random Field.

In ongoing work we expect to increase the performance of the method by further refining and extending the sparse object model description. We suppose to increase the quality of the classification process by making the object appearance descriptors invariant to object orientation and rotation. Additionally, we plan to integrate relational classification based on Markov logic into our segmentation scheme. We assume that the interaction of segmentation/tracking with the results from the classification step can be exploited to drive low-level object detection schemes tending towards more human-like scene perception. First experiments indicate remarkable improvements.

Acknowledgements. The authors gratefully acknowledge the contribution of the German collaborative research center 'SFB/TR 28 – Cognitive Automobiles' granted by Deutsche Forschungsgemeinschaft (DFG).

References

1. Bachmann, A.: Applying recursive EM to scene segmentation. In: Deutsche Arbeitsgemeinschaft fuer Mustererkennung DAGM e.V., Jena, Germany (September 2009)
2. Bachmann, A., Balthasar, M.: Context-aware object priors. In: IEEE IROS 2008; Workshop on Planning, Perception and Navigation for Intelligent Vehicles (PPNIV), Nice, France (2008)

3. Bachmann, A., Dang, T.: Improving motion-based object detection by incorporating object-specific knowledge. International Journal of Intelligent Information and Database Systems (IJIIDS) 2(2), 258–276 (2008)
4. Besag, J.: Spatial interaction and the statistical analysis of lattice systems. Journal of the Royal Statistical Society Series B 36(2), 192–236 (1974)
5. Burl, M.C., Weber, M., Perona, P.: A probabilistic approach to object recognition using local photometry and global geometry. In: Burkhardt, H., Neumann, B. (eds.) ECCV 1998. LNCS, vol. 1407, p. 628. Springer, Heidelberg (1998)
6. Crandall, D., Huttenlocher, D.: Composite models of objects and scenes for category recognition. In: Proc. IEEE Conference on Computer Vision and Pattern Recognition, CVPR 2007, pp. 1–8 (2007)
7. Dang, T., Hoffmann, C., Stiller, C.: Self-calibration for active automotive stereo vision. In: Proceedings of the IEEE Intelligent Vehicles Symposium, Tokyo (2006)
8. Duchow, C., Hummel, B., Bachmann, A., Yang, Z., Stiller, C.: Akquisition, Repraesentation und Nutzung von Wissen in der Fahrerassistenz. In: Informationsfusion in der Mess- und Regelungstechnik 2006, VDI/VDE-GMA, Eisenach, Germany (2006)
9. Fischler, M., Elschlager, R.: The representation and matching of pictorial structures. IEEE Trans. Comput. 22(1), 67–92 (1973)
10. Geman, S., Geman, D.: Stochstic relaxation, Gibbs distribution, and the Bayesian restoration of images. IEEE Transaction on Pattern Analysis and Machine Intelligence 6, 721–741 (1984)
11. Harris, C., Stephens, M.: A combined corner and edge detector. In: Fourth Alvey Vision Conference, Manchester, pp. 147–151 (1988)
12. He, X., Yung, N.: Curvature scale space corner detector with adaptive threshold and dynamic region of support. In: 17th International Conference on Pattern Recognition, Washington, DC, USA, vol. 2, pp. 791–794. IEEE Computer Society, Los Alamitos (2004)
13. Ohm, J.-R., Ma, P.: Feature-Based cluster segmentation of image sequences. In: ICIP 1997, Washington, DC, USA, vol. 3, pp. 178–181. IEEE Computer Society, Los Alamitos (1997)
14. Rentschler, I., Juettner, M., Osmana, E., Mueller, A., Caell, T.: Development of configural 3D object recognition. Elsevier - Behavioural Brain Research 149(149), 107–111 (2004)
15. Rockwell, T.: Skills, judgment, and information acquisition in driving. Human Factors in Highway Traffic Safety Research, 133–164 (1972)
16. Sivak, M.: The information that drivers use: is it indeed 90% visual? Perception 25(9), 1081–1089 (1996)

Hierarchical S(3)-Coding of RGB Histograms

Reiner Lenz[1] and Pedro Latorre Carmona[2]

[1] Dept. Science and Engineering, Linköping University
SE-60174 Norrköping, Sweden
[2] Dept. Lenguajes y Sistemas Informáticos, Jaume I University
Campus Riu Sec s/n 12071 Castellón, Spain

Abstract. In this paper we introduce the representation theory of the symmetric group S (3) as a tool to investigate the structure of the space of RGB-histograms and to construct fast transforms suitable for search in huge image databases. We show that the theory reveals that typical histogram spaces are highly structured. The algorithms exploit this structure and construct a PCA like decomposition without the need to construct correlation or covariance matrices and their eigenvectors. A hierarchical transform is applied to analyze the internal structure of these histogram spaces. We apply the algorithms to two real-world databases (one from an image provider and one from a image search engine company) containing over one million images.

1   Introduction

The number and size of image collections is growing steadily and with it the need to organize, search or browse these collections. These collections can also be used to study the statistical properties of other large collections and to derive models of their internal structure.

In this paper we are interested in the understanding of the statistical structure of large image collections and in the design of algorithms for applications where huge numbers of images have to be processed very fast. We will therefore investigate the color properties of images using one of the simplest and fastest color descriptors available: the RGB histogram [18,8], which has a wide variety of applications in image processing, ranging from image indexing and retrieval [16,19,7,15] to object tracking [2] to cite a few. The approach we use is based on the observation that compression and fast-processing methods are often tightly related to the underlying structure of the input signal space. This structure can often be described in terms of transformation groups. The best-known class of algorithms of this type are the FFT-methods based on the group of shift operations. In the signal processing field these methods were generalized to the application of finite groups in filtering, pattern matching and computer vision. See [3,9,10,11,12,13] for some examples.

In the following we will first argue that a relevant transformation group for the space of RGB histograms is the group S (3) of permutations of three objects. We will describe the basic facts from the representation theory of S (3) and investigate the properties of the resulting transforms of histograms. We will see that the generated structures have a PCA like decorrelation property, leading to a separation of the histogram into blocks.

A. Ranchordas et al. (Eds.): VISIGRAPP 2009, CCIS 68, pp. 188–200, 2010.

Finally, we will analyze the internal structure of each block applying a hierarchical transform (with the help of bin quantization). These transforms will be applied to two image databases, one consisting of 760000 images representing the collection of an image provider and one with 360000 images from the database of an image search engine.

2   Notations and Basic Facts

We first summarize a few facts about permutations and representation theory and then we will describe how to generalize this to representations on spaces of RGB histograms. We only mention the basic facts and the interested reader should consult one of the books in the field, for example [14,4,6,5,1].

The permutations of three objects form the symmetric group $S(3)$. This abstract group comes in several realizations and we will freely change between them. In the most abstract context the permutations π are just elements of $S(3)$. We will use them to investigate color images. We describe colors in the RGB coordinate system described by triples (R, G, B). If we want to denote a triple with some numerical values then we write $(aaa), (aab), (abc)$ in the cases where all three, two or none of the values are equal. If a permutation changes the order within the triple we will simply use the new order of the generic RGB triple as a symbol for the permutation. The permutation (RBG) leaves the first element fixed and interchanges the other two. It should be clear from the context if we mean RGB-triples like (abc) or permutations like (RBG). We define the special permutations π_c as the cyclic shift $\pi_c = (BRG)$ and π_r as the reflection (RBG). These two permutations are the generators of $S(3)$ and all others can be written as compositions of these two. The group $S(3)$ has six elements and we usually order them as $\pi_c^0, \pi_c, \pi_c^2, \pi_r, \pi_c\pi_r, \pi_c^2\pi_r$ or in RGB notation

$$(RGB), (BRG), (GBR), (RBG), (GRB), (BGR)$$

We see that the three even permutations π_c^0, π_c, π_c^2 form a commutative subgroup with the same properties as the group of $0, 120, 240$ degrees rotations in the plane. The remaining odd permutations are obtained by preceding the even permutation with π_r.

If we consider the triples $(R, G, B)'$ as vectors $\boldsymbol{x}$ in a three-dimensional vector space then we can describe the effect of the permutations by a linear transformation described by a matrix. In this way the permutations π_c, π_r are associated with the matrices $T_G(\pi)$

$$T_G(\pi_c) = \begin{pmatrix} 0 & 0 & 1 \\ 1 & 0 & 0 \\ 0 & 1 & 0 \end{pmatrix}; \quad T_G(\pi_r) = \begin{pmatrix} 1 & 0 & 0 \\ 0 & 0 & 1 \\ 0 & 1 & 0 \end{pmatrix} \tag{1}$$

This is the simplest example of a representation of $S(3)$ which is a mapping from the group to matrices, so that group operations correspond to matrix multiplications. In this case the matrices are of size 3×3 and we say that we have a three-dimensional representation. The elements π_c, π_r generate $S(3)$ and therefore we find that also all six permutation matrices are products of $T_G(\pi_c), T_G(\pi_r)$.

Fig. 1. Examples of a three- and a six-orbit

If we apply all six permutations to triples (abc) we obtain the so called orbits. For triples with different values for a, b and c we generate six triples, if we apply them to a triple (abb) we get three triples and the triple (aaa) is invariant under all elements in $S(3)$. The orbits of $S(3)$ have therefore length six, three and one respectively. We denote a general orbit by O and the orbits of length one, three and six by O_1, O_3, O_6. Two such orbits are illustrated in Fig.1 where each stripe shows one element in the orbit. For the three-orbit the colors are repeated for the odd permutations since the last two values in the RGB triple for the red image are identical. We can use the concept of an orbit to construct new representations similar to those in Eq. (1). Take the six-orbit O_6. We describe each element on O_6 by one of the six unit vectors in a six-dimensional vector space. Since permutations map elements in the orbit to other elements in the orbit we see that each permutation π defines a 6×6 permutation matrix $T_6(\pi)$ in the same way as those in Eq. (1). Also here it is sufficient to construct $T_6(\pi_c)$ and $T_6(\pi_r)$. The same construction holds for the three-orbits O_3. For the one-orbit the matrices are simply the constants $T_1(\pi) = 1$. We denote these vector spaces (defined by the orbits) by V_1, V_3, V_6.

The row- and column sums of permutation matrices are one and we see that $T(\pi)\mathbf{1} = \mathbf{1}$ where $T(\pi)$ is a permutation matrix and $\mathbf{1} = \begin{pmatrix} 1 \dots 1 \end{pmatrix}$ is a vector of suitable length with only elements equal to one. This shows that the subspaces V_k^t of $V_k, (k = 1, 3, 6)$, spanned by $\mathbf{1}$ are invariant under all permutations. These spaces define the trivial representation of $S(3)$ [6,5].

Since V_k^t is an invariant subspace of $V_k, (k = 1, 3, 6)$ we see that the orthogonal complements are also invariant and we have thus decomposed the invariant spaces V_k into smaller invariant spaces and each of these subspaces defines a lower-dimensional representation (smaller matrices) of the group. The smallest such invariant spaces define the irreducible representations of the group (for definitions and examples see [14,6,5]).

The decomposition for the three-dimensional space V_3 is given by the matrix

$$P_3 = \frac{1}{\sqrt{3}} \begin{pmatrix} 1 & 1 & 1 \\ \sqrt{2} & \sqrt{2}\cos(2\pi/3) & \sqrt{2}\cos(4\pi/3) \\ 0 & \sqrt{2}\sin(2\pi/3) & \sqrt{2}\sin(4\pi/3) \end{pmatrix} = \begin{pmatrix} \tilde{\mathbf{1}} \\ P_2 \end{pmatrix} \tag{2}$$

with the basis vector of the subspace V_3^t in the first row. The orthogonal complement is spanned by the remaining two basis vectors and it can be shown ([6]) that the space V_3^s spanned by these two cannot be split further. This defines another irreducible representation, the standard representation.

For the six-dimensional space V_6 it can be shown that the decomposition into irreducible representations is given by

$$P_6 = \begin{pmatrix} \hat{\mathbf{1}} & \hat{\mathbf{1}} \\ \hat{\mathbf{1}} & -\hat{\mathbf{1}} \\ \boldsymbol{P}_2 & 0 \\ 0 & \boldsymbol{P}_2 \end{pmatrix} \tag{3}$$

where $\hat{\mathbf{1}}$ represents 3D vectors with entries $\frac{1}{\sqrt{6}}$ and $\boldsymbol{P}_2$ is the matrix with the two basis vectors defined in Eq.(2).

In the final stage of the construction we describe how the group operates on RGB histograms. We start with an orbit O with elements o. The permutations π are maps $\pi :$ $O \to O$. Now take a linear function $f : O \to \mathbb{R}; o \mapsto f(o)$. We then define the new function f^π by $f^\pi(o) = f(\pi^{-1}(o))$. This defines a representation of S (3) on the space of functions on the orbit and we will also decompose them into irreducible parts.

For our application the functions of interest are the histograms. We will however modify this idea slightly. We consider a simple example first. Select an orbit O with elements o and assume that we have a probability distribution on O. Since O has finitely many elements this is a histogram h with the properties that $h(o) \geq 0$ and $\sum_{o \in O} h(o) = 1$. Applying a permutation π to the orbit elements defines a new histogram h^π. In the usual framework of representation theory we have orthonormal matrices $T(\pi)$ transforming vectors according to $h \mapsto T(\pi)h$. We thus have two transformations $h \mapsto h^\pi$ and $h \mapsto T(\pi)h$. The first of this preserves the L_1-norm while the other preserves the L_2-norm. We avoid this conflict and consider the square-roots of the probabilities instead (see also [17]). In the following we use the square root $h(o) = \sqrt{p(o)}$ where p is the probability distribution and h is the modified "histogram".

We summarize the construction so far as follows:

- Split the RGB space into subsets X such that the split is compatible with the permutations in S (3). The elements $x \in X$ are the bins.
- For a set of images compute the probabilities $p(x), x \in X$
- Convert and collect them in histogram vectors h with entries $h(x) = \sqrt{p(x)}$.
- Collect bins x related by permutations in orbits O_i, defining partitions $X = \bigcup_i O_i$
- Every orbit O defines a representation of dimension one, three or six
- Split three-dimensional representations into two parts using P_3 from Eq.(2)
- Split six-dimensional representations into four parts using P_6 from Eq.(3)
- Leave the one-dimensional representations as they are
- The final decomposition is now:

$$V = V^t \oplus V^a \oplus V^s \tag{4}$$

where V is the space defined by the bins. The space V^t is the invariant subspace associated with the one-point orbits and the invariant parts (first rows in P_3, P_6) of the three and six point orbits. V^a is the subspace associated with the six-point orbits and depends on the even/odd properties (second row in P_6) of the six point orbits. The V^s part follows the P_2 parts in the three- and six-point orbit transforms, Eqs.(2, 3).

3   Implementation

In the derivation we only required that the split of the RGB space is compatible with the operation of $S(3)$ but in the rest of the paper we will always split the R, G and B intervals into eight bins each, leading to a 512D RGB histogram. We will also use octal representations of the bin-number and write (klm) for the number $k + 8l + 64m$. One-point orbits are invariant under all permutations, therefore they represent gray-values (kkk). The three-orbits are given by bin numbers (kll). Consider as example the images given by the stripes in the left part of Fig. 1. The histogram for the first stripe has a one at position (700). Applying the six permutations we get the six stripes in this figure and six histograms. Applying the transformation P_3 to the three-orbit section of the histogram space given by $(700), (070), (007)$ we find that the first entry is always one and the positions in the other two dimensions (the P_2 part) transform as in an equal sided triangle. These two-dimensional vectors transform thus as 120 degrees rotations under permutations. The orbit of (740), representing the RGB vector $(255,128,0)$, are the six stripes in the right part of Figure 1. Using the decomposition defined by P_6 we get two two-dimensional vectors (from the last four rows of the matrix). The coordinates of the projections into the alternating and the standard parts are collected in Table 1

Table 1. Coordinates of projections for six-point orbits

	RGB	GBR	BRG	RBG	GRB	BGR
Alternating Representation	0.4082	0.4082	0.4082	-0.4082	-0.4082	-0.4082

	RGB	GBR	BRG	RBG	GRB	BGR
	0.8165	-0.4082	-0.4082	0	0	0
Standard Representation	0	-0.7071	0.7071	0	0	0
	0	0	0	-0.4082	0.8165	-0.4082
	0	0	0	0.7071	0	-0.7071

We have now described how to reorganize the histograms so that the different components show simple transformation properties under channel permutations. This is one of the advantages of this approach. The other is the relation to principal component analysis (PCA) that we will explain now.

We start with a simple example. Consider a vector h defined on an three-point orbit. Generate all different versions h^π under permutations and compute the matrix $C = \sum_\pi h^\pi h^{\pi\prime}$. It is invariant under a re-ordering of the orbit since this will simply re-arrange the sum. This is the simplest example of an $S(3)$-symmetric matrix. We generalize this to the definition of a wide-sense-stationary process as follows: Assume that we have vectors h in a vector space V and the permutations $\pi \in S(3)$ operate on these vectors by $h \mapsto h^\pi$. Assume further that we have a stochastic process with stochastic variable ω and values in $h_\omega \in V$. We define the correlation matrix Σ of this process as $\Sigma = E\left(h_\omega h_\omega{}'\right)$ where $E(.)$ denotes the expectation with respect to the stochastic variable ω. Assume further that we have a representation $T(\pi)$ on V.

Definition 1. *The stochastic process with correlation matrix Σ is T-wide-sense stationary if $T(\pi)\Sigma = \Sigma T(\pi)$ for all $\pi \in S(3)$.*

We will only consider representations for which the matrices T are orthonormal and in this case we have $\Sigma = T(\pi)\Sigma T(\pi)'$ for all $\pi \in S(3)$. But $T(\pi)\Sigma T(\pi)'$ is the correlation matrix of the stochastic process h in the new coordinate system $T(\pi)h$ and we see that wide-sense-stationarity means that the correlation matrix is independent of a certain class of coordinate transforms.

The general theory (Schur's Lemma, [5]) shows that we can find a matrix U (defining a new basis in the vector space) such that the correlation matrix in the new space is block diagonal. This matrix U depends only on the group $S(3)$:

Theorem 3.1. *For an $S(3)$-symmetric process with correlation matrix Σ we can find a matrix U such that:*

$$U\Sigma U' = \begin{pmatrix} \Sigma^t & 0 & 0 \\ 0 & \Sigma^a & 0 \\ 0 & 0 & \Sigma^s \end{pmatrix} \tag{5}$$

This transformation $h \mapsto Uh$ defines a partial principal component analysis of the histogram space by block-diagonalizing the correlation matrix. It is given by the construction described in Section 2.

4   S(3) Experiments

We implemented the transform described above and used it to investigate the internal structure of two large image databases. The image databases denoted by **PDB** contains 754034 (watermarked) images from an image provider. The second database, **SDB**, contains 322903 images collected from the internet by a commercial image search engine. We computed first the distributions p and then the square-roots h. In all experiments we used eight bins/channel. We get 8 one-point orbits, 56 three-point orbits and 56 six-point orbits. The dimensions of the blocks (Eq.(5) are $(120, 56, 336)$. We apply the transform resulting in the new vector $v = (v^t, v^a, v^s)$ corresponding to the vector spaces in Eq.(4).

We describe first some of our experiments regarding the statistical properties of these databases and then we illustrate the compression properties of the group theoretical transform in Section 3.

We first computed the norms of the vectors v^t, v^a and v^s, their mean and max value of $\|v^a\|^2$ for **PDB** and **SDB**. The coefficients in v^a (see also Table 1) are given by differences between contributions from even permutations and odd permutations in a

Table 2. Contributions of the coefficients

Database	$E\left(\|v^t\|^2\right)$	$E\left(\|v^a\|^2\right)$	$E\left(\|v^s\|^2\right)$	Max$(\|v^a\|^2)$	zero vs. non-zero
PDB	0.606	0.042	0.350	0.312	0.057
SDB	0.678	0.031	0.291	0.278	0.144

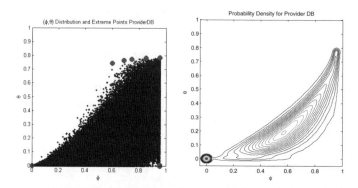

Fig. 2. Location and probability distribution from **PDB**

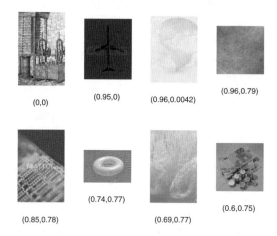

Fig. 3. Extreme images in **PDB**

six-orbit. If we assume that even and odd permutations are statistically equally likely then we expect the value of these coefficients to be small on average. We also computed the histogram (with 1000 bins) of these norms $\|v^a\|^2$ and computed the ratio between the probability of the first bin (with the small values of the norm) and the sum over the remaining bins (representing the non-zero norm values). The results are collected in Table 2.

This shows that the main contribution comes form v^t and the contributions from v^a are indeed low. We also see that there is a difference between the two databases where the contribution of the v^a is higher for **PDB**. One reason for this could be the higher proportion of cartoon-like images with distinct color distributions in **PDB** as compared with **SDB**.

From the construction we know that the modified histograms and their transforms are unit vectors $\|v\|^2 = \|v^t\|^2 + \|v^a\|^2 + \|v^s\|^2 = 1$. Since $\|v^a\|^2$ is small we conclude that the three-dimensional vectors $v = (v^t, v^a, v^s)$ are concentrated in the neighborhood of one quarter of a great circle of the unit sphere. The length of v^t is also larger than the length of v^s. Based on these heuristic considerations we introduce the following polar coordinate system on the unit vectors given by the norms of the projection vectors:

$$\left(v^t, v^a, v^s\right) = \left(\cos\varphi\cos\theta, \cos\varphi\sin\theta, \sin\varphi\right) \tag{6}$$

The angle φ corresponds to the latitude and we think of it as an indication of the unbalance between the three channels (for a value of zero all the contribution is in the v^t part). The (longitudal) angle θ is a measure of the contribution of v^a. The (φ, θ)-distribution of the images (every dot corresponds to one image) in the **PDB** is shown in the left plot of Figure 2. The corresponding probability density distribution is shown in the right plot. This figure shows that the distribution of the images is concentrated around the origin and that the distribution has a banana-like shape in the (φ, θ)-space. The positions of the eight extreme points of the convex hull are marked with filled circles in the left plot of Figure 2. The images belonging to the eight extreme points of the convex hull are shown in Figure 3. Theorem 3.1. shows that wide-sense-stationary processes are partially de-correlated by the transform. In the remaining part of this section we will now investigate if the two databases define wide-sense-stationary processes.

We illustrate the effect of the transform on the correlation matrix in Figure 4 showing the contour plots of the correlation matrices computed from the square-root transformed histograms before and after the transformation. It can be clearly seen that the effect of the transformation is a concentration in the first 120 components given by the vectors v^t. In the following experiment we evaluated the approximation error introduced by reducing the correlation matrix computed from the transformed histograms (Figure 4) to the block-diagonal matrix with block-sizes (120,56, 336). We computed the first 20 eigenvectors of the full correlation matrices and found that they explain about 85% of the summed eigenvalues for both databases. We also computed the 20 eigenvectors for the block-structured correlation matrix. From the construction of the blocks we expect that these eigenvectors of the block-diagonal matrix are elements of the 120, 56 or 336-dimensional subspaces defined by the blocks. In Table 3 we illustrate the accumulated, normed eigenvalues $A_K = (\sum \gamma_{k=1}^{K})/(\sum \gamma_{k=1}^{512})$ where γ_k is the k-th eigenvalue and we list to which block the different eigenvectors belong. We see the minor role of the coefficients in v^a: the only eigenvectors from the second block are in positions nine and eleven. Also here we see that **PDB** has a higher contribution from v^a.

Table 3. Eigenvalues and Block-Number for the Block-Diagonal Eigenvectors

	1	2	3	4	5	6	7	8	9	10	11	12	13	14	15
SDB	0.40	0.51	0.57	0.62	0.65	0.67	0.70	0.72	0.74	0.75	0.76	0.77	0.78	0.79	0.80
Block	1	1	3	1	1	3	1	3	3	3	2	1	1	3	3
PDB	0.41	0.49	0.55	0.59	0.63	0.66	0.68	0.70	0.71	0.72	0.74	0.75	0.76	0.77	0.78
Block	1	3	1	1	3	1	3	3	2	1	3	3	1	3	3

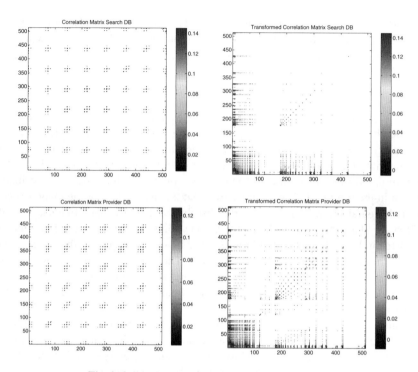

Fig. 4. Original and transformed correlation matrices

To get a more quantitative measure on how good the block-diagonal eigenvalues approximate the full matrix eigenvectors we computed the approximation values:

$$\gamma_{m,n} = \frac{\sum_{k=1}^{n} \left\| \widetilde{B}_m b_k \right\|}{n} \tag{7}$$

where $\widetilde{B}_m$ is the matrix of the m first eigenvectors of the block-diagonal approximation and b_k is the k-th eigenvector of the full correlation matrix. The value of $\gamma_{m,n}$ is a normalized measure on how large part of the n first eigenvectors of the full correlation matrix are projected into the space of the first m eigenvectors of the block-diagonal matrix. Some of the results are shown in Figure 5 where the solid line shows the values of $\gamma_{mm}, m = 1..20$ (equal number of full and block-diagonal eigenvectors) and the dashed line shows $\gamma_{20,n}$, the result for the full set of 20 eigenvectors of the block-diagonal matrix.

We see that the first 20 eigenvectors explain about 85% of the contributions from the first 20 eigenvectors of the full correlation matrix. Since the contribution from the last eigenvectors to the total variation (see also Table 3) is small we find that the approximation computed from the block-diagonal matrix is probably sufficient for most applications.

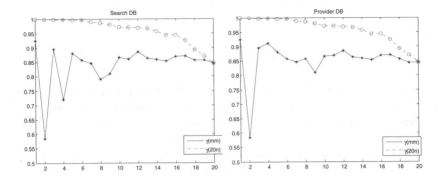

Fig. 5. Projection properties of the approximation.

5   Hierarchical Transforms and Bin Quantization

The experiments described so far show that the transform, derived from the assumption that permutations of the R, G and B channels are likely to occur with the same probabilities, lead to a separation of the histogram space into three clearly separated blocks. From an S (3) point of view nothing can be said about the internal structure of these blocks and if we want to transform them we have to use different sources of information about them. In the following we will introduce additional structure based on the bins defining the histogram. We consider only RGB histogram consisting of $2^n \times 2^n \times 2^n$ bins. We call such a histogram an level n histogram. In the experiments we will use histograms of size $1^3, 2^3, 4^3$ and 8^3, i.e. histograms of levels zero to three. A level-n histogram is the parent of a level-$(n+1)$ histogram.

We start with the parent node describing an orbit with label $(2k, 2l, 2m)$. There are eight possible children $\left\{ (\widetilde{k}, \widetilde{l}, \widetilde{m}) = (2k + \Delta_k, 2l + \Delta_l, 2m + \Delta_m) \right\}, 0 \leq \Delta_k, \Delta_l,$ $\Delta_m \leq 1$. Since $(\widetilde{k}, \widetilde{l}, \widetilde{m})$ is the label of an orbit they have to fulfil the conditions $\widetilde{k} \leq \widetilde{l} \leq \widetilde{m}$. For the case $k < l < m$ we see that $\widetilde{k} < \widetilde{l} < \widetilde{m}$ and all nodes with eight elements have thus eight-element children nodes. For a parent node $(2k, 2l, 2l), k < l$ the labels $\left\{ (\widetilde{k}, \widetilde{l}, \widetilde{l}) = (2k + \Delta_k, 2l + 1, 2l) \right\}$ are not allowed and they have therefore six-element orbits as children. For the case $(2k, 2k, 2k)$ we find four children $(2k, 2k, 2k)$, $(2k+1, 2k+1, 2k+1), (2k, 2k, 2k+1), (2k, 2k+1, 2k+1)$, the first two are one-point orbits, the last two are three-point orbits. We now consider the coefficients related to the trivial representations. Every orbit produces one such coefficient and we can collect the coefficients originating in the same parent orbit into vectors of size four, six and eight. In our experiments we transform these four, six and eight dimensional vectors using the matrices P_4, P_6, P_8:

$$
P_4 = \begin{pmatrix} 1/2 & 1/2 & 1/2 & 1/2 \\ \sqrt{1/2} & -\sqrt{1/2} & 0 & 0 \\ 0 & 0 & \sqrt{1/2} & -\sqrt{1/2} \\ 1/2 & 1/2 & -1/2 & -1/2 \end{pmatrix}
$$

$$P_6 = \left(\begin{array}{cccccc} \sqrt{1/6} & \sqrt{1/6} & \sqrt{1/6} & \sqrt{1/6} & \sqrt{1/6} & \sqrt{1/6} \\ & & \cdots & & & \end{array} \right)$$

and

$$P_8 = \left(\begin{array}{cccccccc} \sqrt{1/8} & \sqrt{1/8} & \sqrt{1/8} & \sqrt{1/8} & \sqrt{1/8} & \sqrt{1/8} & \sqrt{1/8} & \sqrt{1/8} \\ & & & \cdots & & & & \end{array} \right)$$

For the following discussion only the first line in the three matrices is relevant. This choice ensures that we compute the average over the coefficients of the children. The remaining rows are chosen so that the transformation matrix is orthonormal. Only the average is used in the next stage. As a result we get a sequence of decompositions of the 120D space (related to the trivial representation) $120D \mapsto (20D, 100D) \mapsto (4D, 16D, 100D) \mapsto (1D, 3D, 16D, 100D)$ and a final decomposition of the 512D space into a sequence of subspaces:

$$V_1 \subset V_4 \subset V_{20} \subset V_{120} \subset V_{176} \subset V_{512}$$

We investigated the properties of the hierarchical decomposition on a smaller database consisting of 16734 images from the search engine. We call this database the "Small-Search-Engine Database" or **SSDB**. On the (square root) of the histograms we first applied the S(3) transform and then the decomposition of the 120D block. This results in a block-diagonal matrix consisting of six blocks of sizes $1, 3, 16, 100, 76, 336$ We compute the first twenty eigenvectors from this block-diagonal matrix and compute to which block they belong. We found that the first eigenvector comes from block one, the second from block four and the third from block three, etc.. The complete distribution is shown in Figure 6.

    We also evaluated the influence of the transformation on the performance of a database search strategy. For this we first computed for each image the first 20 PCA coefficients. Then we choose 500 random images from the **SSDB** as query images. For each query image we computed the distance to all images in the **SSDB** using the usual Euclidean or L^2-norm based on the feature vectors computed from the PCA coefficients

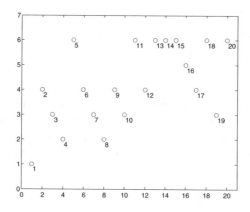

Fig. 6. Blocks and Eigenvectors

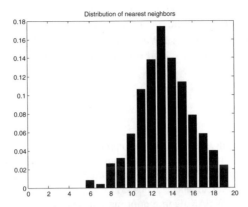

Fig. 7. Histogram over Ranks

in the original and the transformed coordinates. If k is the index of the query image and l denotes the l-th nearest neighbor of this query image computed from the feature vectors in the original space then we define $rank(k, l)$ as the retrieval rank computed from the transformed PCA coordinates. In other words: the image that comes in the l-th position in the ordered distances in the original feature space comes at position $rank(k, l)$ in the distance list computed from the transformed coordinates (Since the query image comes always first in this list we start indexing with zero). Some results obtained are shown in Figure 7 where we computed first for each query image how many of the first 20 retrieved images in the original coordinate space are located in the list of the first 20 images computed from the transformed vectors (which is the case when $rank(k, l) \leq 20$ for $l \leq 20$). We then computed the histogram over these numbers. We see that these numbers are always greater than five, which means that the approximation-based search always found the five most similar images from the full-PCA based retrieval. Most of the times we found twelve of them and never all twenty.

6 Summary

In this paper we showed that the intuitive assumption that R, G and B channels can be interchanged on average motivates the application of tools from the representation theory of the symmetric group S (3). We implemented a fast transform using tools from representation theory and used them to investigate the structure of two large image databases and to develop fast PCA-like compression methods. We further combined the permutation-based transformation with a hierarchical decomposition based on the quantization level of the RGB histogram. The properties of the resulting transformations were illustrated with the help of two large image databases. The quantitative performance of the different approximations shows that the compressed feature vectors are probably sufficient for many retrieval tasks.

Acknowledgements. The support of the Swedish Research Council, the Knowledge Foundation, Sweden and the Ministry of Education and Science of the Spanish

Government through the *DATASAT* project ($ESP - 2005 - 00724 - C05 - C05$) and the *MIPRCV* project ($CSD2007 - 00018$) are gratefully acknowledged. Pedro Latorre Carmona is a *Juan de la Cierva* Programme researcher (Ministry of Education and Science). The databases were provided by Picsearch AB, Stockholm and Matton AB, Stockholm.

References

1. Chirikjian, G.S., Kyatkin, A.B.: Engineering applications of noncommutative harmonic analysis: with emphasis on rotation and motion groups. CRC Press, Boca Raton (2000)
2. Comaniciu, D., Ramesh, V., Meer, P.: Kernel-based object tracking. IEEE Trans. Pattern Analysis and Machine Intelligence 25, 564–577 (2003)
3. Cooley, J.W., Tukey, J.W.: An algorithm for machine calculation of complex Fourier series. Mathematical Computations 19, 297–301 (1965)
4. Diaconis, P.: Group representation in probability and statistics. Institute of Mathematical Statistics, Hayward, Calif. (1988)
5. Fässler, A., Stiefel, E.: Group theoretical methods and their applications. Birkhäuser, Basel (1992)
6. Fulton, W., Harris, J.: Representation Theory. Springer, Heidelberg (1991)
7. Geusebroek, J.M.: Compact object descriptors from local colour invariant histograms. In: Proc. British Machine Vision Conference, BMVC (2006)
8. Hafner, J., Sawhney, H.S., Equitz, W., Flickner, M., Niblack, W.: Efficient color histogram indexing for quadratic form distance functions. IEEE Trans. Pattern Analysis and Machine Intelligence 17(7), 729–736 (1995)
9. Holmes, R.B.: Mathematical foundations of signal processing. SIAM Review 21(3), 361–388 (1979)
10. Lenz, R.: Group Theoretical Transforms in Image Processing. Springer, Heidelberg (1994)
11. Lenz, R.: Investigation of receptive fields using representations of dihedral groups. J. Visual Communication and Image Representation 6(3), 209–227 (1995)
12. Lenz, R.: Crystal vision-applications of point groups in computer vision. In: Yagi, Y., Kang, S.B., Kweon, I.S., Zha, H. (eds.) ACCV 2007, Part II. LNCS, vol. 4844, pp. 744–753. Springer, Heidelberg (2007)
13. Rockmore, D.: Recent progress and applications in group FFT's. In: Computational noncommutative algebra and applications. Kluwer, Dordrecht (2004)
14. Serre, J.P.: Linear representations of finite groups. Springer, Heidelberg (1977)
15. Smeulders, A.W.M., Worring, M., Santini, S., Gupta, A., Jain, R.: Content based image retrieval at the end of the early years. IEEE Trans. Pattern Analysis and Machine Intelligence 22, 1349–1380 (2000)
16. Sridhar, V., Nascimento, M.A., Li, X.: Region-based image retrieval using multiple-features. In: Chang, S.-K., Chen, Z., Lee, S.-Y. (eds.) VISUAL 2002. LNCS, vol. 2314, pp. 61–75. Springer, Heidelberg (2002)
17. Srivastava, A., Jermyn, I., Joshi, S.: Riemannian analysis of probability density functions with applications in vision. In: IEEE Conf. Comp. Vision and Pattern Recognition, Minneapolis, MN, pp. 1–8 (2007)
18. Swain, M.J., Ballard, D.H.: Color indexing. Int. J. Comp. Vision 7(1), 11–32 (1991)
19. Yoo, H.W., Jang, D.S., Jung, S.H., Park, J.H.: Visual information retrieval system via content-based approach. Pattern Recognition 35, 749–769 (2002)

Monocular SLAM Reconstructions and 3D City Models: Towards a Deep Consistency

Pierre Lothe[1], Steve Bourgeois[1], Fabien Dekeyser[1], Eric Royer[2], and Michel Dhome[2]

[1] CEA LIST, Embedded Vision Systems Laboratory
Point Courrier 94, Gif-sur-Yvette, F-91191 France
[2] LASMEA UMR 6602, Université Blaise Pascal/CNRS
24 Avenue des Landais, Aubière, 63177 France
`pierre.lothe@cea.fr, steve.bourgeois@cea.fr,`
`fabien.dekeyser@cea.fr, eric.royer@univ-bpclermont.fr,`
`michel.dhome@univ-bpclermont.fr`

Abstract. Monocular SLAM reconstruction algorithm advancements enable their integration in various applications: trajectometry, 3D model reconstruction, etc. However, proposed methods still have drift limitations when applied to large-scale sequences. In this paper, we propose a two steps post-processing algorithm which exploits a CAD model of the environment to correct SLAM reconstructions. First, a specific non-rigid ICP between the reconstructed 3D point cloud and the known CAD model is proposed. Then, a new constrained bundle adjustment process is presented to improve the accuracy of the obtained reconstructions. Experimental results on both synthetic and real sequences point out that the 3D scene geometry regains its consistency and that the camera trajectory is improved: mean distance between the reconstructed cameras and the ground truth is less than 50 centimetres on several hundreds of meters.

1 Introduction

Simultaneous Localization and Mapping (SLAM) and Structure from Motion (SfM) methods enable the reconstruction of both the trajectory of a moving camera and the environment. However, the first proposed algorithms present a significant computation burden which avoids large-scale sequence reconstruction. Recent works tend to overcome this limit by reducing the problem complexity while still only using easily embeddable and low-cost materials.

For example, Nister et al. [1] do not use any global optimisation. It enables them to speed up the computation time but it is very sensitive to error accumulations since the 3D scene geometry is never questioned. Davison et al. [2] propose a Kalman-filter based solution. This method reaches real-time if the number of landmarks is quite small. Another approach is to use a full non-linear optimisation of the scene geometry: Royer et al. [3] use a hierarchical bundle adjustment in order to build large-scale scenes. Afterwards, Mouragnon et al. [4] propose an incremental non-linear minimisation method in order to almost completely avoid computer memory problem by only optimizing the position of the geometry scene on the few last cameras.

Nevertheless, monocular SLAM and SFM methods still present limitations: the trajectory and 3D point cloud are known up to a similarity. Thus, all the displacements and

A. Ranchordas et al. (Eds.): VISIGRAPP 2009, CCIS 68, pp. 201–214, 2010.

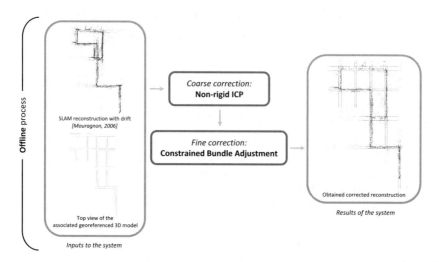

Fig. 1. Summary of the proposed method. We proposed to correct an original distorted SLAM reconstruction thanks to a coarse 3D model of the environment. The result is superimposed on a satellite image.

3D positions are relative and it is not possible to obtain an absolute localisation of each reconstructed element. Besides, as well as being prone to numerical errors accumulation [2,4], monocular SLAM algorithms may present scale factor drift: their reconstructions are done up to a scale factor, theoretically constant on the whole sequence, but it appears that it changes in practice. Even if these errors could be tolerated for guidance applications which only use local relative displacements, it becomes a burning issue for other applications using SLAM reconstruction results like trajectometry or global localization.

To improve SLAM results, a possible approach consists in injecting a priori knowledge about the trajectory [5] or about the environment geometry [6]. This last kind of information can be provided by CAD models. Furthermore, even if high precision models are still unusual, coarse 3D city models are now wide spread in GIS databases.

Thus, we introduce in this paper a solution which consists in correcting SLAM reconstruction thanks to the information provided by a coarse 3D model (i.e. only composed of vertical planes representing buildings fronts) of the environment (see figure 1). First, a model of SLAM reconstruction error is used to establish a specific non-rigid transformations model of the reconstructed environment with few degrees of freedom (section 2). Then, we estimate the parameters of these transformations which allow fitting the SLAM reconstruction on the CAD model through a non-rigid ICP optimisation (section 3). Finally, we optimize all the scene geometry by minimizing in the same time the information provided by both the images and the CAD model (section 4). The complete refinement process is then evaluated on both synthetic and real sequences (section 5).

2 Transformations Model

The registration of 3D point cloud and CAD model has been widely studied. Main used methods are Iterative Closest Point ICP [7,8] or Levenberg-Marquardt [9]. Neverthe-less, these methods only work originally with Euclidean transformations or similarities, which are not adapted to our problem. To overcome with this limit, non-rigid fitting methods have been proposed. Because of their high degree of freedom, this category of algorithm needs to be constrained. For example Castellani et al. [10] use regulariza-tion terms to make the used transformation be in accordance with his problem scope. Therefore we will now introduce the specific non-rigid transformations we use for our problem.

2.1 Non-rigid Transformations Model

The constraints we used to limit the applicable transformations on the 3D SLAM recon-struction are based on experimental results. We observe that the scale factor is nearly constant on straight lines trajectory and change during turnings (see figure 9(c)). So we have decided to consider trajectory straight lines as rigid body while articulations are put in place in each turning. Thus the selected transformations are piecewise similarities with joint extremities constraints.

Thus, the first step is to automatically segment our reconstructed trajectory. We use the idea suggested by Lowe in [11]. He proposes to cut recursively a set of points into segments with respect both to their length and their deviation. So we split the reconstructed trajectory (represented as a set of temporally ordered key cameras) into m different segments $(T_i)_{1 \leq i \leq m}$ whose extremities are cameras denoted $(\mathbf{e}_i, \mathbf{e}_{i+1})$.

2.2 Transformations Parametrisation

Once the trajectory is split into segments, each 3D reconstructed point must be asso-ciated to one camera segment. We say that a segment "sees" a 3D point if at least one camera of the segment observes this point. There are two cases for point-segment asso-ciation. The simplest is when only one segment sees this point: the point is then linked to this segment. The second appears when a point is seen by two or more different seg-ments. In this case, we have tested different policies which give the same results and we arbitrarily decided to associate the point to the last segment which sees it.

We call B_i a fragment composed both of the cameras of T_i (i.e. those included between $\mathbf{e}_i$ and $\mathbf{e}_{i+1}$) and of the associated reconstructed 3D points. Obviously, for $2 \leq i \leq m - 1$, the fragment B_i shares its extremities with its neighbours B_{i-1} and B_{i+1}.

We saw in section 2.1 that applied transformations are piecewise similarities with joint extremities. Practically, those transformations are parameterized with the 3D translation of the extremities $(\mathbf{e}_i)_{1 \leq i \leq m+1}$. From these translations, we will deduce the similarities to apply to each fragment (i.e. its cameras and 3D points). Precisely, since camera is embedded on a land vehicle, the roll angle is not called into question. Then, each extremity $\mathbf{e}_i$ has 3 degrees of freedom and so each fragment has 6 degrees of freedom as expected.

Figure 2 presents an example of extremity displacement.

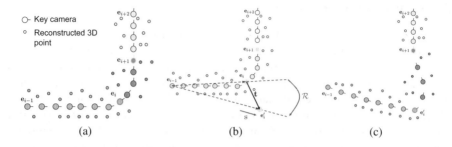

Fig. 2. An example of fragment-based reconstruction transformation. (a) The segmentation of the original reconstruction. (b) A 3D translation of the extremity $\mathbf{e}_i$. The similarity $\mathcal{S}(\mathbf{e}_{i-1}, s, \mathcal{R})$ is then deduced from this 3D displacement and applied to the whole fragment $\mathcal{B}_{i-1}$. An equivalent treatment is realized on $\mathcal{B}_i$. (c) The result of the transformation: the two fragments linked to the moved extremity have been modified.

3   Non-rigid ICP

Once we have defined the used non-rigid transformations (section 2.1) and their parameterisation (section 2.2), we can use additional information provided by CAD model to improve the SLAM reconstruction. Thus, we propose in this part a non-rigid ICP between the reconstructed 3D point cloud and CAD model: first we present the cost function we minimize, the different optimization steps and then parameters initialisation.

Cost Function. Once all the pre-treatment steps are done, we dispose of both the fragmented reconstruction and a simple coarse 3D model of the scene.

In our work, we want to fit the 3D point cloud onto the CAD model. The base cost function ϵ is then the normal distance d between a 3D point and the CAD model $\mathcal{M}$, i.e. the distance between a 3D point $\mathcal{Q}_i$ and the plane $\mathcal{P}_{g_i}$ it belongs to:

$$
\begin{aligned}
\epsilon(\mathcal{Q}_i, \mathcal{M}) &= d(\mathcal{Q}_i, \mathcal{M}) \\
&= d(\mathcal{Q}_i, \mathcal{P}_{g_i})
\end{aligned}
\tag{1}
$$

Non-linear Minimization. The aim of this step is to transform the different fragments to minimise the distance between the reconstructed point cloud and the CAD model, i.e. solving the problem:

$$
\min_{\mathbf{e}_1, \ldots, \mathbf{e}_{m+1}} \sum_i d(\mathcal{Q}_i, \mathcal{M})^2
\tag{2}
$$

Point-Plane Association. The problem in point-plane association is that we do not know in reality on which CAD model plane $\mathcal{P}_{g_i}$ belongs each 3D reconstructed point. So we make the hypothesis that it is the nearest one. Equation 1 becomes:

$$
\epsilon(\mathcal{Q}_i, \mathcal{M}) = \min_{\mathcal{P}_j \in \mathcal{M}} d(\mathcal{Q}_i, \mathcal{P}_j)
\tag{3}
$$

Furthermore, to reduce algorithm complexity, we consider that for a point Q_i, the nearest plane $\mathcal{P}_{h_i}$ does not change during the minimization. Thus, the selection between 3D point and corresponding plane can be done outside the minimization:

$$\forall Q_i, \mathcal{P}_{h_i} = \underset{\mathcal{P} \in \mathcal{M}}{argmin} \; d(Q_i, \mathcal{P}) \tag{4}$$

Besides, the distance d takes into account that the planes are finite: to be associated to a plane $\mathcal{P}$, a 3D point Q must have its normal projection inside $\mathcal{P}$ bounds.

Robust Estimation. There are two cases where the association $(Q_i, \mathcal{P}_{h_i})$ can be wrong: if the initial position of Q_i is too far from its real position or if it is not (in the real scene) on the CAD model. In those two cases, $d(Q_i, \mathcal{P}_{h_i})$ could make the minimization fail. To limit this effect, we insert a robust M-estimator ρ in equation (2):

$$\underset{e_1,\dots,e_m}{min} \sum_i \rho(d(Q_i, \mathcal{P}_{h_i})) \tag{5}$$

We chose to use the Tukey M-estimator [12]. The M-estimator threshold can be automatically fixed thanks to the Median Absolute Deviation (MAD). The MAD works with the hypothesis that the studied data follow a Gaussian distribution around the model. It is to note that this assumption can be done for each individual fragment but not for the whole reconstruction. So we decided to use a different M-estimator threshold ξ_j per fragment. This implies that we have to normalize the Tukey values on each fragment:

$$\rho'_{l_i}(d(Q_i, \mathcal{P}_{h_i})) = \frac{\rho_{l_i}(d(Q_i, \mathcal{P}_{h_i}))}{\max_{Q_j \in \mathcal{B}_{l_i}} \rho_{l_i}(d(Q_j, \mathcal{P}_{h_j}))} \tag{6}$$

where l_i is the index of the fragment owning Q_i and ρ_{l_i} the Tukey M-estimator used with the threshold ξ_{l_i}.

Fragment Weighting. With this cost function, each fragment will have a weight in the minimization proportional to the number of 3D points it contains. Then, fragments with few points could be not optimized in favour of the others. To give the same weight to each fragment, we must unify all the Tukey values of their 3D points with respect to their cardinal:

$$\rho^*_{l_i}(d(Q_i, \mathcal{P}_{h_i})) = \frac{\rho'_{l_i}(d(Q_i, \mathcal{P}_{h_i}))}{card(\mathcal{B}_{l_i})} \tag{7}$$

and the final minimization problem is:

$$\underset{e_1,\dots,e_{m+1}}{min} \sum_i \rho^*_{l_i}(d(Q_i, \mathcal{P}_{h_i})) \tag{8}$$

that we solve using the Levenberg-Marquardt algorithm [13].

Iterative Optimisation. Practically, several non-linear minimisations are done successively with computing the point-plane association before each one of them. It enables 3D points to change their associated plane without losing cost-function computation time.

Initialisation. Non-linear algorithms require a correct initialisation: the 3D reconstruction should be placed in the same frame than the CAD model. To realize this stage, estimating an initial rigid transformation is sufficient when the 3D reconstruction is accurate. However, the drift of the scale factor frequently observed with SLAM reconstruction may induce important geometrical deformations. Therefore, to ensure convergence of the algorithm, we chose to place roughly each extremity e_i around the CAD model. It can be done automatically if the sequence is synchronised with GPS data for example. Otherwise, it could be realized manually through graphic interface.

The figure 5(a) gives an example of the obtained SLAM reconstruction after the ICP step on the synthetic sequence (this sequence is fully studied in section 5.1). It appears that even if the global consistency of the trajectory and 3D point cloud is corrected, local errors can still be important. In fact the error model proposed in the non-rigid ICP step is not perfect. The used transformations are overconstrained to reach fine corrections: even if the scale factor drift occurs mainly during the turnings, it also appends during straight lines. Thus, at the end of the ICP process, errors along the trajectory direction may be still prominent (see figures 5(a) and 8(b)). More results about the non-rigid ICP step can be found in section 5.

In the following section, we will present an algorithm which permits the decrease of those residual errors.

4 Constrained Bundle Adjustment

To reach more accurate corrections, constraints over straight lines must be relaxed. Such a problem is often tackled with bundle adjustment method [14]. This process optimizes each scene parameter (3D point positions and camera poses) with respect to the sensor observations.

In this section, first we expose the limits of classical bundle adjustment methods and then we propose a new constrained bundle adjustment that exploits both camera observations and 3D model information.

4.1 Classical Bundle Adjustment

Classical bundle adjustments [14] minimize the reprojection error of the 3D points $(\mathcal{Q}_i)_i$ in the cameras $(\mathcal{C}_j)_j$. The optimized parameters are then the position of the 3D points $(\mathcal{Q}_i)_i$ and the extrinsic parameters of the cameras $(\mathcal{C}_j)_j$ denoted $(\mathsf{C}_j^E)_j$. The cost function is then:

$$f_{classic}(\mathsf{C}_1^E, \ldots, \mathsf{C}_N^E, \mathcal{Q}_1, \ldots, \mathcal{Q}_M) = \sum_{1 \leq j \leq N} \sum_{i \in \mathcal{A}_j} ||\mathbf{q}_i^j - \pi(\mathsf{P}_j \mathcal{Q}_i)||^2 \qquad (9)$$

where $\mathcal{A}_j$ is the set of indexes of 3D points seen by $\mathcal{C}_j$, P_j is the 3×4 pose matrix of the camera $\mathcal{C}_j$, $\pi(\mathsf{P}_j \mathcal{Q}_i)$ is the projection of $\mathcal{Q}_i$ into the image of camera $\mathcal{C}_j$ and $\mathbf{q}_i^j$ the corresponding feature point.

We have observed that this cost function can induce again incorrect deformations both on the camera trajectory and the 3D point cloud, if it is used after the non-rigid

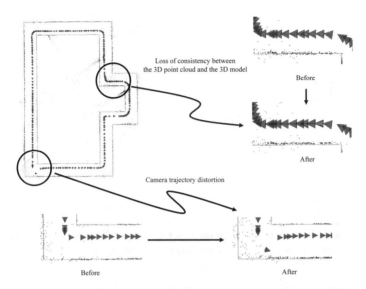

Fig. 3. Result of a classical global bundle adjustment. Applying a classical geometry optimisation, from the non-rigid ICP result, can lead to incorrect scene deformations.

ICP step (see figure 3). This is due to the fact that the geometric consistency between the reconstructed 3D point cloud and the 3D city model is totally suppressed.

Thus, in the following, we will present a way to include the 3D city model information into the bundle adjustment.

4.2   Proposed Constrained Bundle Adjustment

Two kinds of information have to be included in the cost function: the relation between the cameras and the observed 3D points and the geometric consistency between these reconstructed 3D points and the provided 3D city model. An intuitive approach, when having to fuse two kinds of information in a bundle adjustment problem, is to sum those two residual errors (one for each kind of information) up to a factor λ [15,16].

Overview. A usual way to evaluate the consistency between a point cloud and a 3D model consists in measuring the sum of the orthogonal distance between each 3D point and the nearest model surface (see section 3). To combine properly this measure with the usual reprojection error (see equation 9), these two terms must be consistent. For example, it is possible to use the 3D distance between the 3D point and the backprojected ray from its 2D observation [17]. On the other hand, the proposed solution consists in expressing the reprojection error through the 3D distance between the 3D point and the vertical and horizontal interpretation planes associated to its observation. Those planes are two particular planes, which come from the backprojection of the parallel axis to

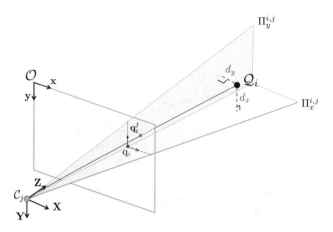

Fig. 4. 3D residue measurement based on interpretation plane. The two residues are the distances d_x and d_y between the point $\mathcal{Q}_i$ and the planes $\Pi_x^{i,j}$ and $\Pi_y^{i,j}$.

Ox and Oy centered on the 2D feature point (figure 4). The function to minimize is then the sum of distances between the 3D points and the three considered plans:

$$f_{LC}(\mathbf{C}_1^E, \ldots, \mathbf{C}_N^E, \mathcal{Q}_1, \ldots, \mathcal{Q}_M) = \sum_{1 \leq j \leq N} \sum_{i \in A_j} \rho\left(d(\mathcal{Q}_i, \Pi_x^{i,j}) + d(\mathcal{Q}_i, \Pi_y^{i,j}) + \lambda \times d(\mathcal{Q}_i, \Pi_i)\right) \ (10)$$

where $\Pi_x^{i,j}$ and $\Pi_y^{i,j}$ are the interpretation planes from the camera $\mathcal{C}_j$ and the 2D point $\mathbf{q}_i$. Π_i is the nearest plane for the 3D point $\mathcal{Q}_i$. λ is the factor to fixe in order to balance the two different constraints. ρ is the Tukey M-estimator [12]. The other notations are the one used in section 4.1.

Evaluation. This function has been evaluated on the synthetic sequence in order to be compared to the known ground truth. The table 1 presents the statistics of the obtained 3D reconstructions for different values of λ. As expected, it appears that for

Table 1. Statistics of the synthetic sequence reconstruction after the bundle adjustment based on residue linear combination

	After ICP (bundle initialisation)	$\lambda = 0.01$	$\lambda = 0.1$	$\lambda = 0.5$	$\lambda = 1$	$\lambda = 1.5$	$\lambda = 2$
Camera mean distance to ground truth (m)	0.51	0.52	0.48	**0.32**	0.35	0.42	0.53
Standard Deviation (m)	0.59	0.89	0.67	**0.23**	**0.23**	0.35	0.77
3D points-Model mean distance (m)	0.11	0.13	0.06	**0.05**	**0.05**	**0.05**	**0.05**
Standard Deviation (m)	0.08	**0.04**	0.06	0.07	0.07	0.07	0.07
Tukey threshold	0.38	×	×	×	×	×	×

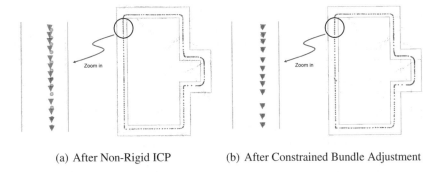

(a) After Non-Rigid ICP   (b) After Constrained Bundle Adjustment

Fig. 5. Result of the reconstruction after the different steps of the proposed method. Red pyramids are the reconstructed cameras while green spheres are the camera positions ground truth.

a small value of λ, the 3D model constraint is too weak and the trajectory is then modified without this constraint (figure 6(a)). On the contrary, when λ is high, the 3D model term in equation (10) is predominant. The 3D points are forced to be on the model planes even if it is not consistent with the camera positions (figure 6(c)). The optimal solution has been found for $lambda = 0.5$ (see figure 6(b) and table 1). The results presented in the following are the ones obtained with this value. It is to note that the value of λ may vary with the processed sequence [15]. Nevertheless, we have observed that using $\lambda = 0.5$ give us satisfactory results (see figures 5(b), 6(b) and 9(e)).

The following section presents more detailed results provided both by the non-rigid ICP and then by the constrained bundle adjustment we propose.

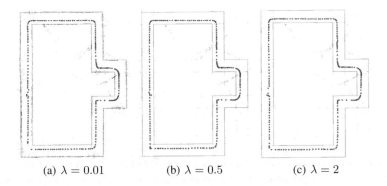

(a) $\lambda = 0.01$ (b) $\lambda = 0.5$ (c) $\lambda = 2$

Fig. 6. Results of bundle adjustment based on residue linear combination for different λ values. When the value of λ increases, the 3D points tend to be flattened on the 3D model.

5 Experimental Results

In this part, we will present results on both synthetic and real sequences. The SLAM algorithm we use for our reconstruction is the one proposed by Mouragnon et al. [4].

5.1 Synthetic Sequence

Figure 7 presents the different steps of the proposed non-rigid ICP. The synthetic sequence (based on 3D model figure 7(a)) have been made by using the SLAM algorithm in a textured 3D world generated with a 3D computer graphics software. The followed trajectory is represented by the red arrows in figure 7(a).

Figure 8(a) underlines the original SLAM method drift. The scale factor is measured by computing the distance between two successive cameras and then computing the ratio for ground truth and reconstruction results. We see that this scale factor decreases in the course of the journey, making the 3D SLAM reconstruction being distorted (figure 7(b)). As consequence, the camera trajectory does not loop anymore.

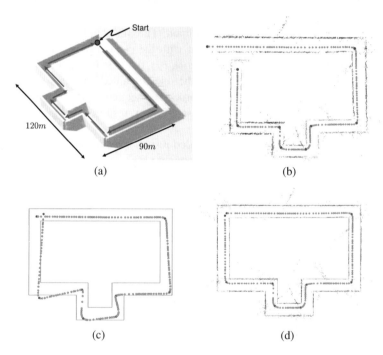

(a)   (b)

(c)   (d)

Fig. 7. Synthetic sequence treatment. (a) Synthetic 3D model. (b) Top view of its 3D reconstruction with [4] algorithm. Orange spheres are cameras while red ones are the fragment extremities. The automatic trajectory and point-fragment segmentation is also represented: the reconstructed 3D points are coloured by fragment belonging. Figure (c) is the user initialisation of the trajectory around the CAD model (in green) before the ICP step. Figure (d) shows the 3D reconstruction after our non-rigid ICP: blue 3D points are inliers and red are outliers.

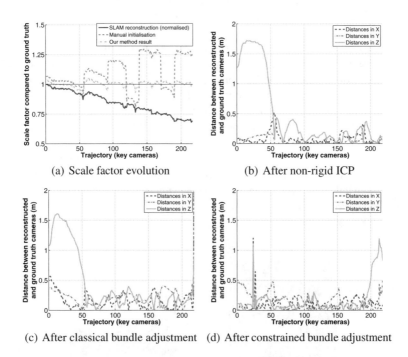

(a) Scale factor evolution   (b) After non-rigid ICP

(c) After classical bundle adjustment   (d) After constrained bundle adjustment

Fig. 8. Positioning error evolution. (a) We can observe the scale factor drift on the original SLAM reconstruction. After our method, scale factor is centred on 1. (b) shows the residual values on distances between reconstructed cameras and ground truth after the non-rigid ICP step. (c) and (d) compare those residual values after the classical and the proposed bundle adjustment. The (X, Y, Z) coordinates frame is relative to each camera: Z is the optical axis, X is the latitude axis and Y the altitude.

Table 2. Numerical results on the synthetic sequence. Each value is a mean over all the reconstruction.

	Before ICP	After ICP	After classical bundle adjustment	After constrained bundle adjustment $lambda = 0.5$
Camera mean distance to ground truth (m)	4.61	**0.51**	0.57	**0.32**
Standard Deviation (m)	2.25	**0.59**	0.46	**0.23**
3D points-Model mean distance (m)	3.37	**0.11**	0.15	**0.05**
Standard Deviation (m)	3.9	**0.08**	0.10	**0.07**
Tukey threshold	×	0.38	×	×

The first step of our method is the non-rigid ICP. For its initialisation, we have manually simulated GPS results: random position error has been assigned to each extremity (figure 7(c)).

Then we observe that after the non-rigid ICP (figure 7(d)) the loop is restored while no loop constraint is directly included into our transformation model. Besides, the 3D reconstructed point cloud regains its consistency. Table 2 confirms those enhancements: the average distance between the reconstructed cameras and the ground truth is reduced from more than 4 meters to about 50 centimetres. Statistics before ICP have been computed on the 5591 reconstructed 3D points (among the 6848 proposed by SLAM) kept as inliers by the ICP step.

Furthermore, we can notice in figure 8(b) that only errors along the direction of the trajectory remain significant. This is due to the fact that we have supposed the error on scale factor strictly constant on each segment. Although this hypothesis reveals to be only a rough approximation.

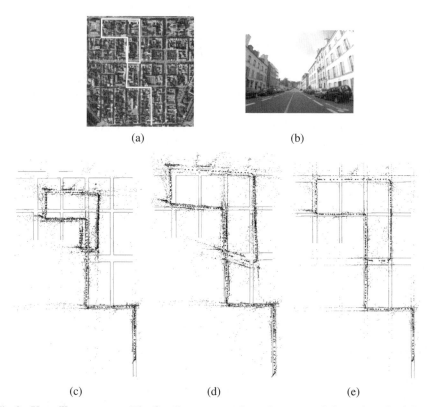

(a)   (b)

(c)   (d)   (e)

Fig. 9. Versailles sequence. The first line presents the real sequence information: the followed trajectory (a) and a frame of the recorded video (b). The second line presents the different configurations of SLAM reconstruction compared to the CAD model: the initial SLAM reconstruction with Mouragnon et al. [4] algorithm (c), the non-rigid ICP initialisation (d) and the result of the full proposed method (e).

Figure 8(d) shows that the proposed constrained bundle adjustment step permits to reduce those residual errors. The mean camera position error reaches about 32 centimetres, that is to say about twice less than after the ICP (table 2).

5.2   Real Sequence

The real sequence is a 640x480 video of a 1500 meters long tour in Versailles, France (see figure 9). The initial SLAM reconstruction is a good example of SLAM method drift: by manually putting it in the same coordinates frame than the model, we observe that the trajectory moves away from its real place from the third bend onwards. After our method, figure 9(e) shows that the drift is corrected along all the tour. Indeed, the camera trajectory follows the road between the buildings and besides, the reconstructed point cloud regains its consistency.

6   Conclusions

We have presented in this paper a post-processing algorithm that improves SLAM reconstruction. First, our method uses a non-rigid ICP between SLAM reconstruction and a coarse CAD model of the environment. Then, a constrained bundle adjustment is applied to refine the obtained reconstructed scene geometry. Synthetic and real experiments point out that method can clearly reduced the 3D positions error, in particular in X and Z directions: trajectory loop are restored and cameras position errors are reduced to less than 50 centimetres on several hundreds meters sequences.

In future work, we would like to find another bundle adjustment cost-function in order both to avoid to fix a λ parameter and to obtain still more accurate results in cameras positioning.

References

1. Nister, D., Naroditsky, O., Bergen, J.: Visual odometry. In: Computer Vision and Pattern Recognition, pp. 652–659 (2004)
2. Davison, A., Reid, I., Molton, N., Stasse, O.: MonoSLAM: Real-time single camera SLAM. Pattern Analysis and Machine Intelligence 26(6), 1052–1067 (2007)
3. Royer, E., Lhuillier, M., Dhome, M., Chateau, T.: Localization in urban environments: Monocular vision compared to a differential gps sensor. In: Computer Vision and Pattern Recognition, pp. 114–121 (2005)
4. Mouragnon, E., Lhuillier, M., Dhome, M., Dekeyser, F., Sayd, P.: Real time localization and 3d reconstruction. In: Computer Vision and Pattern Recognition, pp. 363–370 (2006)
5. Levin, A., Szeliski, R.: Visual odometry and map correlation. In: Computer Vision and Pattern Recognition, pp. 611–618 (2004)
6. Sourimant, G., Morin, L., Bouatouch, K.: Gps, gis and video fusion for urban modeling. In: Computer Graphics International (May 2007)
7. Rusinkiewicz, S., Levoy, M.: Efficient variants of the ICP algorithm. In: 3-D Digital Imaging and Modeling, pp. 145–152 (2001)
8. Zhao, W., Nister, D., Hsu, S.: Alignment of continuous video onto 3d point clouds. Pattern Analysis and Machine Intelligence 27(8), 1305–1318 (2005)

9. Fitzgibbon, A.: Robust registration of 2d and 3d point sets. In: British Machine Vision Conference, pp. 411–420 (2001)
10. Castellani, U., Gay-Bellile, V., Bartoli, A.: Joint reconstruction and registration of a deformable planar surface observed by a 3d sensor. In: 3-D Digital Imaging and Modeling, pp. 201–208 (2007)
11. Lowe, D.G.: Three-dimensional object recognition from single two-dimensional images. Artificial Intelligence 31(3), 355–395 (1987)
12. Huber, P.: Robust Statistics. Wiley, New-York (1981)
13. Levenberg, K.: A method for the solution of certain non-linear problems in least squares. Quart. Appl. Math. 2, 164–168 (1944)
14. Triggs, B., McLauchlan, P.F., Hartley, R.I., Fitzgibbon, A.W.: Bundle adjustment - a modern synthesis. In: International Conference on Computer Vision, pp. 298–372 (2000)
15. Bartoli, A., Gay-Bellile, V., Castellani, U., Peyras, J., Olsen, S., Sayd, P.: Coarse-to-fine low-rank structure-from-motion. In: Computer Vision and Pattern Recognition (2008)
16. Pilet, J., Lepetit, V., Fua, P.: Fast non-rigid surface detection, registration and realistic augmentation. International Journal of Computer Vision 76(2) (2008)
17. Ramalingam, S., Lodha, S., Sturm, P.: A generic structure-from-motion framework. Computer Vision and Image Understanding 103(3), 218–228 (2006)

GPU-Based Euclidean Distance Transforms and Their Application to Volume Rendering

Jens Schneider, Martin Kraus, and Rüdiger Westermann

Technische Universität München, Computer Graphics & Visualization Group
Boltzmannstraße 3, D-85748 Garching bei München, Germany

Abstract. We present discrete 2D and 3D distance transforms based on the vector propagation algorithm by Danielsson. Like other vector propagation algorithms, the proposed method is close to exact, i.e., the error can be strictly bounded from above and is significantly smaller than one pixel. Our contribution is that the algorithm runs entirely on consumer class graphics hardware, thereby achieving a throughput of up to 96 Mpixels/s. Therefore, the proposed method can be used in a wide range of applications that rely on both high speed and high quality. The usability of our approach is demonstrated in the context of hardware-accelerated volumetric isosurface raycasting.

1 Introduction

Algorithms that depend on distance transforms [1] or Voronoi diagrams [2] are ubiquitous. For instance, the automatic analysis of real-time video images at ever increasing resolutions, medical data processing, and artistic applications are just a few examples of a widely established technique. In nearly all cases that require distance transforms, algorithms capable of achieving throughputs of several million pixels per second are highly advantageous. Especially if the results are to be visualized immediately, it is a natural choice to perform data processing and filtering directly on the same commodity class graphics hardware used for visualization. To tap the graphic processing unit's (GPU) superior memory bandwidth and computing power, however, special SIMD-like programming paradigms have to be employed and communication with the host CPU must be minimized. Especially the latter has led to a rich catalogue of GPU-based modules for various tasks. Unfortunately, distance transforms and Voronoi diagrams running directly on the GPU are currently either fast or precise.

To address this disparity, we present a novel algorithm based on the vector propagation paradigm proposed in [3]. Our algorithm is able to approximate discrete Euclidean distance transforms, Voronoi diagrams, and generalized Voronoi diagrams entirely on a GPU, thereby achieving up to 96 Mpixels per second. Like other vector propagation methods it is close to exact, i.e., errors are very unlikely to occur, and each error can be bounded from above [4]. Since the average error is generally negligible, our method can be used for any practical purpose.

The rest of the paper is organized as follows. In the next section, we review related work. After that we briefly state the problem to be solved by our approach. In Sect. 4 we then present our algorithm and we describe the actual implementation using the DirectX

A. Ranchordas et al. (Eds.): VISIGRAPP 2009, CCIS 68, pp. 215–228, 2010.

API. Our results are presented in Sect. 5, and some applications of our 3D algorithm are sketched in Sect. 6. Finally, we present our conclusions and directions for future work.

2 Related Work

In this section we give a short overview of related work. For an exhaustive review of prior art we refer the reader to [5,6]. Furthermore, a broad overview of the construction and applications of Voronoi diagrams is provided in [7,8].

Considerable effort has been spent to accelerate the computation of distance transforms. The most promising algorithms approximate or solve the aforementioned problems by using a sweeping strategy in $\mathcal{O}(N)$ [3,9,10], where N is the number of pixels in the image. In contrast, algorithms following the wavefront propagation principle such as the fast marching method [11,12,13] typically result in a complexity of $\mathcal{O}(\max(N, k \log_2 k))$, where k is the number of features.

Among the first approaches to accelerate the distance transform were algorithms that replace the Euclidean distance metric by more tractable metrics such as the Manhattan distance [14], chamfer metrics [1,15,16], or octagonal metrics [17]. Especially chamfer metrics allow for a trade-off between performance and error, but the distance fields computed with these metrics may not be acceptable in some cases due to the inherent approximation errors.

Another class of methods tries to generate a distance transform that is accurate for virtually all pixels with only spurious errors. The most prominent example is called *vector propagation* [3]. Although being conceptionally simple, highly accurate results can be achieved with good performance [5]. These methods store a vector-valued pointer to a feature candidate for each pixel. These pointers are then propagated using a structuring element called *vector template*. Multiple such templates are swept in a simple fashion across the image. Danielsson [3] describes two methods, 4SED and 8SED (SED being an acronym for *sequential Euclidean distance*), that effectively operate on a von Neumann- and a Moore-neighborhood. 4SED is obviously faster and results in larger approximation errors.

Recently a practical algorithm to compute a precise discrete distance transform in $\mathcal{O}(N)$ was proposed [18]. However, this algorithm relies on frequent concurrent read/write accesses—a very limited feature on GPUs that is not yet exposed in standard graphics APIs.

On a different avenue the use of GPUs has been mandated by several authors. The potential of GPUs for various computational geometry tasks is discussed in [19]. Closely in style to the continuous sweepline algorithm [20], the use of triangle meshes to model a local distance field around each feature is proposed in [21]. Hardware depth-testing is exploited during rendering these meshes to generate a generalized Voronoi diagram. The distance transform can then be obtained from the depth buffer. For applications that only need a distance transform in a shell around features, variations of wavefront propagation methods have been shown to be highly efficient. Using graphics hardware, such methods extrude features to prisms and wedges which can be scan-converted efficiently [22,23]. Although these approaches generate precise results, they rely on generating triangle meshes and/or volumetric primitives, and their complexity is not independent of the number of features. To avoid excessive rasterization of distance meshes, a GPU-based framework to compute 3D distance transforms using slice-based culling and clamping was proposed in [24]. Splatting the distance functions for each feature point [25] avoids the generation of meshes, but these approaches tend to be severely fill-rate-bound due to overdraw.

In [26] the jump flooding paradigm was presented, a communication pattern to quickly propagate information in highly SIMD-parallel computing environments such as GPUs. This method is among the most promising ways to compute distance transforms and generalized Voronoi diagrams since it offers a flexible trade-off between precision and speed. However, compared to vector propagation approaches, the error rate implied by jump flooding is considerably higher.

3 Problem Description

We use the notion of a *feature* to describe the geometric entities that will eventually become Voronoi sites. Features are distinguished by pairwise different IDs. In case of the classical Voronoi diagram, features are points. Among the generalizations commonly made, one allows lines and curve-segments as features. To be able to construct such generalized Voronoi diagrams, we extend the notion of a feature to refer to any non-empty set of (potentially disconnected) points that share an ID.

Given a set of points $P := \{p_i\}_{i=1}^{N} \subset \mathbb{R}^n$ and a set of features $S := \{F_j\}_{j=1}^{k}$, $F_j \subseteq P$, an algorithm that computes a scalar field $\Phi(p_i) := \min_{j \in \{1,...,k\}} \min_{f \in F_j} \|p_i - f\|_2$ is said to compute a discrete Euclidean distance transform of (P, S). Note that according to the definition of S, all points used as a feature are contained in P, which is a convention that does not affect generality. An algorithm that computes a labeling $L(p_i) := \mathrm{argmin}_{j \in \{1,...,k\}} \min_{f \in F_j} \|p_i - f\|_2$ is said to compute a (generalized) discrete Voronoi diagram of (P, S). These two problems are closely related; in fact the above definitions can be turned directly into a naïve algorithm with complexity $\mathcal{O}\left(N \mid \cup_{j \in \{1,...,k\}} F_j\right)$ to compute both. Note that in the continuous case a practical algorithm of complexity $\mathcal{O}(k \log_2 k)$ is only known for the classical Voronoi diagram. Since the bounding curves and surfaces of the regions of continuous generalized Voronoi diagrams can be algebraic surfaces of arbitrary degree, a practical algorithm is not known.

4 Algorithm

We will first review the original vector propagation algorithm before addressing the changes necessary in order to execute the algorithm on the GPU efficiently.

4.1 Vector Propagation

Given an image, a set of features, and a set of vector templates, vector propagation works as described in Alg. 1.

Algorithm 1. Vector Propagation Algorithm

Input:

    an $n \times m$ image of quadratic pixels $P := \{(i,j)\} \equiv \{1, \ldots, n\} \times \{1, \ldots, m\}$

    a set of feature pixels $S \subseteq P$

    a set of vector templates $T := \{\{(k,l)\} \subset \mathbb{Z}^2\}$, where (k,l) specify pixel offsets

Output:

    $v(i,j) : (v(i,j) \in S) \wedge (\forall s \in S : \|v(i,j) - (i,j)\|_2 \leq \|s - (i,j)\|_2) \quad \forall(i,j) \in P$

Initialization:

  1: **for each** $(i,j) \in P$ **do**

  2:     **if** $(i,j) \in S$ **then**

  3:         $v(i,j) \leftarrow (i,j)$

  4:     **else**

  5:         $v(i,j) \leftarrow (\infty, \infty)$

  6:     **end if**

  7: **end for**

Propagation:

  8: **for each** $t \in T$ **do**

  9:     **for each** $(i,j) \in P$ **do**

10:         $v(i,j) \leftarrow v\left((i,j) + \text{argmin}_{(r,s) \in t} \, d_{r,s}\right)$,

11:         where $d_{l,m} := \|v(i+r, j+s) - (i,j)\|_2$

12:     **end for**

13: **end for**

14: **return** $v(i,j) \quad \forall(i,j) \in P$

Note that the sweeping steps (9–12) in Alg. 1 depend on the current template's shape. Each of the propagation update steps (10–11) computes a new best candidate for the feature closest to (i,j) by scanning the neighborhood defined by the template t around (i,j) for possible candidates. The templates originally used for 8SED are depicted in Fig. 1.

Fig. 1. The 8SED vector templates proposed in [3]

The vectors in each cell denote the offset to the current pixel (i,j), since this is the distance that has to be added to the current candidate of the respective cell to compute its distance to (i,j) (hence (i,j) corresponds to the cell marked $0,0$). The arrows on the templates indicate the sweep direction, i.e., the leftmost template can be advanced from left to right and top to bottom in either a row-major or column-major sweep.

4.2 GPU-Based Implementation and Generalizations

The problem with the original vector templates is that two row-major or column-major sweeps are required. Such sweeps cannot be parallelized efficiently. A simple modification however results in a sweepline algorithm that can be efficiently implemented on a SIMD-parallel GPU, albeit at the cost of a slightly higher (by about 11%) memory bandwidth usage. This modification is shown in Fig. 2.

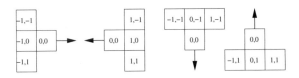

Fig. 2. Modified vector templates that can be swept in four simple line-sweeps

The GPU-based algorithm starts with an ID-texture that stores a value other than 0 for each feature and 0 otherwise. Due to the mutual exclusive read/write access in current graphics APIs, we need two more textures to store 2D vectors. In a first step, initializing proceeds as described by Alg. 1. This step reads from the ID-texture and writes to one of the other 2D textures. Since texture sizes are limited on current GPUs, 2×16 bit are sufficient to store indices to pixels.

In a second step we generate all necessary sweeplines in a single vertex buffer to avoid costly allocations of vertex buffers.

Finally, we rasterize each line of one sweep into one buffer and read potential candidates from the other buffer. We then compute the distance of the current position to each of the candidates to find the new best candidate. This new best candidate is then written to the output buffer. After a single sweep has been completed, the results of odd line indices are stored in one texture and the results of even lines in the other one. In an intermediate step, they are merged. Then, we continue sweeping the image. Since all fragments of a sweep line can be processed independently, we utilize the SIMD-parallelity of current GPUs. For further implementational details we refer the reader to [4].

Once the propagation is finished, each fragment's ID can be obtained by a simple lookup into the ID-texture. Boundaries of Voronoi regions fall between adjacent pixels with differend IDs. The distance transform is obtained by re-computing the distance between the closest feature and the fragment's position for each fagment. Note that generalized Voronoi diagrams are obtained simply by assigning the same ID to multiple pixels in the ID-texture.

The result of a complete run of this algorithm is illustrated in Fig. 3. Each diagram shows the classification of pixels after one sweep, including immediate merging of the two partial ping-pong results. After the first sweep features "fan out" at a 90° angle to the right. The sweep in the opposite direction is not able to correctly classify the two bright cells to the right, since they do not have any additional candidates. Note that such cases will always be removed with the next sweep and that such "islands" cannot occur

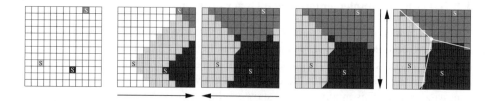

Fig. 3. Example computation of a Voronoi diagram using the proposed algorithm. From left to right: Original image with three features (S), results after sweep to the right and left, and results after sweep down and up. In the final image, a precise continuous Voronoi diagram has been overlaid. Pixels that are colored using two different shades can be associated with either one, since they have exactly the same distance to the respective features.

at the line at which the last sweep begins, since one of the three prior sweeps would have removed them. In this example two pixels have the same distance to different features. Their final classification is dependent on the sweep- and the computation-order.

4.3   Errors in 2D Vector Propagation

Errors in vector propagation only occur if a pixel cannot be "reached" by its closest feature during propagation. This means there is a pixel whose entire Moore-neighborhood points to other features. In terms of Voronoi regions this corresponds to the existence of a Voronoi region that contains the center of a pixel but no center of any of its neighbors. In [4] we further analyze these cases and show that the absolute error is bounded from above by $\sqrt{485} - \sqrt{481} \approx 0.091033$ pixels in the 2D case, which immediately corresponds to a maximum relative error of 0.415%.

4.4   Generalization to 3D

The algorithm can be extended to 3D in an almost straightforward manner by replacing sweep lines by planes. However, current APIs can only render into xy-aligned slices of volumetric textures. Consequently, both sweeps in z-direction are straightforward. For the other directions the volume has to be rotated to make the current sweep-direction z-aligned. This is done after each sweep-pair during the merging of partial results. First, one of the two 3D textures is merged into the other. Then, rotation is performed by rendering a quad per texture slice and fetching from the resource texture using rotated coordinates. Before writing the read vector pointers have to be rotated as well. Once a rotated texture has been obtained, it is copied to the other one and sweeping is repeated. Note that this method only works for volumes that have the same amount of voxels along each dimension.

To reduce the memory requirements from 3×16 bits per voxel and texture to 32 bits, vector pointers can be packed. If the target GPU supports bit operations in the shader (as all DirectX 10 compliant GPUs do), this comes at little if any additional cost.

5   Results and Discussion

In this section we provide results and perform a thorough comparison to the jump flooding algorithm (JFA) [26]. Although other GPU-based methods have been proposed recently, e.g., the fast hierarchical algorithm (FHA) [27], in our opinion JFA offers the best trade-off between speed and approximation error among all previous approaches.

5.1   Bandwidth and Runtime Complexity

First we will compute the memory traffic caused by our method for an image of resolution n^2, since this is a major limiting factor. It is assumed that all references to features will be stored as 2×16 bit integer values. Each read and write access will be counted separately.

During line-sweeps, for each rasterized pixel four vectors are read and one is written. There are $(n - 1) \times n \approx n^2$ intermediate output pixels per sweep. Furthermore, after each pair of sweeps, a merge-operation is necessary. This operation reads a total of $n^2/2$ pixels from one texture and copies them to another buffer. Since this has to be performed in both directions, it results in a total of $2 \times n^2$ accesses. For two pairs of sweeps less than $(2 \times 2 \times 5 + 2)n^2 = 22n^2$ 32-bit accesses are made, thus resulting in less than 88 bytes of memory traffic per pixel.

In comparison, JFA requires $\log_2 n$ passes, each writing n^2 intermediate output pixels. Per pixel, a total of 9 values (modulo boundary cases) is read. Hence, JFA results in about $(9 + 1) \times n^2 \times \log_2 n$ memory accesses, or less than $40 \times \log_2 n$ bytes per pixel. Consequently, our method is less likely to become bandwidth-limited than JFA for large images, since its traffic per pixel is independent of the image resolution.

Our method compares four distances per intermediate output pixel multiplied by four sweeps, while JFA requires nine comparisons per intermediate output pixel. Thus, the theoretical complexity of our method is $\mathcal{O}\left(16n^2\right)$ and $\mathcal{O}\left(9n^2 \log_2 n\right)$ for JFA, where n^2 is the image resolution.

However, it should be noted that the 2D JFA can achieve competitive results, since it generally exploits GPU parallelism better than 2D vector propagation.

5.2   Empirical Validation

All tests were run on an Intel Core2Duo 6600 processor clocked at 2.4 GHz running Windows Vista. The machine was equipped with 2 GB DDR2 RAM and an NVIDIA GeForce 8800GTX with 768 MB of video RAM. The CPU version of our algorithm is carefully hand-tuned and runs on a single core to maximize caching benefits. We were able to run the jump flooding algorithm (JFA) [26] on the very same machine achieving about 185 fps for a resolution of 512^2 pixels. This corresponds to roughly 46.25 Mpixels/sec. JFA is likely to perform differently in other resolutions, but sadly the original OpenGL-based application is locked at 512^2 pixels. Since the timings for JFA are incomplete, they are omitted from Table 1.

Most notable in the results displayed in Table 1 is the sudden decrease in CPU performance at resolutions of 2048^2 which is due to cache limitations. Since we store images on the CPU in x-major order, at a resolution of 2048^2 sweeps in the x-direction are

Table 1. Performance evaluation of our method. We specify both the time per frame in milliseconds and the achieved pixel rate in pixels per second (1 Mpixel = 2^{20} pixels.)

Resolution	CPU time in ms	CPU throughput in Mpixel/s	GPU time in ms	GPU throughput in Mpixel/s	Speedup on GPU
128^2	1.04	14.96	2.50	6.23	0.42×
256^2	4.60	13.60	4.21	14.84	1.09×
512^2	20.02	12.49	7.42	33.68	2.70×
1024^2	91.83	10.89	15.14	66.02	6.06×
2048^2	696.6	5.74	41.68	95.96	16.72×
4096^2	2751	5.82	186.5	85.79	14.74×
8192^2	11366	5.63	1262	50.70	9.00×
32^3	9.67	3.23	3.71	8.42	2.61×
64^3	84.18	2.97	8.21	30.45	10.25×
128^3	1020	1.96	30.85	64.83	33.08×
256^3	9195	1.74	213.0	75.12	43.17×

about five times as expensive as sweeps in the y-direction. The reason is that sweeps in the y-direction are perfectly cache-coherent since in this case x-rows can be processed sequentially. Different storage layouts (i.e., block-major or Z-order) could alleviate this problem to a certain extent. The problem is naturally aggravated in higher dimensions, which is clearly seen in the 3D part of the table. Even for very small volumes, caching issues and the sheer amount of memory traffic prohibit better performance.

On the GPU, caching issues only occur at 4096^2, and they are by far less severe than on the CPU. On the other hand, for small resolutions the GPU's performance is comparable to the CPU implementation or worse. The reason is that in this case the GPU suffers from draw-call overheads and the relatively small amount of parallelism due to the short lines being rasterized. For applications that require to process lots of small images of identical resolutions, the GPU's sweet spot around 2048^2 can still be harnessed by first blocking these images to a larger one. The distance transform can then be computed in parallel for multiple smaller images. This only requires to **not** render the first line of each new image block during sweeps to avoid results from one block of images to leak into the next one. In theory even higher pixel rates than those reported in the table can be achieved in this way, although at the cost of a higher per-image latency.

To validate the likelihood of errors to occur and to measure the magnitude of errors, we reproduced the experiment of [26] in two and three dimensions. Our method was run on images of a resolution of 512^2 (2D) or 64^3 (3D) that were randomly filled with varying amounts of Laplacian-distributed features. Over 10,000 runs were generated for amounts of features between 100 and 10,000. From 100 to 5,000, the amount of features was varied in steps by 100, and between 5,000 and 10,000 in steps of 250.

As can be seen in Figs. 4 and 5, one of the most interesting properties of this algorithm is that the pathological cases leading to errors require a lot of empty area and a very specific configuration of spurious features. Consequently, with increasing amounts of features, the number of errors decreases. This is especially useful for applications

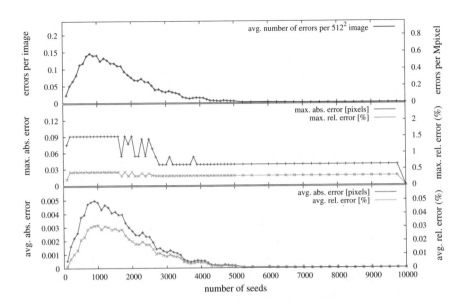

Fig. 4. Top: Likelihood of an error to occur for different amounts of features in the 2D case. Middle: Maximum absolute and relative errors. Bottom: Average absolute and relative errors.

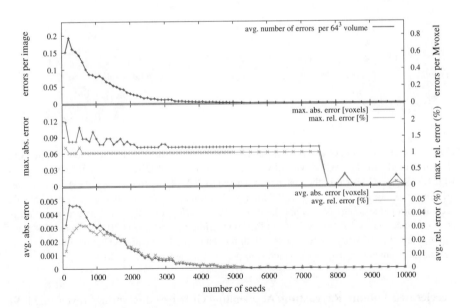

Fig. 5. Top: Likelihood of an error to occur for different amounts of features in the 3D case. Middle: Maximum absolute and relative errors. Bottom: Average absolute and relative errors.

seeking to compute distance transforms of contours, since errors are extremely unlikely to occur in this setting. The errors for the 3D case are still quite low, albeit higher than in the 2D case, and thus make the method acceptable for the vast majority of applications. As already observed in [5], both the error rate and the average error decrease with increasing distance, which is a specific feature of vector propagation.

6   Applications

Three-dimensional Euclidean Distance Transforms can be used in a wide range of applications. In this section we will sketch some of these applications. All these applications require a re-seeding step, i.e., to find those voxels through which a given surface passes, to mark them as features, and to compute the distance transform using these features. After this re-seeding has been performed, each voxel stores the distance to the nearest voxel through which the surface passes.

Morphological Operations. Once the re-seeding has been performed, morphological operations [28], such as dilation and erosion, are trivial to compute on three-dimensional data sets. Dilation and erosion correspond to finding an offset surface that is a fixed distance d away from an input surface. For dilation, d is less than 0 and for erosion it is greater than 0. Figure 6 shows two such dilations for a bone isosurface.

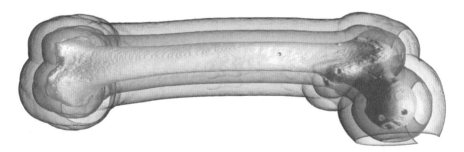

Fig. 6. Volume rendering of a 496^3 distance transform of a femural bone. Our distance transform algorithm used a total of 931 Mbytes of video memory on an NVIDIA Quadro FX 5600 equipped with 1.5 Gbytes. Computing the distance transform took 1860 ms (65.2 Mvoxels/s). In this case, the voxel spacing is 0.373mm $\times$ 0.373mm $\times$ 1.0 mm. The only change necessary to handle such anisotropic spacings is to adapt the distance metric $d_{l,m}$ of Sect. 4.1. The green surface is an iso-surface that is 15 mm away from the bone, while the red one is 30 mm away. Both isosurfaces are clipped where they intersect with the data set's boundaries. The maximum error is significantly smaller than 1 voxel, which is important for medical applications.

Accelerated Volume Raycasting. Accelerating GPU-based isosurface raycasting [29] by means of empty space skipping is another straightforward application if a fast 3D euclidean distance transform is available. The fact that each voxel stores the distance d to the next voxel containing the isosurface is equivalent to saying that there is a sphere with radius d around each voxel that does not contain any part of the surface. Consequently, any ray passing through this voxel can only hit the surface after a distance of at least d. Along this distance, sampling of the volume does not have to be performed. To validate this, we compared a brute-force ray-caster that samples each voxel along the ray with one that utilizes distance-based empty space skipping. In our tests we observed net speedups between a factor of 3 and 8, depending on the data set. Note that we take into account the time required for ray-setup, gradient computation, and lighting for both variants.

Local and Global Accessibility. The local tangent accessibility problem can be stated as follows. Given a radius r, compute for any point p on the surface if there is a sphere with radius r touching p that does not intersect the surface. The global tangent accessibility problem can be stated similarly, but it is additionally required that a sphere of radius r can navigate "from the outside" to p without intersecting the surface along the navigation path. Fast algorithms and applications for both problems are discussed by Miller [30]. Computing the global accessibility is beneficial in medical operation planning, since it can be used to provide surgeons with a visual cue which regions can be accessed without cutting other parts. To compute the global accessibility, we adopted the offset-offset surface algorithm by Miller. Algorithm 2 sketches this method. Figure 8 depicts steps (1–5) of Alg. 2.

Algorithm 2. Offset-Offset Surface Algorithm

Input:
    query radius r
    a surface S voxelized into a volume V
Output:
    a classification $q(p) : p \mapsto \{\text{Accessible} \,|\, \text{Inaccessible}\}$ $\forall$ voxels $p \in V$
Algorithm:
  1: compute distance transform of V
  2: select all voxels with a distance greater or equal to r as features
  3: mark features on V's boundary as seeds
  4: flood-fill features using these seeds; discard non-flooded features
  5: compute distance transform of remaining features
  6: **for each** point $p \in S$ **do**
  7:     **if** distance of p equals r **then**
  8:         $q(p) \leftarrow$ Accessible
  9:     **else**
10:         $q(p) \leftarrow$ Inaccessible
11:     **end if**
12: **end for**

Once the accessibility classification has been obtained, it can be used to color-code the accessibility on the surface. Figure 7 shows some examples of the Visible Human skull [31] where accessible regions are highlit.

Since it is not clear how to implement a runtime-optimal flood-fill (step (4) of Alg. 2) on the GPU using a graphics API, we adopt the line-sweep algorithm presented in this paper as follows. We perform full sweeps with a structuring element that only covers the von Neumann neighborhood. This means that during the sweep to the right each

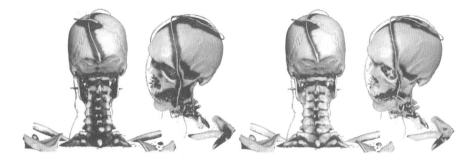

Fig. 7. Left: Two views of the Visible human skull with highlit global accessibility. Dark areas are inaccessible by a sphere with a radius of 20 mm, light areas are accessible. Right: The same two views as in the left part, but with the radius decreased to 12 mm.

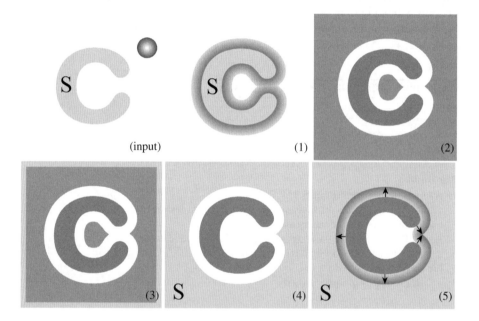

Fig. 8. The offset-offset surface algorithm to compute global accessibility. See also Alg. 2.

fragment on the scanline only reads its immediate left neighbor. If the fragment is itself tagged as a feature (but not as a seed) and the neighbor is tagged as a seed, the fragment is tagged as a new seed. Otherwise, the fragment is discarded. This allows us to detect wether the flood fill has terminated by using an occlusion query. For the data sets we tested, we observed that about 2-3 full sweeps were necessary in order to properly flood the accessible region. Note that one additional full sweep is always require to determine whether the algorithm has terminated.

7   Conclusions

We have presented an algorithm to compute discrete distance transforms, Voronoi diagrams, and generalized Voronoi diagrams entirely on the GPU. We provided empirical evidence that the method is very well suited for the vast majority of applications, since it is both very fast and has an extremely low error rate.

For three exemplary scenarios—morphological operations, isosurface raycasting, and global accessibility computation—we showed that the 3D variant of our method is useful in practise. It is especially benecitial for applications that already perform most of their work on the GPU. Since practical bandwidths from video- to host-memory are currently reaching about 2 Gbyte/s, it could also be interesting for hybrid CPU/GPU algorithms. Although the 3D case results in more memory traffic than other, purely tensor-product-based approaches, the slow-down compared to 2D is less severe than expected. This is mostly due to the fact that the rasterization of slices utilizes the GPU's parallelism better than the rasterization of lines.

In the future, we would like to investigate various avenues of research. Skeletonization algorithms are generally useful but are very sensitive to sporadic errors. We would therefore like to further reduce the errors made by our approach in order to compute stable skeletons. Also, the uses of high-speed, high-quality discrete Voronoi diagrams for artistic purposes are not yet fully explored. Many commercially available painting tools already include filters like mosaicking that are based on Voronoi diagrams. However, with the recent trend to ever higher image resolutions (partly due to advances in CCD technology), the time required to evaluate such filters is likely to become critical. As a side-effect rapid methods that allow for interactivity will offer unprecedented benefits for artists in creating custom filters.

References

1. Rosenfeld, A., Pfalz, J.: Sequential operations in digital picture processing. Journal of ACM 13, 471–494 (1966)
2. Voronoi, G.: Nouvelles applications des paramètres continus à la théorie des formes quadratiques. deuxiéme mémoire: recherches sur les parallélo èdres primitifs. Reine Angewandte Mathematik 134, 198–287 (1908)
3. Danielsson, P.: Euclidean distance mapping. Computer Graphics and Image Processing 14, 227–248 (1980)
4. Schneider, J., Kraus, M., Westermann, R.: GPU-based real-time discrete euclidean distance transforms with precise error bounds. In: International Conference on Computer Vision Theory and Applications (VISAPP), pp. 435–442 (2009)
5. Jones, M., Bærentzen, J., Sramek, M.: 3D distance fields: a survey of techniques and applications. IEEE Trans. Visualization and Computer Graphics 12, 581–599 (2006)
6. Cuisenaire, O.: Distance Transformation: Fast Algorithms and Applications to Medical Image Processing. Phd. thesis, Univ. Catholique de Louvain (1999)
7. Aurenhammer, F.: Voronoi diagrams–a fundamental geometric data structure. ACM Computing Surveys 23, 345–405 (1991)
8. Okabe, A., Boots, B., Sugihara, K., Chiu, S.: Spatial Tesselations: Concepts and Applications of Voronoi Diagrams. John Wiley & Sons Ltd., Chichester (1999)

9. Mullikin, J.: The vector distance transform in two and three dimensions. CVGIP: Graphical Models and Image Processing 54, 526–535 (1992)
10. Satherly, R., Jones, M.: Vector-city vector distance transform. Computer Vision and Image Understanding 82, 238–254 (2001)
11. Tsitsiklis, N.: Efficient algorithms for globally optimal trajectories. IEEE Trans. Automatic Control 40, 1528–1538 (1995)
12. Sethian, J.: A fast marching level set method for monotonically advancing fronts. Nat'l Academy of Sciences US-Paper Ed. 93, 1591–1595 (1996)
13. Helmsen, J., Puckett, E., Colella, P., Dorr, M.: Two new methods for simulating photolithography development in 3D. In: SPIE, vol. 2726, pp. 253–261 (1996)
14. Telea, A., van Wijk., J.: An augmented fast marching method for computing skeletons and centerlines. In: Symp. on Visualization, pp. 251–260 (2002)
15. Butt, M., Maragos, P.: Optimum design of chamfer distance transforms. IEEE Trans. Image Processing 7, 1477–1484 (1998)
16. Svensson, S., Borgefors, G.: Digital distance transforms in 3D images using information from neighborhoods up to $5 \times 5 \times 5$. Computer Vision and Image Understanding 88, 24–53 (2002)
17. Kulpa, Z., Kruse, B.: Methods of effective implementation of circular propagation in discrete images. Internal Report LiTH-ISY-I-0274, Dept. of Electrical Engineering, Linköping Univ., Sweden (1979)
18. Maurer, C., Qi, R., Raghavan, V.: A linear time algorithm for computing exact euclidean distance transforms of binary images in arbitrary dimensions. IEEE Trans. Pattern Analysis and Machine Intelligence 25, 265–270 (2003)
19. Denny, M.: Algorithmic Geometry via Graphics Hardware. Phd. thesis, Universität des Saarlandes, Saarbrücken, Germany (2003)
20. Fortune, S.: A sweepline algorithm for Voronoi diagrams. In: ACM Symp. Computational Geometry, pp. 313–322 (1986)
21. Hoff, K.E., Culver, T., Keyser, J., Lin, M., Manocha, D.: Fast computation of generalized Voronoi diagrams using graphics hardware. ACM Trans. on Graphics 18, 277–286 (1999)
22. Mauch, S.: Efficient algorithms for solving static Hamilton-Jacobi equations. PhD thesis, California Institute of Technology, Pasadena, CA (2003)
23. Sigg, C., Peikert, R., Gross, M.: Signed distance transform using graphics hardware. In: IEEE Visualization, pp. 83–90 (2003)
24. Sud, A., Otaduy, M., Manocha, D.: DiFi: Fast 3D distance field computation using graphics hardware. EG Computer Graphics Forum 23, 557–566 (2004)
25. Strzodka, R., Telea, A.: Generalized distance transforms and skeletons in graphics hardware. In: Joint EG/IEEE TVCG Symp. Visualization, pp. 221–230 (2004)
26. Rong, G., Tan, T.S.: Jump flooding in gpu with applications to Voronoi diagram and distance transform. In: ACM Symp. Interactive 3D Graphics and Games, pp. 109–116 (2006)
27. Cuntz, N., Kolb, A.: Fast hierarchical 3D distance transformations on the GPU. In: Proceedings Eurographics Short Papers, pp. 93–96 (2007)
28. Jähne, B.: Digital Image Processing: Concepts, Algorithms and Scientific Applicartions, 5th edn. Springer, Heidelberg (2002)
29. Krüger, J., Westermann, R.: Acceleration Techniques for GPU-based Volume Rendering. In: Proceedings IEEE Visualization (2003)
30. Miller, G.: Efficient algorithms for local and global accessibility shading. In: Proceedings of ACM SIGGRAPH, pp. 319–326 (1994)
31. US National Library of Medicine: The Visible Human Project®, http://www.nlm.nih.gov/research/visible

Efficient Robust Active Appearance Model Fitting

Markus Storer[1], Peter M. Roth[1], Martin Urschler[1],
Horst Bischof[1], and Josef A. Birchbauer[2]

[1] Institute for Computer Graphics and Vision, Graz University of Technology
Inffeldgasse 16/II, 8010 Graz, Austria
[2] Siemens Biometrics Center, Siemens IT Solutions and Services
Strassgangerstrasse 315, 8054 Graz, Austria
{storer,pmroth,urschler,bischof}@icg.tugraz.at,
josef-alois.birchbauer@siemens.com

Abstract. The Active Appearance Model (AAM) is a widely used approach for model based vision showing excellent results. But one major drawback is that the method is not robust against occlusions. Thus, if parts of the image are occluded the method converges to local minima and the obtained results are unreliable. To overcome this problem we propose a robust AAM fitting strategy. The main idea is to apply a robust PCA model to reconstruct the missing feature information and to use the thus obtained image as input for the standard AAM fitting process. Since existing methods for robust PCA reconstruction are computationally too expensive for real-time processing we applied a more efficient method: Fast-Robust PCA (FR-PCA). In fact, by using our FR-PCA the computational effort is drastically reduced. Moreover, more accurate reconstructions are obtained. In the experiments, we evaluated both, the FR-PCA model on the publicly available ALOI database and the whole robust AAM fitting chain on facial images. The results clearly show the benefits of our approach in terms of accuracy and speed when processing disturbed data (i.e., images containing occlusions).

1 Introduction

Generative model-based approaches for feature localization have received a lot of attention over the last decade. Their key advantage is to use a priori knowledge from a training stage for restricting the model while searching for a model instance in an image. Two specific instances of model-based approaches, the Active Appearance Model (AAM) [1] and the closely related 3D Morphable Model (3DMM) [2], have proven to show excellent results in locating image features in applications such as face detection and tracking [3], face and facial expression recognition [4], or medical image segmentation [5,6].

Despite its large success, the AAM model has one main limitation; it is not robust against occlusions. Thus, if important features are missing, the AAM fitting algorithm tends to get stuck in local minima. This especially credits for human faces since the large variability in the image data such as certain kinds of glasses, makeups, or beards can not totally be captured in the training stage. Similar difficulties also arise in other areas of model-based approaches (e.g., in the medical domain [6]).

A. Ranchordas et al. (Eds.): VISIGRAPP 2009, CCIS 68, pp. 229–241, 2010.

In the recent years some research was dedicated to generative model-based approaches in the presence of occlusions by investigating robust fitting strategies. In the original AAM approach [1] fitting is treated as a least squares optimization problem, which is, of course, very sensitive to outliers due to its quadratic error measure (L_2 norm). To overcome this problem, the work of [7] extended the standard fitting method (a) by learning the usual gray-value differences encountered during training and (b) by ignoring gray-value differences exceeding a threshold derived from these values during fitting. But the main drawback of this method is that the required threshold depends on the training conditions, which makes it improper for real-life situations. In contrast, in [8] a RANSAC procedure is used for the initialization of the AAM fitting in order to get rid of occlusions due to differing poses. However, since the AAM fitting remains unchanged this approach has still problems with appearance outliers.

Another direction of research was dedicated to replacing the least-squares error measure by a robust error measure in the fitting stage [9]. Later this approach was further refined by comparing several robust error measures [10]. The same strategy is also used in [11] and was adapted to a statistical framework in [12]. But the latter approach is limited in several ways: (a) a scale parameter is required, which is hard to determine in general, (b) the framework around the inverse compositional algorithm is specifically tailored to tracking, and (c) the face models are built from the tracked person, which limits its generic applicability.

In the context of medical image analysis a robust AAM fitting approach was presented in [6]. In their method, which is based on the standard AAM fitting algorithm, gross disturbances (i.e., outliers) in the input image are avoided by ignoring misleading coefficient updates in the fitting stage. For that purpose, inlier and outlier coefficients are identified by a Mean Shift based analysis of the residual's modes. Then, an optimal sub-set of modes is selected and only those pixels covered by the selected mode combination are used for actual residual calculation. The Robust AAM Matching (RAAM) approach shows excellent results on a number of medical data sets. However, the mode selection is computationally very complex. Thus, this method is impractical for real-time or near real-time applications.

To overcome these drawbacks we introduce a new efficient robust AAM fitting scheme. In contrast to existing methods the robustness (against occluded features) is not directly included in the fitting step but is detached. In fact, we propose to run a robust pre-processing step first to generate undisturbed input data and then to apply a standard AAM fitting. Since the robust step, which is usually computationally intensive, has to be performed only once (and not iteratively in the fitting process), the computational cost can be reduced.

In particular, the main idea is to robustly replace the missing feature information from a reliable model. Thus, our work is somehow motivated by [13] and [14], where beards and eye-glasses, which are typical problems when applying an AAM approach, are removed. In [14] a PCA model was built from facial images that do not contain any eye-glasses. Then, in the removal step the original input images are reconstructed and the regions with the largest reconstruction errors are identified. These pixels are iteratively replaced by the reconstruction. But this approach can only be applied if the absolute number of missing pixels is quite small. In contrast, in [13] two models are computed in parallel, one for bearded faces and one for non-bearded faces. Then, in the removal step for a bearded face the detected beard region is reconstructed from the non-bearded space.

Since both methods are restricted to special types of occlusion or limited by a pre-defined error level, they can not be applied for general tasks. Thus, in our approach we apply a robust PCA model (e.g., [15,16,17]) to cope with occlusions in the original input data. For that purpose, in the learning stage a reliable model is estimated from undisturbed data (i.e., without any occlusions), which is then applied to robustly reconstruct unreliable values from the disturbed data. However, a drawback of these methods is their computational complexity (i.e., iterative algorithms, multiple hypotheses, etc.), which hinders practical applicability. Thus, we developed a more efficient robust PCA method [18] that overcomes this limitation.

Even though the proposed robust AAM fitting is quite general, our main interest is to apply it to facial images. Thus, this application is evaluated in the experiments in detail. However, we also note that it is necessary that the image patch, where the robust PCA is applied has to be roughly aligned with the feature under consideration. In the case of our face localization this can be ensured by using a rough face and facial component detection algorithm inspired by the Viola-Jones algorithm [19]. Moreover, the applied PCA model can handle a wide variability in facial images.

This paper is structured as follows. In Section 2 we introduce and discuss our Fast-Robust PCA (FR-PCA) approach [18]. In addition, we performed experiments on the publicly available ALOI database, which show that our approach outperforms existing robust methods in terms of speed and accuracy. Next, in Section 3, we introduce our robust AAM fitting algorithm that is based on the robust PCA scheme. To demonstrate its benefits, we also present experimental results using facial images. Finally, we discuss our findings and conclude our work in Section 4.

2   Fast-Robust PCA

If a PCA space $\mathbf{U} = [\mathbf{u}_1, \ldots, \mathbf{u}_{l-1}]$ is estimated from l samples, an unknown sample $\mathbf{x} = [x_1, \ldots, x_m]$, $m > l$, can usually be reconstructed to a sufficient degree of accuracy by p, $p < l$, eigenvectors:

$$\tilde{\mathbf{x}} = \mathbf{U}_p \mathbf{a} + \bar{\mathbf{x}} = \sum_{j=1}^{p} a_j \mathbf{u}_j + \bar{\mathbf{x}} \,, \tag{1}$$

where $\bar{\mathbf{x}}$ is the sample mean and $\mathbf{a} = [a_1, \ldots, a_p]$ are the PCA coefficients obtained by projecting $\mathbf{x}$ onto the subspace $\mathbf{U}_p$.

If the sample $\mathbf{x}$ contains outliers, e.g., occluded pixels, (1) would not yield a reliable reconstruction; a robust method is required (e.g., [15,16,17]). But since these methods are computationally very expensive (i.e., they are based on iterative algorithms) they are often not applicable in practice. Thus, in the following we introduce a more efficient robust PCA approach [18].

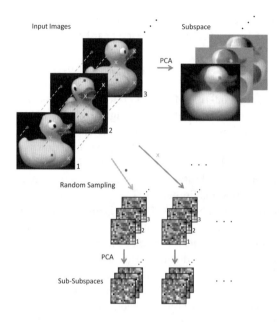

Fig. 1. FR-PCA training. Generation of the subspace and the smaller sub-subspaces derived by randomly sub-sampling the input images.

2.1 Fast-Robust Training

The training procedure, which is sub-divided into two major parts, is illustrated in Figure 1. First, a standard PCA subspace is generated from all training images. Second, in addition, a large number of smaller subspaces (sub-subspaces) is estimated from small sets of randomly selected data points (sub-sampling). Since occlusions are often considered to be spatially coherent the sub-sampling is done in a smart way. Hence, in addition to the random sampling over the whole image region, the random sampling is also restricted to image slices (vertical, horizontal, quadrant).

2.2 Fast-Robust Reconstruction

Given a new unseen test sample $\mathbf{x}$, the robust reconstruction is performed in two stages. In the first stage (*gross outlier detection*), the outliers are detected based on the sub-subspace reconstruction errors. In the second stage (*refinement*), using the thus estimated inliers a robust reconstruction $\tilde{\mathbf{x}}$ of the whole image is generated.

Assuming that in the training stage N sub-subspaces were estimated as described in Section 2.1, first, in the *gross outlier detection*, N sub-samplings $\mathbf{s}_n$ are generated according to the corresponding sub-subspace. In addition, we define the set of "inliers" $\mathbf{r} = \mathbf{s}_1 \cup \ldots \cup \mathbf{s}_N$. This set of points is illustrated in Figure 2(a) (green points). Next, for each sub-sampling $\mathbf{s}_n$ a reconstruction $\tilde{\mathbf{s}}_n$ is estimated by (1), which allows to estimate the (pixel-wise) error-maps

$$\mathbf{e}_n = |\mathbf{s}_n - \tilde{\mathbf{s}}_n| \, , \tag{2}$$

the mean reconstruction errors $\bar{e}_n$ for each of the N sub-samplings, and the mean reconstruction error $\bar{e}$ over all sub-samplings.

Based on these errors we can detect the outliers by local and global thresholding. For that purpose, the sub-samplings $\mathbf{s}_n$ are ranked by their mean error $\bar{e}_n$. The local thresholds (one for each sub-sampling) are then defined by $\theta_n = \bar{e}_n w_n$, where the weight w_n is estimated from the sub-sampling's rank to remove less outliers from first ranked sub-samplings. The global threshold θ is set to the mean error $\bar{e}$. Then, all points $s_{n,i}$ for which

$$e_{n,i} > \theta_n \quad \text{or} \quad e_{n,i} > \theta \tag{3}$$

are discarded from the sub-samplings $\mathbf{s}_n$ obtaining $\tilde{\mathbf{s}}_n$. Finally, we re-define the set of "inliers" by

$$\mathbf{r} = \tilde{\mathbf{s}}_1 \cup \ldots \cup \tilde{\mathbf{s}}_q \, , \tag{4}$$

where $\tilde{\mathbf{s}}_1, \ldots, \tilde{\mathbf{s}}_q$ indicate the first ranked q sub-samplings such that $|\mathbf{r}| \leq k$ and k is the pre-defined maximum number of points. The thus obtained "inliers" are shown in Figure 2(b).

The *gross outlier detection* procedure allows to remove most outliers (i.e., occluded pixels), thus the obtained set $\mathbf{r}$ contains almost only inliers. To further improve the final result in the *refinement* step, the final robust reconstruction is estimated similar to [17]. In particular, starting from the point set $\mathbf{r} = [r_1, \ldots, r_k], k > p$, obtained from the *gross outlier detection*, an overdetermined system of equations is iteratively solved. That is, the following least square optimization problem

$$E(\mathbf{r}) = \sum_{i=1}^{k} \left(x_{r_i} - \sum_{j=1}^{p} a_j \mathbf{u}_{j,r_i} \right)^2 \tag{5}$$

has to be solved obtaining the coefficients $\mathbf{a}$. Hence, the reconstruction $\tilde{\mathbf{x}}$ can be estimated and those points with the largest reconstruction error are discarded from $\mathbf{r}$ (selected by a reduction factor α). These steps are iterated until a pre-defined number of remaining pixels is reached. Thus, finally, an outlier-free sub-set is obtained, which is illustrated in Figure 2(c), and the robust reconstruction $\tilde{\mathbf{x}}$ can be estimated.

Such a robust reconstruction result obtained by the proposed approach compared to a non-robust method is shown in Figure 3. One can clearly see that the robust method considerably outperforms the standard PCA. Note, that the blur visible in the reconstruction of the FR-PCA is the consequence of taking into account only a limited number of eigenvectors.

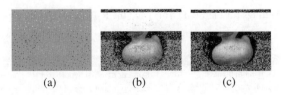

(a)   (b)   (c)

Fig. 2. Data point selection process. (a) Data points sampled by all sub-subspaces. (b) Remaining data points after applying the sub-subspace procedure. (c) Resulting data points after the iterative refinement process for the calculation of the PCA coefficients.

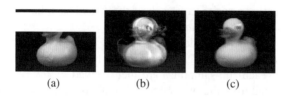

(a)   (b)   (c)

Fig. 3. Demonstration of the insensitivity of the robust PCA to occlusions. (a) Occluded image, (b) reconstruction using standard PCA, and (c) reconstruction using the FR-PCA.

In general, the robust estimation of the coefficients is computationally very efficient and thus very fast. In the *gross outlier detection* procedure only simple matrix operations (standard PCA) have to be performed, which are very fast; even if hundreds of sub-subspace reconstructions have to be executed. The computationally more expensive part is the *refinement* step, where an overdetermined linear system of equations has to be solved iteratively. Since very few refinement iterations have to be performed due to the preceding *gross outlier detection*, the total runtime is kept low.

2.3 Experimental Results

To show the benefits of the proposed Fast-Robust PCA method (FR-PCA) we compare it to the standard PCA (PCA) and the robust PCA approach of [17] (R-PCA). We chose the latter one, because of its proven accuracy and applicability. Our refinement process is similar to theirs.

In particular, the experiments are evaluated on the "Amsterdam Library of Object Images (ALOI)" database [20]. The ALOI database consists of 1000 different objects. Over hundred images of each object are recorded under different viewing angles, illumination angles and illumination colors, yielding a total of 110,250 images. For our experiments we arbitrarily choose 20 categories (018, 032, 043, 074, 090, 093, 125, 127, 138, 151, 156, 174, 200, 299, 354, 368, 376, 809, 911, 926), where an illustrative subset of objects is shown in Figure 4.

In our experimental setup, each object is represented in a separate subspace and a set of 1000 sub-subspaces, where each sub-subspace contains 1% of data points of the whole image. The variance retained for the sub-subspaces is 95% and 98% for the whole subspace, which is also used for the standard PCA and the R-PCA. Unless otherwise noted, all experiments are performed with the parameter settings given in Table 1.

Table 1. Settings for the FR-PCA (a) and the R-PCA (b) for the experiments

(a)

FR-PCA	
Number of initial points k	130p
Reduction factor α	0.9

(b)

R-PCA	
Number of initial hypotheses H	30
Number of initial points k	48p
Reduction factor α	0.85
K2	0.01
Compatibility threshold	100

Fig. 4. Illustrative examples of objects used in the experiments

A 5-fold cross-validation is performed for each object category, resulting in 80% training- and 20% test data, corresponding to 21 test images per iteration. The experiments are accomplished for several levels of spatially coherent occlusions. To sum up, 2100 reconstructions are executed for every level of occlusion. Quantitative results for the root-mean-squared (RMS) reconstruction-error per pixel are given in Table 2. In addition, in Figure 5 we show box-plots of the RMS reconstruction-error per pixel for different levels of occlusions.

Table 2. Comparison of the reconstruction errors of the standard PCA, the R-PCA and the FR-PCA. (a) RMS reconstruction-error per pixel given by mean and standard deviation. (b) RMS reconstruction-error per pixel given by robust statistics: median, upper- and lower quartile. Those results correspond to the box-plots in Figure 5.

(a)

Occlusion	0%		10%		20%		30%		50%		70%	
	mean	std	mean	std	mean	std	mean	std	mean	std	mean	std
PCA	9.96	5.88	21.30	7.24	34.60	11.41	47.72	14.37	70.91	19.06	91.64	19.78
R-PCA	11.32	6.92	11.39	7.03	11.98	8.02	20.40	19.90	59.73	32.54	87.83	26.07
FR-PCA	10.99	6.42	11.50	6.69	11.59	6.71	11.66	6.88	26.48	23.57	73.20	27.79

(b)

Occlusion	0%			10%			20%			30%			50%			70%		
	median	Q_{25}	Q_{75}	median	Q_{25}	Q_{75}	median	Q_{25}	Q_{75}	median	Q_{25}	Q_{75}	median	Q_{25}	Q_{75}	median	Q_{25}	Q_{75}
PCA	9.58	5.77	14.02	21.29	16.56	26.01	34.67	27.71	42.17	47.24	38.22	57.42	70.45	57.03	84.54	89.49	77.55	106.15
R-PCA	10.54	6.39	15.81	10.63	6.50	15.76	10.95	6.60	16.16	13.83	7.96	23.13	62.76	32.47	82.98	87.80	70.64	104.99
FR-PCA	10.46	6.57	15.15	10.97	6.96	15.88	11.01	7.01	16.06	10.98	7.08	16.10	17.25	9.75	36.33	75.04	56.84	92.61

Starting from 0% occlusion, all subspace methods exhibit nearly the same RMS reconstruction-error. Increasing the portion of occlusion, the standard PCA shows large errors whereas the robust methods are still comparable to the PCA without occlusion (best feasible case). The FR-PCA presents the best performance of the robust methods over all occlusion levels.

Finally, we evaluate the runtime[1] for the applied different PCA reconstruction methods, which are summarized in Table 3. It can be seen that compared to R-PCA using FR-PCA speeds up the robust reconstruction by a factor of 18! If more eigenvectors are

---

[1] The runtimes are measured in MATLAB using an Intel Xeon processor running at 3GHz. The resolution of the images is 192x144 pixels.

Table 3. Runtime comparison. Compared to R-PCA, FR-PCA speeds-up the computation by a factor of 18.

Occlusion	Mean Runtime [s]					
	0%	10%	20%	30%	50%	70%
PCA	0.006	0.007	0.007	0.007	0.008	0.009
R-PCA	6.333	6.172	5.435	4.945	3.193	2.580
FR-PCA	0.429	0.338	0.329	0.334	0.297	0.307

used or if the size of the images increases, the speed-up factor gets even larger. This drastic speed-up can be explained by the fact that the refinement process is started from a set of data points mainly consisting of inliers. In contrast, in [17] several point sets (hypotheses) have to be created. The iterative procedure has to run for every set resulting in a poor runtime performance. To decrease the runtime, the number of hypotheses or the number of initial points has to be reduced, which decreases reconstruction accuracy significantly. However, the runtime of our approach only depends slightly on the number of starting points, thus having nearly constant execution times. The runtime of both algorithms depends on the number of eigenvectors used and their length. Increasing one of those values, the gap between the runtime for both methods is even getting larger.

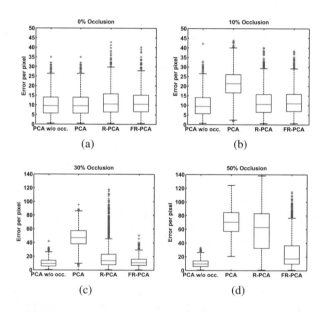

Fig. 5. Box-plots for different levels of occlusions for the RMS reconstruction-error per pixel. PCA without occlusion is shown in every plot for the comparison of the robust methods to the best feasible reconstruction result.

3   Robust AAM Fitting

The Active Appearance Model (AAM) [1] is a widely used and successful method for model based vision. But one of the major drawbacks is its non-robustness to occlusions in the input image. Thus, we propose a robust AAM fitting scheme. In particular, we run a robust pre-processing step based on our FR-PCA (see Section 2) to generate undisturbed input data and then apply a standard AAM fitting. Since the robust step, which is usually computationally intensive, has to be performed only once (and not iteratively in the fitting process), the computational cost can be reduced.

3.1 Active Appearance Model

The AAM [1] is a combination of a parametric model able to generate synthetic images and an efficient fitting algorithm to fit the model to unseen input images.

The model describes the variation in shape and texture of a training set representing an object. By applying PCA to the shape, texture, and the combination of shape and texture, the modes of variation are calculated. By keeping solely a certain percentage of the eigenvalue energy spectrum the model can be represented very compactly.

The AAM model fitting is performed in an analysis-by-synthesis manner, i.e., the parameters of the model are optimized to generate a synthetic image that is as similar as possible to the unseen input image. The optimization of the model parameters is accomplished in a gradient descent optimization scheme. The cost function is defined as the L_2 norm of the intensity differences (between the estimated model and the given input image). To efficiently approximate the Jacobian of the cost function, a learned regression model is used that describes the relationship between parameter updates and texture residual images according to [1]. A local minimum of the cost function corresponds to a model fitting solution, which is not necessarily the global optimal solution. That is, the model fitting is very prone to get stuck in a local minimum because of the very high dimensional parameter space. To overcome this problem, multi-resolution techniques have to be incorporated and the fitting requires a coarse initialization.

3.2 Robust Fitting

Since the parameter updates for the fitting process are estimated from the texture's residual, the standard AAM is not robust against occlusions. To overcome this limitation, we propose to use our FR-PCA, introduced in Section 2, as a pre-processing step to remove disturbances in the input image and to perform the AAM fitting on the thus obtained reconstruction. Occlusions can not only be of artificial spatially coherent nature, which were taken for the quantitative evaluation of the FR-PCA, but also in case of facial images, beards or glasses. Those disturbances of facial images influence the quality of the fitting process of AAMs. Thus, for the pre-processing step we trained the FR-PCA using facial images which do not exhibit any disturbances, i.e., no beards and no glasses.

Figure 6, which was taken from the Caltech Faces data set [21], demonstrates the whole processing chain for robust AAM fitting under occlusion. Figure 6(b) shows the initialization of the AAM on the occluded input image. The rough initialization of the AAM is done using a Viola-Jones face detection approach [19], several AdaBoost-based classifiers for locating eyes and mouth, and a face candidate validation scheme to robustly locate the rough face position [22].

238   M. Storer et al.

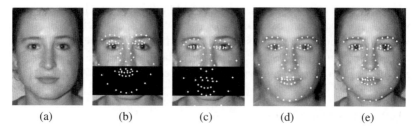

(a)　　　　　(b)　　　　　(c)　　　　　(d)　　　　　(e)

Fig. 6. Handling of occlusions for AAM fitting. (a) Test image. (b) Initialization of the AAM on the occluded image. (c) Direct AAM fit on the occluded image. (d) AAM fit on the reconstructed image. (e) Shape from (d) overlayed on the test image. Image taken from Caltech Faces data set [21].

Figure 6(c) demonstrates the converged fit of the AAM on the occluded image which failed totally. In contrast, using the FR-PCA as a pre-processing step results in the converged fit exhibited in Figure 6(d). In Figure 6(e), the shape from the fitting process on the reconstructed image is overlayed on the original input image. It can be clearly seen that the AAM can not handle occlusions directly whereas the fit on the reconstructed image is well defined.

3.3 Experimental Results

We trained a hierarchical AAM for facial images on three resolution levels (60x80, 120x160, 240x320). Our training set consists of 427 manually annotated face images taken from the Caltech face database [21] and our own collection. Taking also the mirrored versions of those images doubles the amount of training data. For model building we keep 90% of the eigenvalue energy spectrum for the lower two levels and 95% for the highest level to represent our compact model.

As described in Section 3.2, we use the FR-PCA as a pre-processing step and perform the AAM fitting on the reconstructed images. Hence, we trained the FR-PCA (Section 2.1) using facial images which do not exhibit any disturbances, i.e., no beards and no glasses. The variance retained for the whole subspace and for the sub-subspaces is 95%.

A 5-fold cross validation is performed using the manually annotated images, resulting in 80% training- and 20% test data per iteration. For each level of occlusion, 210 AAM fits are executed. Table 4 shows the point-to-point error (Euclidean distance of converged points to the annotated points) comparing the direct AAM fit on the occluded

Table 4. Point-to-Point error. Comparing the direct fit of the AAM on the test image to the AAM fit utilizing the FR-PCA pre-processing (point errors are measured on 240x320 facial images).

Occlusion	0% mean	std	10% mean	std	20% mean	std	30% mean	std	40% mean	std
AAM	4.05	5.77	12.06	11.25	15.19	12.78	18.76	14.89	18.86	13.94
AAM + FR-PCA	5.47	4.97	5.93	5.41	6.06	5.27	9.31	8.75	11.33	9.25

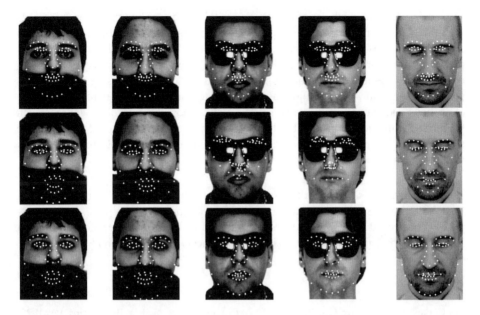

Fig. 7. Examples of AAM fits on natural occlusions like tinted glasses, wearing a scarf or beards. (First row) Test images with AAM initialization. (Second row) Direct AAM fit on the test images. (Third row) AAM fit utilizing the FR-PCA pre-processing. Images are taken from the AR face database [23] and our own database (last column).

image to the AAM fit utilizing the FR-PCA pre-processing. Starting from 0% occlusion, the error for the AAM + FR-PCA is slightly larger than the direct fit, because of the unavoidable reconstruction-blur resulting from the FR-PCA reconstruction. When increasing the size of the occlusion, the big advantage of the FR-PCA pre-processing can be seen.

Up to now, to have a steerable environment, we used artificial spatially coherent occlusions. To show the advantage of FR-PCA pre-processing also on natural occlusions such as tinted glasses, occlusions caused by wearing a scarf or by disturbances like beards, Figure 7 depicts some AAM fits on images taken from the AR face database [23] and from our own database. The FR-PCA pre-processing step takes around 0.69s per image (150x200) measured in MATLAB using an Intel Xeon processor running at 3GHz.

4   Conclusions

We presented a robust AAM fitting scheme. In contrast to existing approaches the robustness is not included in the fitting step but is detached in a pre-processing step. The main idea is to robustly reconstruct unreliable data points (i.e., occlusions) in the pre-processing step and to use the thus obtained undisturbed images as input for a standard AAM fitting. To speed up this robust pre-processing step, we introduced our Fast-Robust PCA method [18]. The main idea is to estimate a large number of small PCA sub-subspaces from a sub-set of points in parallel. By discarding those sub-subspaces with the largest errors the number of outliers in the input data can be reduced, which drastically decreases the computational effort for the robust reconstruction. In the experiments, we showed that our Fast-Robust PCA approach outperforms existing methods in terms of speed and accuracy. In addition, the whole processing chain (robust pre-processing and AAM fitting) was demonstrated on facial images in the presence of artificial and natural occlusion noise. The results show that our robust approach can handle such situations considerably better than a non-robust approach. Moreover, due to the very efficient robust pre-processing the proposed robust AAM fitting method is applicable in practice for real-time applications.

Acknowledgements. This work has been funded by the Biometrics Center of Siemens IT Solutions and Services, Siemens Austria. In addition, this work was supported by the FFG project AUTOVISTA (813395) under the FIT-IT programme, and the Austrian Joint Research Project Cognitive Vision under projects S9103-N04 and S9104-N04.

References

1. Cootes, T.F., Edwards, G.J., Taylor, C.J.: Active appearance models. IEEE Trans. PAMI 23, 681–685 (2001)
2. Blanz, V., Vetter, T.: A morphable model for the synthesis of 3d-faces. In: Proc. SIGGRAPH (1999)
3. Matthews, I., Baker, S.: Active appearance models revisited. International Journal of Computer Vision 60, 135–164 (2004)
4. Blanz, V., Vetter, T.: Face recognition based on fitting a 3D morphable model. IEEE Trans. PAMI 25, 1063–1074 (2003)
5. Mitchell, S.C., Bosch, J.G., Lelieveldt, B.P.F., van der Geest, R.J., Reiber, J.H.C., Sonka, M.: 3-D active appearance models: Segmentation of cardiac MR and ultrasound images. IEEE Trans. Med. Imag. 21, 1167–1178 (2001)
6. Beichel, R., Bischof, H., Leberl, F., Sonka, M.: Robust active appearance models and their application to medical image analysis. IEEE Trans. Med. Imag. 24, 1151–1169 (2005)
7. Edwards, G.J., Cootes, T.F., Taylor, C.J.: Advances in active appearance models. In: Proc. ICCV, pp. 137–142 (1999)
8. Dornaika, F., Ahlberg, J.: Face model adaptation using robust matching and active appearance models. In: Proc. IEEE Workshop on Applications of Computer Vision (2002)
9. Gross, R., Matthews, I., Baker, S.: Active appearance models with occlusion. Image and Vision Computing 24, 593–604 (2006)
10. Theobald, B.J., Matthews, I., Baker, S.: Evaluating error functions for robust active appearance models. In: Proc. FGR, pp. 149–154 (2006)
11. Romdhani, S., Vetter, T.: Efficient, robust and accurate fitting of a 3D morphable model. In: Proc. ICCV, vol. 2 (2003)
12. Yu, X., Tian, J., Liu, J.: Active appearance models fitting with occlusion. In: Yuille, A.L., Zhu, S.-C., Cremers, D., Wang, Y. (eds.) EMMCVPR 2007. LNCS, vol. 4679, pp. 137–144. Springer, Heidelberg (2007)
13. Nguyen, M.H., Lalonde, J.F., Efros, A.A., de la Torre, F.: Image-based shaving. Computer Graphics Forum Journal (Eurographics 2008) 27, 627–635 (2008)
14. Du, C., Su, G.: Eyeglasses removal from facial images. Pattern Recognition Letters 26, 2215–2220 (2005)

15. Rao, R.: Dynamic appearance-based recognition. In: Proc. CVPR, pp. 540–546 (1997)
16. Black, M.J., Jepson, A.D.: Eigentracking: Robust matching and tracking of articulated objects using a view-based representation. In: Proc. ECCV, pp. 329–342 (1996)
17. Leonardis, A., Bischof, H.: Robust recognition using eigenimages. Computer Vision and Image Understanding 78, 99–118 (2000)
18. Storer, M., Roth, P.M., Urschler, M., Bischof, H.: Fast-robust PCA. In: Proc. 16th Scandinavian Conference on Image Analysis, pp. 430–439 (2009)
19. Viola, P., Jones, M.J.: Robust real-time face detection. International Journal of Computer Vision 57, 137–154 (2004)
20. Geusebroek, J.M., Burghouts, G.J., Smeulders, A.W.M.: The Amsterdam Library of Object Images. International Journal of Computer Vision 61, 103–112 (2005)
21. Caltech: Caltech face database (1999),
    http://www.vision.caltech.edu/html-files/archive.html
22. Urschler, M., Storer, M., Bischof, H., Birchbauer, J.A.: Robust facial component detection for face alignment applications. In: Proc. 33rd Workshop of the Austrian Association for Pattern Recognition (AAPR/OAGM), pp. 61–72 (2009)
23. Martinez, A., Benavente, R.: The AR face database. Technical Report 24, CVC (1998)

Semi-supervised Distance Metric Learning in High-Dimensional Spaces by Using Equivalence Constraints

Hakan Cevikalp

Eskisehir Osmangazi University, Meselik, 26480 Eskisehir, Turkey

Abstract. This paper introduces a semi-supervised distance metric learning algorithm which uses pairwise equivalence (similarity and dissimilarity) constraints to discover the desired groups within high-dimensional data. In contrast to the traditional full rank distance metric learning algorithms, the proposed method can learn nonsquare projection matrices that yield low rank distance metrics. This brings additional benefits such as visualization of data samples and reducing the storage cost, and it is more robust to overfitting since the number of estimated parameters is greatly reduced. The proposed method works in both the input and kernel induced-feature space, and the distance metric is found by a gradient descent procedure that involves an eigen-decomposition in each step. Experimental results on high-dimensional visual object classification problems show that the computed distance metric improves the performances of the subsequent classification and clustering algorithms.

1 Introduction

Learning distance metrics is very important for various vision applications such as object classification, image retrieval, and video retrieval [6,5,12,10], and this task is much easier when the target values (labels) associated to the data samples are available. However, in many vision applications, there is a lack of labeled data since obtaining labels is a costly procedure as it often requires human effort. On the other hand, in some applications, side information - given in the form of pairwise equivalence (similarity and dissimilarity) constraints between points - is available without or with less extra cost. For instance, faces extracted from successive video frames in roughly the same location can be assumed to represent the same person, whereas faces extracted in different locations in the same frame cannot be the same person. In some applications, side information is the natural form of supervision, e.g., in image retrieval, there is only the notion of similarities between the query and retrieved images. Side information may also come from human feedback, often at a substantially lower cost than explicit labeled data. Our motivation in this study is that using side information effectively in metric learning can bridge the semantic gaps between the low-level image feature representations and high-level semantic concepts in many visual applications, which enables us to select our preferred characteristics for distinction. A typical example is organizing image galleries in accordance to the personal preferences. For example, one may want to group the images as outdoors or indoors. Similarly, we may want to group face images by race or gender.

A. Ranchordas et al. (Eds.): VISIGRAPP 2009, CCIS 68, pp. 242–254, 2010.

In most of these cases, typical distance functions employed in vision community such as Euclidean distance or Gaussian kernels do not give satisfactory results.

Recently, learning distance metrics from side information has been actively studied in machine learning. Existing distance metric learning methods revise the original distance metric to accommodate the pairwise equivalence constraints and then a clustering algorithm with the learned distance metric is used to partition data to discover the desired groups within data. In [26], a full pseudo distance metric, which is parameterized by positive semi-definite matrices, is learned by means of convex programming using side information. The metric is learned via an iterative procedure that involves projection and eigen-decomposition in each step. Relevant Component analysis (RCA) [2] is introduced as an alternative to this method. But it can exploit only similarity constraints. Kwok and Tsang [13] formulate a metric learning problem that uses side information in a quadratic optimization scheme. Using the kernel trick, the method is also extended to the nonlinear case. Although the authors claim that the learned metric is a pseudo-metric, there is no guarantee that the resulting distance metric yields a positive semi-definite matrix. Shalev-Shwartz et al. [17] proposed a sophisticated online distance metric learning algorithm that uses side information. The method incorporates the large margin concept and the distance metric is modified based on two successive projections involving an eigen-decompsoition. Yang et al. [28] introduced a Bayesian framework for distance metric learning that estimates a posterior distribution for the distance metric from pairwise equivalence constraints. Davis et al. [7] proposed an information-theoretic approach to learn a Mahalanobis distance function. They formulated the metric propoblem as that of minimizing the differential relative entropy between two multivariate Gaussians under equivalence constraints on the distance function. Note that all semi-supervised distance metric learning algorithms mentioned above attempt to learn full rank distance metrics. In addition to these methods, there are some hybrid algorithms that unify clustering and metric learning into a unique framework [4]. A comprehensive survey of distance metric learning techniques can be found at [29].

In this paper we are interested in semi-supervised visual object classification problems. In these tasks, the quality of the results heavily relies on the chosen image representations and the distance metric used to compare data samples. The imagery data samples are typically represented by pixel intensities, multi-dimensional multi-resolution histograms or more sophisticated "bag-of-features" based representations using patch-based shape, texture and color features. Unfortunately, these representations usually tend to be high-dimensional and most of the distance metric learning techniques fail in these situations. This is due to the fact that most dimensions in high-dimensional spaces do not carry information about class labels. Furthermore, learning an effective full rank distance metric by using side information cannot be carried out in such high-dimensional spaces since the number of parameters to be estimated is related to the square of the dimensionality and there is insufficient side information to obtain accurate estimates [5]. A typical solution to this problem is to project the data onto a lower-dimensional space and then learn a suitable metric in the resulting low-dimensional space. There is a large number of dimensionality reduction methods in the literature [9,8,20,21]. But most of them cannot be used in our case since they are supervised methods that require explicit class labels. On the other hand, relying on an unsupervised dimensionality reduction method is also problematic since important discriminatory information may be lost during a completely unsupervised dimensionality reduction. A better approach would be to use a semi-supervised dimensionality reduction method to find a low-dimensional embedding satisfying the pairwise equivalence constraints. To this end, [15] proposed a method which learns a nonlinear mapping that is smooth over the data graph and maps the data onto a unit hypersphere, where two similar points are mapped to the same location while dissimilar samples are mapped to be the orthogonal coordinates. Yan and Domeniconi [27] randomly project data samples onto smaller subspaces and learn the distance metrics in these lower-dimensional spaces using side information. They then use Hybrid-Bipartite-Graph formulation to combine the distance metrics which are learned in the lower-dimensional subspaces. However, there is still risk of losing important discriminatory information during projections onto lower-dimensional subspaces. [5,1] revise the Locality Preserving Projections (LPP) method to exploit side information. In this paper we propose such an algorithm that works in both the input and kernel induced-feature space. In contrast to the traditional full rank distance metric learning methods, the proposed method allows us to learn nonsquare projection matrices that yield low rank pseudo metrics. This brings additional benefits such as visualization of data samples and reducing the storage cost and it is more robust to overfitting since the number of estimated parameters is greatly reduced. The proposed method bears similarity to the semi-supervised dimension reduction method introduced in [5], but it does not assume that samples in a sufficiently small neighborhood tend to have same label. Instead we focus on improving the local margin (separation).

The remainder of the paper is organized as follows: In Section 2, we introduce the proposed method and extend it to the nonlinear case. Section 3 describes the data sets and experimental results. Finally, we present conclusions in Section 4.

2   Method

2.1   Problem Setting

Let $x_i \in \mathbb{R}^d$, $i = 1, \ldots, n$, denote the samples in the training set. We are given a set of equivalence constraints in the form of similar and dissimilar pairs. Let S be the set of similar pairs

$$S = \{(x_i, x_j) | x_i \text{ and } x_j \text{ belong to the same class}\}$$

and let D be the set of dissimilar pairs

$$D = \{(x_i, x_j) | x_i \text{ and } x_j \text{ belong to different classes}\} .$$

Assuming consistency of the constraints, the constraint sets can be augmented using transitivity and entailment properties as in [3].

Our objective is to find a pseudo-metric that satisfies the equivalence constraints and at the same time reflects the true underlying relationships imposed by such constraints. We focus on pseudo-metrics of the form

$$d_A(x_i, x_j) = ||x_i - x_j||_A = \sqrt{(x_i - x_j)^\top A(x_i - x_j)}, \tag{1}$$

where $A \geq 0$ is a symmetric positive semi-definite matrix. In this case there exists a rectangular projection matrix W of size $q \times d$ ($q \leq d$) satisfying $A = W^\top W$ such that

$$||x_i - x_j||_A^2 = ||Wx_i - Wx_j||^2. \tag{2}$$

From this point of view the distance between two points under metric A can be interpreted as linear projection of the samples by W followed by Euclidean distance in the projected space. As a result, optimizing with respect to W rather than A allows us to reduce the dimensionality of the data and find low rank distance metrics. In the following, we will first show how to find a (potentially) full rank distance metric A using side information and then extend the idea to allow low rank metrics.

2.2 Learning Full Rank Distance Metrics

Intuitively, the learned distance metric must pull similar pairs closer and push the dissimilar pairs apart. Additionally, it should generalize well to unseen data. To this end, we minimize the following differentiable cost function defined based on sigmoids

$$J(A) = \frac{1}{N} \sum_{i,j \in S} \frac{1}{1 + \exp[-\beta(||x_i - x_j||_A^2 - t_s)]}$$
$$+ \frac{1}{M} \sum_{i,j \in D} \frac{1}{1 + \exp[\beta(||x_i - x_j||_A^2 - t_d)]}, \tag{3}$$

where N is the number of similar pairs, M is the number of dissimilar pairs, β is a design parameter that controls the slope of the sigmoid functions, and t_s and t_d are the selected thresholds. This cost function has two competing terms as illustrated in Fig. 1. The first term encourages pulling similar points closer, and the second term penalizes small distances between dissimilar pairs. The dissimilar pairs which are closer to each other contribute more to the loss function than the ones which are further from each other for well chosen β (In fact if the dissimilar pairs are too far from each other they do not contribute to the loss function at all). Therefore, just as in the Support Vector Machine's hinge loss, the second term of the above loss function is only triggered by dissimilar pairs in the vicinity of decision boundary which participate in shaping the inter-class decision boundaries. From a dimensionality reduction point of view, this can be thought as paying more attention to the displacement vectors between the dissimilar pairs where classes approach each other since these are good candidates for discriminant directions preserving inter-class separability. Although recent supervised distance learning techniques take the margin concept into consideration during learning [20,25], this issue is largely ignored in semi-supervised distance metric learning methods [13,26]. It should be noted that we need at least one active dissimilar sample pair (the closer dissimilar samples contributing to the lost function) since simply minimizing the above loss function over the set of all similar pairs leads to a trivial solution. Therefore including dissimilar pairs is crucial in our method[1] .We would like to find

---

[1] If the dissimilarity information is not available, we need an additional constraint such as $\sum_{i,j} |A_{ij}| > 0$ in order to avoid a trivial solution. But, we will not consider this case here since dissimilarity information is available in most applications.

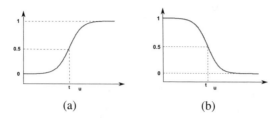

(a)   (b)

Fig. 1. Visualization of sigmoidal functions used in optimization. The first function (a) handles similar pairs, and it takes higher values as the distances between similar pairs increase. The second function (b) is used with dissimilar pairs and it takes higher values if the distances between dissimilar pairs are smaller than the selected threshold.

a positive semi-definite distance matrix that minimizes the above criterion. To do so, we can apply a gradient descent based approach. Let $u = (x_i - x_j)^\top A (x_i - x_j)$ and $dx_{ij} = (x_i - x_j)$. Differentiating $J(A)$ with respect to the distance matrix A gives the following gradient for the update rule

$$
\frac{\partial J(A)}{\partial A} = \frac{1}{N} \sum_{i,j \in S} \frac{\beta \exp[-\beta(u - t_s)]}{(1 + \exp[-\beta(u - t_s)])^2} dx_{ij} dx_{ij}^\top
$$
$$
- \frac{1}{M} \sum_{i,j \in D} \frac{\beta \exp[\beta(u - t_d)]}{(1 + \exp[\beta(u - t_d)])^2} dx_{ij} dx_{ij}^\top. \tag{4}
$$

To optimize the cost function we iteratively take a small step in the direction of the negative of this gradient. However, this updating rule does not guarantee positive semi-definiteness on matrix A. To do so, the matrix A must be projected onto the positive semi-definite cone at each iteration. This projection is performed by taking the eigen-decomposition of the computed distance matrix and removing the components with negative eigenvalues if exist any. At the end, the resulting distance matrix is shaped mostly by the displacement vectors between closer dissimilar pairs and the displacement vectors between far-away similar pairs. The algorithm is summarized below:

Initialization: Initialize A_0 to some positive definite matrix.
Iterate: Do the following steps until convergence:

– Set $\widetilde{A}_{t+1} = A_t - \eta \frac{\partial J(A)}{\partial A}$.
– Apply eigen-decomposition to $\widetilde{A}_{t+1}$ and reconstruct it using positive eigenvalues and corresponding eigenvectors $A_{t+1} = \sum_k \lambda_k e_k e_k^\top$.

2.3   Learning Low Rank Distance Metrics

As we mentioned earlier, distance between two samples under positive semi-definite distance matrix A can be interpreted as linear projection of the samples followed by Euclidean distance in the projected space, i.e., $d_A(x_i - x_j) = \|W x_i - W x_j\|$. Therefore low rank distance metrics satisfying equivalence constraints also allow low-dimensional projections which reduce the dimensionality of the original input space. Reducing the dimensionality offers several advantages: First, projection of samples onto a lower-dimensional space reduces the storage requirements. Secondly, projections onto 2 or 3-dimensional space allow us visualization of data, so we can devise an interactive constraint selection tool and verify the effects of our selections visually.

Unfortunately, optimization of $J(A)$ subject to rank-constraints on A is not convex and difficult to solve [8,20]. One way to obtain a low rank distance matrix is to solve for full rank matrix A using the algorithm described earlier, and then obtain a low rank projection by using its leading eigenvalues and corresponding eigenvectors as in [8]. A more elaborate way to obtain low rank distance matrix is to formulate the optimization problem with respect to nonsingular projection matrix W of size $q \times d$ rather than A. Here $q \leq d$ represents the desired rank of the distance matrix. This formulation is more efficient and robust to overfitting since the number of unknown parameters (elements of W) is significantly reduced. The rank of the resulting distance matrix A is at most q since the equation $A = W^\top W$ holds and the projected samples $W x_i$ lie in $\mathbb{R}^q$.

Our original cost function can be written in terms of W as

$$
\begin{aligned}
J(W) = \frac{1}{N} \sum_{i,j \in S} & \frac{1}{1 + \exp[-\beta(\|W x_i - W x_j\|^2 - t_s)]} \\
&+ \frac{1}{M} \sum_{i,j \in D} \frac{1}{1 + \exp[\beta(\|W x_i - W x_j\|^2 - t_d)]},
\end{aligned} \tag{5}
$$

Now let $u = (x_i - x_j)^\top W^\top W (x_i - x_j)$. If we differentiate $J(W)$ with respect to W, we obtain

$$
\begin{aligned}
\frac{\partial J(W)}{\partial W} = \frac{2W}{N} \sum_{i,j \in S} & \frac{\beta \exp[-\beta(u - t_s)]}{(1 + \exp[-\beta(u - t_s)])^2} dx_{ij} dx_{ij}^\top \\
&- \frac{2W}{M} \sum_{i,j \in D} \frac{\beta \exp[\beta(u - t_d)]}{(1 + \exp[\beta(u - t_d)])^2} dx_{ij} dx_{ij}^\top.
\end{aligned} \tag{6}
$$

As in the first case we have to ensure that the resulting distance matrix is positive semi-definite. To this end, we construct A from W and apply eigen-decomposition on A. This computation can be efficiently done by performing a thin singular value decomposition on W instead of performing a full eigen-decomposition on A. After removing the negative eigenvalues and corresponding eigenvectors we reconstruct the projection matrix as

$$
W = \Lambda^{1/2} E, \tag{7}
$$

where Λ is a diagonal matrix of nonzero eigenvalues of positive semi-definite matrix A, and E is the matrix whose columns are the corresponding eigenvectors. The algorithm is summarized as follows:

Initialization. Initialize W_0 to some rectangular matrix such that $W_0^\top W_0$ is positive semi-definite.

Iterate. Do the following steps until convergence:

- Set $\widetilde{\boldsymbol{W}}_{t+1} = \boldsymbol{W}_t - \eta \frac{\partial J(\boldsymbol{W})}{\partial \boldsymbol{W}}$.
- Construct $\widetilde{\boldsymbol{A}}_{t+1} = \widetilde{\boldsymbol{W}}_{t+1} \widetilde{\boldsymbol{W}}_{t+1}^{\top}$ and apply eigen-decomposition to $\widetilde{\boldsymbol{A}}_{t+1}$ and reconstruct it using positive eigenvalues and corresponding eigenvectors $\widetilde{\boldsymbol{A}}_{t+1} = \sum_k \lambda_k \boldsymbol{e}_k \boldsymbol{e}_k^{\top}$.
- Reconstruct the projection matrix as $\boldsymbol{W}_{t+1} = \Lambda_{t+1}^{1/2} \boldsymbol{E}_{t+1}$.

3 Extensions to Nonlinear Cases

Here we consider the case where the data samples are mapped into a higher-dimensional feature space and the distance metric is sought in this space. We restrict our analysis to nonlinear mappings $\phi : \mathbb{R}^d \rightarrow \mathcal{F}$ where the dot products in the mapped space can be obtained by using a kernel function such that $< \phi(\boldsymbol{x}_i), \phi(\boldsymbol{x}_j) >= k(\boldsymbol{x}_i, \boldsymbol{x}_j)$ for some kernel $k(.,.)$.

Let $\Phi = [\phi(\boldsymbol{x}_1) \ \dots \ \phi(\boldsymbol{x}_n)]$ denote the matrix whose columns are the mapped samples in $\mathcal{F}$. We define $\boldsymbol{k}_{\boldsymbol{x}} = \Phi^{\top} \phi(\boldsymbol{x}) = [k(\boldsymbol{x}_i, \boldsymbol{x}]_{i=1}^n$ as $n \times 1$ kernel vector of $\boldsymbol{x}$ against training samples. As in Kernel Principal Components Analysis [16], we consider parametrizations of $\boldsymbol{W}$ of the form $\boldsymbol{W} = \Omega \Phi^{\top}$, where $\Omega \in \mathbb{R}^{q \times n}$ is some matrix allowing to write $\boldsymbol{W}$ as a linear combinations of the mapped samples. In this setting, the distance matrix $\boldsymbol{A}$ can be written as

$$\boldsymbol{A} = \boldsymbol{W}^{\top} \boldsymbol{W} = \Phi \Omega^{\top} \Omega \Phi^{\top}. \tag{8}$$

By defining the positive semi-definite matrix as $\widehat{\boldsymbol{A}} = \Omega^{\top} \Omega$, the original problem can be converted into looking for a positive semi-definite matrix $\widehat{\boldsymbol{A}}$ since the distance in the mapped space under the distance matrix $\boldsymbol{A}$ can be written as

$$(\boldsymbol{k}_{\boldsymbol{x}_i} - \boldsymbol{k}_{\boldsymbol{x}_j})^{\top} \widehat{\boldsymbol{A}} (\boldsymbol{k}_{\boldsymbol{x}_i} - \boldsymbol{k}_{\boldsymbol{x}_j}) = \hat{\boldsymbol{dx}}_{ij}^{\top} \Phi \Omega^{\top} \Omega \Phi^{\top} \hat{\boldsymbol{dx}}_{ij}, \tag{9}$$

where $\hat{\boldsymbol{dx}}_{ij} = \phi(\boldsymbol{x}_i) - \phi(\boldsymbol{x}_j)$. As can be seen in the equation above, the distance between two samples in the mapped space depends only on dot products which are computed in the original input space. This is equivalent to transformation of the input data into n-dimensional feature space through $\Phi^{\top} \phi(\boldsymbol{x}_i)$ followed by the distance metric learning in the transformed space. Thus, by using the proposed algorithms described earlier, we can search a full rank matrix $\widehat{\boldsymbol{A}}$ or low-dimensional projection matrix Ω in the transformed kernel feature space.

4 Experiments

We perform experiments on three different computer vision applications and attempt to discover the desired unknown groups in these. The proposed Semi-Supervised Distance Metric Learning (SSDML) algorithm is compared to the full rank distance metric learning algorithm followed by dimensionality reduction and the Constrained Locality Preserving Projection (CLPP) method of [5]. The k-means and spectral clustering methods are used as clustering algorithm with the learned distance metric, and pairwise F-measure is used to evaluate the clustering results based on the underlying classes. The pairwise F-measure is the harmonic mean of the pairwise precision and recall measures. To demonstrate the effect of using different number of equivalence constraints, we gradually increased the number of similar and dissimilar pairs. In all visual object classification experiments, constraints are uniformly random selected from all possible constraints induced by the true data labels of the training data, and clustering performance is measured using only the test data. We used the same value for both thresholds t_s and t_d, and it is chosen to be $0.1\mu_S$, where μ_S is the averages of distances between similar pairs under the initial distance metric.

4.1 Experiments on Gender Database

Here we demonstrate how the proposed method can be used to organize image galleries in accordance to the personal preferences. In these applications we determine a characteristic for distinction and group images based on this selection. In our case we group images by gender and use the gender recognition database used in [23]. This database consist of 1892 images (946 males and 946 females) coming from the following databases: AR, BANCA, Caltech Frontal face, Essex Collection of Facial Images, FERET, FRGC version 2, Georgia Tech and XM2VTS. Only the first frontal image of each individual was taken, however because all of the databases have more male subjects than females, the same number of images is taken for both male and female subjects. All images are cropped based on the eye coordinates and resized to 32×40 yielding a 1280-dimensional input space. Then, images are converted to gray-scale followed by histogram equalization. Some samples are shown in Fig. 2. We used 50% of the images as training data and the remaining for testing. The dimensionality $d = 1280$ of the input space is too high, thus we learned a projection matrix of size $10 \times d$ yielding a low rank distance matrix. Since we cannot directly apply the other full rank distance metric learning techniques in this high-dimensional space, we first applied dimensionality reduction methods, Principal Component analysis (PCA) and Locality Preserving Projections (LPP) [11], to the high-dimensional data, and learned a distance metric in the reduced space. The size of the reduced space is chosen such that 99% of the overall energy (sum of the eigenvalues) is retained. To learn the distance metric in the reduced space, we used the method proposed in [13]. The reported clustering performances are

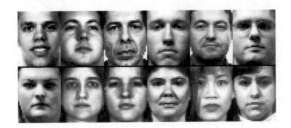

Fig. 2. Some male and female samples from Gender database

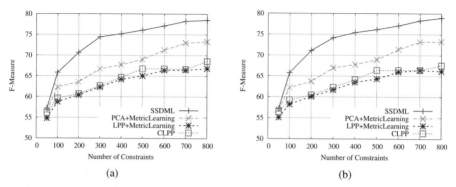

Fig. 3. F-measure as a function of number of constraints for (a) k-means clustering, (b) spectral clustering on Gender database

averages over 10 random test/training splits. Clustering accuracies as a function of constraints are shown in Fig. 3. As can be seen, the proposed method outperforms competing methods for both k-means and spectral clustering in all cases. PCA followed by the distance metric learning comes the second and LPP followed by the distance metric learning performs the worst. CLPP method yields similar accuracies to LPP followed by the distance metric learning. The poor performance of CLPP suggests that the samples coming from male and female subjects in small neighborhoods do not have the same label. Both clustering algorihtms, k-means and spectral clustering, yield similar results.

4.2   Experiments on Birds Database

The Birds database [14] contains six categories, each having 100 images. It is a challenging database since the birds appear against highly cluttered backgrounds and images have large intra-class, scale, and viewpoint variability. We used a "bag of features" representation for the images as they are too diverse to allow simple geometric alignment of their objects. In this method, patches are sampled from the image at many

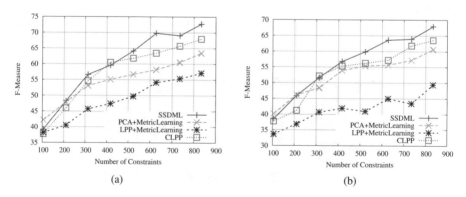

Fig. 4. F-measure as a function of number of constraints for (a) k-means clustering, (b) spectral clustering on Birds database

different positions and scales, either densely, randomly or based on the output of some kind of salient region detector. Here we used a dense grid of patches. Each patch was described using the robust visual descriptor SIFT assignment against a 2000 word visual dictionary learned from the complete set of training patches. The dimensionality of the input space is still high, thus we learned a nonsquare projection matrix with rank 10 and we reduced the dimensionality before applying the full distance metric learning technique as in the first experiment. We used 50% of the images as training data and remaining for testing. Results are again averages over 10 random test/training splits. Results are shown in Fig. 4. Initially, PCA followed by the full rank distance metric learning performs better than the proposed method. As the number of the constraints increases, the proposed method takes the lead and outperforms competing methods. CLPP comes the second and LPP followed by the distance metric learning again performs the worst. This time, k-means clustering yields better results than spectral clustering.

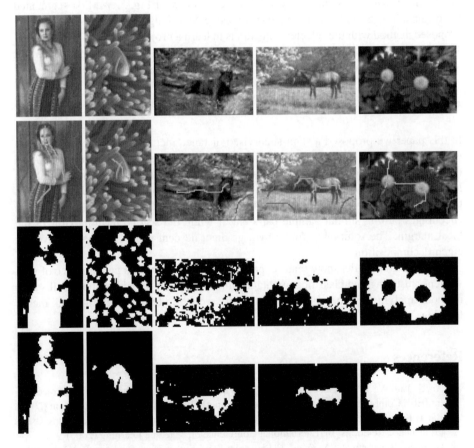

Fig. 5. Original images (top row), pixels used for equivalence constraints (second row), segmentation results without constraints (third row), and segmentation results using constraints (bottom row). Figure is best viewed in color.

4.3   Image Segmentation Applications

We also tested proposed method on image segmentation applications where the dimensionality of the sample space is relatively small compared to the visual object classification problems. We experimented with images chosen from the Berkeley Segmentation dataset[2]. Centered at every pixel in each image we extracted a 20×20 pixel image patch for which we computed the robust hue descriptor of [22]. This process yields a 36-dimensional feature vector which is a histogram over hue values observed in the patch, where each observed hue value is weighted by its saturation. We compared our proposed method to the image segmentation based on Normalized Cuts (NCuts) [19]. The Heat kernel function using Euclidean distance is used as kernel in NCuts segmentation. As in [5], we set the number of clusters to two, one cluster for the background and another for the object of interest.

The pairwise equivalence constraints are chosen from the samples corresponding to pixels shown with magenta and cyan in the second row of Fig. 5. We first segmented the original images without any supervision using NCuts algorithm. Then, we used the proposed method with the selected constraints to learn a projection matrix W with rank 10 and then used NCuts segmentation in the learned space. As can be seen in the figures, simple used added equivalence constraints can improve the segmentations.

5   Summary and Conclusions

In this paper we proposed a semi-supervised distance metric learning method, which uses pairwise equivalence constraints to discover the desired groups in high-dimensional data. The method works in both the input and kernel induced-feature space and it can learn nonsquare projection matrices that yield low rank distance metrics. The optimization procedure involves minimizing two terms defined based on sigmoids. The first term encourages pulling similar sample pairs closer while the second term maximizes the local margin. The solution is found by a gradient descent procedure that involves an eigen-decomposition.

Experimental results show that the proposed method increases performance of subsequent clustering and classification algorithms. Moreover, it yields better results than methods applying unsupervised dimensionality reduction followed by full rank metric learning.

References

1. An, S., Liu, W., Venkatesh, S.: Exploiting Side Information in Locality Preserving Projection. In: IEEE Computer Society Conference on Computer Vision and Pattern Recognition (2008)
2. Bar-Hillel, A., Hertz, T., Shental, N., Weinshall, D.: Learning Distance Functions Using Equivalence Relations. In: International Conference on Machine Learning (2003)
3. Basu, S., Banerjee, A., Mooney, R.J.: Active Semi-Supervision for Pairwise Constrained Clustering. In: The SIAM International Conference on Data Mining (2004)

---

[2] Available at http://www.eecs.berkeley.edu/Research/Projects/CS/vision/grouping/segbench/

4. Bilenko, M., Basu, S., Mooney, R.J.: Integrating Constraints and Metric Learning in Semi-Supervised Clustering. In: International Conference on Machine Learning (2004)
5. Cevikalp, H., Verbeek, J., Jurie, F., Klaser, A.: Semi-Supervised Dimensionality Reduction Using Pairwise Equivalence Constraints. In: International Conference on Computer Vision Theory and Applications (2008)
6. Chen, H.T., Liu, T.L., Fuh, C.S.: Learning effective Image Metrics From Few Pairwise Examples. In: IEEE International Conference on Computer Vision (2005)
7. Davis, J.V., Kulis, B., Jain, P., Dhillon, I.S.: Information-Theoretic Metric Learning. In: International Conference on Machine Learning (2007)
8. Globerson, A., Roweis, S.: Metric Learning by Collapsing Classes. In: Advances in Neural Information Processing Systems (2005)
9. Goldberger, J., Roweis, S., Hinton, G., Salakhutdinov, R.: Neighbourhood Component Analysis. In: Advances in Neural Information Processing Systems (2004)
10. Hadsell, R., Chopra, S., LeCun, Y.: Dimensionality Reduction by Learning and Invariant Mapping. In: IEEE Computer Society Conference on Computer Vision and Pattern Recognition (2006)
11. He, X., Niyogi, P.: Locality Preserving Directions. In: Advances in Neural Information Processing Systems (2003)
12. Hertz, T., Shental, N., Bar-Hillel, A., Weinshall, D.: Enhancing Image and Video Retrieval: Learning Via Equivalence Constraints. In: IEEE Computer Society Conference on Computer Vision and Pattern Recognition (2003)
13. Kwok, J.T., Tsan, I.W.: Learning with Idealized Kernels. In: International Conference on Machine Learning (2003)
14. Lazebnik, S., Schmid, C., Ponce, J.: A Maximum Entropy Framework for Part-Based Texture and Objcect Recognition. In: International Conference on Computer Vision (ICCV) (2005)
15. Li, Z., Liu, J., Tang, X.: Pairwise Constraint Propogation by Semidefinite Programming for Semi-Supervised Classification. In: International Conference on Machine Learning, ICML (2008)
16. Scholkopf, B., Smola, A.J., Muller, K.R.: Nonlinear Component Analysis as a Kernel Eigenvalue Problem. Neural Computation 10, 1299–1319 (1998)
17. Shalev-Shwartz, S., Singer, Y., Ng, A.Y.: Online and Batch Learning of Pseudo Metrics. In: International Conference on Machine Learning (2004)
18. Shental, N., Bar-Hillel, A., Hertz, T., Weinshall, D.: Computing Gaussian Mixture Modles with EM Using Equivalence Constraints. In: Advances in Neural Information Processing Systems (2003)
19. Shi, J., Malik, J.: Normalized Cuts and Image Segmentation. IEEE Transactions on PAMI 22, 885–905 (2000)
20. Torresani, L., Lee, K.C.: Large Margin Component Analysis. In: Advances in Neural Information Processing Systems (2006)
21. Turk, M., Pentland, A.P.: Eigenfaces for Recognition. Journal of Cognitive Neuroscience 3, 71–86 (1991)
22. Van de Weijer, J., Schmid, C.: Coloring Local Feature Extraction. In: Leonardis, A., Bischof, H., Pinz, A. (eds.) ECCV 2006. LNCS, vol. 3952, pp. 334–348. Springer, Heidelberg (2006)
23. Villegas, M., Paredes, R.: Simultaneous learning of a Discriminative Projection and Prototype for Nearest-Neighbor Classification. In: IEEE Computer Society Conference on Computer Vision and Pattern Recognition (2008)
24. Wagstaff, K., Rogers, S.: On subharmonic solutions of a Hamiltonian system. Constrained K-means Clustering with Background Knowledge. In: International Conference on Machine Learning (2001)
25. Weinberger, K.Q., Blitzer, J., Saul, L.K.: Distance Metric Learning for Large Margin Nearest Neighbor Classification. In: Advances in Neural Information Processing Systems (2005)

26. Xing, E.P., Ng, A.Y., Jordan, M.I., Russell, S.: Distance Metric Learning with Application to Clustering with Side-Information. In: Advances in Neural Information Processing Systems (2003)
27. Yan, B., Domeniconi, C.: Subspace Metric Ensembles for Semi-Supervised Clustering of High Dimensional Data. In: Fürnkranz, J., Scheffer, T., Spiliopoulou, M. (eds.) ECML 2006. LNCS (LNAI), vol. 4212, pp. 509–520. Springer, Heidelberg (2006)
28. Yang, L., Jin, R., Sukthankar, R.: Bayesian Active Distance Metric Learning. In: Proceedings of the 23rd Conference on Uncertainty in Artificial Intelligence (2007)
29. Yang, L., Jin, R.: Distance Metric Learning: A Comprehensive Survey (2006), http://wwww.cse.msu.edu/~yangliu1/framesurveyv2.pdf

Orthogonal Distance Least Squares Fitting: A Novel Approach

Sudanthi Wijewickrema[1], Charles Esson[1], and Andrew Papliński[2]

[1] Colour Vision Systems, 11, Park Street, Bacchus Marsh 3340, Australia
[2] School of Information Technology, Monash University, Clayton 3800, Australia

Abstract. Least squares is a common method of conic fitting that minimizes the squared sum of a distance measure between a set of points and a conic. Orthogonal distance, when used as the distance that is minimized, provides more accurate fits as it is the shortest distance between a point and a conic. The problem however lies in the calculation of the orthogonal distance for a general conic, which results in an unstable closed form solution. Existing methods avoid this closed form solution by using non-linear iterative procedures or incorporating conic specific information. This paper introduces a novel method to directly calculate the orthogonal distance for an arbitrary conic, thereby eliminating the need for iterative procedures and conic specific information. It further describes a least squares fitting algorithm that uses the orthogonal distance thus calculated, to fit general conics. This technique is then extended to fit quadrics to three dimensional data.

Keywords: Conic fitting, Quadric fitting, Orthogonal distance least squares fitting.

1 Introduction

Conic fitting is a well known problem and has applications in many fields. Among the methods available for this, the most common are: the Hough transform [1], the moment method [2], and least squares fitting [3]. The two former methods become computationally inefficient when a higher number of parameters are involved, and hence, least squares methods have received more attention in recent years. The objective of least squares fitting is to obtain the curve that minimizes the squared sum of a defined error measure.

$$\min\ \sigma^2 = \sum_{i=1}^{n} d_i^2 \tag{1}$$

where, d_i is the distance measure from of the ith point and σ^2 is the squared sum of the errors over n points.

Depending on the distance measure that is minimized, least squares fitting falls into two main categories: algebraic and orthogonal (geometric/euclidian) distance fitting. The algebraic distance from a point to a geometric feature (*eg.* curve or conic) is defined by the following equation.

$$d_a = f(\mathbf{p}, \mathbf{x}) \tag{2}$$

A. Ranchordas et al. (Eds.): VISIGRAPP 2009, CCIS 68, pp. 255–268, 2010.

where, **p** is the vector of parameters of the geometric feature, **x** is the coordinate vector and f is the function that defines the geometric feature or conic.

Although algebraic fitting is advantageous with respect to computing cost and simplicity of implementation, it has many disadvantages, the most serious of which are the lack of accuracy and the bias of the fitting parameters [4,5]. Changes have been suggested in an effort to improve accuracy and one such error measure is the first order approximation of the orthogonal distance or the normalized algebraic distance [6].

$$d_n = \frac{d_a}{\| \bigtriangledown d_a \|} \tag{3}$$

where, d_a is the algebraic distance, d_n is the normalized algebraic distance and $\bigtriangledown = \frac{\partial}{\partial \mathbf{x}} = [\frac{\partial}{\partial x} \; \frac{\partial}{\partial y}]^T$

Although using the normalized algebraic distance gives better results than algebraic fitting, it also displays most of the drawbacks of the latter.

Orthogonal distance, which is agreed to be the most natural and best error measure in least squares techniques [4], can be used to overcome problems related to algebraic fitting. Although a closed form solution exists for the calculation of the orthogonal point for a general conic, numerical instability can result from the application of the analytic formula [5,7]. Therefore, either non-linear optimization techniques for the general geometric feature [4,8,9] or conic specific characteristics such as semi-axes, center and rotation angle for ellipses [10,11,12] are used to calculate the orthogonal distance.

In contrast, this paper discusses a novel and direct method of calculating the orthogonal distance (and a fitting algorithm based on it), thereby overcoming the above mentioned problems.

The rest of the paper is organized as follows: Section 2 gives a brief review of relevant concepts and section 3 introduces the proposed algorithm, while section 4 discusses experimental results. Section 5 describes how the proposed algorithm can be extended to fit quadratic surfaces (quadrics) in three dimensions.

2   Review of Relevant Concepts

A conic is expressed in the form of a 3×3 symmetric matrix, C. If a point $\mathbf{x} = [x \; y \; 1]^T$, given in homogeneous coordinates is on the conic, it satisfies:

$$\mathbf{x}^T C \mathbf{x} = 0 \tag{4}$$

where,

$$C = \begin{bmatrix} c_{11} & c_{12} & c_{13} \\ c_{12} & c_{22} & c_{23} \\ c_{13} & c_{23} & c_{33} \end{bmatrix} \tag{5}$$

We can extract the five independent parameters of the conic from C by making c_{33} equal to a constant, assuming it's not zero (for example, we use $c_{33} = -1$). Then, the independent parameter vector **p** is as follows:

$$\mathbf{p} = [c_{11} \; c_{12} \; c_{13} \; c_{22} \; c_{23}]^T \tag{6}$$

Similarly, a quadric can be represented in the form of a 4×4 symmetric matrix (with nine independent parameters) Q, which satisfied the following equation for any point $\mathbf{X} = [x \ y \ z \ 1]^T$ that lies on it.

$$\mathbf{X}^T Q \mathbf{X} = 0 \qquad (7)$$

3 Proposed Algorithm

This section describes the orthogonal distance conic fitting algorithm. First, in section 3.1, the orthogonal distance is formulated, while its calculation is explained in section 3.2. Section 3.3 describes the complete conic fitting algorithm.

3.1 Orthogonal Distance from a Conic

The orthogonal distance is the shortest distance from a point to a conic, as shown in figure 1. The closest point on the conic from the given point is called the *orthogonal point*.

Note that any point in space (on, inside or outside the conic) is represented by $\mathbf{a}$, and the corresponding orthogonal point on the conic by $\mathbf{x}$, and that the points are given in homogeneous coordinates. Then, for any point $\mathbf{a}$, the orthogonal distance d, is given by:

$$d = \parallel \tilde{\mathbf{x}} - \tilde{\mathbf{a}} \parallel \qquad (8)$$

where, $\mathbf{a} = [\tilde{\mathbf{a}} \ 1]^T$, $\tilde{\mathbf{a}} = [a_1 \ a_2]^T$, and $\tilde{\mathbf{x}} = [x \ y]^T$ are the non-homogeneous representations of the points $\mathbf{a}$, and $\mathbf{x}$ respectively.

Calculating the orthogonal distance involves the determination of point $\mathbf{x}$ on the curve for a given point $\mathbf{a}$. Since the orthogonal distance is the shortest distance from a point to a conic, the line connecting the points $\mathbf{x}$ and $\mathbf{a}$ is normal to the conic at $\mathbf{x}$. Therefore:

$$\mathbf{n}_1 = \bar{C}\mathbf{x} \qquad (9)$$

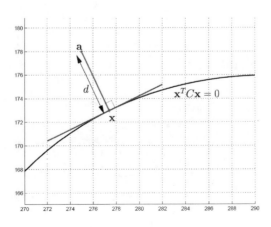

Fig. 1. Orthogonal Distance between a Point and a Conic

where, $\mathbf{n}_1$ is the normal vector, $\bar{C} = [\mathbf{c}_1 \ \mathbf{c}_2]^T$ is the 2×3 matrix formed by the first two rows of C, and $\mathbf{c}_1$ and $\mathbf{c}_2$ are the first and second columns of C respectively.

The vector connecting the two points is given by $\mathbf{n}_2 = \tilde{\mathbf{x}} - \tilde{\mathbf{a}} = [x - a_1 \ \ y - a_2]^T$. The same equation can be written in the following form, to be consistent with equation (9).

$$\mathbf{n}_2 = \bar{A}\mathbf{x} \tag{10}$$

where, $\bar{A} = [\mathbf{a}_1 \ \mathbf{a}_2]^T$, $\mathbf{a}_1 = [1 \ 0 \ -a_1]^T$, and $\mathbf{a}_2 = [0 \ 1 \ -a_2]^T$.

Vectors $\mathbf{n}_1$ and $\mathbf{n}_2$ given in equations (9) and (10) are in the same direction, and lead to equation (11).

$$\bar{C}\mathbf{x} = \alpha \bar{A}\mathbf{x}$$

$$\Longrightarrow \frac{\mathbf{c}_1^T\mathbf{x}}{\mathbf{a}_1^T\mathbf{x}} = \frac{\mathbf{c}_2^T\mathbf{x}}{\mathbf{a}_2^T\mathbf{x}} \tag{11}$$

$$\Longrightarrow \mathbf{x}^T(\mathbf{c}_1\mathbf{a}_2^T - \mathbf{c}_2\mathbf{a}_1^T)\mathbf{x} = 0$$

$$\Longrightarrow \mathbf{x}^T B\mathbf{x} = 0$$

where, $B = \mathbf{c}_1\mathbf{a}_2^T - \mathbf{c}_2\mathbf{a}_1^T$, and α is a scalar parameter.

The relationship obtained in equation (11) is that of a conic, with one exception: the matrix representing the conic B is not symmetric. Without loss of generality, B can be manipulated to get the conventional form of a conic matrix D, which is symmetric but also satisfies the same relationship, as follows:

$$D = B + B^T \tag{12}$$

Therefore, for the orthogonal point $\mathbf{x}$ of any point $\mathbf{a}$, the following equations should be satisfied simultaneously.

$$\mathbf{x}^T C\mathbf{x} = 0$$
$$\mathbf{x}^T D\mathbf{x} = 0 \tag{13}$$

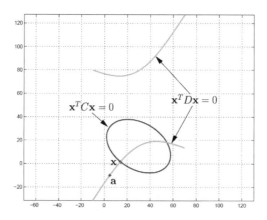

Fig. 2. Orthogonal Point $\mathbf{x}$ on the Conic, for an Arbitrary Point $\mathbf{a}$

These two quadratic equations represent the intersection of two conics and is solved directly using the method discussed in section 3.2. Out of the four possible solutions, the orthogonal point is the point closest to **a**, as shown in figure 2.

3.2 Solving for the Orthogonal Point

To find the orthogonal point **x**, two quadratic equations of two parameters should be solved, resulting in a quartic equation whose closed-form solution is known to be numerically unstable [5,7]. Therefore, iterative methods and/or the introduction of conic specific information as additional constraints are widely accepted as the norm in this calculation [4,10,15]. As explained above, this has undesirable properties such as complex calculations, and inaccurate results when the fitted conic does not resemble the distribution of the data points.

To overcome these problems, we use the method discussed in Miller [16] which uses the properties of conic pencils to solve for the intersection of two conics. Semple and Kneebone [14] show that there exist an infinite number of conics that go through the intersection points of two conics, and that they can be represented by a pencil of conics as follows:

$$C_f = C + \lambda D \tag{14}$$

where, λ is a scalar parameter.

Semple and Kneebone [14] also prove that there are three degenerate members (intersecting, parallel or coincident line pairs) in this pencil of conics. They further show that any member of the pencil (including the three degenerate members) share the intersection points of C and D. Equation (15) gives such a degenerate conic and figure 3 illustrates the relationship between the base conics and a degenerate member.

$$C_d = C + \lambda_d D \tag{15}$$

where, λ_d is the scalar that defines a degenerate conic.

Further, the 3×3 conic matrix of a degenerate conics is singular [13] and therefore satisfies the property shown in equation (16).

$$|C_d| = 0$$
$$\implies |C + \lambda_d D| = 0 \tag{16}$$

The three scalar values (λ_d) that define the degenerate members of the pencil can be calculated by solving the generalized eigen system of equation (16). By substituting a finite, real value of λ_d in equation (15), a degenerate quadric C_d can be obtained. Further, this conic C_d consists of a pair of lines which we define here as $\mathbf{x}^T \mathbf{l} = 0$ and $\mathbf{x}^T \mathbf{m} = 0$. Hartley and Zisserman [13] show that a degenerate conic and the lines that form it, satisfy equation (17).

$$C_d = \mathbf{l}\mathbf{m}^T + \mathbf{m}\mathbf{l}^T \tag{17}$$

Therefore, the vectors that define the line coefficients **l** and **m** can be extracted from C_d by using singular value or eigen decomposition. Once the lines are obtained, the calculation of intersection points is done by solving one of the conic equations ($\mathbf{x}^T C \mathbf{x} = 0$ or $\mathbf{x}^T D \mathbf{x} = 0$) and the line equations ($\mathbf{l}^T \mathbf{x} = 0$ and $\mathbf{m}^T \mathbf{x} = 0$).

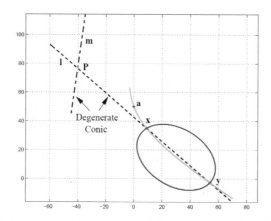

Fig. 3. A Degenerate Member of the Conic Pencil Shares the Intersection Points (**x** and **y**) of the Two Base Conics

The intersection of the conic with the two lines that define a degenerate conic of the pencil gives four solutions (two each for the two lines). Out of these four points, we select the (real) point closest to **a** as the orthogonal point. In figure 3, **x** and **y** are the common intersection points of the pencil of conics and **l** and **m** are the extracted lines. The orthogonal point is **x**, as it is the closest of the two points to **a**.

3.3 Conic Fitting Algorithm

From the method discussed above, the orthogonal distance from the ith point (say $\mathbf{a}_i$) of a set of n points, can be determined directly for a general conic. The next step is to minimize the squared sum of all such distances as shown in equation (1), to find the best fit conic to the given set of points. Note that this is the same quantity that is minimized in the distance based algorithm of Ahn [4] but assumes that the weighting matrix or the error covariance matrix is identity [10]. This results in an unconstrained non-linear optimization procedure.

Out of the algorithms available for solving this non-linear optimization problem, we select the Levenberg-Marquardt method due to its robustness over other methods such as Gauss-Newton. For each step of the iteration for the Levenberg-Marquardt method, the update is done as shown in equation (18).

$$\mathbf{p}_{k+1} = \mathbf{p}_k + \boldsymbol{\delta}_k \qquad (18)$$

where,

$$\boldsymbol{\delta}_k = -(H_k + \alpha_k I)^{-1} J_k^T \mathbf{d}_k \ , \qquad (19)$$

J_k is the Jacobian matrix for the kth step, $H_k = J_k^T J_k$ is an approximation to the Hessian matrix, I is the 5×5 identity matrix, $\boldsymbol{\delta}_k$ is the update vector, $\mathbf{d}_k$ is the orthogonal distance vector for all points at step k, and α_k is a scalar.

An initial guess for the parameter vector (say $\mathbf{p}_0$) has to be given, to start the iterative procedure. The selection of this initial guess is done as discussed at the end of this section. The values for the constant α_k is initially set to a small constant (*eg.* $\alpha_0 = 0.01$). For the consequent steps, if the error increases or if the calculated step yields an imaginary conic, the step is repeated with $\alpha_k = n_{const} \times \alpha_k$. If the error is decreased, the next step is calculated with $\alpha_k = \alpha_k / n_{const}$, where, n_{const} is a scalar constant (*eg.* $n_{const} = 10$).

To calculate the Jacobian matrix for each step, in the conventional way, it is required that the orthogonal distance be expressed as a function of the conic parameters. The method explained in section 3.1, although very convenient for conics with known parameters, makes it difficult, if not impossible for those with unknown parameters. Therefore, an alternative method is used to find the Jacobian matrix, or the matrix of first derivatives of the orthogonal distances with respect to the conic parameters.

First, equation (8) is expressed in the form of equation (20), the derivative of which, with respect to the conic parameter vector $\mathbf{p}$, leads to equation (21).

$$\begin{aligned} d^2 &= \| \tilde{\mathbf{x}} - \tilde{\mathbf{a}} \|^2 \\ &= (\tilde{\mathbf{x}} - \tilde{\mathbf{a}})^T (\tilde{\mathbf{x}} - \mathbf{a}) \end{aligned} \tag{20}$$

$$d\frac{\partial d}{\partial \mathbf{p}} = (\tilde{\mathbf{x}} - \tilde{\mathbf{a}})^T \frac{\partial \tilde{\mathbf{x}}}{\partial \mathbf{p}} \tag{21}$$

Note that for each step, the orthogonal distance and orthogonal point is known. Therefore, the only unknowns in equation (21) are $\frac{\partial d}{\partial \mathbf{p}}$ and $\frac{\partial \tilde{\mathbf{x}}}{\partial \mathbf{p}}$. To find the value of the latter in terms of known quantities, the equations in (13) are differentiated with respect to the parameter vector $\mathbf{p}$, resulting in:

$$2 \begin{bmatrix} \mathbf{x}^T C \\ \mathbf{x}^T D \end{bmatrix} \frac{\partial \mathbf{x}}{\partial \mathbf{p}} = - \begin{bmatrix} \mathbf{x}^T \frac{\partial C}{\partial \mathbf{p}} \mathbf{x} \\ \mathbf{x}^T \frac{\partial D}{\partial \mathbf{p}} \mathbf{x} \end{bmatrix} \tag{22}$$

However, $\mathbf{x} = [\tilde{\mathbf{x}} \; 1]^T$ is the homogeneous representation of the two dimensional point $\tilde{\mathbf{x}}$. Therefore, equation (22) can be rewritten to get equation (23).

$$2 \begin{bmatrix} \mathbf{x}^T \bar{C}^T \\ \mathbf{x}^T \bar{D}^T \end{bmatrix} \frac{\partial \tilde{\mathbf{x}}}{\partial \mathbf{p}} = - \begin{bmatrix} \mathbf{x}^T \frac{\partial C}{\partial \mathbf{p}} \mathbf{x} \\ \mathbf{x}^T \frac{\partial D}{\partial \mathbf{p}} \mathbf{x} \end{bmatrix} \tag{23}$$

where, $\bar{C}$ and $\bar{D}$ are the 2×3 matrices consisting of the first two rows of C and D respectively.

The solution of equations (21) and (23) gives an expression for the first derivative of the orthogonal distance of a point with respect to the parameter vector $\mathbf{p}$ as follows.

$$\frac{\partial d}{\partial \mathbf{p}} = \begin{cases} \dfrac{(\tilde{\mathbf{x}} - \tilde{\mathbf{a}})^T}{d} S^{-1} \mathbf{s} \,, \forall \; \tilde{\mathbf{x}} \neq \tilde{\mathbf{a}} \\ 0 \qquad\qquad , \text{ otherwise} \end{cases} \tag{24}$$

where, $S = 2 \begin{bmatrix} \mathbf{x}^T \bar{C}^T \\ \mathbf{x}^T \bar{D}^T \end{bmatrix}$, and $\mathbf{s} = - \begin{bmatrix} \mathbf{x}^T \frac{\partial C}{\partial \mathbf{p}} \mathbf{x} \\ \mathbf{x}^T \frac{\partial D}{\partial \mathbf{p}} \mathbf{x} \end{bmatrix}$.

Equation (24) gives the 1×5 partial derivative vector of the orthogonal distance at each point. By stacking all such vectors corresponding to n points in a matrix, the $n \times 5$ Jacobian matrix is obtained. The $(k+1)^{th}$ step can then be calculated by substituting the value of the Jacobian at the kth step in equation (18). An iterative minimization is then carried out until the update vector δ_k reaches some threshold, indicating that a minimum is reached, and that further iteration does not significantly affect the results.

As an initialization to start the iteration, we suggest the use of the RMS (root mean squared) circle (as used in the circle fitting algorithm of Ahn et al. [10]). It uses a circle that has the root mean squared central distances as its radius r and the center of gravitation as its center $\tilde{\mathbf{x}}_c$. The initial circle used in the algorithm can thus be represented by:

$$C_0 = \begin{bmatrix} I & -\tilde{\mathbf{x}}_c \\ -\tilde{\mathbf{x}}_c^T & \tilde{\mathbf{x}}_c^T \tilde{\mathbf{x}}_c - r^2 \end{bmatrix} \tag{25}$$

where, $\tilde{\mathbf{x}}_c = \frac{1}{n} \sum_{i=1}^{n} \tilde{\mathbf{a}}_i$, $r = \sqrt{\frac{1}{n} \sum_{i=1}^{n} \| \tilde{\mathbf{a}}_i - \tilde{\mathbf{x}}_c \|^2}$, and $\tilde{\mathbf{a}}_i$ is the ith point in non-homogeneous coordinates.

An example of a conic fitting, which uses the above circle as its initial guess is shown in figure 4(a), along with the square root of the squared sum of orthogonal distances, from the points to the estimated conic at each step of the optimization in figure 4(b).

4   Experimental Results

First, we evaluated the performance of the algorithm for points on randomly generated conics. For this experiment, 1000 random conics were generated, and 5, 10, 15, 20 and 25 points on these conics were selected randomly. Then, the proposed general conic fitting algorithm was run on the points. The type of conic was not restricted in any way, except that a check was done for imaginary conics, and in a situation where one was generated, it was discarded, and another random conic generated in its place. Table 3.3 shows the results of the fitting, where all the values are averaged over the 1000 random conics. σ is the square root of the mean squared orthogonal distance, while σ_n is the same error normalized over the number of points, calculated for the sake of comparison where different numbers of points are involved in the fitting.

Table 3.3 shows that the mean error per point σ_n on average (for all 5000 cases) is less than 0.3 pixels. Furthermore, the results indicate that the number of fits that have

Table 1. Results for the Fitting of Random Conics

Points	Avg. σ (pixels)	Avg. σ_n (pixels)	$\sigma_n < 0.001$ (%)	$\sigma_n < 0.01$ (%)	$\sigma_n < 0.1$ (%)	$\sigma_n < 1$ (%)	Avg. Steps
5	1.2505	0.2501	78.1	85.5	92.4	97.4	17.29
10	1.7653	0.1765	64.6	81.3	91.6	96.2	16.33
15	4.5601	0.3040	60.6	79.3	92.5	95.9	17.11
20	4.7040	0.2352	65.0	81.0	95.3	97.5	15.26
25	7.7385	0.3095	60.3	77.3	92.3	96.7	14.60
Avg.	N/A	0.2551	65.72	80.88	92.82	96.74	16.12

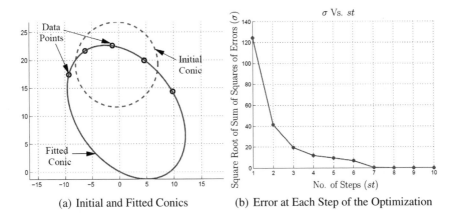

(a) Initial and Fitted Conics   (b) Error at Each Step of the Optimization

Fig. 4. Fitting of a Conic

an error less than $0.001, 0.01, 0.1$, and 1 are $65.72\%, 80.88\%, 92.82\%$, and 96.74% respectively. The average number of iterations to convergence is approximately 16 steps. For a general conic fitting algorithm, these results are very accurate, and the speed of convergence is also acceptable (see Ahn et al. [10]). Figure 5 shows how the proposed algorithm performed on some points on random conics of different types.

Next, we compared the performance of the proposed conic fitting algorithm with other orthogonal distance fitting methods. To this end, first, we compare the time complexities of existing algorithms, iterative and non-iterative in their method of determining the orthogonal distance. Then, we focus on the performance of the proposed algorithm with others that calculate the orthogonal distance directly (but using conic specific information).

The general orthogonal distance fitting algorithm introduced in Boggs et al. [8] determines the model parameters and the orthogonal points simultaneously and has a time/space complexity of $O(n^2)$, while Helfrich and Zwick [9] present a nested iteration scheme with a time complexity of $O(n)$. The general nested iterative method discussed in Ahn [4] has similar time/space complexities. The proposed algorithm also has time and memory usage proportional to the number of data points $O(n)$, but removes the nested iteration scheme of Ahn [4] by calculating the orthogonal distance non-iteratively. The type specific direct fitting methods such as Ahn et al. [10], Gander et al. [11], and Späth [12] also have the same time complexity and require a non-nested iteration.

In light of the similarity in terms of the type of iteration (nested or not) and time/space complexity, the performance of the proposed algorithm can be evaluated against other direct fitting methods [10,11,12]. With respect to the others, the proposed method has a clear advantage in that, it has a time/space complexity of $O(n)$ and that it uses a non-nested iterative scheme. It should also be noted that in most of these methods, accurate initial guesses are required for good performance. Therefore, algebraic (or in some cases, orthogonal) fitting is performed to provide the initialization. The proposed algorithm is more robust and requires only a loose initialization in the form

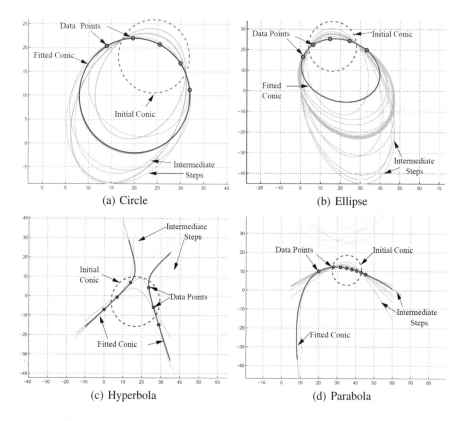

Fig. 5. Fitting of Different Types of Conics with the Proposed Algorithm

of the RMS circle, irrespective of the type of conic the data resembles, as shown in the previous experiment.

Table 4 summarizes the results of the comparison of the direct conic fitting algorithms with respect to the data sets in [11] and [12]. The data sets are for different conic types, and therefore, only the relevant algorithms were run on specific data sets. For example, the data sets provided for ellipse fitting were used only on ellipse specific algorithms. On the contrary, as the proposed algorithm is type independent, it was run on all data sets.

Further, to make the comparison more consistent, the results of the same algorithm, which uses different initializations, were averaged. For example, in the circle fitting of Ahn et al. [10], two initializations were used: the RMS circle, and an algebraically fitted circle. The results in table 4 show the average performance of the two. This is done in an attempt to make the comparison more independent of the type of initialization used. For details of individual performance on various data sets with different initializations, refer to Wijewickrema et al. [17] and Ahn et al. [10].

Note that the error σ_{avg} is the square root of the mean squared orthogonal distance to the fitted conic, and $\| \Delta \mathbf{p} \|_{avg}$ is the average of the norm of the parameter update vector. As seen from the results, even dedicated fitting methods do not achieve

Table 2. Comparison of Direct Orthogonal Distance Fitting Algorithms

Algorithm	Type	Avg. Steps	$\parallel \Delta \mathbf{p} \parallel_{avg}$	Error σ_{avg} (pixels)
Proposed	General	13.1	4.3×10^{-6}	0.8813
Ahn	Circle	8.5	4.5×10^{-6}	1.1080
Gander	Circle	11	2.1×10^{-6}	1.1080
Späth	Circle	116	1.0×10^{-4}	1.1080
Ahn	Ellipse	16.5	4.03×10^{-6}	1.2581
Gander	Ellipse	71	1.0×10^{-6}	1.1719
Späth	Ellipse	30	1.0×10^{-4}	1.4306
Ahn	Hyperbola	6.4	3×10^{-6}	0.8899
Späth	Hyperbola	100	1.0×10^{-4}	1.2532
Ahn	Parabola	11.7	5.9×10^{-6}	1.9263
Späth	Parabola	53.5	5.3×10^{-5}	2.1854

the accuracy of the general algorithm proposed here, which scores the lowest value of $\sigma_{avg} = 0.8813$, over all others. The number of iteration steps, although higher than that of the others, is acceptable considering the rough initialization and type independent nature of the algorithm.

However, it should be noted that, for relatively high levels of noise, the algorithm sometimes converges to local minima, as is the case with algorithms of its kind. To avoid this, a better initialization such as an algebraic fit can be used.

5   Quadric Fitting

The orthogonal distance from a three dimensional point to a quadric is as shown in equation (26).

$$d = \parallel \tilde{\mathbf{X}} - \tilde{\mathbf{A}} \parallel \tag{26}$$

where, $\mathbf{A} = [\tilde{\mathbf{A}} \ 1]^T$ and $\mathbf{X} = [\tilde{\mathbf{X}} \ 1]^T$ are the homogeneous representations of the point in space and its orthogonal point respectively, while $\tilde{\mathbf{A}} = [a_1 \ a_2 \ a_3]^T$ and $\tilde{\mathbf{X}} = [x \ y \ z]^T$ are their non-homogeneous representations.

The normal $\mathbf{n}_1$ to the quadric at the orthogonal point $\mathbf{X}$, and the vector $\mathbf{n}_2$ of the line connecting $\mathbf{X}$ and $\mathbf{A}$ are:

$$\mathbf{n}_1 = \bar{Q}\mathbf{X} \tag{27}$$

$$\mathbf{n}_2 = \bar{E}\mathbf{x} \tag{28}$$

where, $\bar{Q} = [\mathbf{q}_1 \ \mathbf{q}_2 \ \mathbf{q}_3]^T$, $\mathbf{q}_i$ $(i = 1, 2, 3)$ is the ith column of Q, $\bar{E} = [\mathbf{a}_1 \ \mathbf{a}_2 \ \mathbf{a}_3]^T$, $\mathbf{a}_1 = [1 \ 0 \ 0 \ -a_1]^T$, $\mathbf{a}_2 = [0 \ 1 \ 0 \ -a_2]^T$, and $\mathbf{a}_3 = [0 \ 0 \ 1 \ -a_3]^T$.

The vectors $\mathbf{n}_1$ and $\mathbf{n}_2$ are in the same direction, and hence are connected by a scalar value β as $\mathbf{n}_1 = \beta \mathbf{n}_2$, which leads to:

$$\frac{\mathbf{q}_1{}^T \mathbf{X}}{\mathbf{a}_1{}^T \mathbf{X}} = \frac{\mathbf{q}_2{}^T \mathbf{X}}{\mathbf{a}_2{}^T \mathbf{X}} = \frac{\mathbf{q}_3{}^T \mathbf{X}}{\mathbf{a}_3{}^T \mathbf{X}} \tag{29}$$

By performing the same calculation as shown in equations (11) and (12) on equation (29), we get two quadratic equations. These equations are shown below along with the original equation of the quadric giving us three conditions that the orthogonal point $\mathbf{X}$ has to satisfy.

$$\mathbf{X}^T Q \mathbf{X} = 0$$
$$\mathbf{X}^T Q_1 \mathbf{X} = 0 \tag{30}$$
$$\mathbf{X}^T Q_2 \mathbf{X} = 0$$

where, Q_1 and Q_2 are quadrics resulting from the simplification discussed above.

These three equations represent the intersection of three quadrics, which can be solved using Levin's method [18]. It is proven in Levin [18] that there exists at least one (easily parameterized) ruled quadric in the pencil formed by two quadrics, which can be used to determine their intersection curve. Once a ruled quadric is obtained, it is transformed to its canonical form. One of the base quadrics is also transformed to the same coordinate system. The ruled quadric is then written in its parametric form, and substituted in the equation of the (transformed) base quadric to obtain the intersection curve (say ic_1).

To extend this idea to the intersection of three quadrics, the third quadric too has to be converted to the canonical frame of the ruled quadric. Then a similar substitution as explained above gives the intersection curve (say ic_2) between the ruled quadric and the third quadric. The intersection points of the two curves ic_1 and ic_2 are then determined and transformed back to the original coordinate frame. From these points, the one closest to $\mathbf{A}$ is selected as the orthogonal point. Figure 6 shows the points obtained by the intersection of the two curves ic_1 and ic_2 and the orthogonal point of $\mathbf{A}$.

Once the orthogonal distance of a point and a known quadric is calculated, the minimization technique explained in section 3.3 can be extended to fit a quadric to three dimensional points.

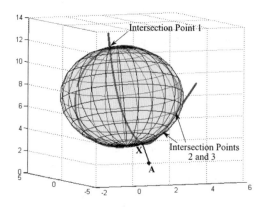

Fig. 6. Orthogonal Distance between a Point and a Quadric

6   Discussion

In this paper, we have introduced a novel algorithm of orthogonal distance least squares fitting for general conics. We have then illustrated the accuracy of the algorithm by testing it on both noiseless and noisy data and comparing with other direct conic fitting methods. The main strength of the method is the simplicity of calculation and the fact that it can be used on any type of conic. Further, the algorithm is robust in terms of requiring only a loose initialization in cases of relatively low noise. It can also be extended to fit quadrics to three dimensional data.

References

1. Hough, P.V.C.: Methods and Means for Recognizing Complex Patterns. US Patent 3 069 654 (1962)
2. Chaudhuri, B.B., Samanta, G.P.: Elliptic Fit of Objects in Two and Three Dimensions by Moment of Inertia Optimization. Pattern Recognition Letters 12(1), 1–7 (1991)
3. Gauss, C.F.: Theory of the Motion of Heavenly Bodies Moving about the Sun in Conic Sections (Theoria Motus Corporum Coelestium in Sectionibus Conicis Solem Ambientium). First published in 1809, Translation by Davis, C.H. Dover, New York (1963)
4. Ahn, S.J.: Least Squares Orthogonal Distance Fitting of Curves and Surfaces in Space. LNCS, vol. 3151. Springer, Heidelberg (2004)
5. Fitzgibbon, A.W., Fisher, R.B.: A Buyer's Guide to Conic Fitting. In: British Machine Vision Conference, Birmingham, UK, pp. 513–522 (1995)
6. Taubin, G.: Estimation of Planar Curves, Surfaces and Nonplanar Space Curves Defined by Implicit Equations, with Applications to Edge and Range Image Segmentation. IEEE Transactions on Pattern Analysis and Machine Intelligence 13(11), 1115–1138 (1991)
7. Press, W.H., Flannery, B.P., Teukolsky, S.A., Vetterling, W.T.: Numerical Recipes in C, 2nd edn. Cambridge University Press, Cambridge (1992)
8. Boggs, P.T., Byrd, R.H., Schnabel, R.B.: A Stable and Efficient Algorithm for Nonlinear Orthogonal Distance Regression. SIAM Journal of Scientific and Statistical Computing 8(6), 1052–1078 (1987)
9. Helfrich, H.-P., Zwick, D.: A Trust Region Method for Implicit Orthogonal Distance Regression. Numerical Algorithms 5, 535–545 (1993)
10. Ahn, S.J., Rauh, W., Warnecke, H.J.: Least Squares Orthogonal Distance Fitting of Circle, Sphere, Hyperbola and Parabola. Pattern Recognition 34, 2283–2303 (2001)
11. Gander, W., Golub, G.H., Strebel, R.: Least-Squares Fitting of Circles and Ellipses. BIT 34, 558–578 (1994)
12. Späth, H.: Orthogonal Squared Distance Fitting with Parabolas. In: Proceedings of the IMACS-GAMM International Symposium on Numerical Methods and Error-Bounds, pp. 261–269. University of Oldenburg (1995)
13. Hartley, R., Zisserman, A.: Multiple View Geometry in Computer Vision. Cambridge University Press, Cambridge (2003)
14. Semple, J.G., Kneebone, G.T.: Algebraic Projective Geometry. Oxford University Press, Oxford (1956)
15. Faber, P., Fisher, R.B.: Euclidean Fitting Revisited. In: Arcelli, C., Cordella, L.P., Sanniti di Baja, G. (eds.) IWVF 2001. LNCS, vol. 2059, pp. 165–172. Springer, Heidelberg (2001)

16. Miller, J.R.: Analysis of Quadric Surface Based Solid Models. IEEE Computer Graphics and Applications 8(1), 28–42 (1988)
17. Wijewickrema, S.N.R., Papliński, A.P., Esson, C.E.: Orthogonal Distance Fitting Revisited. Technical report 2006/205, Clayton School of Information Technology, Monash University, Melbourne, Australia (2006)
18. Levin, J.: A Parametric Algorithm for drawing Pictures of Solid Objects composed of Quadric Surfaces. Communications of ACM 19(11), 553–563 (1976)

Optical Inspection of Welding Seams

Fabian Timm[1,2], Thomas Martinetz[1], and Erhardt Barth[1,2]

[1] Institute for Neuro- and Bioinformatics, University of Lübeck
Ratzeburger Allee 160, D-23538 Lübeck, Germany
[2] Pattern Recognition Company GmbH
Maria-Goeppert-Strasse 1, D-23562 Lübeck, Germany

Abstract. We present a framework for automatic inspection of welding seams based on specular reflections. To this end, we make use of a feature set – called specularity features (SPECs) – that describes statistical properties of specular reflections. For the classification we use a one-class support-vector approach. We show that the SPECs significantly outperform other approaches since they capture more complex characteristics and dependencies of shape and geometry. We obtain an error rate of 3.8%, which corresponds to the level of human performance.

1 Introduction

In many industrial processes individual parts are joined by using welding techniques. Soldering and welding techniques are common in diverse areas such as printed circuit board assembly or automotive line spot welding. The quality of a single welding often defines the grade of the whole product, for example in critical areas such as automotive or aviation industry, where failures of the welding process can cause a malfunction of the whole product. Typically, welds are made by a laser or a soldering iron. During the last few years lasers and their usage in industrial applications have become affordable for many companies. Although the initial cost of a laser-welding system is still high, their wear-out is low and so the service intervals become very long. A laser weld is more precise than a weld by a soldering iron, but the quality can also vary due to shifts of the part towards the laser or due to material impurities. Therefore, an inspection of the welding is required in order to guarantee an accurate quality.

There are several machine vision approaches to automatically classify the quality of solder joints. These approaches can be divided into two groups. The first group deals with special camera and lighting setups to gain the best image representation of relevant features [1,2,3]. In the second group, the camera and lighting setup is often predetermined and the inspection is done by sophisticated pattern recognition methods. In the last few years several approaches for automatic inspection of solder joints concerning feature extraction, feature selection, and classification have been proposed [4,5,1,6,2]. As in many other applications, neural networks and especially the support-vector-machine have become state-of-the-art [7,8,9].

In this work, we focus on the inspection of cathodes welded by an Nd:YAG (neodymium-doped yttrium aluminium garnet) laser during the production of lamps. Due to its position in the whole production process, the camera and lighting setup was fixed and could not be changed.

A. Ranchordas et al. (Eds.): VISIGRAPP 2009, CCIS 68, pp. 269–282, 2010.

Since the welded cathode has specific specular reflections, an appropriate feature extraction is required in order to achieve an accurate performance. Therefore, we apply a feature set called specularity features (SPECs) [10]. The SPECs contain statistics of certain shape characteristics of single components and can cover a wide range of complex shape properties and their dependencies. Since only the class of accurate weldings is sampled properly, we use a one-class support-vector approach [11,12,13] in order to describe features of accurate weldings and to separate them from all other possible inaccurate weldings. We also evaluate those SPECs that are most relevant for the classification and compare them to the physical shape of the cathode. For comparison we use raw pixel intensities, radial encoded raw pixel intensities and the statistical geometric feature (SGF) algorithm that computes simple geometric characteristics of binary components.

In section 2 we give a brief overview of the camera and lighting setting and the image acquisition. The methods for feature extraction and classification are described in section 3. Experiments and the results are shown in section 4. We conclude with a discussion in section 5.

2   Image Acquisition

An unwelded cathode consists of a socket and a pole that may be composed of different materials (see Fig. 1). In a top view with directional parallel light the unwelded cathode simplifies to only four components – two black rings (the slant of the neck and the space between pin and socket), one white ring (neck of the socket) and one white circle (top of the pin, see Fig. 1 bottom right). Hence, a component analysis of the grey value image of the welded cathode can be used to extract specific features.

A correct combination of camera, lens and illumination is very important to achieve the best performance in classification. However, sometimes the best setup can not be chosen due to limited space or other requirements. For this work, there was only one camera setup practicable (see Fig. 2). We used a standard analog monochrome VGA video camera, a single-sided telecentric lens and an LED ring light with a Fresnel lens. Each image contained a single cathode that we extracted by applying a hough-transformation. We removed images of unwelded cathodes and images that are classified easily from the dataset to reduce the amount of images. Thus, the dataset consisted only of images of welded cathodes that are difficult to classify manually. In total, we collected 934 images containing 657 images of non-defective cathodes and 277 images of defective cathodes.

Each image was labelled by experts, scaled to different sizes (10×10, 20×20, 40×40, 80×80 px) and smoothed by a Gaussian filter ($\sigma = 1$). Since we also use raw pixel intensities, we rotated each image four times ($0, \frac{1}{2}\pi, \pi, \frac{3}{2}\pi$) giving a total amount of 3736 images. Since defective cathodes are determined by the mean time to failure, the true class labels are not known in general. Therefore, the experts look for aberrations that were selected by extensive benchmark tests. Example images of defective and non-defective cathodes are shown in Fig. 3. The reflections of cathodes without a defect vary due to differences in material and position of the pin. Also, a slight deflection of the pin just before the welding can affect the quality of the welding. Some of the defective cathodes have holes caused by a slanted pin, others do not have any reflections

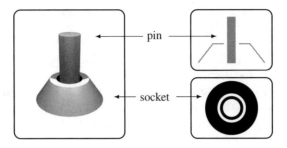

Fig. 1. A 3D drawing of the cathode (left), a cross-section (upper right) and a top-view image are shown (lower right)

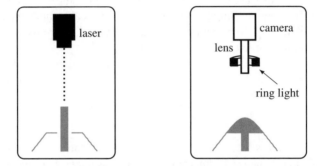

Fig. 2. Drawing of the setup for laser welding (left) and image acquisition (right). The laser and the camera are located on top of the cathode. A Fresnel lens was mounted in front of the ring light to obtain bright illumination at the cathode.

due to a very rough surface. Therefore, the variety of defects cannot be described easily, and a feature extraction method that covers specific image properties such as properties based on specular reflections is required.

3   Methods

Recently, several approaches for the inspection of solder joints were proposed [1,3,4,2,6]. Some of these methods compute simple features in a manually tiled binary image, others use the pixel intensities directly as input features for a neural network or a support vector machine [7,8,9]. Since the number of pixels is very large compared to the number

Fig. 3. Example images of defect-free (left) and defective cathodes (right)

of data samples, the preprocessing often involves a downsampling of the images in order to reduce the dimensionality considerably. Usually, this downsampling reduces the
information contained in the images significantly and therefore yields poor error rates.
A better performance is achieved by extracting specific features that describe relevant
image properties, e.g. specularity features for the case of welding seam inspection.

In the following, we will describe the extraction of SGFs and SPECs. Since the
images were recorded by an 8bit monochrome camera, we focus on grey value images,
but the approach can easily be extended to colour images.

3.1 Statistical Geometric Features

Originally, SGFs were used for texture classification with 16 features for each image
[14]. Further extensions were developed for cell nuclei classification and contained 48
features [15]. SGFs compute simple shape properties of local components. Hence, they
can be used to extract specific features of welding images. Moreover, SGFs are very
intuitive and computed efficiently.

For each l-bit grey value image I a stack of binary images $\mathcal{B} = \{I_\tau\}$ with $\tau \in \{1, 2, 3, ..., 2^l\}$ is created. A single binary image I_τ is computed such that

$$I_\tau(x, y) = \begin{cases} 1 & : & I(x, y) \geq \tau \\ 0 & : & I(x, y) < \tau \end{cases} \tag{1}$$

This decomposition is lossless, since the input image can always be recovered by
summing up all binary images. Furthermore, each binary image I_τ is decomposed into a
set of black and white components, $\{\mathbf{C}_0(\tau), \mathbf{C}_1(\tau)\}$ with $\mathbf{C}_0(\tau) = \{C_{(0,\tau)_1}, ..., C_{(0,\tau)_m}\}$
and $\mathbf{C}_1(\tau) = \{C_{(1,\tau)_1}, ..., C_{(1,\tau)_n}\}$, where m and n are the numbers of black and white
components (see Fig. 4). In the following the subscript 0 denotes a black component and
the subscript 1 a white component.

Each component $C_{(j,\tau)_i} = \{\boldsymbol{x}_k\}$ consists of pixel positions $\boldsymbol{x}_k \in \{1, 2, ..., H\} \times \{1, 2, ..., W\}$, where H and W are the height and the width of the input image, respectively. For convenience we omit the indices of a component if they are not necessary
and we use $C_i = C_{(j,\tau)_i}$ for abbreviation.

The area of a component is defined by the number of its pixels and the relative size
of a single component C_i with respect to all components is then defined as

$$\text{PROP}(C_i) = \frac{\text{AREA}(C_i)}{\sum_k \text{AREA}(C_k)} . \tag{2}$$

Based on the stack of binary images, the feature extraction of the SGF algorithm can
be divided into two stages – a local stage and a global stage. In the local stage several
features for each component are calculated (see Tab. 1). A single binary image is then
described by a set of averaged shape and position properties of all black and white
components.

In the second stage the local features are combined to global features using first order
statistics (see Tab. 2). In total, the SGF algorithm determines 48 shape properties for a
single input image.

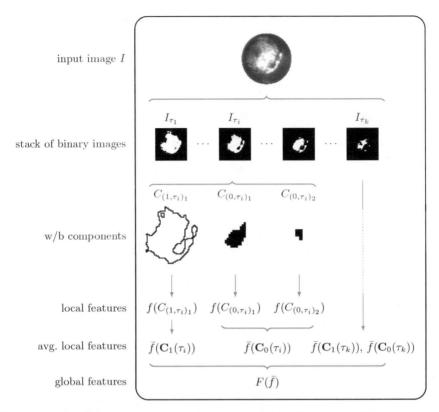

Fig. 4. Decomposition scheme for a grey value input image I. First, the input image is decomposed into a stack of binary images I_τ. Afterwards each binary image is further separated into its black and white components. Local features f, e.g. the area, are computed for all components and averaged according to their component colour. Finally, global features F are generated by computing statistics over all averaged local features.

3.2 Specularity Features (SPEC)

Since the statistical geometric features were mainly developed for classification of textures, i.e. repetitive patterns, they are not suitable for the inspection of welding seams, which usually do not have a repetitive structure. Instead, properties that describe the characteristic shapes of specular reflections are required. For example, some defective cathodes have long narrow reflections at the neck of the socket which can be covered by features such as the formfactor and the extent.

We make use of the general decomposition scheme of binary images and evaluate appropriate features covering the properties of specular reflections. We compute several general properties of each component (see Tab. 3). Using a 4-neighbourhood two successive boundary points are denoted by x_m and x_{m+1}, $F(\alpha)$ is the maximum distance between two boundary points when rotating the coordinate axis by $\alpha \in \mathcal{A} = \{0°, 5°, ..., 175°\}$, w_{BR} and h_{BR} are the width and height of the bounding rectangle and a, b are the major and minor axis of the ellipse that has the same second moments as the region. For a detailed discussion on geometric shapes see chapter 9 of [16].

Table 1. Local features for a single binary image I_τ of size $H \times W$ [15]

description	formula		
number of b/w components	$\texttt{NOC}(\tau)$	$=$	$\lvert \mathbf{C}_i(\tau) \rvert$
averaged irregularity	$\overline{\texttt{IRGL}}(\tau)$	$=$	$\frac{\sum_k \texttt{IRGL}(C_k)\ \texttt{AREA}(C_k)}{\sum_k \texttt{AREA}(C_k)}$
averaged clump displacement	$\overline{\texttt{DISP}}(\tau)$	$=$	$\frac{1}{\texttt{NOC}(\tau)} \sum_k \texttt{DISP}(C_k)$
averaged clump inertia	$\overline{\texttt{INERTIA}}(\tau)$	$=$	$\frac{1}{\texttt{NOC}(\tau)} \sum_k \texttt{DISP}(C_k)\ \texttt{AREA}(C_k)$
total clump area	$\texttt{TAREA}(\tau)$	$=$	$\frac{1}{HW} \sum_k \texttt{AREA}(C_k)$
averaged clump area	$\overline{\texttt{CAREA}}_i(\tau)$	$=$	$\frac{1}{\texttt{NOC}(\tau)} \sum_k \texttt{AREA}(C_k)$

where

$\texttt{IRGL}(C) = \dfrac{1 + \sqrt{\pi}\ \max_{\boldsymbol{x} \in C}\ \lVert \boldsymbol{x} - \mu(C) \rVert}{\sqrt{\texttt{AREA}(C)}} - 1$ is the irregularity of component C,

$\texttt{DISP}(C) = \sqrt{\pi}\ \dfrac{\lVert \mu(C) - \mu_I \rVert}{\sqrt{HW}}$ is the relative displacement of component C,

$\mu(C)$ is the centre of gravity of component C and μ_I is the centre of the image.

Table 2. Global features. f is one of the local features described before.

maximum	$= \max_\tau f(\tau)$	,	mean	$= \frac{1}{\lvert \tau \rvert} \sum_\tau f(\tau)$
sample mean	$= \frac{1}{\sum_\tau f(\tau)} \sum_\tau \tau f(\tau)$	,	sample std.	$= \sqrt{\dfrac{\sum_\tau (\tau - \texttt{sample mean})^2\ f(\tau)}{\sum_\tau f(\tau)}}$

The local features are computed for each component and need to be combined to form a single feature. Hence, we scale each feature in two different ways. First, we calculate the mean weighted by the relative size of the components, and second, we scale the sum by the total number of components. For example, for the averaged perimeter of the binary image I_τ these two scalings are:

$$\overline{\texttt{PERIM}}(\tau) = \sum_k \texttt{PERIM}(C_k)\ \texttt{PROP}(C_k) \quad \text{and} \quad \overline{\texttt{PERIM}}(\tau) = \frac{1}{\texttt{NOC}(\tau)} \sum_k \texttt{PERIM}(C_k)\ , \tag{3}$$

where $\texttt{PROP}(C_k)$ is defined in Eq. 2. By using these two scalings we can evaluate whether the size of a component is relevant for the feature extraction.

We combine the local features by computing $\texttt{minimum}$, $\texttt{variance}$, $\texttt{median}$, and $\texttt{entropy}$ besides the statistics of Tab. 2. Whereas the $\texttt{sample mean}$ and $\texttt{sample std.}$ range over the threshold τ, the others compute statistics over local shape features. Hence, we can, for example, evaluate the variance of the number of white components or the entropy of the formfactor of white components. In total, for a single image, we determine 448 features consisting of:

- 28 local features for a single component (14 for a black component and 14 for a white component),

Table 3. Features for a component C

feature	formula
perimeter (PERIM)	$\sum_{m=1}^{N-1} \|x_m - x_{m+1}\|_2$
distance from centre (DISTC)	$\|\mu(C) - \mu_I\|_2$
maximum Feret diameter (MAXFD)	$\max_{\alpha \in \mathcal{A}} F(\alpha)$
minimum Feret diameter (MINFD)	$\min_{\alpha \in \mathcal{A}} F(\alpha)$
mean Feret diameter (MEANF)	$\frac{1}{|\mathcal{A}|} \sum_{\alpha \in \mathcal{A}} F(\alpha)$
variance Feret diameter (VARF)	$\frac{1}{|\mathcal{A}|} \sum_{\alpha \in \mathcal{A}} \left[F(\alpha) - \mathtt{MEANF} \right]^2$
area of bounding rectangle (AREAB)	$w_{\mathrm{BR}}\, h_{\mathrm{BR}}$
eccentricity (ECCEN)	$\frac{\sqrt{a^2 + b^2}}{a}$
aspect ratio (ASPAR)	$\frac{\mathtt{MAXFD}(\tau)}{\mathtt{MINFD}(\tau)}$
extent (EXTEN)	$\frac{\mathtt{AREA}}{\mathtt{AREAB}}$
formfactor (FORMF)	$\frac{4\,\pi\,\mathtt{AREA}}{\mathtt{PERIM}^2}$
roundness (ROUND)	$\frac{4\,\mathtt{AREA}}{\pi\,\mathtt{MAXFD}^2}$
compactness (COMPT)	$\frac{2\,\sqrt{\mathtt{AREA}}}{\sqrt{\pi}\,\mathtt{MAXFD}}$
regularity of aspect ratio (REGAR)	$\left[1 + \mathtt{VARFD} + \mathtt{MAXFD} - \mathtt{MINFD} \right]^{-1}$

- 2 scaling methods (by the proportional size and by the total number of components) and
- 8 global statistics.

3.3   Radial Encoding

The two approaches mentioned in the previous sections are based on image properties. Alternatively, one could use pixel values as input features. This can be further extended by a radial encoding of pixel values (see Fig. 5). Therefore, we divide the input image into several sectors using 8 angles and 6 radii all sampled equally. For each sector we compute the mean intensity to obtain 48 features for an input image, which reflects the fact that we deal with objects in the image that have a circular outline.

Fig. 5. Radial encoding of an image

3.4 Feature Analysis

Most of the techniques we use for feature extraction generate high-dimensional data. By analysing these feature vectors we want to address two aspects. First, we want to detect features that contain almost no information and remove those features in order to save memory and computation time. Second, we want to evaluate those raw features, SGFs and SPECs that are most discriminative of describing defect-free and defective weldings. Therefore, we use two different approaches, principle component analysis (PCA) and linear discriminant analysis (LDA). For the PCA we take only defect-free samples and evaluate those principle components that have the largest absolute eigenvalues. Although the class of defective weldings is not sampled properly, we also compute the LDA and sort the entries of the resulting weight vector according to their absolute value.

3.5 Classification

The support vector machine (SVM) has become a very useful approach for classification and yields superior performance on several benchmark datasets [7,8,9]. Standard two-class SVMs require samples that describe *both* classes in a proper way. In our case, however, there are only a few defective cathodes that are characterised well. We therefore apply a one-class support-vector machine. Furthermore, we make use of a simple incremental training algorithm with several improvements for fast parameter validation [13,17,12,11]. In contrast to standard two-class SVMs, which separate the input space into two half-spaces, one-class SVMs learn a subspace such as to enclose the samples of only the target class. This increases the robustness against unknown classes of outliers and also extends the time intervals for retraining when new samples are available.

4 Experiments and Results

In the following, we analyse different feature sets with respect to their relevance and we compare them with respect to their classification performance. These feature sets are raw pixel intensities, radially encoded raw pixel intensities, SGFs, and SPECs.

Since the performance of the SGFs can vary depending on the grey level depth of the images we used different depths ranging from 2bit to 8bit [15]. The raw pixel intensities are only used as a baseline.

For the SVM we chose a Gaussian kernel and evaluated the best parameters by 10-fold cross validation. We further scaled the input features to zero mean, unit variance, and unit mean norm and we removed each constant feature to speed up the algorithm and to save memory. For a comparison of the different feature extraction methods we applied a Wilcoxon signed rank test to the test errors.

Since no benchmark datasets of solder joint images are available, we only applied the feature extraction methods to images of laser-weldings.

4.1   Results of Feature Analysis

We analysed the raw pixel intensities using PCA as described in section 3.4. The resulting eigenimages show three important aspects (see Fig. 6).

First, pixels in the centre are more important than pixels at the border of the pole (see Fig. 6, row 2, column 3). This corresponds to the description in Sec. 2 where white reflections (regions) in the centre of the image indicate defect-free weldings. Second, the ring structure, i.e. the area at the neck of the socket, also shows high relevance (see Fig. 6, row 1, column 1). Third, more complex geometric shapes are significant (see Fig. 6, r:1, c:4, r:2, c:1-2). Therefore, a sophisticated feature extraction approach is required in order to describe these complex geometric areas. For describing these areas appropriately than just taking the pixel values we used the radial encoding mentioned in Sec. 3.3. Some of the most significant SGFs are

- the sample std. of irregularity of white components,
- the mean of irregularity of white components,
- the sample std. of total clump area of white components, and
- the mean of displacements of white components.

We analysed the discriminating performance of the SGFs and the SPECs using the LDA as described previously. Therefore, we ranked the features according to their absolute value.

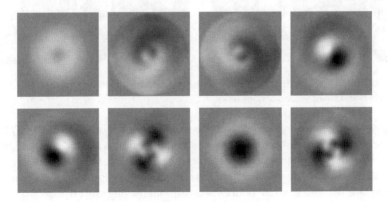

Fig. 6. Eigenimages and eigenvalues using images of size 80×80 and 8 bit grey level depth. Large values (black/white) indicate relevant pixels.

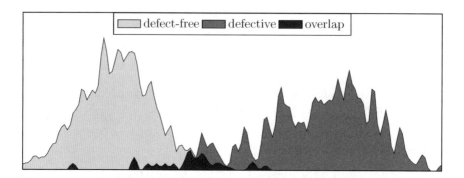

Fig. 7. Class distributions when projecting the SGF features onto the direction obtained by LDA

(a) median of regularity of aspect ratio weighted by area (black components)

(b) median of variance of Feret weighted by NOC (black components)

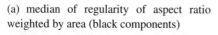

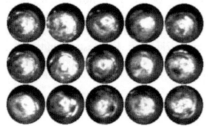

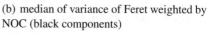

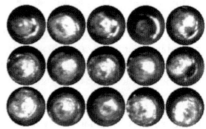

(c) variance of distances from centre weighted by NOC (white components)

(d) sample std. of area of bounding rectangle weighted by NOC (black comp.)

Fig. 8. Example images with large values of the indicated features (top row), medium values (middle row) and small values(bottom row).

This shows that features of white components are more important than those of black components. Further, the shape of components, their positions and their size are relevant properties for the discrimination. If we project the SGFs onto the direction obtained by LDA both classes overlap (see Fig. 7). Thus, in the feature space of SGFs there exists no hyperplane that can separate both classes without making any errors.

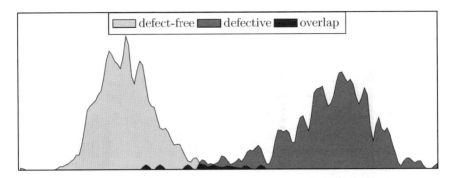

Fig. 9. Class distributions when projecting the SPEC features onto the direction obtained by LDA

Some of the most important SPECs when using the LDA are

- median of regularity of aspect ratio of black components weighted by area (see Fig. 8(a)),
- median of variance of Feret diameter of black components weighted by the number of components (see Fig. 8(b)),
- variance of distances from centre of white components weighted by the number of components (see Fig. 8(c)), and
- sample std. of area of bounding rectangle of black components weighted by the number of black components (see Fig. 8(d)).

This indicates that black components become important when using local features such as the Feret diameter or the bounding rectangle. Since the SGFs are limited to only a few local features, the black components are ignored. Moreover, the area of a component is also relevant as it is used for the scaling of the local features. This becomes more apparent by analysing the ranking of the 100 most relevant SPECs. There, 45 local features are scaled by their area and 55 are scaled by the number of components. Further, 43 local features correspond to black components and 57 correspond to white components. This demonstrates that the properties of the specular reflections cannot be described properly by using raw pixel intensities.

If we project the data onto the LDA direction as we did for the SGFs, the overlap becomes smaller, which indicates that the discrimination power of the SPECs is higher than that of the SGFs (see Fig. 9). However, there also exists no hyperplane separating both classes without an error.

4.2   Results of Classification

The classification results for the different feature extraction approaches to cover complex properties of specular reflections show several aspects.

The radially encoded raw pixel intensities perform significantly better than using raw pixels without any encoding (see Fig. 10). This does not depend on the image size nor on the grey level depth. The best performance of radially encoded raw pixels is obtained using images of size 40×40 pixels and 16 grey levels (error of 13.5%).

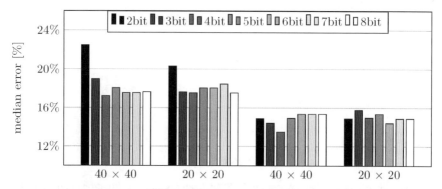

Fig. 10. Classification results using raw pixel intensities and radially encoded pixel intensities for different image sizes and different grey level depths

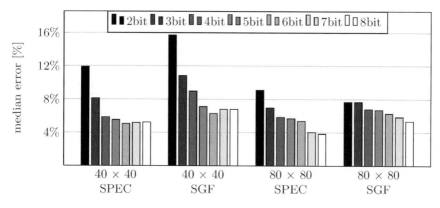

Fig. 11. Classification results using SGFs and SPECs for different image sizes and different grey level depths

Compared to the radial encoding, the SGFs as well as the SPECs improve the classification performance considerably (see Fig. 11). The best performance of the SGFs is achieved by using images of size 80×80 pixels and 256 grey levels with an error of 5.3%. For the same image size and the same number of grey levels the SPECs significantly outperforms ($p = 0.03$) the SGFs with an error of 3.8%. This improvement demonstrates that the SPECs can describe properties of specular reflections more properly than SGFs and radial encoded raw pixels. It further shows that a large number of grey levels is required to describe specular reflections in both cases, for SGFs as well as for the SPECs.

Further, no significant difference between the image sizes could be observed neither for the raw pixel intensities nor for the SGFs and the SPECs, i.e. grey level resolution is more important than spatial resolution (see Fig. 10 and Fig. 11). If the image size is smaller than 10×10 pixels, however, the higher relevance of the grey level depth compared to the image size does not hold, since the structures of the welded pin and the socket are merged, e.g. holes and rings cannot be detected any more.

5   Conclusions

We introduced an approach for the inspection of welding seams using specularity features (SPECs) and showed that these features significantly outperform statistical geometric features as well as raw pixel intensities with and without encoding. We extracted the relevant features of the SPECs and found white regions in the centre of the image and their shape to be of high importance for the classification. The SPECs can cover several complex shape properties and their dependencies and are, nevertheless, intuitive and computed efficiently. Hence, they are well appropriate for the automatic inspection of welding seams and can even be applied to a wider range of machine vision problems concerning complex specular reflections, such as surface inspection or defect detection of specular objects.

The labelling of the datasets of solder joints or other weldings is usually based on experts viewing images and not on the actual functional test. Hence, these labels are very subjective and do not necessarily correspond to the physical and electrical properties of the weldings. Therefore, additional information about the welding, e.g. the conductivity, rigidity, or weld strength, has to be collected and combined with a machine-vision based approach in order to improve the results.

The results may further be improved using other feature selection methods. However, the error rate (3.5%) of the SPEC features are comparable to those obtained by manual inspection.

Acknowledgements. Our research is supported by Philips Technologie GmbH, Global Technology Development Aachen, Germany. Special thanks to Christian Arlt for providing the images and further material.

References

1. Ong, T., Samad, Z., Ratnam, M.: Solder joint inspection with multi-angle imaging and an artificial neural network. The Int. Journal of Advanced Manufacturing Technology 38, 455–462 (2008)
2. Kim, J., Cho, H.: Neural network-based inspection of solder joints using a circular illumination. Image and Vision Computing 13, 479–490 (1995)
3. Chiu, S., Perng, M.: Reflection-area-based feature descriptor for solder joint inspection. Machine Vision and Applications 18, 95–106 (2007)
4. Ko, K., Cho, H.: Solder joints inspection using a neural network and fuzzy rule-based classification method. IEEE Transactions on Electronics Packaging Manufacturing 23, 93–103 (2000)
5. Poechmueller, W., Glesner, M., Listl, L., Mengel, P.: Automatic classification of solder joint images. In: Proc. of the Int. Joint Conf. on Neural Networks, vol. 2, pp. 933–940. IEEE Computer Society Press, Los Alamitos (1991)
6. Driels, M., Lee, C.: Feature selection for automatic visual inspection of solder joints. The Int. Journal of Advanced Manufacturing Technology 3, 3–32 (1988)
7. Cortes, C., Vapnik, V.: Support-vector networks. Machine Learning 20, 273–297 (1995)
8. Boser, B., Guyon, I., Vapnik, V.: A training algorithm for optimal margin classifiers. In: Haussler, D. (ed.) Proc. of the 5th Annual ACM Workshop on Computational Learning Theory, pp. 144–152. ACM Press, New York (1992)

9. Vapnik, V.: The Nature of Statistical Learning Theory. Springer, New York (1995)
10. Timm, F., Klement, S., Martinetz, T., Barth, E.: Welding inspection using novel specularity features and a one-class svm. In: Proc. of the Int. Conference on Imaging Theory and Applications, vol. 1, pp. 146–153. INSTICC (2009)
11. Schölkopf, B., Platt, J.C., Shawe-Taylor, J., Smola, A.J., Williamson, R.C.: Estimating the support of a high-dimensional distribution. Neural Computation 13, 1443–1471 (2001)
12. Tax, D.M.J., Duin, R.P.W.: Support vector data description. Machine Learning 54, 45–66 (2004)
13. Labusch, K., Timm, F., Martinetz, T.: Simple incremental one-class support vector classification. In: Rigoll, G. (ed.) DAGM 2008. LNCS, vol. 5096, pp. 21–30. Springer, Heidelberg (2008)
14. Chen, Y.Q., Nixon, M.S., Thomas, D.W.: Statistical geometrical features for texture classification. Pattern Recognition 28, 537–552 (1995)
15. Walker, R., Jackway, P.T.: Statistical geometric features: Extensions for cytological texture analysis. In: Proc. of the 13th Int. Conf. on Pattern Recognition, pp. 790–794. IEEE Computer Society Press, Los Alamitos (1996)
16. Russ, J.C.: The Image Processing Handbook. CRC Press, Boca Raton (2007)
17. Timm, F., Klement, S., Martinetz, T.: Fast model selection for maxminover-based training of support vector machines. In: Proc. of the 19th Int. Conf. on Pattern Recognition, Florida, USA. IEEE Computer Society Press, Los Alamitos (2008)

A Multiscale Morphological Binarization Algorithm

Leyza Baldo Dorini[1] and Neucimar Jerônimo Leite[2]

[1] Department of Informatics, Federal University of Technology
Paraná, 80230-901, Curitiba, PR, Brazil
[2] Institute of Computing, University of Campinas, 13084-971, Campinas, SP, Brazil

Abstract. Image binarization is widely used to generate more appropriate images to be used in several image analysis and understanding systems, as well as to facilitate data management and decrease storage space requirements. The main difficulties arise from the fact that images are frequently degraded by noise and non-uniform illumination, for example. This paper presents an efficient morphological-based image binarization technique with scale-space properties that is able to cope with these problems. We evaluate the proposed approach for different classes of images, including text images such as historical and machine-printed documents, obtaining promising results.

1 Introduction

Image binarization has been widely applied as a basic preprocessing stage in many image analysis and processing tasks. The main motivation arises from the fact that the data complexity is reduced, thus simplifying further processing.

One possible application is document image binarization, which basically consists on the segmentation of scanned gray level images into text and background. It is essential to threshold the document image reliably in order to extract useful information and perform further processing such as character recognition and feature extraction. The main difficulties are related to the fact that these images can be subjected to different degradation problems that can significantly disturb the results if appropriate methods are not used.

In this paper, we propose a multiscale binarization algorithm that explores the simplification properties of a scale-space toggle operator to define a dynamic thresholding operation. In contrast to other approaches, image maxima and minima interact at the same time, conducing to a region merging that simplifies the image in such a way that important image structures can be identified even in ill-illuminated images. The binarization rule depends on the local convergence of a pixel to a significative extrema, thus taking into account the whole image structure, and not only the local gray level.

The proposed technique is able to cope with general images as well as degraded document images. To assess the robustness of our approach, we compare it against known threshold-based segmentation methods using images of different classes and subjected to different degradation problems. As we will se elsewhere, our approach is computationally efficient and conduce to better results for a wide range of experiments.

Section 2 briefly reviews some image thresholding techniques and Section 3 describes the proposed approach. Section 4 presents the experimental results and Section 5 draws some conclusions and future work perspectives.

A. Ranchordas et al. (Eds.): VISIGRAPP 2009, CCIS 68, pp. 283–295, 2010.

2 Related Work

Image binarization approaches are typically classified into two classes, depending on how the threshold level is obtained: global, when the whole image representation is considered, or local, when only the information in a neighborhood of the pixel being transformed is used.

Global techniques are usually based on histogram analysis, with the threshold value being determined by considering a measure that best separates the histogram peaks. However, since not necessarily all interest features form prominent peaks, these techniques cannot be applied in images with non-uniform illumination, for example [1]. A well-known general purpose global thresholding approach is the Otsu's algorithm [2]. Briefly, it selects as an optimal threshold the one which minimizes the ratio between the total variance and the "between-class"(defined as the deviation of the mean values for each considered class - background and object - from the overall mean of the pixels).

Local thresholding approaches provide an adaptive solution where the threshold value is determined pixelwise and depends on regional image characteristics. Due to the computational cost, it is important to define efficient transformations. We compare our approach against some of these methods, described below.

The Niblack's algorithm defines a local threshold based on the mean and standard deviation values calculated over a rectangular window around the pixel according to the following formula [3]:

$$T = m + k * s, \tag{1}$$

where m is the mean and s the standard deviation of the pixels in the window. The k value determines how much of the object is retained and assumes a value between -1 and 1. The main drawbacks are the low thresholding speed, the sensitivity to the size of the window and the occurrence of noise in the background.

In order to minimize the background noise, Sauvola proposed an extension to Niblack's algorithm where the threshold value is computed with the dynamic range of the standard deviation, R, according to the equation [4]:

$$T = m * \left(1 + k \left(\frac{s}{R} - 1\right)\right) \tag{2}$$

where, again, m and s are the mean and standard deviation of the window. Here, k takes a positive value between 0 and 1. To properly determine the R value, it is necessary to know the document contrast. The influence of the window size and the threshold speed still remains a problem.

Gatos et al. [5] proposed a locally adaptive binarization scheme that can deal with degraded document images. The method consists of five basic steps: (a) remotion of undesired details and noise with the Wiener filter, (b) definition of a foreground approximation by using the Sauvola's algorithm (Equation 2), (c) estimation of the background by interpolation, (d) thresholding of the interest objects based on the combination of the background estimate with the original image and (e) post-processing stage to improve the quality of the letters.

The moving averages method considers a threshold based on the mean gray level of the last n pixels and is designed for images containing text. n summary, any pixel with a value lower than a fixed percentage of its moving average is set to black; otherwise it is set to white.

More complete reviews of image thresholding techniques can be found in [1][6][7].

3   Proposed Operator

In the image processing context, multiscale approaches have also been largely considered, playing an important role when designing automatic methods to cope with real world measurements where, in most of the cases, there is no prior information about which would be the appropriate scale.

In this work, we consider an operator based on the scale-space approach [8], in which the inherent multiscale nature of real-world images is represented by embedding the original signal into a family of simplified signals, created by successively removing image structures across scales while preserving the essential features. Since the representation of an interest signal feature describes a continuous path through the scales, it is possible to relate information obtained in different representation levels, a drawback in many multiscale approaches.

Due to the inherent problems of the linear approaches [8], non-linear scale-space operators have been frequently used [9]. In the mathematical morphology context, scale-spaces are generated by filtering gray-scale signals with specific combinations of the scaled erosion and dilation operations, defined as follows [10].

Definition 1. *(Dilation) The dilation of the function* $f(x)$ *by the structuring function* $g_\sigma(x)$, $(f \oplus g_\sigma)(x)$, *is given by:*

$$(f \oplus g_\sigma)(x) = \sup_{t \in \mathcal{G} \cap \mathcal{D}_x} \{f(x - t) + g_\sigma(t)\} \tag{3}$$

Definition 2. *(Erosion) The erosion of the function* $f(x)$ *by the structuring function* $g_\sigma(x)$, $(f \ominus g)(x)$, *is given by:*

$$(f \ominus g_\sigma)(x) = \inf_{t \in \mathcal{G} \cap \mathcal{D}_x} \{f(x + t) - g_\sigma(t)\} \tag{4}$$

where $f : \mathcal{D} \subset \mathbb{R}^n \to \mathbb{R}$ is the image function, $\mathcal{D}_x$ is the translate of $\mathcal{D}$, $\mathcal{D}_x = \{x + t : t \in \mathcal{D}\}$, and $g_\sigma : \mathcal{G}_\sigma \subset \mathbb{R}^2 \to \mathbb{R}$ is the scaled structuring function

$$g_\sigma(x) = |\sigma| g(|\sigma|^{-1}x) \quad x \in \mathcal{G}_\sigma, \ \forall \ \sigma \neq 0. \tag{5}$$

To ensure reasonable scaling behavior, g_σ must be a monotonic decreasing function along any radial direction from the origin (i.e., anti-convex). To avoid level-shifting and horizontal translation effects, respectively, one must also observe the conditions [10]

$$\sup_{t \in \mathcal{G}_\sigma} \{g_\sigma(t)\} = 0 \text{ and } g_\sigma(0) = 0. \tag{6}$$

In a previous work, we have proposed a morphological based operator with scale-space properties [11], further named Self-Dual Multiscale Morphological Toggle (SMMT) and defined as follows.

Definition 3. *(Self-dual Multiscale Morphological Toggle operator) Let the primitives be defined as* $\phi_1^n(x) = (f \oplus g_\sigma)^n(x)$ *and* $\phi_2^n(x) = (f \ominus g_\sigma)^n(x)$, *that is, the dilation and erosion, respectively, of* $f(x)$ *with the scaled structuring function* g_σ *n times. The Self-dual Multiscale Morphological Toggle (SMMT) operator is defined as [12]:*

$$(f \oslash g_\sigma)^n(x) = \begin{cases} \phi_1^n(x), & \text{if } \phi_1^n(x) - f(x) < f(x) - \phi_2^n(x), \\ f(x), & \text{if } \phi_1^n(x) - f(x) = f(x) - \phi_2^n(x), \\ \phi_2^n(x), & \text{otherwise.} \end{cases} \tag{7}$$

Briefly, the transformation replaces the original value of each pixel with the most similar one between its *scaled* dilation and erosion (in contrast to Kramer's [13] and Bernsen's [14] approaches, which does not deals with scale-space transformation properties). If the difference is the same to both transformed values, the pixel is not modified.

The SMMT operator has interesting characteristics, such as self-duality, i.e., there is a symmetric treatment of foreground and background, thus reducing the gray-level bias. Also, it leads to an image simplification that does not displace the boundaries.

Idempotence is usually desired when dealing with toggle-like transformations to avoid undesirable effects, such as halos and oscillations [15]. Since the previously defined operator is not idempotent, it is important to ensure that it has a well-controlled behavior for any parameter set (i.e., for varying scale and number of iterations).

It has been proved that the operator obeys the necessary conditions to constitute a scale-space operator for varying scale [11]. The monotonicity property (requiring that the number of features must necessarily be a monotonic decreasing function of scale) holds when using as features image extrema (there is no need to consider image maxima and minima separately as in previous approaches [10]). The other properties, including fidelity and Euclidean invariance, can be easily proved.

On the other hand, when considering iterative applications of the operator, a stronger simplification is obtained and regions are merged as discussed below. To make calculations easier and more intuitive, let us consider the pyramid structuring function given by

$$g_\sigma(x, y) = -|\sigma|^{-1} \max\{|x|, |y|\} \tag{8}$$

in its scaled version. Under these conditions, we have the following equivalence for the SMMT operator (for a fixed scale σ):

$$(f \oslash g_{\sigma_3})^n(\mathbf{x}) == (f \oslash g_{\sigma_{2n+1}})^1(\mathbf{x}) \tag{9}$$

where the subscript on σ denotes the structuring element size. In a few words, n iterations of the primitives using a 3×3 structuring element is equivalent to one iteration using a structuring element of size $2n + 1$. Since the transformed value of a pixel depends on the dominant extrema in the region being considered, the increasing on the number of iterations simplifies the image so that these extrema create wider "attraction zones", leading to a homogenization of the gray levels. The defined operator can be seen as a *quasi-connected* operator, in the sense that it simplifies the image by creating quasi-flat zones as explained next.

Definition 4. *[16] (R-flat-zone) Two pixels* x, y *belong to the same R-flat zone of a function* f *if and only if there exists an n-tuple of pixels* $(p_1, p_2, \ldots, p_n)$ *such that*

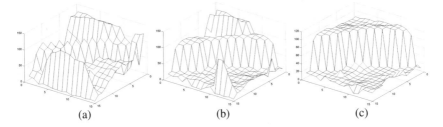

Fig. 1. Simplification obtained by considering successive iterations (1, 3 and 5) of the operator at scale $\sigma = 1$

$p_1 = x$ and $p_n = y$, and for all i, (p_i, p_{i+1}) are neighbors and satisfy the symmetrical relation $f_{p_i} R f_{p_{i+1}}$.

In this paper, R corresponds to the relation $|p_i - p_{i+1}| \leq \lambda$. When R is the equality, we are dealing with flat zones, which consist on connected components where the pixel value is constant. In Figure 1, we show the transformation of the gray levels of a small portion of an image when applying successive iterations of the defined operator, $n = 1 \ldots 5$, with $\sigma = 1$. Observe that quasi-flat zones are created.

We can observe that, unlike other approaches [9][10], the SMMT conduces to a transformation where maxima and minima interact at the same time, creating a simplified image where regions are merged and the gray-level of a pixel depends on its convergence to a specific extrema. In such a way, relevant structures can be identified even in images with uneven illumination.

Figure 2 illustrates the way pixels are transformed by the SMMT operator, emphasizing the fact that different structures are affected depending on the scale, σ, and on the number of iterations, k. Pixels replaced by the dilated values are set to white while those replaced by the eroded values are set to black. Finally, pixels that were not modified are set to gray.

This characteristics can be explored in different ways depending on the specific application. Note that while the increasing on scale and/or number of iterations conduces to a stronger image simplification (less pixels are set to gray), the use of lower scales enables us to extract information related to regions with higher variation, such as edges. Consider Figure 2(e), for example. In this case, if the pixels that did not have their values modified were set to white, we would obtain a binary image where only the characters are set to black. We explore these properties to define an adaptive multiscale local thresholding operator as follows:

Definition 5. *(Binary Self-dual Multiscale Morphological Toggle - BSMMT) Let the primitives of a toggle operation be defined as $\phi_1^n(x) = (f \oplus g_\sigma)^n(x)$ and $\phi_2^n(x) = (f \ominus g_\sigma)^n(x)$, that is, the dilation and erosion, respectively, of $f(x)$ with the scaled structuring function g_σ n times. We call BSMMT operator:*

$$(f \oslash g_\sigma)^n(x) = \begin{cases} 1, & \text{if } \phi_1^n(x) - f(x) <= f(x) - \phi_2^n(x), \\ 0, & \text{otherwise.} \end{cases} \qquad (10)$$

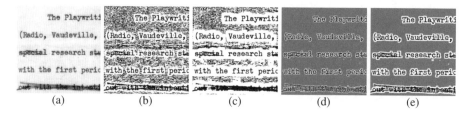

Fig. 2. SMMT resulting transformation of the (a) original image when considering the parameters (b) $\sigma^{-1} = 1$ e $k = 5$, (c) $\sigma^{-1} = 1$ e $k = 15$, (d) $\sigma^{-1} = 15$ e $k = 1$ and (e) $\sigma^{-1} = 15$ e $k = 5$

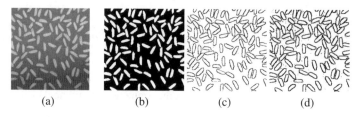

Fig. 3. Effect when changing the BSMMT parameters: (a) original image, (b) $\sigma^{-1} = 1$ and $k = 25$ and (c) $\sigma^{-1} = 40$ and $k = 5$

Basically, if the value of a pixel is closer to the eroded value, it is set to black (zero). Otherwise, it is set to white (one), even if the difference between the eroded and dilated values is the same. Figure 3 illustrates how the parameter changing influences the transformation of an image with non-uniform illumination. Since the background is darker than the grains (Figure 3(a)), the values of the pixels in this area tend to be closer to the eroded ones when higher scales are considered (that is, when small variations on the gray levels are enough to change them).

The iterative application avoids that non-significative extrema - like the ones present due to illumination inconsistencies - disturb the results (Figure 3(b)). For a lower scale, the regions with homogeneous gray levels are not modified and, thus, the defined operator set their corresponding pixels to white. The values of the pixels close to the edges, on the other hand, are closer to the eroded values and are set to black (Figure 3(c)). Observe that a stronger representation of the contour can be obtained by increasing the number of iterations, k (Figure 3(d)).

Thus, depending on the specific objectives, different combinations of parameter must be considered. While higher scales tend to define homogeneous regions, lower scales tend to delimit these regions by identifying edges.

4   Results

In the following, we discuss some possible applications of the proposed binarization approach, namely binarization of ill-illuminated images and of degraded document images.

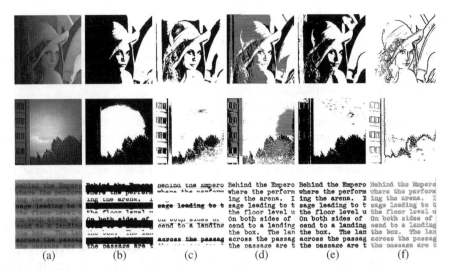

Fig. 4. Binarization results: (a) original images, (b) Otsu, (c) Niblack, (d) moving averages and BSMMT for (e) $k = 50$ and $\sigma^{-1} = 1$, $k = 50$ and $\sigma^{-1} = 2$, $\sigma^{-1} = 2$ and $k = 20$ and (f) $k = 2$ and $\sigma^{-1} = 8$, $k = 2$ and $\sigma^{-1} = 25$), $\sigma^{-1} = 10$ and $k = 1$

arena. arena.

Fig. 5. Note that the white stripes produced by the (a) moving averages algorithm are not present in the (b) BSMMT result

4.1 Binarization of Ill-Illuminated Images

The first experiment assess the performance of the BSMMT when dealing with images having non-uniform illumination. The results were compared against the ones obtained by the following methods: Otsu [2], moving averages [17], Niblack [3] and Gatos *et al.* [5]. Since Bernsen's method [14] has shown to produce worse results than other local binarization methods, we do not consider it in the experimental tests. Figure 4 shows the results when considering images with linear, Gaussian and senoidal illumination variation, respectively.

Note that the results of some methods are seriously disturbed by the uneven illumination. Otsu's algorithm, for example, does not yield satisfactory results in any case, while Niblack's approach presents noise in the background region. Although the moving averages algorithm produces good results for the text image, it contains some white "stripes" (Figure 5) that can disturb further optical character recognition (OCR) procedures.

The BSMMT, on the other hand, conduces to sound results in all cases. As discussed previously, depending on the chosen parameters, different results can be obtained (observe, for example, columns (e) and (f) in Figure 4).

4.2   Document Image Binarization

Briefly, document image binarization consists on the segmentation of scanned gray level images into text and background. Besides generating more appropriate images to be used in several image analysis and understanding systems, the binarization of text images has been used to facilitate data management.

Since the accuracy of the resulting images strongly affects the performance of subsequent high level tasks, such as OCR and feature extraction, it is essential to find thresholding methods that correctly keep all useful information while removing undesirable details corresponding to noise.

These images are frequently subject to degradation problems, which may occur, for example, as a result of aging and bad environmental conditions. In historical document images, for example, it is very common to have seepage of ink, uneven illumination, smear and smudge. When working with scanned images, the main difficulties are related to poor printing quality and low contrast due to shadows.

The BSMMT properties can be explored in this context. As mentioned in the previous section, different structures are modified depending on the set parameters. To detect text regions, which have a higher variation in gray levels, we consider lower scales. This procedure treats appropriately different kinds os noise and illumination inconsistencies, as discussed below.

Experimental Results. The BSMMT results were compared against the ones obtained by the binarization methods discussed in Section 2 using degraded images of three different categories: historical handwritten documents, old newspapers and poor quality modern documents. Based on one example of each class, we discuss the overall aspects of the different approaches.

Figure 6 shows a small part of the binarization result of an old newspaper image. Besides the traditional problems of uneven illumation and smudges, these images are usually degraded by an extra noise caused mainly due to the old printing matrix precision.

The results of the moving averages and Niblack algorithms present noise in the background region. Sauvola's approach yields thin or even broken characters, which consequently disturbs the results of the Gatos *et al.* method. The proposed approach presents satisfactory results, eliminating most part of the noise without disturbing the characters' definition.

In historical manuscripts it is common the occurrence of seepage of ink, shadows and strain. It is very difficult to eliminate these problems, mainly due to the similarity with the textual properties (like gray levels and component sizes, for exemple). Figure 7 illustrates some results for this kind of images.

The moving averages algorithm yields noise in the background. The approach suggested by Gatos *et. al* [5] presents regular results, but the use of Sauvola's algorithm to obtain an initial estimate of the text regions produces ill-defined or even discaded characters that cannot be retrieved by the post-processing stage. In this sense, the proposed approach has a superior performance.

When considering scanned images from modern documents, the main problems are usually related to irregular contrast and poor print quality. In the following, we compare

Fig. 6. Binarization results: (a) original image and results considering (b) moving averages, (c) Niblack ($k = -0.2$), (d) Sauvola ($k = 0.5$), (e) Gatos *et al.* and (f) BSMMT for $\sigma^{-1} = 20$ and $k = 5$

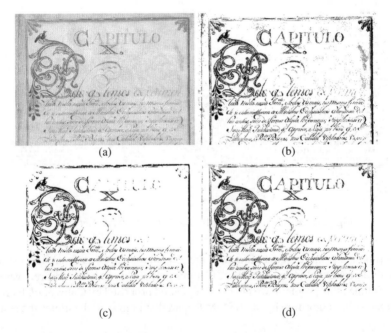

Fig. 7. Binarization results: (a) original image and results for (b) moving averages (c) Gatos *et al.* and (d) BSMMT for $\sigma^{-1} = 15$ and $k = 5$

the BSMMT operator against the approach proposed by Gatos *et al.*, which presented the best results between the methods considered for comparison. Figure 8 shows the original images.

The first line of Figure 9 shows the binarization results of our approach. Note that the BSMMT operator did not identify letters only in very critical regions (as in the right bottom corner of the image in the first column). For the approach defined by Gatos *et.*

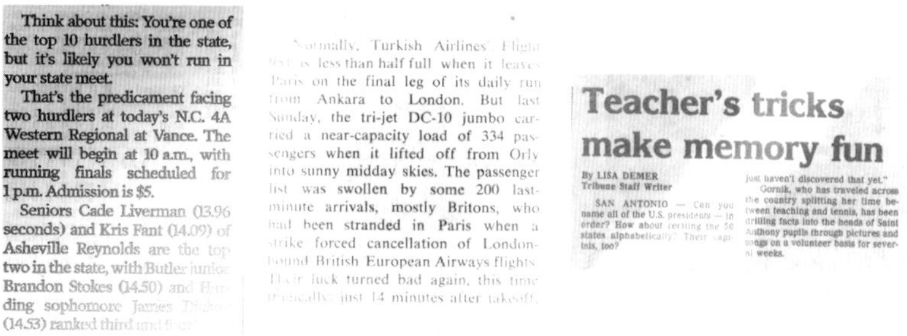

Fig. 8. Images considered for tests: (a) Doc 01, (b) Doc 02 and (c) Doc 03

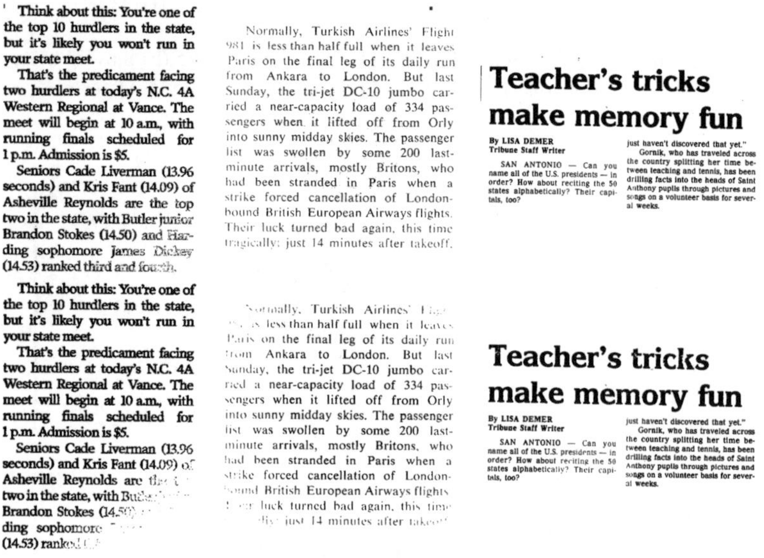

Fig. 9. Binarization results for BSMMT (first line) and Gatos *et. al*

al, this problem is more frequent (as was the case in the previous examples, the use of Sauvola's algorithm eliminated interest features that could not be further recovered).

To minimize this problem, we change the method proposed by Gatos *et al.* by replacing the Sauvola's algorithm by the BSMMT operator. Figure 10 illustrates the resulting images.

In order to better assess the quality of the resulting images, we have performed some OCR tests (we use the Abbyy sotware [18]). As evaluation metric, we consider the precision, P, and recall, R, given by:

$$P = \frac{TP}{TP + FP} \qquad \text{and} \qquad R = \frac{TP}{TP + FN} \tag{11}$$

where TP is the number of words correctly retrieved (true positive), FP represents the words (or noise) wrongly retrieved (false positive), and FN indicates the amount of not retrieved words (false negative).

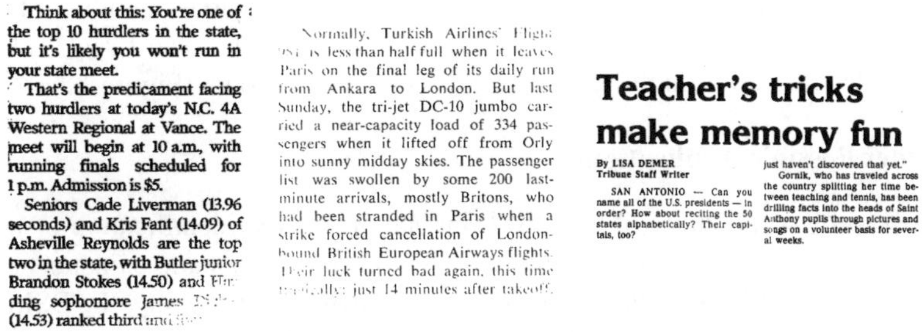
Think about this: You're one of the top 10 hurdlers in the state, but it's likely you won't run in your state meet.
That's the predicament facing two hurdlers at today's N.C. 4A Western Regional at Vance. The meet will begin at 10 a.m., with running finals scheduled for 1 p.m. Admission is $5.
Seniors Cade Liverman (13.96 seconds) and Kris Fant (14.09) of Asheville Reynolds are the top two in the state, with Butler junior Brandon Stokes (14.50) and

Normally, Turkish Airlines' Flight ... is less than half full when it leaves Paris on the final leg of its daily run from Ankara to London. But last Sunday, the tri-jet DC-10 jumbo carried a near-capacity load of 334 passengers when it lifted off from Orly into sunny midday skies. The passenger list was swollen by some 200 last-minute arrivals, mostly Britons, who had been stranded in Paris when a strike forced cancellation of London-bound British European Airways flights. Their luck turned bad again, this time ... just 14 minutes after takeoff.

Teacher's tricks make memory fun

By LISA DEMER
Tribune Staff Writer

SAN ANTONIO — Can you name all of the U.S. presidents — in order? How about reciting the 50 states alphabetically? Their capitals, too?

just haven't discovered that yet."
Gornik, who has traveled across the country splitting her time between teaching and tennis, has been drilling facts into the heads of Saint Anthony pupils through pictures and songs on a volunteer basis for several weeks.

Fig. 10. Resulting images for the Gatos *et. al* approach when replacing the Sauvola's algorithm by the BSMMT operator

Table 1. Precision and Recall scores

Method	Doc 01		Doc 02		Doc 03	
	Precision	Recall	Precision	Recall	Precision	Recall
Gatos *et al.*	0.81	0.87	0.81	0.83	0.91	0.92
BSMMT	0.87	0.90	0.88	0.91	0.93	0.95
BSMMT + Gatos *et al.*	0.92	0.91	0.91	0.92	0.95	0.95

Table 1 shows the precision and recall scores for the three example images.

Note that the approaches proposed in this paper conduce to better results. The modification in the Gatos *et al.* method, for example, increased the scores from 82.99% to 91.66% (in average).

Since most document processing systems analyze a large number of documents, having different styles and layouts, it is important to develop automatic techniques that do not require user intervention to set the corresponding parameters each time it is applied.

In this sense, we propose an alternative approach that explores the multiscale nature of the binarization operator discussed here. First, we apply the BSMMT operator for n different scales. The final result is defined by a voting algorithm, that is, it is given by the pixels classified as text in at least m scales out of 8.

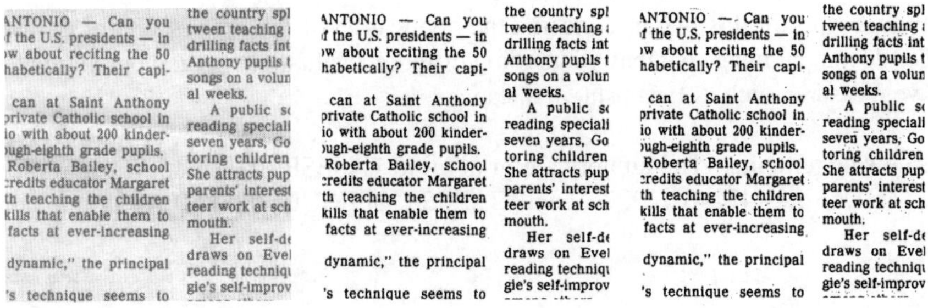
ANTONIO — Can you
f the U.S. presidents — in
w about reciting the 50
habetically? Their capi-

can at Saint Anthony
private Catholic school in
io with about 200 kinder-
ugh-eighth grade pupils.
Roberta Bailey, school
credits educator Margaret
th teaching the children
kills that enable them to
facts at ever-increasing

dynamic," the principal

's technique seems to

the country spl
tween teaching
drilling facts int
Anthony pupils t
songs on a volun
al weeks.
A public s
reading speciali
seven years, Go
toring children
She attracts pup
parents' interest
teer work at sch
mouth.
Her self-d
draws on Evel
reading techniq
gie's self-improv

(a) (b) (c)

Fig. 11. Multiscale approach to automatic binarizarion. (a) original image and results when considering (b) at least 5 scales out of 8, and (c) only the lowest scale

Note that the most significant structures persist for a larger number of scales (Figure 11(b)). The result contains some noise when only the lowest scale, identifying the greater variations on the gray levels, is taken into account (Figure 11(c)).

4.3 Other Possible Applications

Another possible application of the BSMMT operator is the identification of moving objects in video sequences, a challenging problem even when static cameras are used for capture. Figure 12 illustrates one possible approach [19]. Basically, the BSMMT is applied to a reference image of the background (without moving objects) and to each sequence frame. The moving object is identified by subtracting the resulting binary images.

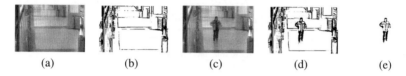

(a)   (b)   (c)   (d)   (e)

Fig. 12. Identifying moving objects: background reference image (a) original and (b) processed; sequence frame (c) original and (d) processed; (e) final result

5 Conclusions

We have defined an adaptive multiscale local binarization operator named BSMMT. Depending on the chosen parameters, regions are identified or delimited. In both cases, the operator has shown to be robust even when the images present problems like uneven illumination and some kinds of noise.

Besides, we apply the BSMMT to degraded document images, performing a qualitative analysis (based on visual evaluation) and OCR procedures. The experimental results comprove the superior performance of the proposed approach when compared to well-known binarization methods, being robust to a wide range of degradation problems without yielding ill-defined characters.

Future work in this matter concerns the application of the proposed approach in a larger document image database, including different evaluation method based on alternative measures such as Levenshtein distance.

Acknowledgements. The authors are grateful to FAPESP (07/52015-0; 05/04462-2) and MCT/CNPq (472402/2007-2) and CAPES/COFECUB (592/08) for the financial support.

References

1. Sahoo, P., Soltani, S., Wong, A.: A survey of thresholding techniques. Comput. Vision, Graphics and Image Processing 41(2), 233–260 (1988)
2. Otsu, N.: A threshold selection method from grey-level histograms. IEEE Transactions on Systems, Man and Cybernetics 9(1), 377–393 (1979)

3. Niblack, W.: An Introduction to Digital Image Processing. Prentice-Hall, Englewood Cliffs (1986)
4. Sauvola, J., Pietikainen, M.: Adaptive document image binarization. Pattern Recognition 33, 225–236 (2000)
5. Gatos, B., Pratikakis, I., Perantonis, S.: Adaptative degraded image binarization. Pattern Recognition 39, 317–327 (2006)
6. Trier, O., Jain, A.: Goal-directed evaluation of binarization methods. IEEE Trans. Pattern Anal. Mach. Intell. 17, 1191–1201 (1995)
7. Sezgin, M., Sankur, B.: Survey over image thresholding techniques and quantitative performance evaluation. J. Electron. Imaging 13, 146–165 (2004)
8. Witkin, A.P.: Scale-space filtering: a new approach to multi-scale description. In: Image Understanding, pp. 79–95. Ablex, Greenwich (1984)
9. Bosworth, J., Acton, S.: Morphological scale-space in image processing. Digital Signal Processing 13, 338–367 (2003)
10. Jackway, P.T., Deriche, M.: Scale-space properties of the multiscale morphological dilation-erosion. IEEE Transactions on Pattern Analysis and Machine Intelligence 18, 38–51 (1996)
11. Dorini, L.E.B., Leite, N.J.: A scale-space toggle operator for morphological segmentation. In: 8th ISMM, pp. 101–112 (2007)
12. Dorini, L.E.B., Leite, N.J.: Multiscale image representation using scale-space theory. In: XXXI Congresso Nacional de Matemática Aplicada e Computacional, pp. 103–110 (2008)
13. Kramer, H.P., Bruckner, J.B.: Iterations of a non-linear transformation for enhancement of digital images. Pattern Recognition 7, 53–58 (1975)
14. Bernsen, J.: Dynamic thresholding of grey-level images. In: International Conference on Pattern Recognition, pp. 1251–1255 (1986)
15. Serra, J., Vicent, L.: An overview of morphological filtering. Circuits, Systems and Signal Processing 11(1), 47–108 (1992)
16. Maragos, P., Meyer, F.: A pde approach to nonlinear image simplification via levelings andreconstruction filters. In: International Conference on Image Processing, pp. 938–941 (2000)
17. Wellner, P.: Adaptive thresholding for the digital desk. Technical Report EPC1993-110, Xerox (1993)
18. ABBYY (2008), http://www.finereader.com
19. Dorini, L.E.B., Simões, N.C., Leite, N.J.: A scale-dependent morphological approach to motion segmentation. In: IWSSIP, pp. 122–125 (2007)

On the Suitability of Different Features for Anomaly Detection in Wire Ropes

Esther-Sabrina Platzer[1], Herbert Süße[1], Josef Nägele[2],
Karl-Heinz Wehking[2], and Joachim Denzler[1]

[1] Chair for Computer Vision, Friedrich Schiller University of Jena, Germany
[2] Institute of Mechanical Handling and Logistics, University Stuttgart, Germany
{Esther.Platzer,Joachim.Denzler,Herbert.Suesse}@uni-jena.de,
{Naegele,Karl-Heinz.Wehking}@ift.uni-stuttgart.de
http://www.inf-cv.uni-jena.de, http://www.uni-stuttgart.de/ift

Abstract. Automatic visual inspection of wire ropes is an important but challenging task, as anomalies in the rope are usually unobtrusive. Certainly, a reliable anomaly detection is essential to assure the safety of the ropes. A one-class
classification approach for the automatic detection of anomalies in wire ropes
is presented. Furthermore, the performance of different well-established features
from the field of textural defect detection are compared with respect to this task.
The faultless rope structure is thereby modeled by a Gaussian mixture model and
outliers are regarded as anomaly. To prove the practical applicability, a careful
evaluation of the presented approach is performed on real-life rope data. In doing
so, a special interest was put on the robustness of the model with respect to un-
intentional outliers in the training and on its generalization ability given further
data from an identically constructed rope. The results prove good recognition
rates accompanied by a high generalization ability and robustness to outliers in
the training set.

1 Introduction

Wire ropes are used in many fields of logistics. They are deployed as load cable for
bridges, elevators and ropeways. This implies a high strain by external powers every
day. Unfortunately, this can lead to structural anomalies or even defects in the rope
formation. A defective rope bears a high risk for human life. This motivates the strict
rules summarized in the European norm [1], which instruct a regular inspection of wire
ropes.

Risky defects, prominent in wire ropes, are small wire fractions, missing wires, and
damaged rope material due to lightening strokes. Furthermore, structural anomalies
caused by interweavement of the rope ends or a reduced stress are also in the focus
of interest. In Fig. 1, two exemplary defects are marked in the rope. Visual inspection
of wire ropes is a difficult and dangerous task. Besides, the inspection speed is quite
high (on average 0.5 meters/second) which makes it a hard effort, to concentrate on the
passing rope without missing small defective rope regions.

A prototypic acquisition system was developed to overcome these limitations [2].
Four line cameras record the passing rope and yield four different views. By this, the

A. Ranchordas et al. (Eds.): VISIGRAPP 2009, CCIS 68, pp. 296–308, 2010.
© Springer-Verlag Berlin Heidelberg 2010

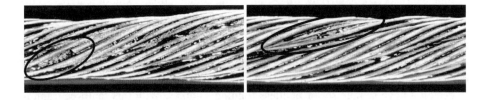

Fig. 1. Rope defects: in the left image you can see a wire fraction and in the right image a wire is missing

rope can be inspected in the office without time pressure. The images in Fig. 1 were acquired with this system.

Defects and anomalies in wire ropes are unimposing and small. The image quality is deranged by mud, powder, grease or water and the lighting conditions change frequently. Therefore, the choice of features for the detection task is important. Recent approaches for defect or anomaly identification focus on fault detection in material-surfaces. In [3] we introduced a one-class classification approach for anomaly detection in wire ropes using linear prediction (LP) coefficients as features and a Gaussian mixture for model learning. This former work is extended now by two main aspects. First of all, we compare the performance of LP features to that of well-established features from the field of textural defect detection as well as to that of features based on histograms of oriented gradients (HOG). Secondly, the robustness to outliers in the training set as well as the generalization ability of the presented approach are carefully evaluated. The last point is of particular interest for the practical relevance of the method.

Features based on local binary patterns (LBP) were first introduced by Ojala [4] for texture classification. Recently, they were used for defect detection in fabrics [5] and for real-time surface inspection [6]. Textural features, extracted from co-occurrence matrices, were proposed by Harlick in the early 70's [7] and are frequently used for texture description [8]. Iivarinen [9] compares two histogram-based methods for surface defect detection using LBP and co-occurrence matrices. Rautkorpi et al. [10] used shaped-based co-occurrence matrices for the classification of metal surface defects. Vartiainen et al. [11] focus on the detection of irregularities in regular, periodic patterns. They separate the image data in a regular and an irregular part. Based on the resulting irregularities, we compute local histograms, which serve as features. In addition to our previously published work [12] on this topic, also features based on histograms of oriented gradients (HOG) are considered. They were originally introduced for human detection by Dalal and Triggs [13] and have gained in importance in the last years. As it is obvious, the regular rope structure results in some eminent gradient orientations. For this reason, HOG features seem to be a suitable choice for the problem of rope anomaly detection.

Another important category of features for texture analysis and textural defect detection are wavelet-based features. Kumar and Pang [14] for example use Gabor features for the detection of defects in textured material. However, the computation of these features requires large filter banks and high computational costs. Due to the huge size of rope data sets (20-30 GB) the time-consuming computation of Gabor features seems to be not the best choice. In [15] the authors state, that similar results to that obtained by the usage of wavelet features can be resolved with help of joint neighborhood distributions and less computational effort.

The one-class classification strategy proposed in [3] was chosen due to a lack of defective training samples for a supervised classification. In contrast, it is no problem to design a huge sample set of faultless training samples. With this faultfree training set a model of the intact rope structure can be learned. In the detection step outliers with regard to this model are classified as defect. However, the only available ground truth information about this training data is the labeling of the human expert. In the following, there remains a small uncertainty of underdiagnosed defects in the training set. For this reason, the robustness of the proposed method to outliers in the training set is evaluated. Results obtained by learning from a faultless training set are compared to those, obtained by learning from a training set with intentionally added, faulty samples. The generalization ability of a learned model is a further important point, especially for the practical relevance of the presented method. There exist only a limited number of different construction types for wire ropes. The differences between them are mainly a different number of wires and strands, different thickness of single wires, the length of twist and the diameter. If just one model for every possible rope type would have to be learned in advance, this would save a lot of computational effort. However, the rope data from different ropes differs significantly due to the changing acquisition conditions and a different mounting of the ropes. Nevertheless, it is desirable to have just one model for every construction type and to overcome the challenges of a changing acquisition environment. Therefore, the generalization ability of the learned models is evaluated by learning and testing on different rope data from nearly identical constructed ropes.

The paper is structured as follows: in Sect. 2 we briefly review the feature extraction using linear prediction. A short description of the used textural and HOG features and their extraction is given. The one-class classification of wire rope data is shortly summarized in Sect. 3. Experiments, revealing the usability and robustness of our approach, have been performed on real-life rope data and results are presented in Sect. 4. A conclusion and a discussion about future work is given in Sect. 5.

2   Feature Extraction

In this section, the different features are briefly reviewed. Their extraction from the underlying rope data is described, as it differs for the LP features in contrast to the remaining ones. Furthermore, we will shortly motivate the choice of every feature with respect to the rope analysis task.

Local binary patterns (LBP) code the local graylevel-structure of a pixel neighborhood. Histograms based on the resulting codes lead to a local feature distribution. Since local binary patterns incorporate contextual information from a local neighborhood, a comparison of their performance with that of the LP features is of particular interest.

Harlick [7] introduced a set of 14 different textural features computed from co-occurrence matrices. They reveal the spatial distribution of gray-levels and though seem to be an interesting choice for structures with a certain regularity.

The detection of irregularities, proposed in [11] focuses on anomalies in regular, periodic patterns. Since the structure of wire ropes is not perfectly periodic, but offers some regular periodicities, we used the detected irregularities for the computation of local, histogram-based features.

Finally, HOG features [13] were used as they are based on gradient orientations. The regular structure of the rope features articulated gradients within a certain orientation range, related to the twist direction. Gradients with a perpendicular orientation can be considered as noise or anomaly.

2.1   Linear Prediction Based Features

Linear prediction can be seen as one key technique in speech recognition [16]. It is used to compute parameters determining the spectral characteristics of the underlying speech signal.

The behavior of the underlying signal is modelled by forecasting the value $x(t)$ of the signal x at time t by a linear combination of the p past values $x(t-k)$ with $k = 1, \ldots, p$, where p is the order of the autoregressive process. The prediction $\hat{x}(t)$ of a 1-D signal can be written as

$$\hat{x}(t) = -\sum_{k=1}^{p} \alpha_k x(t - k) \tag{1}$$

with the following prediction error

$$e(t) = x(t) - \hat{x}(t) = x(t) + \sum_{k=1}^{p} \alpha_k x(t - k) \ . \tag{2}$$

This motivates the choice of linear prediction for feature extraction. For the prediction of the actual value the contextual information of the past values is used and is implicitly incorporated in the resulting feature.

Based on a least-squares formulation, the optimal parameters $\alpha = (1, \alpha_1 \ldots \alpha_p)$ can be obtained by solving the normal equations [17]. The optimal coefficients are derived by use of the auto-correlation method and the Levinson-Durbin recursion [17,16]. Free parameters of this method are framesize and the order of the process. In experiments the optimal framesize was found to be 20 camera lines with an incremental overlap of 10 lines. Best results were achieved for order $p = 8$.

Rope data, obtained from the acquisition system, can be seen as a sequence of 2-d images. Thus, with 1-d linear prediction it is not possible to analyze the 2-d signal. To overcome this, the rope data is considered as a multichannel time series. The signal x consists of c channels $x = (x_1 \ x_2 \ldots x_c)^T$ and every channel represents a 1-dimensional time series $x_i(t) = (x_i(1), \ldots, x_i(t))$. For every channel i of this signal an individual 1-d linear prediction is performed, leading to the estimate $\hat{x}_i(t)$, the squared prediction error for the whole frame, and the coefficient vector α_i. These components are used as corresponding feature for the actual frame and the channel i. Best results were obtained with a combined feature vector, including prediction coefficients and the squared error. In the training step, a separate model for every channel is learned. This is schematically depicted in Fig. 2. By this, the different appearance of the rope at different positions in the images is taken into consideration.

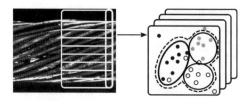

Fig. 2. Multichannel version of the classification model. For every channel (horizontal white boxes) a feature is extracted and examined in a separate feature space. The vertical white box marks the signal values, which are actually predicted.

2.2   Local Binary Pattern

For the local binary pattern (LBP) a texture region is seen as a joint distribution of $P + 1$ pixel-graylevels in a predefined neighborhood. Often a circular neighborhood with radius R and P equally spaced samples is chosen. The center pixel grayvalue g_c serves as threshold for the binarization of the neighborhood pixels g_p, $p = 1, \ldots, P$. The local binary pattern operator can be summarized as follows:

$$LBP_{P,R}(g_c) = \sum_{p=1}^{P} s(g_p - g_c)2^{p-1} \quad \text{with} \quad s(x) = \begin{cases} 1, & x \geq 0 \\ 0, & x < 0 \end{cases} . \tag{3}$$

Transforming the binary vector into a decimal number (3) results in a pixel label, based on the neighborhood information. Ojala et al. [18] developed a rotational invariant and uniform extension of the local binary pattern. For the anomaly detection task there is no need for rotational invariance due to the constant rope orientation. The uniformity of the pattern is defined based on the number of 0/1 transitions U in the binary vector. The resulting LBP code is computed as follows:

$$LBP_{P,R}^u(g_c) = \begin{cases} \sum_{p=1}^{P} s(g_p - g_c), & U \leq 2 \\ P + 1, & \text{otherwise} \end{cases} . \tag{4}$$

A histogram with a predefined number of bins is built from the underlying code distribution and serves as feature. The optimal parameters P and R and the number of quantization levels for the local histograms were determined in extensive experiments. We found the optimal parameter setting to be $R = 1$, $P = 8$ with 16 quantization levels for the histogram. As already mentioned, defects usually have just a small elongation. Hence, the histogram computation resulting in the feature vector is done for a small detection window (20×20 pixels), which moves over the underlying frame of rope data. By this, more than one feature is obtained for every frame.

2.3   Co-occurrence Features

Features for texture classification based on co-occurrence matrices were first introduced by [7]. A co-occurrence matrix is defined with respect to a certain displacement vector $d = (d_x, d_y)$ and results in the joint distribution of co-occurring grayvalues. The relative frequency p_{ij}, which defines the co-occurrence of two neighboring grayvalues (with respect to $\boldsymbol{d}$) i and j, is defined as

$$p_{ij}(\boldsymbol{d}) = \lambda|\{(x,y) : I(x,y) = i, I(x + d_x, y + d_y) = j\}| \tag{5}$$

with $i, j \in \{0 \ldots G - 1\}$ and G the number of gray levels. I represents an image of size $M \times N$ and λ is a normalization factor such that $\sum_{ij} p_{ij}(\boldsymbol{d}) = 1$.

Harlick introduced 14 different textural features [7]. Experiments for the determination of the most discriminative ones were performed. As the information theoretic texture features named difference entropy, information measure one, information measure two and the maximum correlation coefficient lead to the best results, a combination of these four features is used. Furthermore, a parameter evaluation resulted in an optimal displacement vector of 2 pixels length with an angle of 90 degrees. As co-occurrence matrices lead to a global representation of the underlying texture, they are usually computed for a local region of interest. For the detection of small, regional anomalies in the rope structure this is important, as small defects will not be recognized with global features. Again, a detection window of 20 × 20 pixels was used for the feature computation.

2.4 Features Based on Pattern Irregularity

Vartianinen et al. [11] describe an approach for irregularity detection in regular patterns based on the Fourier transform. By filtering out the distinct frequency peaks of a regular pattern in the Fourier domain, followed by an inverse transformation a perfectly regular pattern can be obtained. On the other hand, it is possible to substract this regular part from a unit function in the frequency domain, which results in the irregular part of the pattern:

$$I(x,y) = \mathcal{F}^{-1}(I(u,v)) \tag{6}$$
$$= \mathcal{F}^{-1}((\mathbf{1} - \mathcal{M}(u,v) + \mathcal{M}(u,v))I(u,v)) \tag{7}$$
$$= \underbrace{\mathcal{F}^{-1}(\mathcal{M}(u,v)I(u,v))}_{\text{regular part}} + \underbrace{\mathcal{F}^{-1}((\mathbf{1} - \mathcal{M}(u,v))I(u,v))}_{\text{irregular part}} .$$

$I(x,y)$ is the input image, $I(u,v)$ is the Fourier transformed image, $\mathcal{F}$ is the Fourier transform and $\mathcal{M}(u,v)$ is the filter function in the frequency domain. $\mathbf{1}$ represents the unit function. Without prior knowledge about the pattern structure a reasonable filter function is self-filtering [19]. Filtering is performed with the magnitude of the Fourier spectrum $\mathcal{M}(u,v) = |I(u,v)|$. As the rope consists of regular structures, filtering is done with regard to the irregular part of the data. For the computation of the local histograms again a detection window of size 20 × 20 is used. Experimental evaluation has led to an optimum of 16 quantization levels for histogram computation.

2.5 HOG Features

Descriptors based on histograms of oriented gradients can be computed from gradient images. For predefined portions of the input image, the cells, an evenly spread gradient orientation histogram is computed given a predefined number N of histogram bins.

Thereby, the histogram entries are weighted by the gradient magnitude. In a last step a descriptor or feature vector is formed, by concatenating and normalizing the cell histograms given a larger block consisting of $m \times n$ cells. In our experiments in analogy to the detection windows cell sizes of 20×20 pixels are used, with a block dimension of $m \times h$. h is the height (in pixels) of the segmented rope and m was chosen to be of 20 pixels width. We found out, that histograms with just 4 bins performed best in our application, as the distinct number of gradient orientations in the rope data is limited. As it is important for rope analysis, to discriminate between noise (caused by dirt or reflections) and actual defects, we further add the entropy given the gradient orientations of each HOG cell to the feature vector, which results in a dimension $d = \frac{h}{n}(N+1)$. In our case d is 35.

3   One-Class Classification

In order to exclude as many rope meters as possible from a further inspection, the theory of one-class classification seems to be a good choice. A separation between faultless and faulty samples is required. In this case, the faultless samples represent the target class ω_T and the defects are considered as outliers ω_O. As it is no problem to construct a large training set of defect-free feature samples, a representation for this target density $p(x \mid \omega_T)$ has to be found without any knowledge about the outlier density $p(x \mid \omega_O)$ [20]. Here, x is the feature vector.

For one-class classification problems the false negative rate (FNR) is the only rate which can be measured directly from the training data. The false positive rate (FPR) is the most important measure for defect detection, but cannot be obtained without a sample set containing a sufficient number of defective samples. In case of a uniform distributed outlier density, however, a minimization of the FNR in combination with a minimization of the descriptive volume of the target density $p(x \mid \omega_T)$ results in a minimization of the FNR and FPR [20].

There exist many different methods for one-class classification (also called novelty detection) [21,22]. In [3] two approaches, namely the K-means clustering and a Gaussian mixture model (GMM), were compared. In contrast to our former work, where the training sample set contained only faultless samples, the learning step is now modified. Model learning is performed on a sample set with intentionally included samples from defective rope regions. The aim is to evaluate the robustness of the method against outliers in the training set. This would reduce the need of a human inspector, who determines an optimal, faultfree rope region for model learning.

3.1   Decision Making

For a classification into target class and outliers, a threshold is defined on the density. This threshold is based on the mean and the minimal probability reached in the training. It is stated, that an optimal threshold should be within the range of mean and minimum probability. As the training samples are all considered as defect-free, the minimum probability gives the lower bound for the likelihood of faultless samples. To account for possible outliers, the threshold is varied in this range and the evaluation is done

Fig. 3. In this rope region a wire is missing. The window marks the frame, which was detected as an outlier by the described system.

by means of receiver operating characteristics (ROC). Since anomaly detection is a security relevant application, it is important not to miss any defect. As a consequence, the optimal threshold maximizes the TPR (number of samples correctly classified to the target class) while keeping the FPR zero.

Due to feature extraction with a detection window (or in case of the LP features based on one single channel), a rope frame consists of more than one feature. Accordingly, the decision for the overall frame is based on the decisions for the single windows/channels. In case of feature extraction by a detection window, the frame is classified as outlier, if one of the corresponding windowsor blocks (for HOG features) is rejected as outlier. For the channel-based LP features a further pre-processing is necessary. As the channels have no spatial extension like the detection window, one single channel is prone to noise. Therefore, a local channel-neighborhood consisting of 15 channels is scanned for potential outliers and only if the number of channel-votes exceeds five channels, the whole frame is rejected as defect.

Since a defect usually lasts over several frames, the whole defect is regarded as detected, if one frame in this range is rejected as outlier. Consequently, defects are detected but not localized at the moment. Figure 3 displays one defect, detected by the described system. The borders of the frame, detected as outlier are depicted by the window.

4   Experiments and Results

In the following section, experiments and their outcomes are presented. All experiments were performed on authentic rope data, acquired from real ropeways. In the generalization experiment (Subsect. 4.3) the data used for model learning was acquired in a controlled environment, but testing was again performed on data from a real ropeway. Model learning was done with a Gaussian mixture composed of five mixture components and rope data belonging to one of the four views. Testing was performed on all four views and the resulting ROC curves were averaged over the different views. Interference between the views was not yet considered. The length of the used rope regions in all experiments is given by the number of camera lines, followed by the corresponding length in meters put into brackets. Learning on 20.000 camera lines (2m rope) of one view takes between 25 seconds and one minute on a Intel Pentium 4 with 3,4GHz, according to the choice of features. Surely, the LP model learning needs the most time due to the separate computation of one model for every channel. In testing, we reach an average detection speed of 10-25 seconds per meter of rope (10.000 camera lines).

4.1   Comparison of Features

To compare the performance of the different features, model learning was done for every feature on the same training set, consisting of 20.000 lines (2m rope) of defect-free rope data from a real ropeway. Experiments were performed on a connected region of rope data, containing 600.000 camera lines (60m rope) and covering all known defects in the rope. The receiver operating characteristics in Fig. 4 point out, that the HOG features outperform all other features, since the goal is to maximize the TPR for an FPR= 0. However, for all used features respectable results were obtained, whereas the context-sensitive features seem to be the best choice. Their overall characteristics show a more robust behavior. Features based on detected irregularities perform the worst. A lot of noise is contained in the rope raw data and the structure is not perfectly regular, so that a certain amount of irregularities are detected in every frame. This results in a less discriminative behavior. Table 1 summarizes the maximum TPR for every view and feature, which was reached for a FPR of zero. For the HOG features sometimes a threshold equal to the minimum probability obtained in training was not enough to result in an FPR greater zero. This emphasizes the discriminative ability of these features. The reason for the decreased TPR of the LP features in view 4 is just one underdiagnosed error. A manual inspection depicted that this defect is spread over more than one view and was discovered correctly in the remaining views. Accordingly, results could be improved by incorporating interference between the different views. In summary,

Table 1. Comparison of the maximum TPR for a FPR of zero for all features and all views

view#	LP	CoOccurrence	LBP	Irregularity	HOG
view1	0.96	0.78	0.96	0.62	0.95
view2	0.93	0.77	0.82	0.89	> 0.97
view3	0.94	0.77	0.88	0.71	> 0.95
view4	0.62	0.88	0.93	0.78	0.90

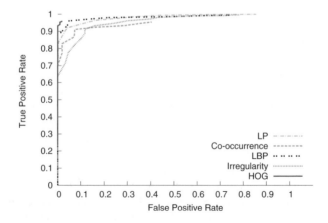

Fig. 4. Comparison of the ROC curves for the different choice of features

these results reveal the importance of context-sensitive features for the challenging task of defect detection in wire ropes.

4.2 Robustness to Outliers

To evaluate the robustness to outliers in the training set, model learning was performed on a training set containing 200.000 (20m rope) lines of rope data. For learning, the view containing the most defects (9 defects) was chosen. Testing was performed on the remaining three views, also containing each at least seven defects. For comparison, the same experiment was performed with a model, learned from 200.000 defect-free camera lines (20m rope). The resulting ROC curves are compared in Fig. 5. The ROC curve in Fig. 5(a) gives the averaged ROC for the model, learned on defect-free training data. Figure 5(b) visualizes the results obtained with a model, learned from a training set including outliers. Obviously, the method is robust to few outliers in the training set, as the results differ not significantly from each other. Where especially the HOG and LP features show the most robust behavior, the LBP features seem to be error-prone if outliers are contained in the training set. The size of the training set was increased in the experiment, to incorporate as many defects as possible.

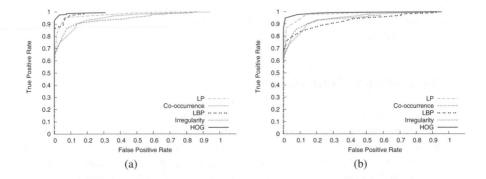

Fig. 5. Comparison of ROC curves for learning with a defect-free training set (a) and a training set including defects (b)

4.3 Generalization Ability

For the evaluation of the generalization ability, learning was performed on a real, fault-less rope, acquired in a controlled environment. Testing on the other hand was performed on different rope data from a real ropeway containing defective regions. Both ropes belong to the same construction type and they only differ in their diameter by 10 pixels. In Fig. 6 the results are depicted by the corresponding ROC curves, averaged over all views. Figure 6(a) is generated by learning and testing on the same rope from the ropeway and Fig. 6(b) shows the result for learning in the controlled setup and testing on real-life rope data. In both cases the size of the learning set was 20.000 camera

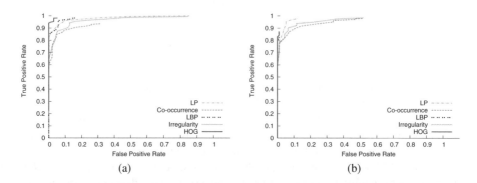

Fig. 6. Comparison of the ROC curves for learning and testing on the same data set (a) and learning and testing on two different, identically constructed rope data sets (b)

lines (2m rope). The HOG features still outperform all other features, but their performance reduces distinctly. The same can be stated for the LP features, whereas the global features like the co-occurrence features and the features based on irregularities seem not to suffer from a big loss of performance. Especially, for context-sensitive features this performance loss can be explained by the modified context, which is the fact in case of learning and testing on different datasets. But nevertheless, these results indicate a quite good generalization ability of the overall approach.

5   Discussion and Outlook

As an important and meaningful extension of our former work [3,12] we extended the one-class classification approach for anomaly detection in wire ropes by a performance comparison of five well-established and interesting features. The results emphasize the necessity of context-sensitive features for this challenging task and especially reveal the suitability of HOG features for this application domain. With the presented approach about 90 percent of the defect-free rope can be excluded from a reinspection by a human expert and only a region of 10 cm around a detected defect has to be re-examined again. Furthermore, experiments emphasizing the robustness and generalization ability of the approach were presented. They pointed out that a perfect, faultless training set is not essential for model learning. Especially from the practical point of view, this is an important insight, precisely because one cannot assure a completely defect-free training set. With regard to the generalization ability it was shown, that learning and testing on different datasets of identical constructed ropes still results in good recognition rates and therefore implies a good generalization ability of the learned models. Concerning the practical applicability, this is a remarkable finding, as it is a difficult and time consuming task to learn an individual model of the respective rope previous to every detection run.

In the meantime our research already revealed a significant improvement of defect detection by the usage of context-based classification methods like Hidden Markov Models (HMM). The permit defect localization instead of pure detection [23]. Hence, future work will be focused on a fusion of all available rope views to make a robust decision for a whole rope section.

Acknowledgements. This research is supported by the German Research Foundation (DFG) within the particular projects DE 735/6-1 and WE 2187/15-1.

References

1. EN 12927-7: Safety requirments for cableways installations designed to carry persons. ropes. inspection, repair and maintenance. European Norm: EN 12927-7:2004 (2004)
2. Moll, D.: Innovative procedure for visual rope inspection. Lift Report 29, 10–14 (2003)
3. Platzer, E.-S., Denzler, J., Süße, H., Nägele, J., Wehking, K.-H.: Challenging anomaly detection in wire ropes using linear prediction combined with one-class classification. In: Proceedings of the 13th International Fall Workshop Vision, Modeling and Visualization, pp. 343–352 (2008)
4. Ojala, T., Pietikäinen, M., Harwood, D.: A comparative study of texture measures with classification based on featured distributions. Pattern Recognition 29, 51–59 (1996)
5. Tajeripour, F., Kabir, E., Sheikhi, A.: Fabric Defect Detection Using Modified Local Binary Patterns. EURASIP Journal on Advances in Signal Processing 8, 1–12 (2008)
6. Mäenpää, T., Turtinen, M., Pietikäinen, M.: Real-time surface inspection by texture. Real-Time Imaging 9, 289–296 (2003)
7. Harlick, R.M., Shanmugam, K., Dinstein, I.: Textural Features for Image Classification. IEEE Transactions on Systems, Man and Cybernetics 3, 610–621 (1973)
8. Chen, C.H., Pau, L.F., Wang, P.S.P. (eds.): The Handbook of Pattern Recognition and Computer Vision, 2nd edn. World Scientific Publishing Co., Singapore (1998)
9. Iivarinen, J.: Surface Defect Detection with Histogram-Based Texture Features. Society of Photo-Optical Instrumentation Engineers (SPIE) Conference Series, vol. 4197, pp. 140–145 (2000)
10. Rautkorpi, R., Iivarinen, J.: Shape-Based Co-occurrence Matrices for Defect Classification. In: Kalviainen, H., Parkkinen, J., Kaarna, A. (eds.) SCIA 2005. LNCS, vol. 3540, pp. 588–597. Springer, Heidelberg (2005)
11. Vartiainen, J., Sadovnikov, A., Kamarainen, J.-K., Lensu, L., Kälviäinen, H.: Detection of irregularities in regular patterns. Machine Vision and Applications 19, 249–259 (2008)
12. Platzer, E.-S., Denzler, J., Süße, H., Nägele, J., Wehking, K.-H.: Robustness of Different Features for One-class Classification and Anomaly Detection in Wire Ropes. In: Proceedings of the 4th International Conference on Computer Vision Theory and Applications (VISAPP), vol. 1, pp. 171–178 (2009)
13. Dalal, N., Triggs, B.: Histograms of oriented gradients for human detection. In: Proceedings of the IEEE Computer Society Conference on Computer Vision and Pattern Recognition (CVPR), pp. 886–893 (2005)
14. Kumar, A., Pang, K.H.: Defect Detection in Textured Materials Using Gabor Filters. IEEE Transactions on Industry Applications 38, 425–440 (2002)
15. Varma, M., Zisserman, A.: Texture Classification: Are Filter Banks Necessary?. In: Proceedings of the IEEE Computer Society Conference on Computer Vision and Pattern Recognition (CVPR), vol. 2, pp. 691–698 (2003)
16. Rabiner, L., Juang, B.-H.: Fundementals of speech recognition. Prentice Hall PTR, Englewood Cliffs (1993)
17. Makhoul, J.: Linear Prediction: A Tutorial Review. Proceedings of the IEEE 63, 561–580 (1975)

18. Ojala, T., Pietikäinen, M., Mäenpää, T.: Gray Scale and Rotation Invariant Texture Classification with Local Binary Patterns. In: Vernon, D. (ed.) ECCV 2000. LNCS, vol. 1842, pp. 404–420. Springer, Heidelberg (2000)
19. Bailey, D.: Frequency domain self-filtering for pattern detection. In: Proceedings of the first New Zealand Conference on Image and Vision Computing, pp. 237–243 (1993)
20. Tax, D.M.J.: One-Class classification: Concept-learning in the absence of counter-examples. Phd thesis, Delft University of Technology (2001)
21. Hodge, V.J., Austin, J.: A Survey of Outlier Detection Methodologies. Artificial Intelligence Review 22, 85–126 (2004)
22. Markou, M., Singh, S.: Novelty detection: a review - part 1: statistical approaches. Signal Processing 83, 2481–2497 (2003)
23. Platzer, E.-S., Nägele, J., Wehking, K.-H., Denzler, J.: HMM-based Defect Localization in Wire Ropes - A new Approach to Unusual Subsequence Recognition. In: Denzler, J., Notni, G., Süße, H. (eds.) Pattern Recognition. LNCS, vol. 5748, pp. 442–451. Springer, Heidelberg (2009)

Importance Sampling as One Solution to the Data Association Problem in Multi-target Tracking

Nicolai v. Hoyningen-Huene and Michael Beetz

Intelligent Autonomous Systems Group, Technische Universität München
Boltzmannstr. 3, D-85748 Garching, Germany
{hoyninge,beetz}@cs.tum.edu

Abstract. Tracking multiple targets with similar appearance is a common task in many computer vision applications as surveillance or sports analysis. We propose a Rao-Blackwellized Resampling Particle Filter (RBRPF) as a real-time multi-target tracking method that solves the data association problem by a Monte Carlo approach. Each particle containing the whole target configuration is predicted by using a process model and resampled by sampling associations and fusing of the predicted state with the assigned measurement(s) instead of the common dispersion. As each target state is modeled as a Gaussian, Rao-Blackwellization can be used to solve some of these steps analytically. The sampling of associations splits the multi-target tracking problem in multiple single target tracking problems, which can be handled by Kalman filters in an optimal way. The method is independent of the order of measurements which is mostly predetermined by the measuring process in contrast to other state-of-the-art approaches. Smart resampling and memoization is introduced to equip the tracking method with real-time capabilities in the first place exploiting the discreteness of the associations. The probabilistic framework allows for consideration of appearance models and the fusion of different sensors. A way to constrain the multiplicity of measurements associated with a single target is proposed and – along with the ability to cope with a high number of targets in clutter – evaluated in a simulation experiment. We demonstrate the applicability of the proposed method to real world applications by tracking soccer players captured by multiple cameras through occlusions in real-time.

Keywords: Multi-target tracking, Data association problem, Particle filter, Rao-Blackwellization, Kalman, Resampling.

1 Introduction

Tracking multiple targets is needed in a wide range of computer vision applications like surveillance, air-traffic control or sports analysis. The difference of multiple target tracking to parallel single target tracking constitutes the so called data association problem, where measurements and targets have to be matched. Computation of all possible matchings is highly exponential and therefore improper for real time tracking. Existing approaches limit the associations to feasible ones (MHT, JPDAF [2]) or explore only the highly probable subspace of possible associations accompanied by Rao-Blackwellization (RBMCDA [21], RBMCMC [15]).

A. Ranchordas et al. (Eds.): VISIGRAPP 2009, CCIS 68, pp. 309–325, 2010.

In this paper we propose a Rao-Blackwellized Resampling particle filter (RBRPF) for real-time tracking of a fixed number of multiple targets. Our non-backscan target-oriented approach follows the framework of Sampling Importance Resampling particle filter. We solve the data association problem by sampling the most probable associations similar to RBMCDA [21]. As we want to estimate the positions of all targets, one particle holds the complete arrangement. We model each target as a Gaussian distribution allowing for fast computation and Rao-Blackwellization of the SIR particle filter. Therefore the particle filter tracks a mixture of Gaussians, where the multi-modality is caused by possible mix-ups of associations and one Gaussian refers to the uncertainty of the dynamics of an individual player. Sampling of new target configurations contains a Rao-Blackwellized prediction step analogous to the Kalman filter, the sampling of associations and the fusion of associated measurements with predicted target states. The association problem is ergo handled by a Monte Carlo approach avoiding the exponential effort to list all possible associations. Taking advantage of the fact that the (discrete) number of probable associations for given target positions and measurements are usually low, the particle filter focuses on the most likely associations and can avoid unnecessary computations by smart resampling and memoization thus adapting to the complexity of the tracking problem. The Bayesian framework allows the integration of kinematic and appearance models to determine the most probable target locations through occlusions.

As the order of measurements in real world application is usually determined by the sensors, for example in a top-down and left-right fashion for camera images, we avoid the dependency of the method on the order of measurements by firstly associating measurements in parallel, followed by fusing the informations to form updated target estimates. A simple example shows that the one measurement at a time approach by [20,21] is dependent on the order of the measurement sequence uncovered by different sampling probabilities. We allow to constrain the multiplicity of associations according to single measurements only or to a Poisson distribution.

The method is developed as part of the ASPOGAMO system [4,5,6], that aims to extract knowledge from broadcasted soccer games, and is evaluated by applying it to real soccer games, showing robust real-time performance over challenging sequences. The sports domain provides a challenging testbed for concurrent tracking of multiple targets with similar appearance through frequent occlusions captured from different views. The handling of constraints on the measurements is inspected in a simulation experiment tracking a high number (100) of objects through clutter.

The remainder of this paper is organized as follows. We briefly talk about related work in the next section. In section 3 we derive the Rao-Blackwellized Resampling particle filter and continue in the next section with showing the independence of the proposed algorithm on the order of measurements and a way how to state constraints on the multiplicity on associations. Section 5 describes the two experiments we conducted. We finish in section 6 with our conclusions.

2 Related Work

Multiple-target tracking algorithms can be differentiated by their data association methods. Nearest-Neighbor tracking constitutes the straight forward approach, assigning all targets to their closest measurement. Multiple hypothesis tracking (MHT) [2] builds a tree of all possible association sequences of each measurement with close targets. Gating, the assumption of single associations and the use of Kalman filtering as well as the Hungarian algorithm reduce the computational costs to polynomial time, but inhibit to handle multiple or merged associations. The Joint Probabilistic Data Association Filter (JPDAF) assigns each target to all measurements weighted according to the probability of the association. Khan et al., [15] propose a real-time Rao-Blackwellized MCMC-based particle filter where associations are sampled by a Markov chain. The Markov chain allows also sampling of merged measurement assignments but demands computation time that reduces the number of particles degrading the approximation of the posterior to a search for the MAP estimate. In their experiments real-time could only be provided for a small number of particles (less than 6) i.e. the tracker can cope with three parallel mix-ups of targets max. Interaction of targets are modeled as correlations between target positions which does not hold for many applications.

The Rao-Blackwellized particle filter approach by [20,21] samples the associations directly and handles dependencies between them by data associations priors. The performance of the method was demonstrated only on synthetic simulations without statements about computation time. Our approach inherits their idea of sampling the associations, but overcomes the dependency on the order of measurements and offers real-time tracking due to smart resampling and memoization.

Tracking of soccer players is distinguished by [16] in category and identity tracking. Category tracking extracts trajectories with team affiliation where in the other case each single player is traced with its identity. Barceló et al., [3] and [11] label the measurements by nearest neighbor assignment. In [12] MHT was applied, but Particle filters constitute the mostly used method in the literature for category tracking (i.e. [23,7]). Du et al., [9,10] aim on combining local particle filters to fuse measurements captured from different views. A MCMC method for team labelling is proposed by [17] to link observations of soccer players over time.

Identity tracking is often performed in a second stage by consistent labelling of the trajectory graph generated by category tracking. Hung & Hilton [14] propose an assignment in batch mode by shortest path algorithm, [19] solve the association of the trajectory graph by Bayesian network inference, and [22] combine trajectories of unoccluded players in a graph structure by clustering. Barceló et al., [3] resolve collisions of nearest neighbor Kalman tracking by constraints in the trajectory graph. To the best of our knowledge no real-time identity tracking method for soccer player that allows multiple measurements and fuses different camera views was proposed in the literature yet.

3 Rao-Blackwellized Resampling Particle Filter

A particle filter for complete player configurations constitutes the base of our algorithm. The idea is that for each particle every player position can be modeled as a Gaussian. The different particles reflect the distribution over possible mix-ups, which are the source for multi-modality. Instead of sampling new particles by prediction with noise, Rao-Blackwellization can be used to predict the Gaussians analytically and the sampling of associations followed by the fusion with corresponding measurements replaces

the noise step. The Rao-Blackwellization already reduces the number of needed particles, but exploiting the fact that the number of highly probable discrete associations is
typically low, we further save computation time by memoization of precomputed samples and probabilities. Sampling and weighting is done by using the Kalman filter for
the Gaussian target states.

3.1 Bayesian View of Tracking

The problem of tracking is to recursively estimate a state x_k knowing the evolution of
the state sequence

$$x_k = f_k \left(x_{k-1}, v_{k-1} \right) \tag{1}$$

from measurements

$$z_k = h_k \left(x_k, n_k \right) \tag{2}$$

where f_k is called system or motion model and h_k is called measurement model, v_{k-1}
and n_k denote the process and measurement noise, respectively. The tracked state x_k is
represented as the configuration of all player states stacked into one vector

$$x_k = (x_{j,k} = \mathcal{N} \left(x; m_{j,k}, V_{j,k} \right)) \; j = 1, \ldots, T \tag{3}$$

where $x_{j,k}$ contains the position and velocity of player j at time k. An individual target
state $x_{j,k}$ is assumed to be Gaussian with mean $m_{j,k}$ and corresponding covariance
matrix $V_{j,k}$.

Although the state can contain arbitrary variables depending on the application, we
depict the method for moving targets in a 2D-plane with constant velocity resulting in
a single target state

$$x_{j,k} = (x, y, \dot{x}, \dot{y})^T . \tag{4}$$

In a Bayesian framework, the problem of tracking can be formulated as one of es-
timating the *posterior* probability density function $p \left(x_k | z_{1:k} \right)$ for the state x_k given a
sequence of measurements $z_{1:k}$ up to time k.

3.2 Particle Filtering

In *Sampling Importance Sampling* (SIS) particle filtering, the posterior probability density function is approximated by a weighted sum of random samples x_k^i also called
particles [1]. The weights are normalized such that $\sum_i w_k^i = 1$:

$$p \left(x_k | z_{1:k} \right) \approx \sum_i w_k^i \delta \left(x_k - x_k^i \right) \tag{5}$$

with Dirac function δ.

We draw the samples x_k^i by importance sampling from a proposal $q(.)$ called an
importance density. Doucet [8] showed that the optimal importance density function
that minimizes the variance of the true weights conditioned on x_{k-1}^i and z_k is

$$q_{opt} \left(x_k | x_{k-1}^i, z_k \right) = \frac{p \left(z_k | x_k, x_{k-1}^i \right) p \left(x_k | x_{k-1}^i \right)}{p \left(z_k | x_{k-1}^i \right)}. \tag{6}$$

3.3 Sampling New Configurations

In our case the importance density $q\left(x_k|x_{k-1}^i, z_k\right)$ is the probability distribution of data associations, while the actual sample is deduced by Rao-Blackwellization from an association J_k by the use of Kalman fusion of assigned measurements and predicted target state x_k':

$$q = \sum_{J_k} p\left(x_k'|x_{k-1}^i\right) q\left(J_k|x_k', z_k\right) \delta\left(x_k - \arg \max_x p\left(x|J_k, x_k', z_k\right)\right) \qquad (7)$$

For known associations between measurements z_k and predicted targets x_k', the newly sampled configuration x_k is Gaussian and can be evaluated analytically as an optimal fusion between the assigned measurements and the predicted player positions. The Kalman filter provides the method to find the parameter of the Gaussian, where the first two probabilities in the numerator of equation 7 equal and thus their product is maximized. The sampling problem reduces therefore to sample associations between measurements and the predicted player configuration and solving multiple single target tracking problems by Kalman filtering. The analytical sampling part forms the Rao-Blackwellization of the particle filter. To supply an optimal solution, the Kalman filter assumes state and measurement noise to be zero-mean, white Gaussian and the measurement as well as the motion model to be linear. If the last assumption does not hold, an extended or unscented Kalman filter can be applied instead, exhibiting a theoretically suboptimal solution only. The posterior probability density function of configurations forms a mixture of Gaussians, where the multi-modality originates from ambiguities in the associations.

Predicting by the System Model. We can sample from $p\left(x_k'|x_{k-1}^i\right)$ analytically by the Kalman prediction step according to the system dynamics of eq. 1, because the analytical solution complies with an infinite sampling. For the 2D case, each player state is predicted independently using the discretized Wiener velocity model $A_{\Delta t}$ [2] for time difference Δt between $k - 1$ and k as a linear motion model:

$$m_{j,k}' = \begin{pmatrix} x_{j,k}' \\ y_{j,k}' \\ \dot{x}_{j,k}' \\ \dot{y}_{j,k}' \end{pmatrix} = \begin{pmatrix} 1 & 0 & \Delta t & 0 \\ 0 & 1 & 0 & \Delta t \\ 0 & 0 & 1 & 0 \\ 0 & 0 & 0 & 1 \end{pmatrix} \begin{pmatrix} x_{j,k-1}^i \\ y_{j,k-1}^i \\ \dot{x}_{j,k-1}^i \\ \dot{y}_{j,k-1}^i \end{pmatrix} \qquad (8)$$

The covariance matrix evolves to

$$V_k' = A_{\Delta t} V_{k-1} A_{\Delta t}^T + \begin{pmatrix} \frac{\Delta t^3}{3} & 0 & \frac{\Delta t^2}{2} & 0 \\ 0 & \frac{\Delta t^3}{3} & 0 & \frac{\Delta t^2}{2} \\ \frac{\Delta t^2}{2} & 0 & \Delta t & 0 \\ 0 & \frac{\Delta t^2}{2} & 0 & \Delta t \end{pmatrix} \tilde{q} \qquad (9)$$

with power spectral density $\tilde{q}$ as a constant factor.

Sampling Associations. We introduce associations

$$J_k : \{1, \ldots, |z_k|\} \to \wp\left(\{1, \ldots, T\}\right) \qquad (10)$$

as mappings from all measurements at time k to a (possibly empty) subset of all targets. We denote $\hat{J}_k = (J_k)^{-1}$ as the inverse mapping from targets to their assigned observations for convenience. The space of data associations equals the finite and discrete set of all possible associations of measurements to targets containing $2^{|z_k| \times T}$ elements. If we restrict the data associations J_k to assign a measurement to one target max, the number of possible associations reduce to $(T+1)^{|z_k|}$. We can further reduce this number to

$$\sum_{i=0}^{\min(T,|z_k|)} \binom{\min(T, |z_k|)}{i} \max(T, |z_k|)^{\min(T,|z_k|)-i} \text{ if we prohibit multiple measure-}$$

ments per target, also named as the exclusion principle [18]. Enumerating this set and solving each single target tracking problem is still intractable even for a small number of targets and measurements. Fortunately only a few associations have high probability, but to sample them efficiently, we have to assume the associations for single measurements to be independently or the dependency between them to be determined in constant time.

Individual Independent Associations. If we look at sampling an individual association for measurement $z \in z_k$, we can enumerate all possible assignments easily as z can be clutter viz. a false alarm or assigned to one of the targets. While the importance distribution $\pi(z)$ for an association of a specific measurement z can be evaluated only up to a constant factor, we normalize the probabilities $\hat{\pi}(z)$ for each possible association.

Clutter measurements are assumed to be independent from target positions and uniformly distributed in the measurement space with volume $\mathcal{M}$

$$\hat{\pi}_\varnothing(z) = p\left(J_k(z) = \varnothing | z_k\right) \sim \mathcal{M}^{-1}. \tag{11}$$

$\hat{\pi}_\varnothing(z)$ functions as a soft gating: because of the normalization it decreases the probability for far targets to be sampled.

The probability for a data association between target t and an observation z is up to a constant factor:

$$\hat{\pi}_t(z) \sim p_a\left(t \in J_k(z)\right) \mathcal{N}\left(z; H_z m'_{t,k}, H_z V'_{t,k} H_z^T + R_z\right) \tag{12}$$

with measurement model $H_z = \begin{pmatrix} 1 & 0 & 0 & 0 \\ 0 & 1 & 0 & 0 \end{pmatrix}$ and R_z as measurement noise covariance.

$p_a\left(t \in J_k(z)\right)$ denotes the propability of an association based on the appearance model only, which is independent from player and measurement positions. The Gaussian in the second part refers to the probability of the association by the kinematic model. We included the appearance model in difference to [21] to allow a realistic influence of additional information from segmentation beside spatial data only.

Importance Density. Utilizing the independence of single associations the importance density for a sampled state x_k^j can be computed as a product over probabilities of assignments for each single measurement that are given by the normalized importance distribution π of equations 11 and 12.

$$q\left(J_k | x'_k, z_k\right) = \prod_{z_k} \pi\left(z_k\right) \tag{13}$$

Determination of State from Associations. For sampled associations J_k the predicted player positions x'_k can be updated individually by Kalman update with the assigned observations maximizing the last term of eq. 7

$$x^i_{j,k} = x'_{j,k} + V'_{j,k}H^T \left(HV'_kH^T + R\right)^{-1} \left(\hat{J}_k(j) - Hx'_{j,k}\right),$$ (14)

with H denoting the linear measurement model (2) as H_z stacked $|\hat{J}_k(j)|$ times and R as diagonal matrix of measurement covariances of observations $\hat{J}_k(j)$. The covariances are updated as

$$V^i_{j,k} = \left({V'_{j,k}}^{-1} + H^TR^{-1}H\right)^{-1}.$$ (15)

3.4 Weighting

For a good performance of the particle filter the computation of the weights of each sampled state is crucial. To approximate $p(x_k|z_{1:k})$ correctly, the weights w^i_k have to be defined recursively as

$$w^i_k \propto w^i_{k-1} \frac{p\left(z_k|x^i_k\right) p\left(x^i_k|x^i_{k-1}\right)}{q\left(x^i_k|x^i_{k-1}, z_k\right)}.$$ (16)

The denominator was already computed in the sampling phase and is depicted in equation 13. The likelihood of the measurements given the sampled state x^i_k with known associations and the likelihood of x^i_k given the former state x^i_{k-1} and the dynamics can be computed for each player and measurement separately. The measurement likelihood can be computed analogously to eq. 12 but substituting x'_k by x^i_k and V'_k by V^i_k, respectively:

$$p\left(z_k|x^i_k\right) = \prod_{z \notin \hat{J}^i_k} \pi_\varnothing(z) \prod_j p\left(\hat{J}^i_k(x^i_{j,k})|x^i_{j,k}\right).$$ (17)

The likelihood of the new sample according to the motion model can be computed by reusing the already predicted state x'_k of eq. 8

$$p\left(x^i_k|x^i_{k-1}\right) = \prod_j \mathcal{N}\left(m^i_{j,k}; m'_{j,k}, V^i_{j,k} + V'_{j,k}\right).$$ (18)

3.5 Resampling

Sequential Importance Sampler (SIS) particle filters suffer from the so called degeneracy phenomenon, where only a small amount of all particles have non-negligible weights. This implies that most of the computation time will be spent on particles that contribute only marginally to the approximation of the posterior probability density function of equation 5. To reduce the degeneracy problem resampling has been proposed to eliminate particles with small weights and clone the others according to their weights. We include the resampling step by sampling $w^i_{k-1} \times N_{max}$ associations for particle x^i_{k-1}. Particles with larger weights will therefore allocate more particles in the next time step, while particles with small weights are dropped.

Sampling several times from the same particle the number of distinct sampled particles will approach the number of ambiguities in the associations because a specific assignment leads to the same sampled configuration. Due to their discreteness there are usually only a small number of distinct probable associations. This allows a chance for noticeable improvement in computation time by smart memoization. Caching and testing sampled associations for equality can save computation time considering not only the update to generate a new state of equation 14 but also the prediction in the next particle filtering step in equation 8.

After resampling the weights are usually reset to $w_k = 1/N_{max}$ to reflect the equal probability of all particles. In our case we count the times n_{J_k} the same association J_k was sampled for a specific particle and provide only one single particle for the next filtering step having the weight set to $w_k = n_{J_k}/N_{max}$. Then the weights are recursively updated as in equation 16 and normalized at the end of the filtering step. The actual number of particles can therefore vary between 1 and N_{max} using more particles in situations with high association ambiguities. This smart resampling reduces the computation time and allows real time in the first place.

3.6 Estimate of the State

An estimate of the target positions at time k i.e. of the state x_k can be found by either selecting the particle with maximum weight or by clustering the particles and taking the weighted mean of the most probable cluster. Calculating the weighted mean of all particles should not be considered here because it can lead to the so called ghost phenomenon for multi-modal distributions i.e. it leads to a state estimated as the mean of two modes that is known to be wrong.

4 Aspects of Multiple Associations

In computer vision applications there are usually multiple measurements per sweep or image, repectively, and sometimes we may have also multiple measurements per target.

4.1 Parallel Association Sampling

As described earlier we sample all associations for one measurement sweep preliminary to the fusion and the Kalman update of the assigned targets respectively. That approach is independent of the order of the measurements. This is important because in most applications, the order of measurements is predetermined as for example in computer vision measurements are read top-down from left to right.

While the fusion of Gaussians is mathematically equivalent independently of parallel or sequential processing, this does not hold for the sampling process (contrary to the assumption in [21]). We look at a simple one-dimensional counterexample containing just one target $x_t \sim \mathcal{N}(x; 0, 1)$ and two measurements $a \sim \mathcal{N}(x; -1, 0.01)$ and $b \sim \mathcal{N}(x; 1, 100)$. Figure 1 shows the state distributions for the target t, the measurements and the different intermediate fused estimates with labels on the x-axis above and/or beneath the modes of each distribution. One can see that the fusion of t with a and the fusion of the resulting (t, a) and b is equivalent to the fusion of (t, b) with a

(the Gaussian curves of (t, a, b) and (t, b, a) coincide). But the probabilities that these associations have been sampled differ. One can imagine that a target Gaussian associated with a measurement with very low uncertainty is rarely associated with another measurement afterwards. In the figure, a bar at the mean of each estimate depicts the probability for that estimate to be sampled with the corresponding probability value displayed on the right in an exp-scale. Fusing immediately after the association, the association of the target with both measurements is significantly more likely to be sampled, if the measurement sequence is a followed by b, $(P((t, a, b)) = 0.638)$ than sampling associations of the measurement sequence in the reverse order $(P((t, b, a)) = 0.015)$:

$$P((t, a, b)) = P((t, a, b)|(t, a)) = \pi_t(a) * \pi_{(t,a)}(b)$$
$$\neq \pi_t(b) * \pi_{(t,b)}(a) = P((t, b, a)|(t, b)) = P((t, b, a)) \tag{19}$$

Associating all measurements first and then fusing the assigned measurements with the corresponding targets at once results in the same target posteriors sampled with the correct probability independently of the association sequence.

$$P((t, a, b)) = P((t, a)) P((t, b)) = \pi_t(a) * \pi_t(b)$$
$$= \pi_t(b) * \pi_t(a) = P((t, b)) P((t, a)) = P((t, b, a)) \tag{20}$$

4.2 Restricting the Associations

The JPDAF and also the MHT approach [2] omit other than feasible associations to lower their computational demand. Associations are called feasible if they associate measurements to at most one target and no more than one measurement can originate from a single target. In general this assumption does not hold, especially for tracking in computer vision with several pixels belonging to one object. There is no restriction for our approach, but it is sometimes desirable to state constraints on the number of measurements assigned to a single target.

Säärkka et al introduced a joint data association prior to handle dependencies between associations and so RBMCDA allows also to restrict the association of multiple measurements to a single target. Usually one draws the number of measurements assigned to one single target from a Poisson distribution with the expected number of detections in a sweep. In a generative approach, associations for the pulled number of measurements for the specific target would have to be sampled. But this can lead to sampling of configurations with low probability, especially if the drawn number overestimates the real one, and therefore more particles would be needed for balancing.

We draw an association for each measurement with the normalized importance distribution $\pi(z)$ one at a time. If a target was associated, it is excluded from further associations according to

$$F(x, \lambda) = 1 - \frac{f(x, \lambda)}{1 - \sum_{k=0}^{x-1} f(k, \lambda)} \tag{21}$$

with Poisson distribution $f(k, \lambda) = e^{-\lambda} \frac{\lambda^k}{k!}$ and x being determined by the number of assignments of this specific target. After each exclusion, the importance distribution is

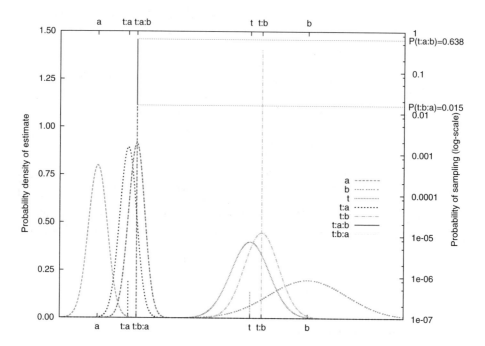

Fig. 1. Example depicting the relevance of the order of intermediate fusions for the sampling probabilities

renormalized omitting the removed target. To model the number of measurements per target with a different distribution than Poisson, the pdf $f(x, \lambda)$ has to be substituted in eq. 21 accordingly. As the distribution has to be evaluated on integer numbers only (up to a given maximal bound), a look-up table can be precomputed and used. If the mentioned exclusion principle holds i.e. targets can be assigned to one measurement at max, every target should be excluded after been associated. As the factor for the multiplicity in the importance sampling pdf and in $p\left(z_k, x_k^i\right)$ equal, these cancel in eq. 16 remaining in an unchanged weight calculation.

Again the order of the measurements influences the sampling probability. Therefore we repeatedly sample an ordering on the measurements of one sweep uniformly at random preliminary to the generation of new particles x_k^j, reducing the relevance of the ordering and the induced dependencies on the tracking result.

4.3   Implementation

The complete algorithm is depicted in figure 2 following the derivation of the former section. The individual importance distributions π as well as $\hat{\pi}$ and the Kalman prediction and updates are cached for reuse in the next sampling iteration to improve efficiency. Like most particle filters, the algorithm can easily be parallelized. The importance distribution, all probabilities and weights are calculated in log-space to avoid numerical problems.

$$\left[\{x_k^i, w_k^i\}_{i=1}^{N_k}\right] = RBRPF\left[\{x_{k-1}^i, w_{k-1}^i\}_{i=1}^{N_{k-1}}, z_k\right]$$

```
Nₖ = 0
FOR  i = 1 : Nₖ₋₁
  Predict x'ₖ as in 8
  C = ∅
  FOR  j = 1 : (wⁱₖ₋₁ × Nₘₐₓ)
    Sample an association Jₖ:
      τ = {1,...,T}
      Init  Jₖ : ∀p ∈ τ.Ĵₖ(p) = ∅
      Reorder measurements zₖ randomly
      FOR  l = 1 : |zₖ|
        Compute π̂() as in 11 and 12
        π = normalized π̂
        Draw assoc. for lth measurement with player p ∈ τ by π
        Jₖ(p) = Jₖ(p) ∪ {l}
        IF random(0,1) > F(|Jₖ(p)|,λ): τ = τ \ p and renormalize π

      END FOR

    IF  Jₖ not in C
      Nₖ = Nₖ + 1
      n_{Jₖ} = 1
      Compute x_k^{Nₖ} by Kalman update if not done prev. as in 14
      ŵ_k^{Nₖ} = 1/Nₘₐₓ
      Update ŵ_k^{Nₖ} as in 16
      C = C ∪ {Jₖ}

    ELSE
      n_{Jₖ} = n_{Jₖ} + 1
      ŵₖ = ŵₖ (n_{Jₖ})/(n_{Jₖ}-1)

    END IF

  END FOR

END FOR
Calculate total weight: t = Σ_{j=1}^{Nₖ} ŵ_k^j
FOR  j = 1 : Nₖ
  Normalize:  w_k^j = t⁻¹ ŵ_k^j

END FOR
```

Fig. 2. Algorithm for one iteration of the proposed Rao-Blackwellized Resampling particle filter

5 Experimental Results

We conducted two experiments. A simulation provides a comprehensible experiment with a high number of targets in clutter, and a real-world experiment tracking soccer players evaluates the performance in a computer vision application.

5.1 Simulation

To investigate the ability of the proposed method to track a high number of targets with multiple measurements through clutter, we adopted a simulation similar to the one described in [13]. 100 targets are drawn with an initial position, which is uniformly distributed in $[-2000; 2000]^2$, and a velocity with distribution $\mathcal{N}\left(0; 10^2\right)$. The targets are tracked for 100 measurement sweeps with the time between measurement sweeps set to 1. Measurements are taken of the true targets' positions, while each position measurement having an independent error which has distribution $\mathcal{N}\left(0; 20^2\right)$. The number of measurements generated by one single target is Poisson distributed with $\lambda = 3$. Clutter is drawn according to a Poisson with $\lambda_c = 100$ uniformly distributed over the whole tracking area $\mathcal{M} = [-4000; 4000]^2$. An examplar simulation with tracked targets is shown in fig. 4 at the last timestep.

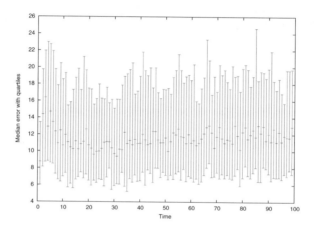

Fig. 3. Median error with quartiles for tracking 100 targets with multiple measurements in clutter

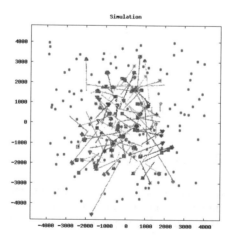

Fig. 4. Tracking of 100 simulated targets with multiple measurements in clutter

Table 1. Tracking result for simulation experiment

Assignment	Single only	Multiple
Failures	37.01	8.21
Time(ms)	473.5	561.1

We inited our tracker with the true target positions and zero velocity, the uncertainty in the target state was set to $100.0I_4$. The power spectral density of the process noise was set to $\tilde{q} = 1.0$. We used $n = 50$ particles to track the distributions.

We counted a failure if the tracked target position differed more than 100.0 from the true target position at the last timestep. We tracked the targets firstly assuming single assignments only and secondly assuming the correct Poisson distribution. Table 1 depicts the mean number of failures during 100 simulation runs. Failed tracking is mostly due to very close initial target positions getting swapped or misleading by clutter in the beginning. One can see the higher robustness due to the incorporation of more measurements and hence more information. Figure 3 graphs the median distance of the tracked targets to their true position with 0.25 and 0.75 quantiles for a single simulation run tracking with multiple measurements. This error expectedly stays inside the measurement generation distribution $\mathcal{N}\left(0; 20^2\right)$.

The original simulation of [13] generated 400 tracks without clutter. Unfortunately Horridge did not provide tracking errors but computation time only. We also conducted the same experiment but tracking seemed futile since the measurement density is very high accompanied by comparatively high uncertainty of each measurement, so arbitrary traces could be supported by observations resulting in low tracking performance.

5.2 Tracking of Soccer Players

The proposed tracking method is evaluated as part of the ASPOGAMO system [4,5], that aims to extract knowledge from broadcasted soccer games. ASPOGAMO is able to track multiple dynamic pan-tilt-zoom cameras and segment the soccer players and referee by a combination of variance filter and color templates. Segmentation influences the tracking process as the Kalman filters smooth assigned measurements. A qualitative evaluation of the used methods can be found in [5]. Noteworthy, segmentation by background subtraction for static cameras is usually of higher quality. Digital videos captured by two dynamic cameras with a frame rate of 25Hz provide the basic raw material. Tracking results in both camera perspectives are depicted in figures 5 and 6 and are presented quantitatively in table 3. The extracted players spatial measurements of each camera are fused by the proposed tracking algorithm as different measurement sweeps with same time stamps.

Player positions have been measured in meters and were initialized manually in the image with covariance $V_0 = 2I_4$, initial velocity was set to zero. The factor for the kinematic process noise $\tilde{q} = 0.0008$ is derived from maximal human speed. A confusion matrix between different categories was used as a simple appearance model p_{app} and is depicted in table 2. The measurement space is determined by the number of pixels in

Fig. 5. Tactical camera view of the World Cup final 2006

Fig. 6. Identity tracking of soccer players in the broadcasted highangle camera view of the World Cup final 2006

Table 2. Confusion matrix between different categories

	Italy	France	Referee
Italy	0.6	0.1	0.3
France	0.1	0.8	0.1
Referee	0.3	0.1	0.6

Table 3. Tracking performance on the final of the world cup 2006

Game	Frames	Fail	Time(ms)	Particles
Tactical	1262	13	23.3± 4	43.5±10
Highangle	1262	7+54	8.5± 5	12.1±12
Fused	1262	11	30.2±20	33.3±16
Fused II	3202	98	33.4±18	34.1±14

each camera frame and evaluates to $\mathcal{M} = 720 \times 576$. We used $N_{max} = 50$ particles to track all of the 22 players and the referee.

There is no ground truth available for broadcasted soccer games because players can be tracked only visually and camera parameters are unknown. We abandon to present a spatial error as this is influenced mainly by camera estimation and segmentation. Instead we tried to find a error measure that is related with the number of false associations. A failure was counted when the projected player position differed from the real player in the image by more than 10 pixels for longer than 3 frames. In this case the tracker was reset in the failed player positions and run again on the rest of the sequence. We tracked both camera views separately and also ran the same sequence fusing the measurements of both perspectives. Because the broadcasted highangle camera shows only a part of the field and is panning and zooming fast, in average only 9.9 players are visible (with standard deviation of 3.2). We splitted the number of failures into association errors and assigning emerging players (second number) to be comparable with the other results. The second row of table 3 shows the number of frames that were tracked in the according experiment. The computation time was taken for one update step, where all experiments have been conducted on a 2.2 GHz Dual-core PC. As the complexity of the proposed algorithm is linear in the number of measurements and targets, the actual needed time is more significant since the input data do not scale but stay in fixed boundaries (number of players is 22, number of measurements usually lower than 200). The last row depicts the average number of particles and the corresponding standard deviation. Table 3 clearly evidences the real-time tracking ability of the proposed method with low failure rate for single cameras. Fusion of different cameras reduces the occurrence of occlusions and therewith failure rate and number of particles even further.

The fourth soccer experiment states a challenging sequence including several fouls and header duels where kinematic and appearance model have often been to weak to differentiate between players causing a higher number of failures. The amount of measurements (lower for the highangle view) correlates obviously with the number of particles and the computation time demonstrating the adaptiveness of the proposed method to the complexity of the tracking problem. Also we observed assignment errors if segmentation could not extract a specific player for longer than 20 frames (e.g. fouled player on the ground).

We also implemented the method as proposed by [15] and tested it on the World Cup final. We encountered problems of two kind: low variance in sparse particles and misleading interaction handling. The real-time requirement allowed only a small number of particles (6 in our case) which had a low variance because the Markov chain converged to very similar associations. This misled the tracker to remember the most probable configuration only, which often did not equal the true positions. Interactions were handled by dependencies in the positions via symmetric entries in the configuration covariance matrix. Unfortunately, this modeling is inappropriate for interacting soccer players, where e.g. the player on the ball shows contrary motion to his competitor. Both drawbacks resulted in poor tracking performance for the inspected soccer game sequences.

6   Conclusions

In this article we have proposed a real-time multiple target tracking method based on Rao-Blackwellized Resampling particle filtering that solves the data association problem with a Monte Carlo approach. As the sampling of associations replaces the noise in usual particle filters, smart resampling and memoization was introduced to equip the tracking method with real-time capabilities exploiting the discreteness of the drawn assignments. We showed the independence of the order of measurements for the proposed algorithm contrary to the RBMCDA method by [21] due to the processing of measurements of one sweep in parallel instead of one at a time. The handling of constraints on the multiplicity of measurements assigned to a single target has been integrated in our framework and evaluated in a simulation experiment with a high number of targets in clutter. Further experimental results demonstrate robustness and real-time performance of the developed method in challenging soccer game sequences including increased achievements by fusion of measurements from different cameras. A comparison with another recent multi-target tracking method explains the supremacy of our approach for the soccer domain. For future research we plan to examine more complex appearance models for automatic reinitialization of the identities especially regarding broadcasted single view sports videos.

Acknowledgements. This work was partially funded by the German Research Foundation DFG.

References

1. Arulampalam, M.S., Maskell, S., Gordon, N., Clapp, T.: A tutorial on particle filters for online nonlinear/non-gaussian bayesian tracking. IEEE Trans. on Signal Processing 50(2) (2002)
2. Bar-Shalom, Y., Li, X.-R., Kirubarajan, T.: Estimation with Applications to Tracking and Navigation. Wiley Interscience, Hoboken (2001)
3. Barceló, L., Binefa, X., Kender, J.R.: Robust methods and representations for soccer player tracking and collision resolution. In: Leow, W.-K., Lew, M., Chua, T.-S., Ma, W.-Y., Chaisorn, L., Bakker, E.M. (eds.) CIVR 2005. LNCS, vol. 3568, pp. 237–246. Springer, Heidelberg (2005)
4. Beetz, M., Bandouch, J., Gedikli, S., von Hoyningen-Huene, N., Kirchlechner, B., Maldonado, A.: Camera-based observation of football games for analyzing multi-agent activities. In: Proc. of Intl. Joint Conf. on Autonomous Agents and Multiagent Systems, AAMAS (2006)

5. Beetz, M., Gedikli, S., Bandouch, J., Kirchlechner, B., von Hoyningen-Huene, N., Perzylo, A.: Visually tracking football games based on tv broadcasts. In: Proc. of Intl. Joint Conf. on Artificial Intelligence, IJCAI (2007)
6. Beetz, M., von Hoyningen-Huene, N., Kirchlechner, B., Gedikli, S., Siles, F., Durus, M., Lames, M.: ASPOGAMO: Automated Sports Games Analysis Models. International Journal of Computer Science in Sport 8(1) (2009)
7. Dearden, A., Demiris, Y., Grau, O.: Tracking football player movment from a single moving camera using particle filters. In: European Conf. on Visual Media Production, CVMP 2006 (2006)
8. Doucet, A.: On sequential Monte Carlo methods for Bayesian filtering. Technical report, Dept. End., Univ. Cambridge, UK (1998)
9. Du, W., Hayet, J.-B., Piater, J., Verly, J.: Collaborative multi-camera tracking of athletes in team sports. In: Workshop on Computer Vision Based Analysis in Sport Environments (CVBASE), pp. 2–13 (2006)
10. Du, W., Piater, J.H.: Multi-camera People Tracking by Collaborative Particle Filters and Principal Axis-Based Integration. In: Yagi, Y., Kang, S.B., Kweon, I.S., Zha, H. (eds.) ACCV 2007, Part I. LNCS, vol. 4843, pp. 365–374. Springer, Heidelberg (2007)
11. Figueroa, P.J., Leite, N.J., Barros, R.M.L.: Tracking soccer players aiming their kinematical motion analysis. Computer Vision and Image Understanding 101(2), 122–135 (2006)
12. Gedikli, S., Bandouch, J., von Hoyningen-Huene, N., Kirchlechner, B., Beetz, M.: An Adaptive Vision System for Tracking Soccer Players from Variable Camera Settings. In: Proc. of Intl. Conf. on Computer Vision Systems, ICVS (2007)
13. Horridge, P., Maskell, S.: Real-time tracking of hundreds of targets with efficient exact jpdaf implementation. In: 9th International Conference on Information Fusion, pp. 1–8 (2006)
14. Huang, P., Hilton, A.: Football player tracking for video annotation. In: European Conf. on Visual Media Production (2006)
15. Khan, Z., Balch, T., Dellaert, F.: MCMC data association and sparse factorization updating for real time multitarget tracking with merged and multiple measurements. IEEE Trans. on Pattern Analysis and Machine Intelligence 28(12), 1960–1972 (2006)
16. Li, Y., Dore, A., Orwell, J.: Evaluating the performance of systems for tracking football players and ball. In: IEEE Intl. Conf. on Advanced Video and Signal Based Surveillance (2005)
17. Liu, J., Tong, X., Li, W., Wang, T., Zhang, Y., Wang, H., Yang, B., Sun, L., Yang, S.: Automatic player detection, labeling and tracking in broadcast soccer video. In: British Machine Vision Conference (2007)
18. MacCormick, J., Blake, A.: A probabilistic exclusion principle for tracking multiple objects. In: Proc. of Intl. Conf. on Computer Vision (ICCV), pp. 572–578 (1999)
19. Nillius, P., Sullivan, J., Carlsson, S.: Multi-target tracking - linking identities using bayesian network inference. In: Proc. of Computer Vision and Pattern Recognition, pp. 2187–2194 (2006)
20. Särkkä, S., Vehtari, A., Lampinen, J.: Rao-Blackwellized Monte Carlo data association for multiple target tracking. In: Proc. of Intl. Conf. on Information Fusion, Stockholm, vol. 7 (2004)
21. Särkkä, S., Vehtari, A., Lampinen, J.: Raoblackwellized particle filter for multiple target tracking. Information Fusion Journal 8(1), 2–15 (2007)
22. Sullivan, J., Carlsson, S.: Tracking and labelling of interacting multiple targets. In: Leonardis, A., Bischof, H., Pinz, A. (eds.) ECCV 2006. LNCS, vol. 3953, pp. 619–632. Springer, Heidelberg (2006)
23. Yang, C., Duraiswami, R., Davis, L.: Fast multiple object tracking via a hierarchical particle filter. In: Proc. of Intl. Conf. on Computer Vision, vol. 1, pp. 212–219 (2005)

Photo Repair and 3D Structure from Flatbed Scanners Using 4- and 2-Source Photometric Stereo

Ruggero Pintus[1], Thomas Malzbender[2], Oliver Wang[3], Ruth Bergman[4],
Hila Nachlieli[4], and Gitit Ruckenstein[4]

[1] CRS4 (Center for Advanced Studies, Research and Development in Sardinia)
Parco Scientifico e Tecnologico, POLARIS, Edificio 1, 09010 Pula (CA), Italy
[2] Hewlett-Packard Laboratories, 1501 Page Mill Road, Palo Alto, CA 94304, U.S.A.
[3] University of California, Santa Cruz, 1156 High Street, Santa Cruz, CA 95064, U.S.A.
[4] Hewlett-Packard Laboratories, Technion City, Haifa 32000, Israel
ruggero@crs4.it, tom.malzbender@hp.com,
owang@soe.ucsc.edu,{ruth.bergman,hila.nachlieli}@hp.com

Abstract. We recently introduced a technique that allows 3D information to be captured from a conventional flatbed scanner [22]. The technique requires no hardware modification and allows untrained users to easily capture 3D datasets. Once captured, these datasets can be used for interactive relighting and enhancement of surface detail on physical objects. We have also found that the method can be used to scan and repair damaged photographs. Since only the 3D structure on these photographs will typically be surface tears and creases, our method provides an accurate procedure for automatically detecting these flaws without any user intervention. Once detected, automatic techniques, such as infilling and texture synthesis, can be leveraged to seamlessly repair such damaged areas. We here provide a more thorough exposition and significant new material. We first present a method that is able to repair damaged photographs with minimal user interaction and then show how we can achieve similar results using a fully automatic process.

Keywords: Scanners, 3D reconstruction, Photo repair, Photometric stereo.

1 Introduction

Flatbed scanners are commonly available, low cost, and commercially mature products that allow users to digitize documents and photographs efficiently. Recently, flatbed scanner products that incorporate two separate and independently controlled illumination bulbs have become available [14]. The original intent of such a two bulb design is to improve color fidelity by illuminating the document or photograph with separate chromatic spectra, effectively making a 6 channel measurement of color instead of the conventional 3 channel measurement, improving color fidelity. We demonstrate that such hardware can also be used to estimate geometric information, namely surface normals, by a novel approach to photometric stereo.

These extracted surface normals can be used in several ways. Scanned objects can be relit interactively, effectively conveying a sense of 3D shape. Normal information

A. Ranchordas et al. (Eds.): VISIGRAPP 2009, CCIS 68, pp. 326–342, 2010.

can also be used to automatically repair damaged surfaces of old photographs. We have found that tears and creases in old photographs can be reliably detected since they are associated with surface normals that are not strictly perpendicular to the surface of the scanner plate. Once detected, these imperfect pixels can be replaced by leveraging infilling and texture synthesis methods, effectively repairing the print in an automatic manner. Although products do exist on the market that specialize in recovery of 3D information from physical objects, these are 2-4 orders of magnitude more expensive than commercial flatbed scanners and involve significant mechanical complexity. Our method requires no hardware modification to current products, no additional user interaction, and can scan objects in a very short amount of time.

Many of details of our method were presented in [22]. We here provide a more thorough exposition and also significant new material in terms of theoretical approach and real test cases. Finally, we further clarify all steps in order to facilitate the implementation of the photo repair algorithm.

The rest of the paper is organized as follows. Section 2 provides an overview of related work. Section 3 presents the entire procedure used to estimate the surface gradient from a flatbed scanner with two bulbs. Sections 4 and 5 describe the photograph repair application and the automatic process to remove tears and creases. Two methods are presented, one that works on two pairs of images with an intermediate manual rotation, and another method that achieves fully automatic repair from a single pair of images. Section 6 summarizes other applications and Section 7 provides paper summary and conclusions.

2 Related Work

In this paper we use principles from photometric stereo to recover per-pixel surface normals of a 3D object or photograph. This is only recently possible because of the introduction of flatbed scanners with 2 separately controllable light sources (fig.2). As an alternative approach to gathering 3D structure from flatbed scanners, [23] demonstrates how they can be used to collect stereoscopic images. Although no explicit extraction of depth or 3D information is performed, a good percept of 3D shape can be achieved with this approach. Schubert leverages the fact that in such CCD-based scanners the resulting scanned images perform an orthographic projection in the direction of the carriage movement, y, but a perspective projection in the orthogonal direction, x. By repositioning the object with variation in the x placement, views of the object from multiple perspectives are achieved. Stereograms can be produced to good effect by arranging and viewing these images appropriately.

Although the hardware prototype has significantly more complexity than a flatbed scanner, [11] shows an elegant approach using Lego Mindstorm and linear light sources to collect normal and albedo information, along with higher-order reflectance properties. This approach can not be leveraged on today's flatbed scanners due to the fixed geometric relationship between the light sources and imagers in conventional scanners. A related, unpublished approach was independently developed by [6]. Their acquisition methodology is similar, and also discusses the approach of simultaneously performing registration and photometric stereo. However, applications such as photo repair and reflectance transformation are not pursued. [4] describe an approach for

Fig. 1. Left: Original scan of a damaged photograph. Middle: 3D structure present on the surface of the print extracted by our method. Right: Automatically repaired photograph using 3D structure information and infilling methods.

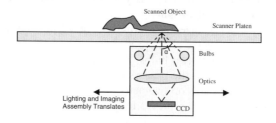

Fig. 2. Typical flatbed scanner – side view. Note the lighting assembly moves with the imager effectively providing two lighting directions across the entire scan.

digitizing geometry, normals and albedo of wall painting fragments using the combination of a 3D scanner and a conventional flatbed scanner. Surface normals are acquired with a flatbed scanner by combining 2D scans. They demonstrate the improved normal fidelity that can be achieved by photometric stereo as opposed to 3D scanning.

Our image repair application is motivated by earlier work on removing dust and scratch from scanned images. [2] describe a range of solutions for dust and scratch removal. For scans of transparent media, i.e. negative or slides, [7] introduced the use of Infra-red (IR) hardware. The IR light is blocked by dust and scattered by scratches, thereby enabling very accurate defect detection. For prints, detection is based upon characteristics of the defects in the digital image, e.g., defects that are light and narrow.

While this approach correctly identifies defects, it is prone to false detection of image features with similar characteristics. We propose a detection method for scanned prints based on 3D surface normals.

3 Normal Capture from Four Images

Given at least 3 images of a surface taken with different lighting directions, it is possible to recover per-pixel estimates of surface normals and albedo using photometric stereo. Flatbed scanners currently capture a single image under static lighting conditions, but they often employ 2 bulbs to illuminate the subject. These two bulbs provide illumination from either side of the scan line being imaged. If we independently control these 2 bulbs, the scanner is capable of taking 2 scans, effectively one with lighting from above, and another with lighting from below. We have experimented with two hardware platforms that allow such scans to be acquired. First, we modified an HP Scanjet 4890 to allow us to manually activate each of the two bulbs separately. Later, when the HP ScanJet G4050 became available with separate control of each bulb supported in software, we switched to this platform.

Both platforms provide 2 images with different lighting. For the first approach we describe, we retrieve another pair of images under new lighting directions by prompting the user to manually rotate the object they are scanning by roughly 90 degrees. At this point, two new scans are taken, again with each bulb activated independently yielding 4 images of the object with 4 different light source direction (fig.3). However, the two sets of images are not registered relative to each other, so we have introduced a difficult registration problem since the images are all taken under varying lighting directions. We have developed a method to robustly solve this registration problem called SIRPH, which stands for SImultaneous Registration and PHotometric stereo.

In section 4.2 we present a method that avoids any approximate manual rotation and works directly with just 2 images.

SIRPH exactly solves for the two translation and one rotation parameters, (x,y,θ), that are introduced by the user rotating the object by roughly 90 degrees. At the same time it solves for the surface orientation (normals) at each pixel. The SIRPH method initializes the rotation and translation parameters, then uses photometric stereo [1] on three of the images to compute surface albedo and normals per pixels. Two of the images used are from one set of scans and a third is taken from the other set and rotated and translated according to the current best guess of the rotation and translation parameters. Photometric stereo gives us and estimation of normals and albedo of the scanned object, which can be used to estimate the 4th image by the Lambertian reflectance model:

$$I' = \rho(N \bullet L) \qquad (1)$$

where ρ is surface albedo, N is normal vector and L is the vector pointing to the light source. The estimated image, I', is then compared to the actual 4th image, I4 giving us a prediction error (fig.3) for parameters (x,y, θ) as follows:

$$E_{prediciton} = \sum_{p \subset P}(I'_p - I^4_p)^2 \qquad (2)$$

where P is the set of all pixels in an image, and Ip corresponds to the pth pixel in image I.

Fortunately, this prediction error is typically well behaved, and iterative nonlinear optimization techniques can be employed to find the well defined minimum. After experimenting with several nonlinear optimization methods, namely Levenberg-Marquart, Gauss-Newton and Simplex, we finally settled on a simple hierarchical approach that was both robust and fast. In our technique, we perform an iterative search starting at a low resolution working up to the original size image. At each resolution level, samples are taken at the current position and at a +/- step size

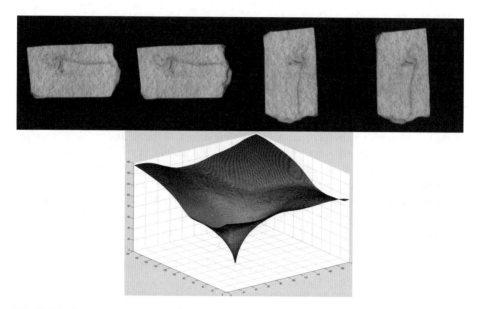

Fig. 3. Up: Images captured by our modified HP Scanjet 4890. Pairs of scans are captured with only one of two bulbs actuated independently. For the second pair, the user has manually rotated the fossil by roughly 90 degrees. This effectively yields 4 lighting directions. Low: Prediction error for the fossil shown in Fig. 2 using the SIRPH algorithm. X: rotation, Y: translation in y, Z: error.

increment in each of the 3 dimensions of our search space. The lowest error of these 8 + 1 sample points is chosen as the base for the next iteration. If the same base point is chosen, the step size is halved and further iterations are taken. Once the step size is below a threshold, convergence is achieved and we start the search at the next resolution level with the current convergence state. At each level, this technique is commonly known as compass-search.

Because compass-search can get stuck in local minima, a good starting point is key to convergence. We therefore perform the entire search multiple times at the lowest resolution, each "seeded" with a different starting point. Because the optimization occurs very quickly at low resolution, we are able to use many different starting points that cover a large area of the sample space. We then take the best match from all these to start the search at the next level. After we converge on the original resolution image, we will have robustly recovered the required translation and rotation parameters to register the 2 pairs of images, as well as a surface normal per pixel. We tested this method on a variety of objects and notice that it is capable of achieving correct convergence in almost all cases, including very difficult ones such as circular objects with low amounts of texture.

4 Photograph Repair Application

We have outlined our procedure for extracting 3D normals and albedo from objects using a flatbed scanner. We now present several applications of this method, the most significant being the automatic detection and repair of creases and tears in scanned photographs. Almost everyone has a one of a kind photo of their child, parent or grandparent that has been battered over the years. Old photographs often have tears, creases, stains, scratches and dust. Fortunately, the technology to restore such images exists today through a variety of digital imaging tools. Your local photo-finishing lab can do it for a fee. It can also be done in the home using a scanner, printer and photo editor such as Adobe Photoshop. This path to photo restoration is fairly tedious and requires some expertise in the use of the photo editor.

Although a reliable capability exists already to detect and repair defects in transparencies such as dust and scratches (using IR illumination), no such robust counterpart exists for the detection and repair of damaged prints. Infilling techniques from the transparency domain can be leveraged for the repair process, but the robust detection of damaged regions of a print is lacking. Our method provides such a capability, since the damage one that is looking for is associated with 3D perturbations. Fig.1 shows one example of this capability that we have prototyped with a HP 4890 scanner. The next two sections describe the procedures used for this application. We first present the 4 image procedure, which has the drawback that it requires the user to rotate the photograph. In section 4.2 we introduce a 2 image process that performs the same task, but without any user intervention.

4.1 Defect Maps from Normals

The 3D normals give a general indication of the location of the defects in the scans. In principle, high normal perturbations from the z axis (defined to be pointing up from the photograph) indicate a defect, and low normal perturbations indicate undamaged portions of the print. However, simply taking a threshold of such perturbations produces a defect map with insufficient accuracy.

Such a defect map might miss portions of the defect, e.g., very fine portions of a crease, and it is likely to have some false detections, e.g., the red pixels near the boy's left sleeve in Fig.4 (left). To overcome these issues, we use a two step approach. We first expand the set of candidate pixels, along features such as creases, then apply a refinement stage on the expanded mask to select a subset of these pixels that will need repair. The expansion phase thresholds the 3D normal information at two levels. Pixels with very high normal perturbations are marked as defective. Pixels with less high normal perturbations are marked as candidates. A voting algorithm, closely related to [19], extends the defects. Connected components of the marked pixels are computed. Each component exerts a field of influence based on its shape and size. For example, a crease extends a field in the direction of the crease. The fields of influence from all the components are added for an overall vote at each pixel. Defective pixels are marked pixels with high votes and unmarked, connected pixels with very high votes.

The purpose of the refinement step is to select a subset of pixels identified in the expansion phase as the final selection that will require repair. The refinement step uses a grayscale representation of the image and creates a smoothed reference image that does not contain the defects by applying a median filter. Defective pixels can either be too light or too dark. In both cases the difference between the grayscale representation and the reference image is significant for defective pixels. Thresholding the difference image is prone to detection of some small, bright image features, hence we label pixels as defective only if they are both in the expanded set of candidate pixels and yield a big difference between the grayscale and reference images. We further refine the defect map by detecting the contour of the defect using classification. Looking at a neighborhood near a defect we have gray-level data and a label for each pixel of clean, defect-light or defect-dark. We label several pixels around the contour of the defect as unknown and classify them using Quadratic Discriminant Analysis [13]. Without contour classification, a trace of the tear would remain after repair.

Fig. 4. Constructing defect maps using the 4-image procedure. Left: Expansion labeling computed from the normals. Right: Refinement detection map for light defects.

This refinement step is repeated once for light defects and again for dark defects. From a normal viewing distance the white areas are the most striking defect. A closer look usually reveals dark shadows adjacent to the white tear. Indeed, if we only repair the white defects, we are left with an apparent crease in the image due to the shadowed pixels. We obtained the best results by detecting and repairing (infilling) light defects and then detecting and repairing dark defects.

4.2 Normal Component From Two Images

The 4-image procedure has the drawback that the user must rotate the photograph to compute normals (or both surface derivatives along x and y). It is well known that photometric stereo requires at least three images for a complete gradient computation [1]. We have developed a method to use two images to estimate one component of the derivative (in our case the derivative along y, i.e. along image columns). In this way, we avoid needing the user to rotate the sample manually. However, we encounter two limitations. First, we have less information to detect defects, and second, the algorithm can't recover tears and creases that are precisely aligned with the image columns. We can address the first issue with a more complex procedure.To avoid perfectly vertical defects, we recommend that the user reorient the photo in the scanner.

An unmodified, commercial HP ScanJet G4050 scanner, which we used for these experiments, introduces the further complication that the chromatic spectra of each bulb is intentionally designed to be different. As mentioned, this was done to improve color fidelity effectively making a 6 channel measurement of color. This chromatic difference is problematic for photometric stereo. We overcome this issue by recovering 2 separate 3x1 color transform matrices that map each image into a similar one dimensional 'intensity' space, in which we perform photometric stereo computations.

Fig. 5. From left to right: one of the scanned images, absolute difference of the two scanned images after color calibration in which we can clearly see the misalignment, absolute difference after the alignment step based on the gradient minimization. We have scaled the intensity in the middle and right images by the same constant value in order to make the images more visible.

These color transform matrices have been derived by scanning a Macbeth color chart exposed with each bulb independently, and then minimizing the difference in transformed response.

A second problem with flatbed scanners is that the mechanical repeatability of the scan mechanism is not perfect, causing slight vertical misalignment between the pair of scans. To correct this we upsample each scanned image in the vertical direction, and then we find the misalignment by minimizing the integral of the surface gradient in y direction.

In fig.5 we show one acquired image and, if we perform a simple per pixel difference of the two acquired images and take its absolute value, we realize that there is an evident vertical misalignment along the columns; we can see some white lines at the edges of machbeth colorchart squares. If we try to translate one image with respect to the other we discover that this misalignment is a sub-pixel displacement, so overcoming this issue is not so trivial. In order to understand our simple alignment approach we need first to define an image formation model that interprets the physical and optical behavior of the scanner.

We approximate the lighting geometry with lighting direction vectors

$$\begin{cases} l_1 = [\sin \alpha_1 \cos \beta_1 & \sin \alpha_1 \sin \beta_1 & \cos \alpha_1] \\ l_2 = [\sin \alpha_2 \cos \beta_2 & \sin \alpha_2 \sin \beta_2 & \cos \alpha_2] \end{cases} \tag{3}$$

with

$$\alpha_1 = \alpha_2 = \alpha = \frac{\pi}{6}, \beta_1 = +\frac{\pi}{2}, \beta_2 = -\frac{\pi}{2} \tag{4}$$

Using the Lambertian reflectance map [15] we obtain

$$I_1 = R_1(p,q) = L_0 \rho \frac{-q \sin \alpha + \cos \alpha}{\sqrt{1+p^2+q^2}}, I_2 = R_2 = L_0 \rho \frac{q \sin \alpha + \cos \alpha}{\sqrt{1+p^2+q^2}} \tag{5}$$

where I1 and I2 are the images, p and q are surface derivative along x and y respectively, L0 is the light source magnitude and ρ is the surface albedo. Solving for q, we obtain:

$$q(x,y) = \frac{1}{\tan \alpha} \frac{I_2(x,y) - I_1(x,y)}{I_2(x,y) + I_1(x,y)} \tag{6}$$

Fig. 6. From left to right: Scanned image, repaired image, absolute value of the y derivative before the alignment step, after alignment

In this way, we can recover the surface derivative value in one direction. Note that although this derivative along y is exactly recovered, the estimation of the other component of the surface gradient with just a pair of images is not possible without making some assumption on p, such as convexity or smoothness assumptions.

To solve for the misalignment, we assume, for now, that most of our scanned photograph is flat (q=0). We find the best alignment minimizing the function

$$\sum_{i=1}^{N}\sum_{j=1}^{M}\left|q_{i,j}^{us}\right| = \sum_{i=1}^{N}\sum_{j=1}^{M}\frac{1}{\tan\alpha}\left|\frac{I_{2\ i+\Delta i,j+\Delta j}^{us} - I_{1\ i,j}^{us}}{I_{2\ i+\Delta i,j+\Delta j}^{us} + I_{1\ i,j}^{us}}\right| \tag{7}$$

where $I_{1,2}^{us}$ and q^{us} are the gray level upsampled images and scanned surface derivative along y, $(\Delta i,\Delta j)$ is the misalignment and N and M are respectively the number of rows and columns. We used upsampled images to compute subpixel misalignments. After correcting the misalignment, we downsample images to their original resolution.

Fig.5 shows the result of alignment algorithm on the machbeth chart images, while fig.6 shows its application in a real photo repairing case. We have the derivative along y before and after the alignment step. We can see, in Fig. 6, that there are some image edges that should not be in an albedo independent signal (such as the surface gradient), while such image content dramatically decreases after the images are aligned as shown in Fig. 6, furthest right.

This kind of alignment algorithm proves to be very robust, but is computationally expensive. If we need to speed up the algorithm the best solution is to adopt a fourier based approach. For this reason we have implemented a method based on the Fourier Shift Theorem [3] that is suited for the registration of translated images (i.e. our case). After computing the fourier transform of the two input images, we compute the cross-power spectrum

$$\frac{F(I_1)F(I_2)^*}{\left|F(I_1)F(I_2)^*\right|} = e^{2\pi i(ux_0+vy_0)} \tag{8}$$

and measure the peak of its inverse. The displacement between this peak and the image center is the offset between the images. Our spatial alignment method that minimizes the gradient is more robust, but this fourier method is faster and is well

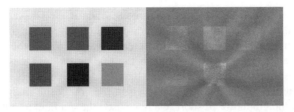

Fig. 7. Top: Scanned image; Bottom: Recovered radient component along y

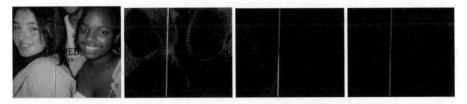

Fig. 8. From left to right: scanned image, gradient component absolute value along x, absolute value of the difference between the two acquired images, mask is $\hat{m}(x, y)$ the input of the defect trimap generation step.

suited to align images with different lighting conditions, as those ones scanned with our device.

After the color transformation and alignment operations, these two source images can be used as input to compute a defect map that will indicate where tears and creases on the surface of the photograph are present. Unfortunately, the q image recovered at this point suffers from numerical noise in regions where the colors are dark (fall near the origin if the RGB color cube). Fig. 7 shows two kind of signals: 1) the numerical noise that makes the darkest square be noisier than the others, while the brightest gray one on the bottom right is practically invisible; 2) the shading due to the real shape of the paper. Recall that our goal (regarding the repairing task) is to differentiate pixels associated with tears and creases from flat regions of the photograph, not necessarily to recover exact estimates of the gradient component. To this end, we have found it useful to combine the gradient and color difference information to define a composite image

$$\hat{m}(x, y) = \frac{m(x, y)}{\max[m(x, y)]} \tag{9}$$

which is the normalized version of the product of the color differences multiplied by the estimated vertical derivative:

$$m(x, y) = |I_2(x, y) - I_1(x, y)| \cdot |q(x, y)| \tag{10}$$

The gray level difference image has a value near zero where q is near zero and doesn't contain numerical errors due to the albedo. This feature is useful to eliminate the numerical errors in q, even if it adds some albedo dependent signal in regions containing defects. Note that we could still have a problem if a defect pixel has dark albedo. In practice we find that for these pixels, even if the (I_1, I_2) vector has a low magnitude, the difference of its components is big enough to distinguish the defect. In Fig.8 we can compare the gradient and difference images. While the noise in the gradient image is evident (we can distinguish the outline of the faces), the difference image has almost no numerical noise. Note that the defective pixels are also less visible in the difference image, but are enhanced in the composite image, m, due to the strong signal in the gradient. In short, we have used the gradient to enhance the signal in defect regions and use the difference image to avoid noise in the flat zones. Note that in figure 8 we display the scanned images rotated 90 degrees for clarity, effectively placing the light sources to the left and right in the figure.

Fig.8 shows the mask is $\hat{m}(x, y)$ the computed from the source images. This obtained mask has gray level values that must be thresholded in some way to decide how high the value must be to identify a defect pixel. A single threshold across all photos fails to be adequately robust. To this end, we define a function $\tilde{m}$:

$$\tilde{m}(x, y, \gamma) = \begin{cases} 0 \rightarrow \hat{m}(x, y) < \gamma \\ 1 \rightarrow \hat{m}(x, y) \geq \gamma \end{cases} \tag{11}$$

This function is simply a binary image, with γ as threshold. The percentage of the image lying above this threshold is simply

$$A(\gamma) = \frac{1}{NM} \int\int \tilde{m}(x, y, \gamma) dx dy \tag{12}$$

where N and M are respectively rows and columns number.

We compute a trimap by classifying each pixel as being either 'defect', 'uncertain' or 'non-defect'. We choose the 2 thresholds for this classification by finding the knee in the relationship between A and γ. Specifically, we set two thresholds on the angle the curve makes, namely $-\pi/8$ and $-3\pi/8$ which are 25% and 75% respectively of the angular range. A concrete example may clarify this approach. Fig.9 shows the function $A(\gamma)$ for the sample in fig.8. This is a display of the image area as a function of threshold γ. Choosing the angle thresholds above corresponds to γ thresholds of 0.005 and 0.0094 for constructing the tri-map. Fig.9 shows also the trimap in which red pixels are defect, bright grey pixels are non-defect and black pixels are the unknown ones. In this example the defects are fairly easy to detect yielding a small number of unknown pixels.

Once such a trimap is constructed we need to classify the unknown pixels. For this we use Quadratic Discriminant Analysis (QDA) [13]. As features we use the q and difference images as well as the following image:

$$f(x, y) = \frac{\left| \rho(x, y) - \dfrac{E_1(x, y)}{\cos \alpha} \right| + \left| \rho(x, y) - \dfrac{E_2(x, y)}{\cos \alpha} \right|}{2} \tag{13}$$

This equation is derived from eq. 5 by setting L_0 to 1 and $p(x,y)=0$. After normalizing, $f(x,y)$ has low values in the non-defect pixels and high values (albedo dependent) in the defect pixels. Note that we have computed the albedo using classical

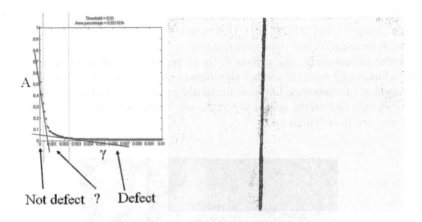

Fig. 9. Left: The function $A(\gamma)$ for Fig. 8. Right: The trimap for Fig. 8: red pixels are defect, light grey are non-defect and black are unknown (appear sparse and small in this case).

Fig. 10. Subtle, low frequency creases are avoided in the albedo image. Left: Scanned image. Middle: Recovered albedo. Right: repaired image.

photometric stereo methods and assuming $p=0$. Although in practice the unknown p does not always equal zero, especially for defective pixels, this assumption still yields the function, $f(x,y)$, which is useful in distinguishing defect from non-defect pixels.

We apply QDA, trained on the known defect and non-defect pixels, and applied to the unknown pixels, for each photograph independently. This yields a labeling of all pixels as being either defective or not, which along with the albedo image, is processed by the refinement step, as described in 4.1. We use the albedo instead of one of the original images because some low frequency creases are removed by simply computing the albedo, even when they are present in the source images, as shown in Fig.10. We also apply the infilling procedure to the albedo image, not one of the original source images, since the albedo image is not prone to darkening introduced by the interaction of the non-perpendicular lights and subtle low frequency curvature on the surface of the photograph. Fig.11 shows the automatically detected defect map, which is the input for the refinement step and the repaired image after the infilling algorithm.

Methods do exist in the literature that attempt to compute all gradient information from two images [20] [25] [26] [21]. Unfortunately, after prototyping several of these, we find them insufficiently robust in practice.

In order to summarize our approach, fig.12 presents a scheme of the entire algorithm, while fig.13 presents another significant real test case. This photo has a lot of different kind of structures, like low frequency creases, big and very thin tears, and defects in dark and bright zones. We show one of the original damaged photo, the defect map and the repaired one.

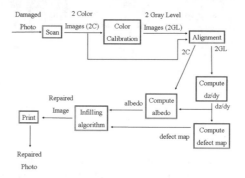

Fig. 11. Left: Defect map before refinement step. Right: Repaired image after infilling algorithm.

Fig. 12. The workflow of the photo repair algorithm

Fig. 13. From left to right: scanned photo, defect map, repaired Image

5 Infilling Algorithms

The input to the infilling algorithm is a digital image in which every pixel is classified as either defective or non-defective. The non-defective pixels can be further classified as candidates or non-candidates for replication. A data structure is provided in which defective pixels are arranged in connected components.

Our algorithm essentially replaces every defective pixel by a value computed from selected candidate pixels. A candidate pixel may be any non-defective pixel of the image. The selection is based on (1) the spatial distance between the defect location and the candidate location and (2) the similarity of pixel values in the local neighborhoods of the two pixels. Two parameters govern the selection: the width W of a square region around the defect in which candidates are examined and the width w of a square local neighborhood surrounding and including a pixel. Typically, the region width W is much greater than the neighborhood width w. For example, we used a region of 200×200 pixels and neighborhoods of 7×7, 9×9, and 11×11 pixels.

As a pre-processing step, we compute texture descriptors of all the local neighborhoods of candidate pixels in the image. In our implementation, we used mean and standard deviation of values in a surrounding w×w neighborhood as texture descriptors. The computations are done once for every candidate pixel and do not depend on any defective context. Pixel reconstruction is done for groups of connected components sequentially. The recommended order of pixel reconstruction within a single connected component is from the outside in. This order of computation creates fewer image artifacts. To reconstruct a defective pixel, we examine its surrounding w×w neighborhood while ignoring defective pixels in that neighborhood. The texture measures of the local neighborhood are computed, namely the mean and standard deviation of the non-defective pixel values. We then find 10% of the candidates in the W×W region around the defect whose texture measures best match the texture measures of the target neighborhood. To accelerate the search for the best 10% of all candidates, we use an efficient data structure where all the candidates in a region are sorted by both the mean and the standard deviation of their surrounding w×w neighborhoods.

For each of the 10% of selected candidate pixels, we further compare its w×w neighborhood relative to the defective pixel and its neighborhood. Neighborhoods are compared by the sum of squared differences (SSD) of respective values. Two approaches were used to compute the output pixel value, resulting in two different algorithms. The first approach, which is based on [8], takes the best pixel, i.e. lowest SSD. The second approach computes a weighted average of all the candidates, where the weighting is based on the SSD measure as follows. Let $Q = q_1, q_2, \ldots, q_{w \cdot w}$ be the two dimensional neighborhood surrounding the pixel to repair and let C be the set of candidate neighborhoods. For a neighborhood P in C, we use the notation $P = p_1, p_2 \ldots, p_{w \cdot w}$ and denote its central pixel by p. Let $G = g_1, g_2 \ldots, g_{w \cdot w}$ be a Gaussian spatial filter, and let h be a real value weight filter. For a defective pixel i in the neighborhood P, the corresponding value of the Gaussian filter g_i is set to 0. The new value for the pixel is

$$\bar{q} = \frac{\sum_{p \in C} \exp\left(\dfrac{-\sum_{i=0}^{w \cdot w} g_i \cdot (p_i - q_i)^2}{h^2}\right) \cdot p}{\sum_{p \in C} \exp\left(\dfrac{-\sum_{i=0}^{w \cdot w} g_i \cdot (p_i - q_i)^2}{h^2}\right)} \tag{14}$$

This method is adapted from the NL-Means denoising algorithm [5]. By applying SSD comparisons to only 10% of the candidate neighborhoods instead of all the neighborhoods in the surrounding region, we attain approximately a factor of ten speed up, and no visible degradation in image quality. This speed up makes these algorithms applicable in practical infilling tasks, as those described in subsequent sections.

Fig. 14. UL: scanned image. UR: albedo. LL: automatically computed defect map before refinement. LR: repaired image using infilling algorithms.

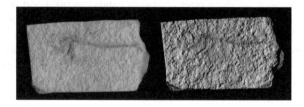

Fig. 15. Left: The first of the four scans shown in Fig. 3. Right: Interactively relit to enhance surface detail.

Note that the accelerated infilling algorithms are still slower than simple local operations such as median filtering or averaging. These local algorithms however tend to blur image details, so they are not acceptable for a photo repair application. Fig.14 shows the entire automatic procedure (using two images, the automatic defect detection, the refinement procedure and the infilling algorithm.

6   Additional Applications

In addition to allowing the repair of old photographs, the combination of color and normal or reflectance data taken from physical objects can be applied in other ways. Transforming reflectance data based on normal information to enhance surface perception of detail has already been demonstrated [18], [24], [10]. A further example on data captured by our flatbed scanner is shown in fig. 15. Combing multiple images taken under multiple lighting in a spatially varying manner can also yield enhanced visualizations [9]. Data captured from our scanners can also be used for these methods. Lastly, normal information from photometric stereo can of course be integrated to recover a 3D model of surface structure [15]. This geometry will typically suffer from a number of artifacts, such as low-frequency warping from the integration of inaccuracies and mishandling of discontinuities in the object geometry.

7 Conclusions

We have presented a technique to recover the 3D normal structure of an object using a conventional flatbed scanner. This allows relighting, and limited geometry capture. We have also demonstrated an application to the automatic repair of damaged photographs exhibiting creases or tears. Although we prototyped this functionality on a particular HP scanner, the approach is applicable to any flatbed scanner that uses 2 bulbs to illuminate the platen, which is the common case.

Outstanding challenges still remain. First, the depth of geometry we can handle is limited by the optics of the scanner. For the unmodified scanners we used in our work, we measured this to be approximately 1 cm. Second, a geometric warp must be applied to the raw scanner data to rectify the images before registration. This must be done to sub-pixel accuracy to obtain reliable normal estimates. Also, a limitation of the 2 image approach we have taken (but not our 4 image approach) is our inability to detect perfectly aligned defects. This can however be accommodated in most cases by the user simply avoiding such defects with a rotation of the photograph to re-align it.

We have investigated techniques in the literature that attempt to recover both surface derivatives components, (p,q), from a single pair of images, but have found them insufficiently robust. In future work, we would like to develop such a robust method.

Acknowledgments. Justin Tehrani with Hewlett-Packard's Imaging and Printing Group in Ft. Collins, Colorado was instrumental in initiating the investigation into the feasibility of recovering shape information from multiple lighting. Greg Taylor, also with Hewlett-Packard's Imaging and Printing Group, modified a Scanjet 4890 to allow us to control the bulbs independently. Dan Gelb at Hewlett-Packard Laboratories, Palo Alto collaborated on developing the relighting methods that led to this work.

References

1. Barsky, S., Petrou, M.: The 4-Source Photometric Stereo Technique for Three-Dimensional Surfaces in the Presence of Highlights and Shadows. IEEE Transaction on Pattern Analysis and Machine Intelligence 25(10), 1239–1252 (2003)
2. Bergman, R., Maurer, R., Nachlieli, H., Ruckenstein, G., Chase, P., Greig, D.: Comprehensive Solutions for Automatic Removal of Dust and Scratches from Images. Journal of Electronic Imaging (2007)
3. Bracewell, R.N.: The Fourier Transform and Its Applications. McGraw-Hill, New York (1965)
4. Brown, B., Toler-Franklin, C., Nehad, D., Burns, M., Dobkin, D., Vlachopoulos, A., Doumas, C., Rusinkiewicz, S., Weyrich, T.: A System for High-Volume Acquisition and Matching of Fresco Fragments: Reassembling Theran Wall Paintings. ACM Transactions on Graphics 27(3), 83 (2008)
5. Buades, A., Coll, B., Morel, J.: A Review of Image Denoising Algorithms, With a New One. Multiscale Modeling and Simulation (SIAM Interdisciplinary Journal) 4(2), 490–530 (2005)

6. Chantler, M., Spense, A.: Apparatus and Method for Obtaining Surface Texture Information, Patent GB 0424417.4 (2004)
7. DIGITAL ICE™, Eastman Kodak Company,
   http://asf.com/products/ice/FilmICEOverview/
8. Efros, A., Leung, T.: Texture Synthesis by Non-parametric Sampling. In: Proceedings of IEEE Internation Conference on Computer Vision (September 1999)
9. Fattal, R., Agrawala, M., Rusinkiewicz, S.: Multiscale Shape and Detail Enhancement from Multiple-light Image Collections. ACM Transactions on Graphics 26(3) (2007)
10. Freeth, T., Bitsakis, Y., Moussas, X., Seiradakis, J., Tselikas, A., Mangou, H., Zafeiropoulou, M., Hadland, R., Bate, D., Ramsey, A., Allen, M., Crawley, A., Hockley, P., Malzbender, T., Gelb, D., Ambrisco, W., Edmunds, M.: Decoding the Ancient Greek Astronomical Calculator known as the Antikythera Mechanism. Nature 444, 587–591 (2006)
11. Gardner, A., Tchou, C., Hawkins, T., Debevec, P.: Linear Light Source Reflectometry. ACM Transactions on Graphics 22(3), 749–758 (2003)
12. Hammer, O., Bengston, S., Malzbender, T., Gelb, D.: Imaging Fossils Using Reflectance Transformation and Interactive Manipulation of Virtual Light Sources. Palaeontologia Electronica, August 23 (2002)
13. Hastie, T., Tibshirani, R., Friedman, J.: The Elements of Statistical Learning - Data Mining, Inference, and Prediction. Springer, Heidelberg (2001)
14. Hewlett-Packard G4050 Photo Scanner (2007), http://www.hp.com
15. Horn, P.: Robot Vision. MIT Press, Cambridge (1986)
16. Klette, R., Schluns, K., Koschan, A.: Computer Vision: Three-Dimensional Data from Images. Springer, Heidelberg (1998)
17. Kschischang, F.R., Frey, B.J., Loeliger, H.A.: Factor Graphs and the Sum-Product Algorithm. IEEE Transaction on Information Theory 47(2) (2001)
18. Malzbender, T., Gelb, D., Wolters, H.: Polynomial Texture Maps. In: Fiume, E. (ed.) Proceedings of ACM Siggraph 2001. Computer Graphics Proceedings, Annual Conference Series, pp. 519–528. ACM Press / ACM SIGGRAPH, New York (2001)
19. Medioni, G., Lee, M., Tang, C.: A Computational Framework for Segmentation and Grouping. Elsevier, Amsterdam (2000)
20. Onn, R., Bruckstein, A.: Integrability Disambiguates Surface Recovery in Two-Image Photometric Stereo. International Journal of Computer Vision 5, 105–113 (1990)
21. Petrovic, N., Cohen, I., Frey, B.J., Koetter, R., Huang, T.S.: Enforcing Integrability for Surface Reconstruction Algorithms Using Belief Propagation in Graphical Models. In: 2001 IEEE Conf. on Computer Vision and Pattern Recognition (CVPR), vol. 1, pp. 743–748 (2001)
22. Pintus, R., Malzbender, T., Wang, O., Bergman, R., Nachlieli, H., Ruckenstein, G.: Photo Repair and 3D Structure from Flatbed Scanners. In: VISAPP International Conference on Computer Vision Theory and Applications (February 2009)
23. Schubert, R.: Using a Flatbed Scanner as a Stereoscopic Near-Field Camera. IEEE Computer Graphics and Applications, 38–45 (2000)
24. Toler-Franklin, C., Finkelstein, A., Rusinkiewics, S.: Illustration of Complex Real-World Objects using Images with Normals. In: International Symposium on Non-Photorealistic Animation and Rendering, NPAR (2007)
25. Tu, P., Mendonca, P.R.S.: Surface Reconstruction via Helmholtz Reciprocity with a Single Image Pair. In: Proc. of 2003 IEEE Computer Society Conference on computer Vision and Pattern Recognition (CVPR 2003), pp. 541–547 (2003)
26. Yang, J., Ohnishi, N., Sugie, N.: Two Image Photometric Stero Method. In: Proc. SPIE, Intelligent Robots and Computer Vision XI, vol. 1826, pp. 452–463 (2003)

Markerless Human Motion Capture Using Hierarchical Particle Swarm Optimisation

Vijay John, Spela Ivekovic, and Emanuele Trucco

School of Computing, University of Dundee, Dundee, U.K.
{vijayjohn,spelaivekovic,manueltrucco}@computing.dundee.ac.uk

Abstract. In this paper, we address full-body articulated human motion tracking from multi-view video sequences acquired in a studio environment. The tracking is formulated as a multi-dimensional nonlinear optimisation and solved using particle swarm optimisation (PSO), a swarm-intelligence algorithm which has gained popularity in recent years due to its ability to solve difficult nonlinear optimisation problems. Our tracking approach is designed to address the limits of particle filtering approaches: it initialises automatically, removes the need for a sequence-specific motion model and recovers from temporary tracking divergence through the use of a powerful hierarchical search algorithm (HPSO). We quantitatively compare the performance of HPSO with that of the particle filter (PF), annealed particle filter (APF) and partitioned sampling annealed particle filter (PSAPF). Our test results, obtained using the framework proposed by Balan et al [1] to compare articulated body tracking algorithms, show that HPSO's pose estimation accuracy and consistency is better than PF, APF and PSAPF.

1 Introduction

Tracking articulated human motion from video sequences is an important problem in computer vision with applications in virtual character animation, medical posture analysis, surveillance, human-computer interaction and others. In this paper, we formulate the full-body articulated tracking as a nonlinear optimisation problem which we solve using particle swarm optimization (PSO), a recent swarm intelligence algorithm with growing popularity [3,2].

Because the full-body articulated pose estimation is a high-dimensional optimisation problem, we formulate it as a hierarchical PSO algorithm (HPSO) which exploits the inherent hierarchy of the human-body kinematic model, thus reducing the computational complexity of the search.

HPSO is designed to address the limits of the particle filtering approaches. Firstly, it removes the need for a sequence-specific motion model: the same algorithm with unmodified parameter settings is able to track different motions without any prior knowledge of the motion's nature. Secondly, it addresses the problem of divergence, whereby the filter loses track after a wrongly estimated pose and is unable to recover unless interactively corrected by the user or assisted by additional, higher-level motion models [4]. In contrast, our tracking approach is able to automatically recover from an incorrect pose estimate and continue tracking. Last but not least, in line with its ability to recover

A. Ranchordas et al. (Eds.): VISIGRAPP 2009, CCIS 68, pp. 343–356, 2010.

from an incorrect pose estimate, our HPSO tracker also initialises automatically on the first frame of the sequence, requiring no manual intervention.

This paper is organised as follows. We describe the related work in Section 2. Section 3 presents the PSO algorithm. In Section 4 we describe the body model and cost function used in our tracking approach and in Section 5 present the HPSO algorithm. We show the experimental results including a comparison of our algorithm with the particle filter (PF), the annealed particle filter (APF) and partitioned sampling annealed particle filter (PSAPF) in Section 6. Section 7 contains conclusions and ideas for future work.

2   Related Work

The approaches to articulated motion analysis can generally be divided into *generative* and *discriminative* methods. The generative methods use the *analysis-by-synthesis* approach, where the candidate pose is represented by an explicit body model and the appropriate likelihood function is evaluated to determine its fitness. The discriminative methods, on the other hand, represent the articulated pose implicitly by learning the mapping between the pose space and a set of image features. Combinations of both approaches have also been reported.

Our method fits under the umbrella of generative analysis-by-synthesis and we review the related work accordingly. We do not attempt to provide an exhaustive list of related research and instead refer the reader to one of the many recent surveys on this topic [13].

Particle filtering approaches, with their ability to use non-linear motion models and explore the search space with a number of different hypotheses, have become very popular for the estimation of articulated pose. An early attempt was the Condensation algorithm [20], which in its original form quickly became computationally unfeasible when applied to high-dimensional problem of articulated tracking [19].

Efforts to reduce the computational complexity and the required number of particles resulted in various extensions, some focusing on ways of partitioning the search space according to the limb hierarchy or modifying the sampling process [9,21] and others advocating trained prior models [6,4]. Partitioning the search space to reduce the computational complexity of the search is formulated as a hierarchical search problem, where the poses of the body parts are estimated sequentially with each estimate constraining the possible configurations of subsequent limbs in the chain [21].

In our work, we also formulate the pose estimation as a hierarchical search problem, however, instead of using a particle filter to estimate the pose, we employ a powerful swarm intelligence global search algorithm, called particle swarm optimisation (PSO) [12]. Similarly to the annealed particle filter (APF) and its genetic crossover extension [19], the idea is to allow the particles to explore the search space for a number of iterations per frame. The advantage of our method lies in the way the particles communicate with each other to find the optimum. Our method does not use any motion priors and we are able to demonstrate experimentally that our approach outperforms the APF with crossover operator by [19].

PSO is a swarm intelligence search technique which has been growing in popularity and has in the past 13 years been used to solve various non-linear optimisation problems in a number of areas, including computer vision [3]. A recent publication by [15] demonstrated an application of a variant of PSO, called sequential PSO, to box tracking in video sequences. Application of PSO to articulated tracking from stereo data have also been reported [16,18].

The work presented in this paper is an extension of our previous work [17,8], where a PSO-based hierarchical framework is used to estimate the articulated upper-body pose with multi-view still images. In this work, we extend the existing approach to tracking the full-body pose in multi-view video sequences.

3   Particle Swarm Optimisation

PSO is a swarm intelligence technique introduced by [12]. The idea originated from the simulation of a simplified social model, where the agents were thought of as collision-proof birds and the original intent was to graphically simulate the unpredictable chore-ography of a bird flock in their search for food. The original PSO algorithm was later modified by several researchers to improve its search capabilities and convergence prop-erties. In this paper we use the PSO algorithm with inertia introduced by [11].

3.1   PSO with Inertia

Assume an n-dimensional search space $\mathbb{S} \subseteq \mathbb{R}^n$ defined by a pair of constraint vectors $\mathbf{a}, \mathbf{b} \in \mathbb{R}^n$, a swarm consisting of N particles, each particle representing a candidate so-lution to the search problem and a cost function $f : \mathbb{S} \to \mathbb{R}$ defined on the search space. The i-th particle is represented as an n-dimensional vector $\mathbf{x}^i = (x_1, x_2, ..., x_n)^T \in \mathbb{S}$ subject to $\mathbf{a} \leq \mathbf{x}^i \leq \mathbf{b}$. The velocity of this particle is also an n-dimensional vector $\mathbf{v}^i = (v_1, v_2, ..., v_n)^T \in \mathbb{S}$. The best position encountered by the i-th particle so far (*personal* best) is denoted by $\mathbf{p}^i = (p_1, p_2, ..., p_n)^T \in \mathbb{S}$ and the value of the cost function at that position $pbest^i = f(\mathbf{p}^i)$. The index of the particle with the overall best position so far (*global* best) is denoted by g and $gbest = f(\mathbf{p}^g)$. The PSO algorithm can then be stated as follows:

1. **Initialisation**:
   - Initialise a population of particles $\{\mathbf{x}^i\}, i = 1 \ldots N$, with positions randomly within $\mathbb{S}$ and velocities randomly within $[-1, 1]$. For each particle evaluate the desired cost function f and set $pbest^i = f(\mathbf{x}^i)$. Identify the best particle in the swarm and store its index as g and its position as $\mathbf{p}^g$.
2. **Repeat** until the stopping criterion is fulfilled:
   - Move the swarm by updating the position of every particle $\mathbf{x}^i$, $i = 1 \ldots N$, according to the following two equations:

$$\mathbf{v}_{t+1}^i = \omega \mathbf{v}_t^i + \varphi_1(\mathbf{p}_t^i - \mathbf{x}_t^i) + \varphi_2(\mathbf{p}_t^g - \mathbf{x}_t^i)$$
$$\mathbf{x}_{t+1}^i = \mathbf{x}_t^i + \mathbf{v}_{t+1}^i \tag{1}$$

where subscript t denotes the time step (iteration).

- Ensure that $\mathbf{a} \le \mathbf{x}^i \le \mathbf{b}$. Search constraints are easily enforced through particle velocities. If the particle violates the search space boundary in some dimension, its position in that dimension is set to the boundary value and the corresponding velocity entry reversed.
- For $i = 1 \ldots N$ update $\mathbf{p}^i$, $pbest^i$, $\mathbf{p}^g$ and $gbest$.

The stopping criterion is usually either a maximum number of iterations or a threshold on $gbest$ improvement. The parameters $\varphi_1 = c_1 rand_1()$ and $\varphi_2 = c_2 rand_2()$, where c is a constant and $rand()$ is a random number drawn from $[0, 1]$, influence the *social* and *cognition* components of the swarm behaviour, respectively. In line with [12], we set $c_1 = c_2 = 2$, which gives the stochastic factor a mean of 1.0 and causes the particles to "overfly" the target about half of the time, while also giving equal importance to both social and cognition components. Parameter ω is the inertia weight which we describe in more detail next.

3.2   The Inertia Weight

The inertia weight ω plays an important role in directing the exploratory behaviour of the particles: higher inertia values push the particles to explore more of the search space and emphasise their individual velocity, while lower inertia values force particles to focus on a smaller search area and move towards the best solution found so far.

The inertia weight can remain constant throughout the search, or change with time. In this paper, we use a time-varying inertia weight. We model the change over time with an exponential function which allows us to use a constant sampling step while gradually guiding the swarm from a global to a more local search:

$$\omega(c) = \frac{A}{e^c}, \quad c \in [0, \ln(10A)], \tag{2}$$

where A denotes the starting value of ω when the sampling variable $c = 0$ and c is incremented by $\Delta c = ln(10A)/C$, where C is the desired number of inertia weight changes. The optimisation terminates when $\omega(c) < 0.1$.

4   Body Model and Cost Function

In this section, we present a short summary of the body model and the cost function proposed by Balan et al. [1], which we adopt in our implementation. We adopt this framework to ensure a fair comparison with other body tracking algorithms reported.

4.1   Body Model

The human body shape is modelled as a collection of truncated cones (Figure 1(a)). The underlying articulated motion is modelled with a kinematic tree containing 13 nodes, each node corresponding to a specific body joint. For illustration, the indexed joints are shown overlaid on the test subject in Figure 1(b). Every node can have up to 3 rotational DOF, while the root node also has 3 translational DOF. In total, we use 31 parameters to describe the full body pose (Table 1).

Table 1. Joints and their DOF

JOINT (index)	#	DOF
Global body position (1)	3	r_x, r_y, r_z
Global body orientation (1)	3	$\alpha_x^1, \beta_y^1, \gamma_z^1$
Torso orientation (2)	2	β_y^2, γ_z^2
Left clavicle orientation (3)	2	α_x^3, β_y^3
Left shoulder orientation (4)	3	$\alpha_x^4, \beta_y^4, \gamma_z^4$
Left elbow orientation (5)	1	β_y^5
Right clavicle orientation (6)	2	α_x^6, β_y^6
Right shoulder orientation (7)	3	$\alpha_x^7, \beta_y^7, \gamma_z^7$
Right elbow orientation (8)	1	β_y^8
Head orientation (9)	3	$\alpha_x^9, \beta_y^9, \gamma_z^9$
Left hip orientation (10)	3	$\alpha_x^{10}, \beta_y^{10}, \gamma_z^{10}$
Left knee orientation (11)	1	β_y^{11}
Right hip orientation (12)	3	$\alpha_x^{12}, \beta_y^{12}, \gamma_z^{12}$
Right knee orientation (13)	1	β_y^{13}
TOTAL	31	

4.2   Cost Function

The cost function measures how well a candidate body pose matches the pose of the person in the video sequence. It consists of two parts, an edge-based part and a silhouette-based part.

In the edge-based part, a binary edge map is obtained by thresholding the image gradients. This map is then convolved with a Gaussian kernel to create an edge distance map, which determines the proximity of a pixel to an edge. The model points along the edge of the truncated cones are projected onto the edge map and the mean square error (MSE) between the projected points and the edges in the map is computed.

In the silhouette-based part, a silhouette is obtained from the input images by statistical background subtraction with a Gaussian mixture model. A predefined number of points on the surface of the 3-D body model is then projected into the silhouette image and the MSE between the projected points and the silhouette computed.

Finally, the MSEs of the edge-based part and silhouette-based part are combined to give the cost function value $f(\mathbf{x}^i)$ of the i-th particle :

$$f(\mathbf{x}^i) = MSE_{edge}^i + MSE_{silhouette}^i \tag{3}$$

5   HPSO Algorithm

HPSO tracking algorithm is designed to estimate and track the full-body pose in multi-view video sequences. The tracking algorithm consists of three main components: the initialisation, the hierarchical pose estimation and the next-frame propagation, which we describe next.

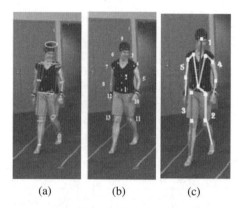

(a)   (b)   (c)

Fig. 1. (a) The truncated-cone body model. (b) Joint positions. (c) Kinematic tree.

5.1   Initialisation

The initialisation is fully automatic. Each particle in the swarm is assigned a random position within the constrained 31-dimensional search space $\mathbb{S}$ and a random 31-dimensional velocity vector drawn from [-1.0,1.0], giving it an exploratory direction in the search space. A particle's position represents a possible body pose configuration, with the position vector specified as:

$$\mathbf{x}_i = (r_x, r_y, r_z, \alpha_x^1, \beta_y^1, \gamma_z^1, ..., \alpha_x^K, \beta_y^K, \gamma_z^K), \tag{4}$$

where r_x, r_y, r_z denote the position of the entire body (root of the kinematic tree) in the world coordinate system, and $\alpha_x^k, \beta_y^k, \gamma_z^k, k = 1 \ldots K$, refer to rotational degrees of freedom of joint k around the x, y, and z-axis, respectively, where K is the total number of joints in the kinematic tree.

5.2   Hierarchial Pose Estimation

PSO has been successfully applied to various nonlinear optimisation problems [3,2]. However, as pointed out by [18,17], it becomes computationally prohibitive with increasing numbers of optimised DOF.

   In order to make the implementation computationally feasible, we solve the pose estimation in a hierarchical manner, where the kinematic tree modelling the articulated motion is estimated in several stages, starting at the root and proceeding downwards towards the leaves. This is possible because the kinematic structure of the human body contains an inherent hierarchy in which the joints lower down the kinematic tree (e.g., elbows) are constrained by the joints higher up the tree (e.g., shoulders).

   We use this property to subdivide the search space into several subspaces containing only a subset of DOF each, thus reducing the search complexity. The hierarchy of the kinematic structure starts with the position and orientation of the entire body in the world coordinate system. Changing either of these affects the configuration of every joint in the model. The kinematic tree then branches out into 5 chains: one for the neck and head, two for left and right arm, and two for left and right leg. The chains modelling

Table 2. Hierarchy of optimisation

(Step 1) Global body pos.: 3DOF: r_x, r_y, r_z	(Step 5) Left lower arm orient.: 2DOF: γ_z^4, β_y^5	(Step 9) Left upper leg orient.: 2DOF: $\alpha_x^{10}, \beta_y^{10}$
(Step 2) Global body orient.: 3DOF: $\alpha_x^1, \beta_y^1, \gamma_z^1$	(Step 6) Right upper arm orient.: 4DOF: $\alpha_x^6, \beta_y^6, \alpha_x^7, \beta_y^7$	(Step 10) Left lower leg orient.: 2DOF: $\gamma_z^{10}, \beta_y^{11}$
(Step 3) Torso orient.: 2DOF: β_y^2, γ_z^2	(Step 7) Right lower arm orient.: 2DOF: γ_z^7, β_y^8	(Step 11) Right upper leg orient.: 2DOF: $\alpha_x^{12}, \beta_y^{12}$
(Step 4) Left upper arm orient.: 4DOF: $\alpha_x^3, \beta_y^3, \alpha_x^4, \beta_y^4$	(Step 8) Head orient.: 3DOF: $\alpha_x^9, \beta_y^9, \gamma_z^9$	(Step 12) Right lower leg orient.: 2DOF: $\gamma_z^{12}, \beta_y^{13}$

the upper body form a subtree with the torso orientation as the root node. From the root node they then branch out independently.

The 5 branches of the kinematic tree are shown overlaid on the test subject in Figure 1(c). We split the search space into 12 different subspaces and correspondingly perform the hierarchical optimisation in 12 steps (Table 2), where each step in the optimisation follows the PSO algorithm described in Section 3. Finally the subspaces are chosen so that only one limb segment at a time is optimised.

5.3   Next-Frame Propagation

Once the pose in a particular frame has been estimated, the particle swarm for the next frame is initialised by sampling the individual particle positions from a Gaussian distribution centred on the position of the best particle from the previous frame, with the covariance set to a low value, in our case 0.01, to promote temporal consistency. This implements, in practice, a zero-velocity predictive model, the simplest possible, as no informed prediction for the next state is actually formulated.

6   Experimental Results

Balan et al [1] published a Matlab implementation of an articulated full-body tracking evaluation software, which includes an implementation of PF and APF. This provided us with a platform to quantitatively evaluate our tracking algorithm. We implemented our tracking approach within their framework by substituting the particle filter code with our HPSO algorithm. Additionally, we implemented the PSAPF algorithm [21] within the software by substituting the particle filter code. All other parts of their implementation were kept the same to ensure a fair comparison.

Datasets. In our experiments, we used 4 datasets: the *Lee walk* sequence included in the Brown University evaluation software and 3 datasets courtesy of the University of Surrey: *Jon walk*, *Tony kick* and *Tony punch* sequences. The *Lee walk* dataset was captured with 4 synchronised grayscale cameras with resolution 640×480 at 60 fps and came with the ground truth articulated motion data acquired by a Vicon system, allowing for a quantitative comparison of the tracking results. The Surrey sequences were acquired by 10 synchronised colour cameras with resolution 720×576 at 25 fps.

HPSO Setup. HPSO was run with only 10 particles and without any hard prior. The PSO parameters (inertia weight model, stopping condition) and the covariance of the

Gaussian distribution used for propagating the swarm into the next frame were kept the same across all the datasets to demonstrate the versatility of our algorithm. The starting inertia weight A (Equation 2) was kept at 2 and number of inertia weight changes C (Section 3.1) was fixed at 60, which amounted to 60 PSO iterations per step in the hierarchical optimisation and with 12 hierarchical steps to 720 iterations in total.

PF/APF Setup. Balan et al [1] use a zero-velocity motion model, where the noise drawn from a Gaussian distribution is equal to the maximum inter-frame difference and different for each dataset. Unlike the original APF algorithm [19], the Brown software uses a motion-capture-trained hard prior for the *Lee walk* sequence to initialise the tracking and eliminate particles with implausible poses. This significantly improves the accuracy of the APF tracking algorithm [1] and also confirmed by our experiments. Since we wanted to compare our algorithm with the original APF algorithm by [19], we ran our tests without the hard prior, except for initialisation which otherwise failed, as described later.

PSAPF Setup. In addition to adopting the APF/PF setup described above (zero-velocity motion model without hard prior), we decompose the search space to 12 subspaces corresponding to the HPSO hierarchical steps described in Table 2 in order to ensure a fair comparision between HPSO and PSAPF, a hierarchical annealed particle filtering algorithm.

Testbed Choice. To select the appropriate comparison testbed for PF, APF and HPSO, we ran two tests. In the first one, all three algorithms were set up to use the same number of likelihood evaluations to find the solution. In the second one, all three were given the same computation time. The setup was normalised to HPSO which required 7200 evaluations and took 70 seconds per frame. We therefore ran the PF with 7200 particles and the APF with 1440 particles and 5 annealing layers in the first experiment (Setup A), and PF with 3000 particles and APF with 600 particles and 5 annealing layers in the second experiment (Setup B).

The results of the first experiment showed that the same number of likelihood evaluations increased the temporal complexity of APF and PF to thrice that of PSO. Our results (Table 3), show that the tracking accuracy does not increase significantly with the increased number of particles. This result is parallel to the results observed in [7], where increasing the particle numbers beyond 500 does not result in any additional improvement. When comparing on the basis of temporal complexity, HPSO also outperformed both PF and APF (Table 3). Due to the high temporal complexity of PF and APF associated with Setup A, which did not significantly improve the accuracy, we decided to perform the rest of the experiments based on the Setup B.

In case of PSAPF, a hierarchical approach, we chose to compare the algorithms (HPSO and PSAPF) based on the number of likelihood evaluations per each hierarchical step (600 evaluations). Thus PSAPF had 120 particles and 5 annealing layers or 7200 evaluations for 12 hierarchical steps (partitions).

Lee Walk Results. The results obtained at 60 fps show that the performance of HPSO is better than that of PF, APF and PSAPF. Table 4 shows the error calculated as the distance between the ground-truth joint values and the values from the pose estimated in each frame, averaged over 5 trials. We also performed a comparison with a temporally

Table 3. MAP error in mm for the *LeeWalk* sequence with varying number of likelihood evaluations

Algorithm	testbed	MAP error
PF	(Setup A)	70.0 ± 21.2
APF	(Setup A)	68.38 ± 17.5
PF	(Setup B)	72 ± 20.5
APF	(Setup B)	68.83 ± 25
HPSO	(Setup A,B)	46.5 ± 8.48mm

Table 4. The distance error calculated for the Lee Walk sequences

Sequence	LeeWalk60hz Mean and Std.Dev (5 trials)	LeeWalk30hz Mean and Std.Dev (5 trials)
PF	72 ± 20.55mm	92.58 ± 25.12mm
APF	68.38 ± 25mm	88.4 ± 20mm
PSAPF	63.8 ± 19mm	87.2 ± 30.1mm
HPSO	46.5 ± 8.48mm	52.5 ± 11.7mm

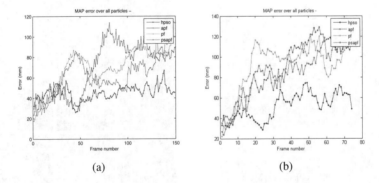

(a)   (b)

Fig. 2. The distance error graph for the 60 fps (a) and the 30 fps (b) Lee walk sequence

subsampled Lee walk sequence by downsampling to 30 fps to increase the inter-frame motion. The distance error tabulated in Table 4 shows that the HPSO performs better than the particle filtering based algorithms at the reduced frame rate. The graph comparing the distance-error for 30 fps and 60 fps sequences are shown in Figure 2. Furthermore, the accuracy of HPSO is not significantly affected by faster motion, while the performance of the APF, PF and PSAPF deteriorates (Figure 3,a).

Surrey Sequence Results. The Surrey test sequences contained faster motion than the Lee walk sequence.

For rapid and sudden motion in the punch and kick sequence, HPSO performed better than APF, PF and PSAPF (Figure 4). In line with results of the *Lee walk* sequence, the performance of HPSO on the *Jon walk* sequence was better than the particle filtering algorithms (Figure 3,b). Since we do not have the ground truth data for the Surrey

352 V. John, S. Ivekovic, and E. Trucco

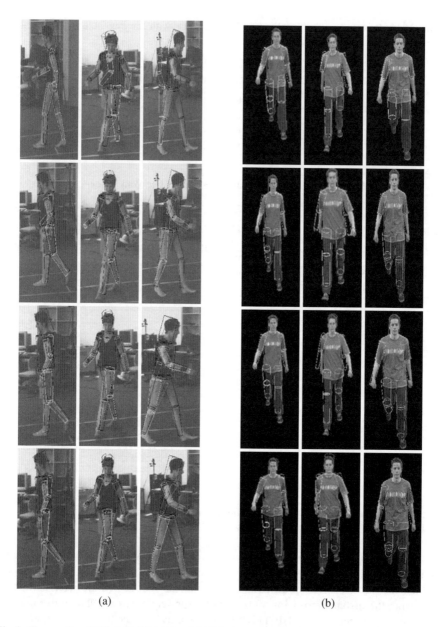

(a)   (b)

Fig. 3. The results of PF, APF, PSAPF and HPSO for the 30 fps Lee Walk sequence (a) and Jon walk sequence (b) are illustrated in the first, second, third and last row respectively. The black cylindrical body models (a) represent the ground-truth, while the coloured cylindrical body model (a,b) in represent the estimated pose.

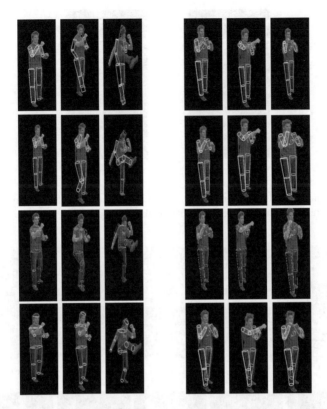

Fig. 4. a) Results of Tony kick sequence illustrated for frames 1, 15 and 25 and b) Results of Tony punch sequence, illustrated for frames 1, 15 and 25. The PF, APF, PSAPF and HPSO results are displayed in the first, second, third and fourth row respectively.

dataset, we could not compute numerical errors as in the case of the *Lee walk* sequence. Instead, we chose to compare the cost function values of the estimated pose as a better estimated pose would have a lower cost function value. The results averaged over 5 trials are tabulated in Table 5.

Recovery. Our experiments also confirmed that HPSO has the ability to recover from a wrong estimate, unlike PF, APF and PSAPF, where the error after a wrong estimate

Table 5. The cost function values of the estimated pose for the Surrey sequence. Smaller number means better performance.

Sequence	JonWalk (5 trials)	Tony Kick (5 trials)	Tony Punch (5 trials)
PF	0.38±0.03	0.616±0.1183	0.869± 0.1828
APF	0.338±0.02	0.507 ±0.0519	0.861 ± 0.1805
PSAPF	0.334±0.032	0.496±0.04	0.861±0.18
HPSO	0.3046±0.0184	0.398±0.03	0.84±0.2

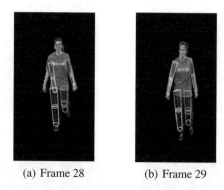

(a) Frame 28   (b) Frame 29

Fig. 5. (a) an incorrect HPSO estimate due to error propagation resulting from an ambiguous silhouette constraint (b) the estimate is corrected in the next frame

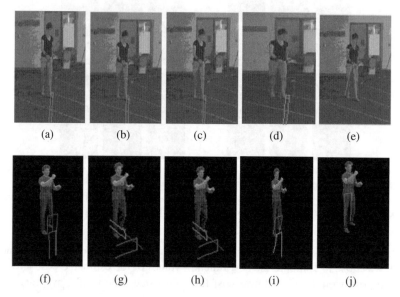

(a)   (b)   (c)   (d)   (e)

(f)   (g)   (h)   (i)   (j)

Fig. 6. The automatic initialisation results for the Lee walk (top) and Tony Kick (bottom) sequence. (a,f) The canonical initial pose for all three algorithms. (b,g) Unsuccessful PF, (c,h) unsuccessful APF and (d,i) unsuccessful PSAPF initialisation. (e,j) successful HPSO initialisation.

normally increases (the problem of *divergence*). In the *Tony kick* sequence (Figure 4a), the right elbow is wrongly estimated by APF and is never recovered. This behaviour is even more pronounced in the PF. HPSO, on the other hand, recovers and finds the correct estimate in the following frame, in spite of wrongly estimating it in the previous frame (Figure 5).

Automatic Initialisation. HPSO initialises automatically on the first frame of the sequence, using a model in the canonical pose. The only manual intervention must set the model's front-back orientation in the direction of motion, which is necessary due to the front-back ambiguity of the cylindrical body model. We tested the automatic initialisation on all 4 test sequences. The initial canonical pose is shown in Figure 6(a,f). In our experiments, the HPSO algorithm, initialised by sampling from a random distribution centered at the canonical pose, consistently found the correct position and orientation of the person in the initial frame, whereas the implementations of PF, APF and PSAPF available to us fails.

7 Conclusions and Future Work

We presented a hierarchical PSO algorithm (HPSO) for full-body articulated tracking and demonstrated that it performs better than APF, PF, and PSAPF. Furthermore our algorithm does not need a pre-trained motion model and does not rely on the prior knowledge of the motion in the sequence. HPSO also demonstrates the ability to automatically initialise. Finally HPSO successfully addresses the problem of particle filter divergence through its search strategy and particle interaction.

An inherent limitation of algorithms with a weak motion model is the dependence of its accuracy on the observation. In case of noisy silhouettes or missing body parts the accuracy would decrease. Another limitation that became evident during the experimental work, was error propagation: due to the hierarchical and sequential structure of the HPSO algorithm, an incorrect estimate higher up in the kinematic chain influenced the accuracy of all the subsequent hierarchical steps. Although undesired, the error propagation was not fatal for the performance of the HPSO tracker, as it was still able to recover from a bad estimate in the subsequent frames (Figure 5).In our future work, we will address the error propagation problem as well as incorporate a better next frame strategy to further increase the accuracy and decrease the time complexity of the search.

Acknowledgements. This work is supported by EPSRC grant EP/080053/1 Vision-Based Animation of People in collaboration with Prof. Adrian Hilton at the University of Surrey (UK). We refer the readers to [10] for further information on the Surrey test sequences.

References

1. Balan, A.O., Sigal, L., Black, M.J.: A Quantitative Evaluation of Video-based 3D Person Tracking. In: Proceedings of ICCCN, pp. 349–356 (2005)
2. Poli, R., Kennedy, J., Blackwell, T., Freitas, A.: Editorial for Particle Swarms: The Second Decade. Journal of Artificial Evolution and Applications 1(1), 1–3 (2008)
3. Poli, R.: An Analysis of Publications on Particle Swarm Optimisation Applications. Technical Report, University of Essex, Department of Computer Science (2007)
4. Caillette, F., Galata, A., Howard, T.: Real-Time 3-D Human Body Tracking using Learnt Models of Behaviour. Computer Vision and Image Understanding 109(2), 112–125 (2008)
5. Poppe, R.: Vision-based human motion analysis: An overview. Computer Vision and Image Understanding 108(1-2), 4–18 (2007)
6. Vondrak, M., Sigal, L., Jenkins, O.C.: Physical Simulation for Probabilistic Motion Tracking. In: Proceedings of CVPR, pp. 1–8 (2008)

7. Husz, Z., Wallace, A., Green, P.: Evaluation of a Hierarchical Partitioned Particle Filter with Action Primitives. In: CVPR 2nd Workshop on Evaluation of Articulated Human Motion and Pose Estimation (2007)
8. Ivekovic, S., Trucco, E., Petillot, Y.: Human Body Pose Estimation with Particle Swarm Optimisation. Evolutionary Computation 16(4) (2008)
9. MacCormick, J., Isard, M.: Partitioned Sampling, Articulated Objects, and Interface-Quality Hand Tracking. In: Vernon, D. (ed.) ECCV 2000. LNCS, vol. 1843, pp. 3–19. Springer, Heidelberg (2000)
10. Starck, J., Hilton, A.: Surface Capture for Performance Based Animation. IEEE Computer Graphics and Applications 27(3), 21–31 (2007)
11. Shi, Y.H., Eberhart, R.C.: A Modified Particle Swarm Optimizer. In: Proceedings of CEC, pp. 69–73 (1998)
12. Kennedy, J., Eberhart, R.: Particle Swarm Optimization. In: Proceedings of ICNN, vol. 4, pp. 1942–1948 (1995)
13. Poppe, R.: Vision-based human motion analysis: An overview. Computer Vision and Image Understanding 108(1-2), 4–18 (2007)
14. Sminchisescu, C., Triggs, B.: Estimating Articulated Human Motion With Covariance Scaled Sampling. International Journal of Robotic Research 22(6), 371–392 (2003)
15. Zhang, X., Hu, W., Maybank, S., Li, X., Zhu, M.: Sequential Particle Swarm Optimization for Visual Tracking. In: Proceedings of CVPR (2008)
16. Robertson, C., Trucco, E., Ivekovic, S.: Dynamic body posture tracking using evolutionary optimisation. Electronics Letters 41(25), 1370–1371 (2005)
17. Ivekovic, S., Trucco, E.: Human Body Pose Estimation with PSO. In: Proceedings of CEC, pp. 1256–1263 (2006)
18. Robertson, C., Trucco, E.: Human body posture via hierarchical evolutionary optimization. In: Proceedings of BMVC, III, p. 999 (2006)
19. Deutscher, J., Reid, I.: Articulated Body Motion Capture by Stochastic Search. International Journal of Computer Vision 61(2), 185–205 (2005)
20. Isard, M., Blake, A.: CONDENSATION- conditional density propagation for visual tracking. International Journal of Computer Vision 29(1), 5–28 (1998)
21. Bandouch, J., Engstler, F., Beetz, M.: Evaluation of Hierarchical Sampling Strategies in 3D Human Pose Estimation. In: Proceedings of British Machine Vision Conference (2008)

Textured Image Segmentation Using Active Contours

Xianghua Xie

Department of Computer Science, University of Wales Swansea, Swansea, U.K.
x.xie@swansea.ac.uk
http://www.cs.swan.ac.uk/~csjason

Abstract. In this paper, we propose a novel level set based active contour model to segment textured images. The proposed method is based on the assumption that local histograms of filtering responses between foreground and background regions are statistically separable. In order to be able to handle texture non-uniformities, which often occur in real world images, we use rotation invariant filtering features and local spectral histograms as image feature to drive the snake segmentation. Automatic histogram bin size selection is carried out so that its underlying distribution can be best represented. Experimental results on both synthetic and real data show promising results and significant improvements compared to direct modeling based on filtering responses.

1 Introduction

Deformable models, particularly active contours, have been widely used for image segmentation and shape extraction due to their natural ability in capturing shape variations [1,2,3,4]. They deform under the influence of internal and external forces to delineate object boundaries. Explicit representations of active contours [5,6] track the points on the curves across time, and hence generally have difficulties in dealing with topological changes, e.g. splitting and merging. Implicit representation based on the level set method [1,2] embeds contours in a higher-dimensional scalar function and deforms the contours through evolving the scalar function, which conveniently facilitates necessary topological changes.

Active contours have been increasingly used in analyzing textured images, e.g. [7,8,9,10]. Despite recent advances in edge based approaches, e.g. [11,12], region based approaches have some obvious advantages when analyzing heavily textured images in that edge based boundary description can easily be compromised by texture patterns. Region based approach generally deforms initial contours towards the region/object boundaries of interest by minimizing an energy function, whose minimum ideally collocates with those boundaries. Thus, it is vitally important to use robust features and region indication/separation functional.

Various features have been investigated in the contour segmentation framework, such as co-occurrence matrices [13], structure tensor [14], and local binary patterns [10]. However, filtering responses are among the most popular approaches, e.g. [15,7,16,17,18]. In [7] the authors decompose the image using Gabor filters. The collected filtering responses at each pixel are used to measure the difference between pixels in a piecewise constant model. However, it largely ignores the spatial distribution

A. Ranchordas et al. (Eds.): VISIGRAPP 2009, CCIS 68, pp. 357–369, 2010.

among local filtering coefficients and this direct comparison of filter responses is error prone since the responses can be misaligned due to the anisotropic nature of most of the filters. Wavelet packet transform is used in [16] and the energy distributions in sub-bands are used to characterize textures. One of the main difficulties in dealing with filtering responses is their large dimensionality. It is also challenging to handle textural variations within regions of interest due to, for example, rotation or view point changes, since most of the filters are orientation sensitive.

Once the features are derived, one also needs to decide how to model their distribution so that correct features are included in describing the object of interest. In other words, this modeling provides a region indication or separation functional to drive the active contours. Modeling based on global distribution is a popular approach. For example, in [15,17] Mixture of Gaussians are used to model the image features. Another powerful approach is based on the piecewise constant assumption [19]. It also has been recently adopted in texture segmentation, e.g. [7,18,8]. However, how to cope with texture inhomogeneity is a major challenge.

2   Proposed Approach

In this paper, we propose a novel region based active contour model, which is based on the assumption that local histograms of filtering responses between object of interest and background regions are statistically separable. Briefly, we first apply a bank of filters to the image, from which we have a set of filter responses at different scales and orientations. These responses are then grouped and condensed so that it can handle textural non-uniformity which may occur in real world images. Reduced, invariant features are thus obtained. This process also effectively decreases the dimensionality of filter feature space, which is beneficial for single image segmentation. We then collect local distributions of these features at each pixels, known as local spectral histograms. These local histograms contains not only direct filtering responses but also their spatial distributions in their local neighborhoods. The optimal bin size for these histograms are obtained by minimizing a mean integrated square error based cost function. An energy minimization problem is thus formulated by fitting two spectral histograms, one of which is used to approximate the foreground region and the other for the background. We will show that this approach is effective to handle texture inhomogeneity, compared to, for example, direct modeling based on filtering responses [7] or local intensity distributions [8].

Next, Section 2.1 describes the filter bank and rotation invariant feature selection. Local spectral histogram extraction is presented in Section 2.2 and automatic optimal histogram bin size computation is given in Section 2.3. Finally, Section 2.4 introduces the level set based snake model using these invariant features for image segmentation.

2.1   Filters and Feature Selection

Texture is one of the most important characteristics in identifying objects. It provides important information for recognition and interpolation. Numerous techniques have been reported in the literature to carry out texture analysis. They can be generally categorized in four ways: statistical approaches, which measure the spatial distribution of

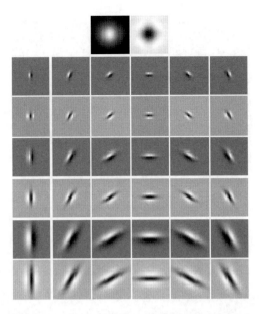

Fig. 1. The filter bank consists 38 filters in total, which include one Gaussian filter, one Laplacian of Gaussian filter, and 36 edge and bar filters across 6 orientations and 3 scales

pixel values, structural approaches, that are based on analyzing texture primitives and the spatial arrangement of these primitives, filter based approaches, which analyze local pixel dependencies using a bank of filters, and model based approaches, which often use derived model parameters as texture features. Filter bank based approaches have been very popular since they can analyze textures in arbitrary orientations and scales and have been strongly motivated by psychological studies of human vision system. They have been shown as an effective approach to classifying [20], segmenting [21] and synthesizing [22] textured images.

However, filter bank based methods often result in high dimensional feature space which can be difficult to handle for certain applications. For example, in [23] the authors found it ineffective to condense the high dimensional Gabor features for the purpose of novelty detection. Unlike image classification, in snake based image segmentation, we may not have enough features extracted from a single image to populate the high dimensional feature space in order to accurately estimate the underlying feature distributions. Moreover, there are usually significant amount of redundant information among the filtering responses. For example, a set of anisotropic filters will get the same responses from isotropic image regions. Fig. 1 shows a bank of filters which has been used in [24] for image classification. It contains two isotropic filters and thirty six anisotropic filters.

The two isotropic filters are Gaussian and Laplacian of Gaussian both with $\sigma = 10$. Those thrifty six anisotropic filters come from two families, edges and bars, each of which consists filters at three progressive scales, i.e. $(\sigma_x, \sigma_y) = \{(1, 3), (2, 6), (4, 12)\}$, and six uniformly spaced different orientations. This moderate size filter bank will produce a thirty eight dimensional feature space, which is considerably large for features extracted from a single image to populate. Fig. 3 gives the filter response images for

Fig. 2. An example testing image

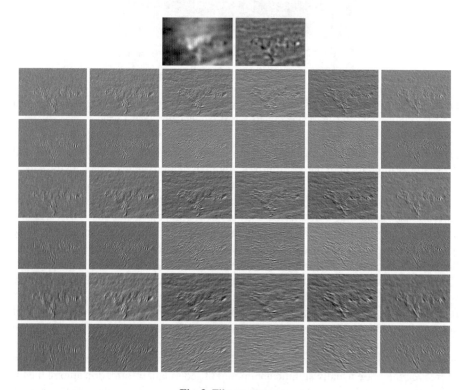

Fig. 3. Filter responses

the example image shown in Fig. 2. It is evidently clear that there are certain correlations among these filter responses and not all the channels are effectively revealing the image structures. Thus, it is natural to condense the feature space, which is particularly desirable for our application.

It is also worth noting that object in the scene may have inhomogeneous textures due to, for example, perspective projection. This inhomogeneity will exhibit nonuniform responses after applying directional filters, e.g. animal stripe texture (see zebra example

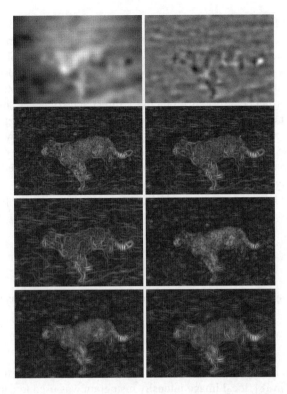

Fig. 4. Maximum filter responses - The first row shows the filter responses from the isotropic Gaussian and Laplacian of Gaussian are kept the same. The rest six filter responses are collected from the 36 directional (isotropic) filter responses. Each of them contains the maximum responses across 6 different orientations (i.e. the six rows of the directional filter responses in Fig. 3 are collapsed into six rotational invariant filter responses).

in Fig. 7) and brick wall texture (see Fig. 8). Rotation invariance is thus desirable in such circumstance. We follow [24] to condense the filter responses by collecting only the maximum filter response across all the six orientations, i.e. those thirty six directional filter responses are reduced to six. Alternative methods, such as steerable filters [25] can also be used. Thus, this not only reduces the dimensionality of the feature space but also simultaneously improve rotational invariance. Instead of applying convolution operators, the recursive technique [26] is used to efficiently filter the images. Fig. 4 shows the collected maximum responses from those thirty eight filter coefficients. Note the isotropic filter responses are remain unchanged since they are inherently rotationally invariant.

2.2   Local Spectral Histogram

The filtering responses can be directly used to drive the active contours as in, for example, [7]. However, we can further incorporate local spatial dependency of filtering responses by computing the marginal distributions of filter responses over a local window.

Thus, it captures local pixel dependency through filtering and global patterns through histograms. Local spectral histogram has been found useful, for example, texture classification [27]. The maximum filter responses are largely local dominant features, such as edges and bars (e.g. see 4). Their spatial distribution conveys important information regarding the nature of the texture. Misaligning of filter responses due to inhomogeneity of filter responses can be a serious problem for direct approaches. Using local spectral histogram further enhances our model in dealing with texture inhomogeneity and helps to produce more coherent segmentation. Fig. 8 provides an example where directly using filter response without taking into account texture inhomogeneity resulted in a very poor segmentation, whereas the proposed method correctly segmented the foreground object from the texturally nonuniform background.

Let $\mathbf{W}$ denote a local window and $\mathbf{W}^{(\alpha)}(\mathbf{x})$ a maximum filter response patch centered at $\mathbf{x}$, where $\alpha = 1, 2, ..., 8$. Thus, for $\mathbf{W}^{(\alpha)}$ the histogram is defined as [28]:

$$P_{\mathbf{W}}^{(\alpha)}(z_1, z_2) = \sum_{\mathbf{x} \in \mathbf{W}} \int_{z_1}^{z_2} \delta(z - \mathbf{W}^{(\alpha)}(\mathbf{x})) dz, \quad (1)$$

where z_1 and z_2 specify the range of the bin. The spectral histogram is then defined as:

$$P_{\mathbf{W}} = \frac{1}{\mathbf{W}} \left(P_{\mathbf{W}}^{(1)}, P_{\mathbf{W}}^{(2)}, ..., P_{\mathbf{W}}^{(8)}, \right). \quad (2)$$

Example spectral histograms extracted from the testing image can be found in Fig. 6.

Very recently in [8], local image intensity histogram was used to carry out segmentation in the Chan-Vese piecewise constant framework. However, this method may have difficulties in dealing with highly textured images where intensity alone is not sufficient to describe the texture. Intensity variation, for example, due to illumination variation can also cause severe problems. A comparative example is given in Fig. 9 where the best result reported in [8] is still significantly less accurate than the proposed approach.

2.3   Deducing Optimal Bin Size

Although histogram based methods have been routinely used in various image processing tasks, the importance of automatically selecting appropriate histogram bin size has been largely ignored. However, if a too small bin size is selected, the frequency value at each bin will suffer from significant fluctuation due to the paucity of samples in each bin. On the other hand, if the bin size is chosen too large, the histogram will not be a good representation of the underlying distribution. Thus, it is necessary to select optimal bin size. It also avoids practical problems associated with manual parameter tunning.

We follow the method in [29] to estimate the optimal bin size. Let us consider a histogram as a bar graph. Also, let Δ denote the bin size and Z the range of the coefficients. The expected frequency for $s \in [0, \Delta]$ is:

$$\theta = \frac{1}{\Delta} \int_0^\Delta \lambda_s ds, \quad (3)$$

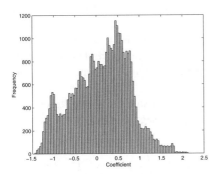
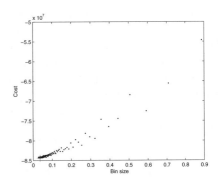

Fig. 5. Optimal bin size selection - left: A typical spectral histogram for a single maximum response filter; right: The plot shows the relationship between the MISE based cost function and bin size (the red cross indicates the optimal bin size with the lowest MISE value).

where λ_s is the underlying true frequency which is not known. The goodness of fit of the estimated $\hat{\lambda}_s$ to λ_s is measured according to mean integrated squared error (MISE):

$$\text{MISE} = \frac{1}{\Delta} \int_0^\Delta \langle E(\hat{\theta} - \lambda_s)^2 \rangle ds, \tag{4}$$

where E denotes expectation and the empirical bar height $\hat{\theta}_i \equiv k_i/\Delta$ (k_i is the frequency count for ith bin). The associated cost function is then defined as:

$$\mathcal{O}(\Delta) = \text{MISE} - \frac{1}{\Delta} \int_0^\Delta \langle (\lambda_s - \langle \theta \rangle)^2 \rangle ds. \tag{5}$$

The second term represents a mean squared fluctuation. By assuming the number of events counted in each bin obeys a Poisson distribution, the cost function can be written as:

$$\mathcal{O}(\Delta) = \frac{2}{\Delta} \langle E\hat{\theta} \rangle - \langle E(\hat{\theta} - \langle E\hat{\theta} \rangle)^2 \rangle. \tag{6}$$

The optimal bin size thus is obtained by minimizing the above cost function, i.e.

$$\hat{\Delta} = \arg\min_\Delta \mathcal{O}(\Delta). \tag{7}$$

Thus, the testing image is first filtered through the bank of isotropic and anisotropic filters and their responses are condensed into eight channels. Before generating the local spectral histograms at each pixel, global spectral histograms for every eight channels are produced. Then, this optimal bin size selection for each channel is taken place, based on which local spectral histograms are computed. Fig. 5 gives an example of optimal bin size computation.

2.4 Active Contour Based on Wasserstein Distance

The snake based segmentation can be viewed as a foreground-background partition problem (in the case of bi-phase). The snake evolves in the image domain, attempting to minimizing the feature similarity for those inside and outside the contours. Meanwhile, it tries to minimize the feature difference for those that belong to the same region. Thus, we can formulate our snake based on the piece-wise constant assumption [19,8]. However, since we are using invariant image features and local spectral histograms, the proposed method can cope with texture inhomogeneity much better (see Figs. 8 and 9 as comparative examples).

Let Ω be the image domain, Λ_+ denote the regions inside the snake (foreground) and Λ_- those outside the snake (background). The snake segmentation can be achieved by solving the following energy minimization problem:

$$\inf_{\Lambda_+} \mathcal{E}(\Lambda_+) = \alpha \mathcal{L}(\Lambda_+) + \int_{\Lambda_+} \mathcal{D}(P(\mathbf{x}), P_+)d\mathbf{x} + \int_{\Lambda_-} \mathcal{D}(P(\mathbf{x}), P_-)d\mathbf{x}, \qquad (8)$$

where α is a constant, $\mathcal{L}$ denote length, $\mathcal{D}$ is the metric which measures the difference between two histograms, and P_+ and P_- are the foreground and background spectral histograms to be determined. The first term is the length minimization term which regularize the contour. The next two terms are data fitting terms, which carry out the binary segmentation.

Among many other candidates, such as χ^2 distance and normalized cross correlation, The Wasserstein distance (also known as the earth mover's distance) [30] is used to compute the distance between two normalized spectral histograms. since it is a true metric (unlike χ^2 distance) and has been found very useful in various applications, e.g. image retrieval [30]. Let $H_a(y)$ and $H_b(y)$ be two normalized spectral histograms. The Wasserstein distance between these two histograms is defined as:

$$\mathcal{D}(P_a, P_b) = \int_T |F_a(y) - F_b(y)|dy, \qquad (9)$$

where T denotes the range of the histogram bins, and F_a and F_b are cumulative distributions of P_a and P_b, respectively.

The level set method is implemented to solve this energy minimization problem so that topological changes, such as merging and splitting, can be effectively handled. Let ϕ denote the level set function. The foreground is identified as $\Lambda_+ = \{\mathbf{x} \in \Omega : \phi(\mathbf{x}) > 0\}$, which can be computed using the Heaviside function, i.e. $\int_\Omega \mathcal{H}(\phi)d\mathbf{x}$ where $\mathcal{H}$ is the Heaviside function. The level set formulation can be expressed as:

$$\begin{aligned}
\inf_{\Lambda_+} \mathcal{E}(\Lambda_+) =\; &\alpha \int_\Omega |\nabla \mathcal{H}(\phi)|d\mathbf{x} \\
&+ \int_\Omega \mathcal{D}(P(\mathbf{x}), P_+)\mathcal{H}(\phi)d\mathbf{x} \\
&+ \int_\Omega \mathcal{D}(P(\mathbf{x}), P_-)(1 - \mathcal{H})(\phi)d\mathbf{x}
\end{aligned} \qquad (10)$$

The regularized Heaviside function proposed in [19] is used to allow larger support in the vicinity of the zero level set so that the contours can be initialized anywhere across the image (e.g. see Fig. 7):

$$\mathcal{H}_\epsilon(z) = \frac{1}{2}\left(1 + \frac{2}{\pi}\arctan(\frac{z}{\epsilon})\right). \qquad (11)$$

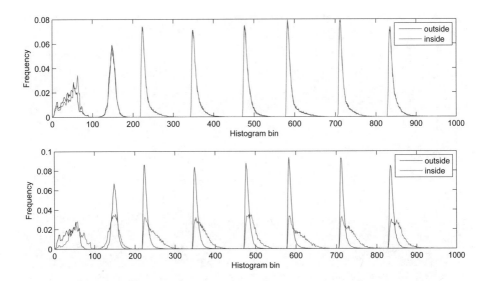

Fig. 6. The average local spectral histogram inside and outside the snake - top: These two histograms are largely overlapping each other; bottom: It clearly shows the difference between the histograms when the snake converged to the object boundaries.

Thus, minimizing $\mathcal{E}$ with respect to ϕ gives us the following partial differential equation:

$$\frac{\partial \phi}{\partial t} = \delta(\phi) \left[\alpha \nabla \cdot \left(\frac{\nabla \phi}{|\nabla \phi|} \right) - (\mathcal{D}(P(\mathbf{x}), P_+) - \mathcal{D}(P(\mathbf{x}), P_-)) \right]$$

$$= \delta(\phi) \left[\alpha \nabla \cdot \left(\frac{\nabla \phi}{|\nabla \phi|} \right) \right.$$

$$\left. - \int_T |F_\mathbf{x}(y) - F_+(y)| dy + \int_T |F_\mathbf{x}(y) - F_-(y)| dy \right], \qquad (12)$$

where $\delta(x) = \frac{d}{dx} \mathcal{H}(x)$, F_+ and F_- are the spectral cumulative histogram inside and outside the contours, respectively. The minimization process thus moves the contours towards object boundaries through competing pixels by measuring the similarity of local cumulative spectral histogram with those inside and outside current foreground.

Fig. 6 shows an example of spectral histogram changes between the initial stage and the stabilized result. The corresponding segmentation result can be found in the first row of Fig. 7.

3 Results

The proposed method has been tested on both synthetic and real world images. Fig. 7 shows some typical example results obtained using the proposed method. The first row shows the result of the running example given earlier. Good segmentation was achieved despite the large variations in the body region. In the second example, reasonable result

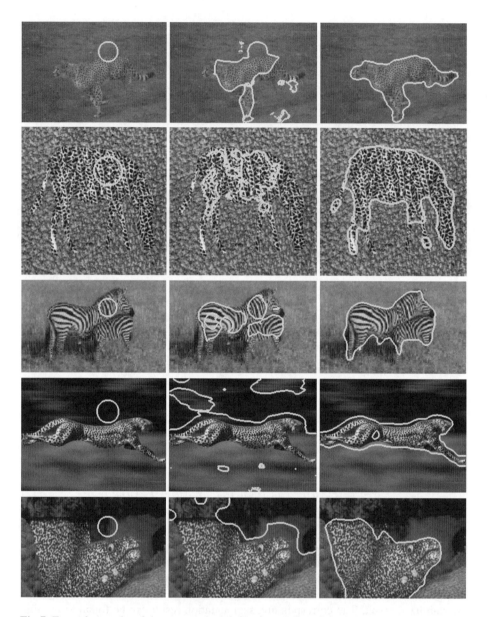

Fig. 7. Examples results of the proposed method - from left to right: initial snake, intermediate stages, and stabilized result

was obtained, missing some very fine and thin structures. In the third example, there are clearly texture orientation variations. In the last two rows, the initial snakes were placed outside the objects of interest but still managed to localize them. Particularly, in the last example, there are significant texture variations both in foreground and background regions, which made it very difficult to segment.

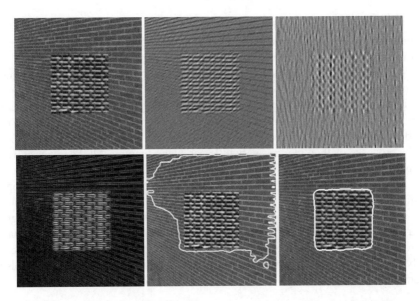

Fig. 8. Top row - a synthetic texture collage which contains an inhomogeneous background due to orientation and scale changes, and two filter responses to particular orientations; Bottom row - the maximum response derived across different orientations which highlights edge features in various directions, including vertical; segmentation result obtained using the Chan-Vese model based on Gabor features [18]; segmentation result obtained using the proposed method.

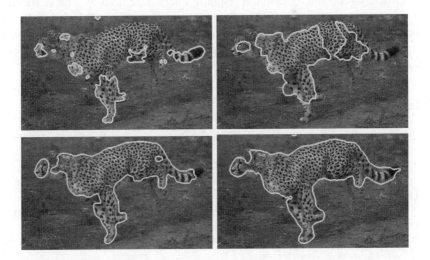

Fig. 9. Comparative analysis. Top row - results obtained using edges based methods, namely geodesic snake and generalized GVF snake [3]; bottom row - the left image shows the best result on the testing image reported in [8] using a region based approach; the last image shows the result obtained using the proposed method.

In Figs. 8 and 9, we mainly compare our work with two extensions of the piece-wise constant model, which is also our fundamental model. Fig. 8 demonstrates when dealing with inhomogeneous textures, the proposed method performs significantly better than that directly using filter responses [7]. The proposed method also showed improvements against a very recent method based on local histograms [8]. It illustrates the effectiveness of using invariant filtering technique. Fig. 9 also gives example results obtained from geodesic snake and generalized GVF snake [3]. It is expected that these edge based techniques are not appropriate when dealing with highly textured images.

The proposed method requires very little parameter tunning. All the images given in this paper are using a fixed set of parameters. The parameters used to generate the filter bank are given in Section 2.1. The local window used to collect the spectral histogram is empirically fixed as 19. For a too small window size, the local spectral histogram may have difficulties in reflecting underlying distribution and can result in isolated regions. For a too large window, the segmentation can be less accurate around object boundaries. We found that a window size of 19 is a good tradeoff, however, we attempt to automatically select the window size as part of our future work. The parameter α controls the smoothness of the contour and very rarely needs to be adjusted.

4   Conclusions

In this paper, we introduced a novel region based snake method which is based on the assumption that foreground and background local filtering response distributions are statistically separable. Maximum response filters were used to achieve rotational invariancy and their local spectral histograms were used as image features to drive the snake. The experimental studies showed some promising results. As part of our future work, we will further investigate optimal filter selection and automatic local spectral histogram window selection.

References

1. Caselles, V., Kimmel, R., Sapiro, G.: Geodesic active contour. International Journal of Computer Vision 22, 61–79 (1997)
2. Malladi, R., Sethian, J.A., Vemuri, B.C.: Shape modelling with front propagation: A level set approach. IEEE Transations on Pattern Analysis and Machine Intelligence 17, 158–175 (1995)
3. Xu, C., Prince, J.: Snakes, shapes, & gradient vector flow. IEEE Transactions on Image Processing 7, 359–369 (1998)
4. Xie, X., Mirmehdi, M.: RAGS: Region-aided geometric snake. IEEE Transactions on Image Processing 13, 640–652 (2004)
5. Kass, M., Witkin, A., Terzopoulus, D.: Snakes: Active contour model. International Journal of Computer Vision 1, 321–331 (1988)
6. McInerney, T., Terzopoulos, D.: Deformable models in medical image analysis: A survey. Medical Image Analysis 1, 91–108 (1996)
7. Sandberg, B., Chan, T., Vese, L.: In: A level-set and gabor-based active contour algorithm for segmenting textured images. Technical Report 39, Math. Department UCLA, Los Angeles, USA (2002)

8. Ni, K., Bresson, X., Chan, T., Esedoglu, S.: Local histogram based segmentation using the Wasserstein distance. In: Scale Space and Variational Methods in Computer Vision, pp. 697–708 (2007)
9. Houhou, N., Thiran, J.: Fast texture segmentation model based on the shape operator and active contour. In: IEEE Conference on Computer Vision Pattern Recognition, pp. 1–8 (2008)
10. Savelonas, M., Iakovidis, D., Maroulis, D.: LBP-guided active contours. Pattern Recognition Letters 29, 1404–1415 (2008)
11. Paragios, N., Mellina-Gottardo, O., Ramesh, V.: Gradient vector flow geometric active contours. IEEE Transations on Pattern Analysis and Machine Intelligence 26, 402–407 (2004)
12. Xie, X., Mirmehdi, M.: MAC: Magnetostatic active contour model. IEEE Transations on Pattern Analysis and Machine Intelligence 30, 632–646 (2008)
13. Pujol, O., Radeva, P.: Texture segmentation by statistical deformable models. International Journal of Image and Graphics 4, 433–452 (2004)
14. Rousson, M., Brox, T., Deriche, R.: Active unsupervised texture segmentation on a diffusion based feature space. In: IEEE Conference on Computer Vision Pattern Recognition, pp. 1–8 (2004)
15. Paragios, N., Deriche, R.: Geodesic active regions and level set methods for supervised texture segmentation. International Journal of Computer Vision 46, 223–247 (2002)
16. Aujol, J., Aubert, G., Blanc-Féraud, L.: Wavelet-based level set evolution for classification of textured images. IEEE Transactions on Image Processing 12, 1634–1641 (2003)
17. He, Y., Luo, Y., Hu, D.: Unsupervised texture segmentation via applying geodesic active regions to Gaborian feature space. World Academy of Science, Engineering and Technology 2, 200–203 (2005)
18. Sagiv, C., Sochen, N., Zeevi, I.: Integrated active contours for texture segmentation. IEEE Transactions on Image Processing 15, 1633–1645 (2006)
19. Chan, T., Vese, L.: Active contours without edges. IEEE Transactions on Image Processing 10, 266–277 (2001)
20. Azencott, R., Wang, J., Younes, L.: Texture classification using windowed fourier filters. IEEE Transations on Pattern Analysis and Machine Intelligence 19, 148–153 (1997)
21. Dunn, D., Higgins, W., Wakeley, J.: Texture segmentation using 2-d gabor elementary functions. IEEE Transations on Pattern Analysis and Machine Intelligence 16, 130–149 (1994)
22. Heeger, D., Bergen, J.: Pyramid-based texture analysis/synthesis. In: Computer graphics and interactive techniques, pp. 229–238 (1995)
23. Xie, X., Mirmehdi, M.: TEXEMS: Texture exemplars for defect detection on random textured surfaces. IEEE Transactions on Pattern Analysis and Machine Intelligence 29, 1454–1464 (2007)
24. Varma, M., Zisserman, A.: Classifying images of materials: Achieving viewpoint and illumination independence. In: IEEE European Conference on Computer Vision, pp. 255–271 (2002)
25. Jacob, M., Unser, M.: Design of steerable filters for feature detection using Canny-like criteria. IEEE Transactions on Pattern Analysis and Machine Intelligence 26, 1007–1019 (2004)
26. Geusebroek, J., Smeulders, A., van de Weijer, J.: Fast anisotropic gauss filtering. IEEE Transactions on Image Processing 12, 938–943 (2003)
27. Liu, X., Wang, D.: Texture classification using spectral histograms. IEEE Transactions on Image Processing 12(6), 661–670 (2003)
28. Liu, X., Wang, D.: Image and texture segmentation using local spectral histograms. IEEE Transactions on Image Processing 15, 3066–3077 (2006)
29. Shimazaki, H., Shinomoto, S.: A method for selecting the bin size of a time histogram. Neural Computation 19, 1503–1527 (2007)
30. Rubner, Y., Tomasi, C., Guibas, L.: A metric for distributions with applications to image databases. In: IEEE Conference on Computer Vision Pattern Recognition, pp. 59–66 (1998)

Author Index

Printing: Mercedes-Druck, Berlin
Binding: Stein+Lehmann, Berlin